ANTEBELLUM
ARCHITECTURE
OF KENTUCKY

ANTEBELLUM ARCHITECTURE OF KENTUCKY

CLAY LANCASTER

THE UNIVERSITY PRESS OF KENTUCKY

Frontispiece: Liberty Hall (1796-1804), Frankfort. Photo, 1930s, by Theodore Webb, courtesy of the Library of Congress.

Copyright © 1991 by The University Press of Kentucky
Scholarly publisher for the Commonwealth,
serving Bellarmine College, Berea College, Centre
College of Kentucky, Eastern Kentucky University,
The Filson Club, Georgetown College, Kentucky
Historical Society, Kentucky State University,
Morehead State University, Murray State University,
Northern Kentucky University, Transylvania University,
University of Kentucky, University of Louisville,
and Western Kentucky University.

Editorial and Sales Offices: Lexington, Kentucky 40508-4008

Library of Congress Cataloging-in-Publication Data
Lancaster, Clay.
    Antebellum architecture of Kentucky / Clay Lancaster.
        p.   cm.
    Includes bibliographical references and index.
    ISBN 0-8131-1759-3 (alk. paper) :
    1. Architecture, Modern—17th-18th centuries—Kentucky.
2. Architecture, Modern—19th century—Kentucky.   3. Architecture
—Kentucky.   I. Title.
NA730.K4L36 1991
720'.9769—dc20   91-2419

CONTENTS

To the Founding Members of
The Blue Grass Trust for Historic Preservation

THE BLUE GRASS TRUST had been smoldering in the heart of its patriarch, Joseph C. Graves, long before it became a reality. Its actual inception was prompted by a disaster and an opportunity, both of which occurred in 1955. The disaster was the razing of the late-eighteenth-century Col. Thomas Hart House at the southwest corner of Mill and Second streets for a parking lot. Henry Clay had married Hart's daughter Lucretia in the house, and Kentucky's first newspaper publisher, John Bradford, had lived in it for about a quarter of a century. The Hart House was diagonally across from Gratz Park, the site of Transylvania University through the first third of the nineteenth century, and the persisting center of Lexington's most fashionable neighborhood. The finest house on the park, built for John Wesley Hunt in 1814, stood across Second Street from the demolished building. Recently it had been rented out as apartments, and it was up for sale. The possibility of its suffering a fate similar to that of the Hart House was imminent. On 18 April Joseph C. Graves formed a group calling itself the Foundation for the Preservation of Historic Lexington and Fayette County. Advised by Mrs. A.W. (Lucretia) Johnson, a realtor who lived on the fourth corner of the intersection at Second and Mill streets, and backed by Mrs. Victor (Carolyn Reading) Hammer and other residents on the park, on 1 July the foundation became the purchaser of Hunt's house for $37,334, making a down payment of $2,666, with the balance to be distributed over annual installments (at 6 percent interest) for a period of fifteen years. The house was the first of many architecturally significant monuments to be saved by the organization.

The Foundation for the Preservation of Historic Lexington and Fayette County was the initial name of what was to become the Blue Grass Trust for Historic Preservation. Another title considered was the John Hunt Morgan Foundation, which memorialized the grandson of John Wesley Hunt, a dashing Confederate general and former resident of the house; but it was discarded as being too limited. It focused on the headquarters instead of the purpose of the organization. The builder's great-grandson and general's nephew, Thomas Hunt Morgan, who was brought up in the residence, distinguished himself through his contributions to science. He clarified the laws and mechanics of heredity and the mutation of species and was awarded the Nobel Prize for Medicine in 1933. The building was henceforth called the Hunt-Morgan House, but the title of the society remained autonomous. For the time being, however, the house remained the center of the group's attention.

The dual purpose of building an organization and renovating a building tended to divide the affiliates between those who held office and those who directed and themselves performed manual labor. There was, of course, overlapping, and fluctuation of personnel both in committee and volunteer-work groups. Officers were elected at the first organization meeting in April. By general assent Joseph C. Graves was named chairman. Three committees were appointed: finance, headed by Frank van Deren Coke, and including Edward S. Dabney, Sidney S. Combs, and Alfred D. Powell; publicity and organization, headed by Mrs. Hammer, and including William H. Townsend, Thomas D. Clark, Mrs. Joseph Estes, and Mrs. Waller Jones; and open house, headed by Mrs. Anderson Gratz, and including Mrs. F.H. (Retta) Wright, Mrs. Sterling Coke, Mrs. Waller Bullock, and Mrs. W. Clay Shropshire. The third committee anticipated the acquisition of the Hunt-Morgan House.

The work program was launched by the purchase

of the building in July 1955. Apartment facilities, such as the bathroom that had been installed in the service stair hall, had to be removed from the first floor (the second story was not to be restored for thirty years). Cellars and the stable had to be cleaned out, and the yard had to be made presentable. Mr. and Mrs. Lawrence Crump had espoused the cause by this time, and they, Mrs. Joseph C. (Lucy) Graves, her sister Mrs. Wright, Mrs. Hammer, Mrs. Johnson with her two domestics, and a number of Boy Scouts attacked the job. Van Deren Coke organized a Saturday paving party for laying bricks in the courtyard and walks on the north side of the house. Professionals were engaged to paint the outside of the building. The interior work was largely undertaken by volunteers. Rooms had to be cleared and decorated. Curtains had to be made for the windows. The former owner, Mrs. Carey Gratz Johnstone Thomas, had generously included a number of furnishings and family mementos in the sale of the house, and other interested parties contributed heirlooms and artifacts having to do with early Kentucky. Most of the latter did not relate to the Hunt-Morgan House historically, but they accorded in period and helped to fill it with a museum sufficiency. Recessed lights were installed in the dining-room ceiling for wall displays. The building was officially opened by a reception on 16 October 1955. Burton Milward wrote the first publication, a twenty-two page booklet entitled *The Hunt-Morgan House*, which gave biographical sketches of the various former residents and was accompanied by architectural notes. Besides serving as a museum the house was used for meetings, social events, exhibitions, lectures, and other cultural purposes to build up membership and much needed funds. Dues were set at $2 per year, with life membership at $100.

The officers formally elected in 1956 included Joseph C. Graves, president; Frank Van Deren Coke, first vice-president and chairman of exhibition and special events; Mrs. Victor Hammer, second vice-president and chairman of the calendar committee; Robert Landrum, treasurer and chairman of the finance committee; Mrs. A.W. Johnson, membership secretary; Mrs. Holman Hamilton, recording secretary; Mrs. F.H. Wright, chairman of the garden committee; Mrs. Henry Holladay, chairman of the decorating committee; Mrs. Elmer Deiss, chairman of the hostess committee; Mrs. Louis Beard, chairman of special events and arrangements committee (including refreshments); Edward W. Rannells,

chairman of the acquisition committee; A.D. Kirwan, chairman of the research committee; Mrs. Robert W. Miles, chairman of publicity; Mrs. Joseph Desha McDowell, chairman of the house; and Dr. Jacqueline Bull, architivist.

Other committee members and supporters of the cause not mentioned before were: Mrs. W.E. Bach, Mrs. Caperton Burnham, Miss Ann W. Callihan, Mrs. Johnson Camden, Miss Henrietta Clay, Mrs. Blanton Collier, Miss Mary Didlake, Miss Rebecca Edwards, Mrs. Augustus Gay, Miss Mary Frances Haner, Mrs. Elizabeth Van Meter Hutchinson, Mrs. Robert Jewell, Mrs. Waller Jones, Mrs. Sam B. Marks, Miss Katherine Meng, Miss Kathleen Mulligan, Mrs. John Jacob Niles, Mrs. William Pettit, Mrs. Virginia Moore Rice, Mrs. Elvis Stahr, Miss Sunshine Sweeney, Mrs. Harry St. George Tucker, Miss Anna Rebekah Van Meter, and Mrs. Joseph Wile; John Harris Clay, James L. Cogar, J. Winston Coleman, Jr., William A. Combs, Louis Hillenmeyer, Jr., Lafon Ingels, Clay Lancaster, J.S. Lansill, A.Z. Looney, Gene Markey, William Wickman, and William Worth.

The first momentous event of the foundation was the Blue Grass Preservation Short Course held during 25-27 July 1957. It was cosponsored by the National Trust for Historic Preservation in Washington. The National Trust had been chartered in 1949, and it had held its first Preservation Short Course at Cooperstown, New York, in September 1955 and repeated it a year later. The Lexington venture was the third of its kind. The National Trust for Historic Preservation publicized it throughout the country, and financial aid was furnished by Lilly Endowment, Inc., Indianapolis, Indiana. Richard H. Howland was president of the National Trust, and the Trust's historian, Mrs. Helen Duprey Bullock, acted as deputy director. Former assistant to the director of the Trust, Mrs. Betty Walsh Morris, currently living in Lexington, was registrar for the short course. Besides lectures having to do strictly with preservation, there were talks on Civil War music, costumes of the nation's first ladies, and local subjects such as Shakertown and Henry and Cassius M. Clay. Speakers included Mrs. Margaret Brown Klapthor, curator of the Smithsonian Institution; Mrs. Lida Mayo, historian with the U.S. Department of Defense; Miss Barbara Snow, managing editor of *Antiques* magazine; James L. Cogar, former curator at Colonial Williamsburg; Frederick D. Nichols, associate professor of architecture at the University of Virginia; Earl H. Reed, fellow of the American Institute of Architects; and Richard Bales, conductor of the orchestra of the National Gallery of Art. There was also a walking tour through downtown Lexington, as well as an all-day bus tour with lunch at Pleasant Hill; it included Danville, Harrodsburg, Versailles, and Frankfort, ending with a buffet supper in the Gold Room of the Lafayette Hotel.

At the regular monthly meeting of the executive committee on 30 September 1957 it was suggested that the name of the foundation be changed to the Bluegrass Trust. At the full membership meeting a week later a resolution regarding the transformation of title was presented and passed. As stated in the minutes, "The primary reason for this change was to broaden the scope of this organization and to simplify its name." Thus the Foundation for the Preservation of Historic Lexington and Fayette County officially became the Blue Grass Trust for Historic Preservation. The change recognized a relationship with the National Trust, of which it had become an institutional member.

New names appearing in the roles of officers or committee members in late 1957 were Hilary J. Boone, treasurer; Robert Jewell and Edward Wilder, board of directors; Mrs. William Robb and Mrs. William Talbert, house committee; Mrs. Frank Zorniger, special events and also acquisition committees, which later also included Mrs. Henry Graddy and (later) Mrs. Lawrence Brewer; Warfield Gratz, historical committee; and Mrs. Henry Martin, Jr., decorating committee. Although holding no office at this time (he later was to serve as president), young Joseph Graves, Jr., became a dedicated member.

Joseph C. Graves, Sr., died 2 June 1960, only five years after the inception of the Trust. The board of directors pledged themselves to carry on his ideals. Included on the board at this time were Robert Houlihan, Philip Noffsinger, and Harry Tucker. Hilary J. Boone was elected president to succeed Graves, and Mrs. F.H. Wright and Charles Graves were made vice-presidents. Mrs. Hamilton remained secretary.

A tribute is due Joseph C. Graves, Sr., for his promotion of publications pertaining to the Blue Grass Trust, the Hunt-Morgan House, and Kentucky architecture. Mention has been made of Burton Milward's booklet *The Hunt-Morgan House*, brought out at the time the house was opened to the public. Issued a month later was a large architectural map, *Ante Bellum Suburban Villas and Rural Residences of Fayette County, Kentucky, and Some Outstanding Homes of Lexington*, showing perspective sketches of well over three hundred buildings and floor plans of more than fifty. It was accompanied by a twenty-page explanatory booklet printed by the Thoroughbred Press, Lexington. In March 1956 there appeared *An Architectural Ramble in Historic Ante-Bellum Lexington*, a bird's-eye-view map covering from Gratz Park northward to beyond Limestone and Fifth streets, and eastward to the Episcopal Cemetery on Third Street. The printing, in two colors on tan paper, was by Clarke and Way of New York City. No record indicates that the Trust subsidized either of the maps—although it received all proceeds from their sales—and it is presumed that Mr. Graves financed them himself. At the 4 March 1957 meeting of the executive committee of the board of trustees he proposed that the Trust publish the book by the creator of the two maps, *Ante Bellum Houses of the Bluegrass*. As it turned out, the project was submitted to the University of Kentucky Press, which brought out the book in December 1961, eighteen months after Graves died; but its production was financed partly by funds the Trust channeled into it from the Margaret Voorhies Haggin legacy and by personal donations from Mrs. Lucy Graves and Mrs. Retta Wright. *Ante Bellum Houses of the Bluegrass* was dedicated to Joseph Clark Graves, Sr., as founder and first president of the trust, and it is entirely fitting that the present publication of wider scope, *Antebellum Architecture of Kentucky*, be inscribed to those who joined him in his noble venture.

7 January 1991

ACKNOWLEDGMENTS

THE ACCUMULATION of names of institutions and persons who have helped an author on a project that has lasted more than a half century is considerable. Investigation of buildings included in this book began in 1938 for a master's thesis suggested by and written under Professor Edward W. Rannells, chairman of the art department of the University of Kentucky. The subject was the architectural work of John McMurtry (1812-90), and the thesis was completed and a master's degree received in 1939. By this time the author's field had broadened to include all of Kentucky architecture. Special thanks is due Mr. Alfred Andrews, who was then working on a master's thesis on Gideon Shryock for a degree at Columbia University, and who invited the author to accompany him on his state-wide expeditions. Equal appreciation is due Mrs. John S. Gardner, who had a penchant for visiting old (often dilapidated) houses and frequently asked the author to share these excursions. By these means some of the most valuable photographs and measured drawings, many of them of buildings no longer in existence, were obtained.

The author is indebted to a coterie of local historians of that period for facts about and appreciation of the early Bluegrass region. They include Mr. (referred to as "Colonel") James Maurice Roche, who had known personally John McMurtry and Thomas Lewinski; Mr. William H. Townsend; Mr. John Wilson Townsend; Mrs. Willis S. Field, daughter of Cincinnatus Shryock; Mrs. Maude Ward Lafferty; Mr. C. Frank Dunn; Mr. Charles R. Staples; and Mr. J. Winston Coleman, Jr. The last shared his extensive file of photographs of early Kentucky architecture, many of which he had taken himself. His collection also included numerous historic photographs. Similar collections had been made by Mr. Dunn and Mr. Staples, and by Dr. Waller O. Bullock, who also made

them available to the author, to which testify a number of illustrations in the present book.

Institutions and a commercial house from which old pictures were obtained during early researches were the Lexington Public Library, Transylvania University Library, the University of Kentucky Libraries, the Filson Club, the University of Louisville Library, and Lafayette Studio in Lexington.

Others who were helpful in various ways in furthering the author's pursuit of Kentucky architecture were the two grandchildren of John McMurtry, John and Elizabeth Watkins; Mr. and Mrs. Joseph C. Graves; the latter's sister, Mrs. F.H. (Retta) Wright; Mrs. Margaret Preston Johnston; Mrs. Eleanor Parker Hopkins; Miss Anne Worthington Callihan; Miss Virginia Hayes; Miss Carolyn Reading (later Mrs. Victor Hammer); Mrs. Amelia Buckley; Mrs. John Johnstone, and Mr. Burton Milward. Not to be overlooked is a history class on the commonwealth at the University of Kentucky given by Dr. Thomas D. Clark, who has remained a source of inspiration to the present time. Association with others is noted in the dedication to the Blue Grass Trust.

After his move to New York in 1943, the author specialized in Asian studies at Columbia University, and American architecture took second place. It was kept alive through contact with Avery librarian Talbot F. Hamlin and with Professors Everard M. Upjohn and Emerson Swift of the fine arts department at Columbia. There was also correspondence with Professor Rexford Newcomb of the University of Illinois and Professors Justus Bier and Walter Creese of the University of Louisville. Research facilities included not only Avery Library but the New York Public Library and the Metropolitan Museum of Art Library.

A John Simon Guggenheim Fellowship in 1963 made possible a year of study of Kentucky architecture that was concentrated outside of the Lexington area.

A commission from the *Courier-Journal* permitted a three-months' sojourn for study in Louisville in 1973. Dr. Samuel W. Thomas, editor of books published by the *Courier-Journal* and himself a writer on historic Kentucky subjects, has been one of the author's most loyal and persisting patrons. Dr. Thomas's associate, Mrs. Mary Lawrence Young, rendered inestimable service by adding to Dr. Thomas's research contributions and checking references.

A corresponding period of three months was spent in Lexington in 1974 through sponsorship of the Lexington–Fayette County Historic Commission, directed by Mr. Richard S. DeCamp. The visit resulted in the book on Lexington *Vestiges of the Venerable City*, published in 1978.

Foremost of enthusiasts over historic Kentucky architecture is Miss Bettye Lee Mastin of the *Lexington Herald-Leader,* whose articles on old houses and related topics are frequently referred to in the notes of this book. The author is deeply indebted to her, and to Dr. Samuel W. Thomas, as well as to Dr. Patrick Snadon and Mr. William Blair Scott, Jr., for going over early versions of this manuscript and submitting valuable suggestions for its improvement.

The author is grateful to the owners and occupants of the numerous buildings that he has chosen for allowing him to investigate and photograph them. To a host of residents, most of them met since the author's return to Kentucky in 1978, he is indebted for various contributions to this project. Among them are Mr. and Mrs. James D. Birchfield, Mrs. Helen E. Abell, Mrs. Hunter Adams, Mr. Ben Ardery, Mrs. Edith S. Bingham, Mr. Jamie Clark, Mrs. Carole Cogswell, Mrs. Rebecca Conover, Mrs. Dorothy H. Crutcher, Mrs. Mary Louise Duke, Mr. William Barrow Floyd, Mr. Martin Ginocchio, Mr. Joseph C. Graves, Jr., Mr. Howard Gregory, Mr. David H. Hall, Mrs. Frances Keightley, Mr. Stanley Kelly, Miss Bettie Kerr, Mr. and Mrs. Robert McMeekin, Mrs. Eleanor O'Rear, Mr. Calvin Shewmaker, Mr. Gary Stone, Mr. James C. Thomas, Mrs. Mai Noy VanArsdall, Mr. and Mrs. Robert Wilson, Jr., and Mrs. Carolyn Murray-Wooley.

The author appreciates the fine editorial work performed by Dr. Samuel W. Thomas, and by Ms Joanne Ainsworth.

INTRODUCTION

Antebellum Architecture of Kentucky is not a history of Kentucky architecture, and it certainly is not a survey of pre–Civil War building here either. Its concern is with architectural heritage, with the manifestation and derivation of architectural forms, with building as a fine art, and with its quality as opposed to its quantity. The examples are a selection. In contrast, the author's *Vestiges of the Venerable City* (1978) was both an architectural history and an inventory of old Lexington buildings, and *Ante Bellum Houses of the Bluegrass* (1961), together with the map *Ante Bellum Suburban Villas and Rural Residences of Fayette County* (1955), dealt extensively with surviving dwellings of the early period. The Kentucky Heritage Council, in collaboration with various local resources, has since published a number of county surveys, and that program continues. A catalog of buildings in the entire state obviously would be too voluminous for a single presentation and is far from the object of this undertaking.

The present book deals with intangibles and concentrates on essences. It is preoccupied with original forms rather than in what buildings may have become later. The silent and crumbling ruins of the Parthenon hardly relay the intense devotion of the ancient Greeks to their goddess Athena. The remains are only a partial shell of the colorful and perfect edifice that was erected in Athena's honor. The superposition of a monstrous office tower on Boston's 1848 Custom House reduces Ammi B. Young's Greek Revival Pantheon to the podium of a Pharos lighthouse. And the conversion of James H. Dakin's Bank of Louisville into a theater lobby diminishes an architectural masterpiece—complete in itself—to a mere passageway into an entertainment facility unrelated in architectural style. Guide books state these changes as facts. To the author they are desecrations, though the last is infinitely to be preferred to its destruction.

These buildings, as initially realized, were Platonic eidolons, perfect models, of which they now fall far short. The temple on the Acropolis, the customhouse in Boston, and the bank in Louisville were all notable monuments, symbols of a culmination of culture. As built, they were full-voiced proclamations of architecture. As ruins, or segment, or compartment, they are less than half statements.

Although the original forms of most of Kentucky's notable early buildings have been lost, it was in that condition that they figured in our architectural heritage, and not in any of the various shapes that time and chance renovations have made them. A few important examples of early building have been carefully preserved and restored, such as Liberty Hall in Frankfort and Farmington in Louisville, and they may take a place among the intangibles mentioned. The expanded group constitutes a collection worthy of our utmost consideration. These examples are the links of a chain that spans the beginning to culmination of the first efflorescence of Kentucky architecture. It lasted little more than a century, all but ending with the Civil War. The building slowdown occasioned by the conflict serves as a fitting terminus for the present study. Purity of architectural expression was not generally resumed afterward, except for a few instances that will be pointed out in due time.

Like the book on houses of the Bluegrass, *Antebellum Architecture of Kentucky* is divided into chapters determined by well-defined phases of architecture. Part 1 concerns the use of primary building materials. Its chapters have to do with construction in log, frame, stone, and brick. Then follows an examination of Shaker building, which remained somewhat isolated from the mainstream of Kentucky architecture. Much of its character was determined by the Shaker hierarchy in New York and Ohio, and by the brilliance of a local master builder. Part 2 takes up the establishment of architecture per se, which occurred during the Federal period. The monuments are divided into three styles: Georgian survival, the geometric, and classic revival. Part 3 deals with the regional manifestation of the popular national architectural modes that prevailed during the decades preceding the outbreak of the Civil War: Greek Revival, Gothic Revival, and Italianate. Each is subdivided into several types.

While adhering to the chronology and organization of the Bluegrass book, *Antebellum Architecture of Kentucky* embraces a broader scope. Besides residences, it includes fortifications and communal complexes, commercial and entertainment buildings, as well as educational and religious edifices. But the current work is not limited to Lexington; it expands to other centers and to other areas. The seedbed of early architecture was not evenly distributed throughout the state. It was determined by the most desirable locations, by fertility of land and provision of water, and by the accessibility of those places, via navigable watercourses, preexistent trails, and later roads. The broad and irregular district rich in early architecture may be said to include Maysville, Mount Sterling, curving through Richmond and Crab Orchard, taking in central Kentucky, continuing up through Bardstown, and ending in and around Louisville. The initial leadership of Lexington, where the earliest trails and roads converged, had begun to shift to the river port of Louisville by the second quarter of the nineteenth century. This was due largely to the introduction of the steamboat, though tempered by the ensuing complement of steam-powered trains.

Kentuckians' pride in preserving their architecture dates back at least to 1854-56 when Thomas Lewinski was commissioned by James B. Clay to rebuild his father's house, Ashland, which had become structurally unsound. The new building followed the old layout and massing, and although the bracketed style was much in evidence, early features such as the colonnetted doorway and the Palladian window above it reappeared. Gideon Shryock's statehouse at Frankfort (1827–30) was supplemented by a detached office building in 1869–71, yet it continued to serve as the capitol until 1912, when a considerably larger successor replaced it. Afterward the Shryock building became a museum and the headquarters of the Kentucky Historical Society. Shortly after World War I, the preservation-restoration movement began in Kentucky. Federal Hill at Bardstown

was made a state park in 1923, with the house being opened to the public under the false assumption that Stephen Collins Foster had written "My Old Kentucky Home" about and in it. In 1926 a smaller reproduction of Harrod's Fort was built at Harrodsburg, and it also was made a state park as part of a historic compound encompassing the old pioneer burying ground, the "Mansion House" of Major James Taylor, and the Lincoln Marriage Temple. Duncan Tavern in Paris was refurbished and became a museum in 1940. About the same time Cane Ridge Meeting House in Bourbon County was restored, and two decades later it was sheltered under a large brick building. Other restorations followed, among them the Dr. Ephraim McDowell House and apothecary shop in Danville; Sportsman's Hill near Crab Orchard; Locust Grove and Farmington in Louisville; the John Wesley Hunt House, Ashland, and the Palmateer-Todd House in Lexington; Riverview in Bowling Green; and Cassius Clay's White Hall in Madison County. Old Mud Meeting House in Mercer County and Big Spring Meeting House in Versailles underwent restoration in the mid-1970s. The town of Washington had been the scene of similar activities for several years, and Mefford's Fort was moved from an isolated location into Washington for protection. The most ambitious undertaking has been the restoration of the Shaker village at Pleasant Hill, opened in 1968. Three years later the first of the extant Shaker buildings at South Union was purchased for a similar endeavor.

Many nineteenth-century religious and secular buildings have continued to serve their original purposes, although some have been drastically altered (such as Saint Martin of Tours in Louisville, the Abbey of Our Lady of Gethsemani in Nelson County, Cottage Grove near Bardstown, and Pleasant Lawn in Woodford County). Some have been enlarged (Oxmoor in Jefferson County), and some abbreviated (the Alberti House in Fayette County). Others serve different purposes, which have caused them to be altered accordingly (Morrison College in Lexington). Of the key examples dealt with in the following pages, less than half continue to function in the purpose for which they were built, and about one-tenth serve other requirements. Approximately one-seventh, plus those in the Shaker villages, have become museums. At least one-third have been allowed to deteriorate to a hopeless stage or have been demolished. About two-thirds of the latter have been casualties to twentieth-century expansion, of which 50 percent postdate World War II. Largely, their destruction cleared the way for mass construction to accommodate an overwhelming influx of people and businesses having little concern for local culture, although a few of the newcomers later showed an interest in regional tradition and have supported preservation.

The author began investigating Kentucky architecture in the late 1930s, which was before Lexington had grown to ungainly size and obliterated so much of its historic architecture. He graduated from the University of Kentucky in 1938 and began a master's thesis on the work of John McMurtry (1812-90), which study was rewritten later and published as *Back Streets and Pine Trees* (1956). It was accompanied by twenty other publications on Kentucky architecture and related subjects, some of which were cited at the beginning of this introduction. After returning to Kentucky in 1978, following an absence of thirty-five years, the author gave numerous lectures and courses on Kentucky architecture at Transylvania University, the College of Architecture at the University of Kentucky, and as Morgan Professor at the University of Louisville. Although all of these writings and classes were beneficial to the present study, the author holds no illusions regarding its completeness. He feels that it is fortunate he was able to investigate and record many buildings that are now gone, but that their survival had been a matter of fate, and that his choice of other examples has been largely subjective. Despite whatever shortcomings this book may have, the author trusts that *Antebellum Architecture of Kentucky* will impart worthwhile information and an appreciation for historic buildings in this region to those who peruse it. Hopefully it will encourage more intelligent restoration, and less thoughtless renovation and imitation.

Unless otherwise noted, drawings and photographs illustrating this book have been made by the author. For all floorplans drawn by the author, the scale marker equals 20 feet.

PART ONE

EXPLORATIONS IN TECHNIQUES AND MATERIALS

1 LOG STRUCTURES

IT MAY SEEM REMARKABLE that in wooded America log houses were not built and used by the earliest settlers from across the Atlantic. The only precedent for log construction which the English brought was the stake fence. In the Massachusetts Bay Colony, the Pilgrims replaced their temporary wigwams with half-timber shelters. In Virginia, before the middle of the seventeenth century, buildings both of half-timber and brick were erected, and the latter material was given increasing preference. Horizontal log construction was introduced to the New World by the Swedes, who settled along the Delaware River in 1638.[1] As in Swedish peasant dwellings, rooms usually were square and had a fireplace in the corner. About 1710, German settlers in Pennsylvania began constructing log buildings, but it is not clear whether they acquired the practice from the Swedes or brought it with them from the northern Alps. Both groups initially built houses of round tree trunks, and later they squared the timbers and made neatly fitted joints. The Scotch-Irish were the first English-speaking immigrants to adopt the log cabin, and its use spread throughout the seaboard frontier. Wood being a good thermal insulator, the log house was cool in summer and by use of the fireplace could be heated in winter. The English were fully aware of the advantages of log construction by the time settlers began moving westward.

The earliest record of a log building in what would become Kentucky is in Dr. Thomas Walker's journal for 23 April 1750. Walker, a surveyor for the Loyal Land Company of Virginia, had entered the inland territory through a cleft in the mountains he later was to name Cumberland Gap. He divided his party into two groups, directing one to remain and establish a post while he led the other into the wilderness. Upon his return, Walker recorded: "The People I left had built an House 12 by 8, clear'd and broke up some ground, & planted Corn, and Peach Stones." This log house was four miles below Barbourville in Knox County. The site was later determined by J. Stoddard Johnston from landmarks recorded by Walker and "a pile of chimney debris."[2] A twentieth-century reconstruction includes a chimney, although Walker's description does not mention one, and it is very unlikely that one existed until much later. Photographs taken over the years indicate that the cabin has been rebuilt several times and the chimney has changed ends.

During the middle of the eighteenth century, a more temporary type of shelter was usually fashioned by hunters, trappers, fur traders, and surveyors. Victor Collot, a French military surveyor, later called them "Forest Men." He reported that they devised a "hut covered with the bark of trees, and supported by two poles; [with] a large fire place on the side of the opening; [and they carried] a great blanket, in which they wrap themselves up when they sleep, placing their feet towards the fire and their head in the cabin."[3] Constructing these huts required only the use of an ax, which like the blanket, they brought with them.

Joseph Doddridge termed this crude lean-to a "hunting camp" or "half-faced cabin" and described it in detail.[4]

The back part of it was sometimes a large log; at the distance of eight or ten feet from this two stakes were set in the ground a few inches apart, and at the distance of eight or ten feet from these two more, to receive the ends of the poles for the sides of the camp. The whole slope of the roof was from the front to the back. The covering was made of slabs, skin and blankets, or, if in the spring of the year, the bark of hickory or ash trees. The front was left entirely open. The fire was built directly before this opening. The cracks between the logs were filled with moss. Dry leaves served for a bed. It is thus that a couple of men, in a few hours, will construct for themselves a temporary, but toler-

Fig. 1.1 Sketch of a half-faced cabin.

ably comfortable, defense from the inclemencies of the weather [fig. 1.1]. . . . A cabin ten feet square, bullet proof and furnished with port holes, would have enabled two or three hunters to hold twenty Indians at bay for any length of time. But this precaution I believe was never attended to; hence the hunters were often surprised and killed in their camps.

Early settlers who came to stay devised the "improvement" cabin, so designated because it was not only better built than the half-faced but also a symbol of a man's right to land occupancy, being part of the improvement he made to his property. This type was built like the Walker cabin, of felled trees, stripped of their branches, and the logs notched at the ends to fit into one another. Thus was raised a square pen, with an entrance hole in one wall and covered by a sloping roof. The walls were only a few timbers in height, as logs were upward of a foot in diameter, and the open spaces between them were half that. The roof was covered with clapboards (fig. 1.2). One could stand upright only in the middle of the pen. Improvement cabins were virtually bunkhouses; cooking was done outside.

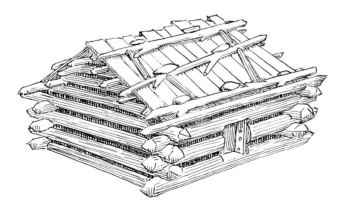

Fig. 1.2 Sketch of an improvement cabin.

The first improvement cabins were built at the site of Harrodsburg by James Harrod and his party of some thirty Pennsylvanians, who camped on the south side of Big Spring Branch early in 1774. They planned a town, planted corn, and surveyed for land claims. Attacked by Indians and suffering a casualty, they went back home. Harrod returned with more allies the following spring, and they reoccupied the improvement cabins. James Norse, head of a company taking up lands in Kentucky, visited the little community on 5 June 1775. He described "Hardwoodtown" as consisting of "about 8 or 10 log cabins without doors nor stopped" (chinked).[5] At this time Harrod was at his preemption, Boiling Springs, about six miles away, and Norse called on him en route to "Boonesburg." He recorded that Harrod had "a tolerable good house having a floor and a Chimney but not stopt."[6] The split-puncheon floor and fireplace were features incorporated in cabins to be built in Fort Harrod.

Examples of the earliest structures of round logs are now rare because of the natural deterioration of wood and an aversion later generations had for rusticity. A domestic survivor is an eighteen-foot-square addition to a shaped-log house about five miles west of Harrodsburg on the Johnson Road. It is remarkable that the primitive addition is later than the more sophisticated core. Logs of both parts are saddle-notched at the corners. Ends of the round logs adjoining the older cabin are hewn into vertical tenons, which have been inserted between double pun-

Fig. 1.3 Junction of a round-log pen with an older square-log cabin on Johnson Road, Mercer County. Photo, 1982.

cheons pinned into the corners of the original pavilion (fig. 1.3). A door and window were in each of the front and rear walls, and a chimney was centered on the outer flank. The building has almost a full second story. In the old section, upper-floor joists rest on horizontal strips of wood pegged to the walls like the puncheons for the addition, perhaps indicating a contemporary improvement.

A number of round-log dependencies are extant in Kentucky. In Mercer County, between the Johnson Road cabin and Central Pike, stands a well-preserved barn that serves as a mow in an enlarged barn, which has protected it from the weather for many years. A corncrib of slender round logs is on the nearby Turner Bottom tract on Chaplain River, near Bruners Chapel Road. Two examples in Woodford County accompany the General Scott House on Soard Ferry Road and the Joel DuPuy House on Grier's Creek (fig. 1.4). These outbuildings are probably several decades later than the earliest dwellings.

Shortly after the settlers from Pennsylvania returned to their improvement cabins on Big Spring Branch in 1775, downstream from the settlement they erected a fort named for their leader.

FORT HARROD. Its northern palisade ran parallel to a stretch of the stream, which flowed directly from east to west, and about sixteen feet distant. One of its two gateways was centered in this side. Fortunately, a

Fig. 1.4 Corner detail of log outbuilding at the Joel DuPuy House, Woodford County. Photo, 1964.

detailed description of this first permanent settlement in Kentucky was made in 1791 by Benjamin Van Cleve, a young man with "a strong penchant for visiting and mapping old forts." Although the fort had been changed and enlarged, Van Cleve recorded from interviews with older inhabitants how it had been built originally.[7]

[It is]a square of 264 feet [fig. 1.5]. The S.W. and S.E. corners are block houses about 25 by 44 feet each. In the N.W. corner is a spring and on the eastern side is another spring. The south line of the fort or the hill is a solid row of log cabins. . . . The east, north and west sides are stockades. Gates of stout timber ten feet wide open on the west and on the north sides . . . defended by port holes, the doors are secured by heavy bars.

The pickets are round logs of oak, grown near by, and all of them more than a foot in diameter. They are set four feet in the ground leaving ten feet clear and the earth rammed tight. They are held together with stout wall pieces pinned in through holes with inch tree nails on the side.

The corner buildings are blockhouses, the upper stories extend two feet from the walls on each side providing for gunfire along the walls.

Seven . . . cabins are between the [two south] block houses. . . . The cabins are 20 by 20, with a space of ten feet between them. They are built of round logs, a foot in diameter, chinked and pointed with clay in which straw has been mixed as a binder. The doors and the window shutters are of oaken puncheons, secured by stout bars on the inside with the latch-string of leather hanging out.

The buildings are a story-and-a-half structures the slope of the roof being entirely to the inside. In the attic of each cabin is a puncheon of water, always filled, and to be used in case of fire. The Indians, on several occasions succeeded in firing the roofs with burning arrows and these casks of water was all that saved them.

The eave bearers are the end logs which project over to receve the butting poles, against which the lower tier of clapboards rest in forming the roof. The trapping is the roof timbers composing the gable ends and the ribs upon which the course of clapboards lie. The weight poles are those small logs on the roof which weigh down the clapboards upon which they lie and against which the next course is laid. The knees are pieces of heart timber laid above the butting poles to prevent the poles rolling off [fig. 1.6].

A ladder of five rounds occupies the corner near the window and the walls are hung with articles of clothing that give some seclusion. Floor boards are hewn with ax [and] adz and are half the length of the floor they are intended to cover. The floors are usually earthen, which by careful handling have become hard and firm. Puncheon floors are all right as long as it is cold enough to let them be covered with furs, but when warm weather comes and people go barefooted splinters become a source of annoyance. These floors however have now been used so long, and scraped so frequently that they no longer yield splinters.

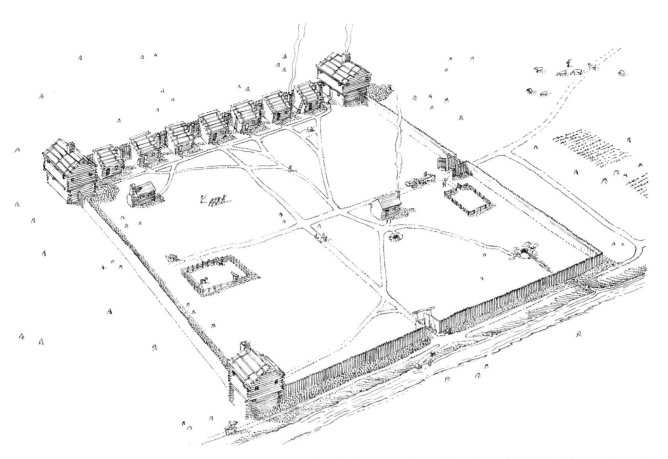

Fig. 1.5 Reconstruction of Fort Harrod (1776), looking southwest.

The walls of this fort are none of them bare, some are chinked with white clay, in which straw has been used as a binder, but several of the houses have the entire walls covered with mortar and rubbed down smooth. A mantle over the fireplace extending across the room supported pewter plates, basins and dishes, while above it hangs the rifle, horn and bullit pouch. The doors are made by cutting out the logs to a proper width with frames set in and pinned fast in holes bored into the logs. . . . Now each household possesses one or more bed, looking glass and a few chairs.

Van Cleve recorded structures other than dwellings in the fort: "A small single-room cabin of one story is to the right of the east corner and is built as a school. It has a dirt floor pounded hard and no chinking in the walls. The fire place is larger than usual, extending along the east wall with an opening at the south end for sections of logs that are hauled in and fit over the andirons. The windows are of heavy paper greased with bear's fat." Though built a few years after the fort, the schoolhouse may have been the first of its kind in Kentucky. Oiled paper windowpanes were an improvement over wood shut-

ters, and the absence of chinking may signify that the logs were squared and fitted together sufficiently close to preclude its need.

He also mentioned that "close to the spring near the center of the fort is the blacksmith shop." On his plan of the fort, there is a square by the inner spring, presumably the blacksmith shop, but labeled

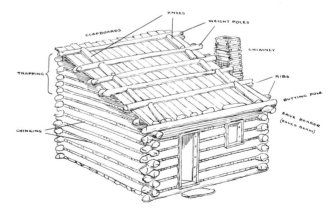

Fig. 1.6 Sketch of a cabin with Van Cleve's terms applied to its members.

"spring." It also indicates a third blockhouse at the northeast corner of the stockade, not mentioned in the description.

A census of the settlement in 1777 lists 85 men, 24 women, 70 children, and 19 slaves, a total of 158 people.[8] About half may have been living in the fort proper, the balance sheltered in the detached cabins along the stream. After some of these were burned by Indians, the garrison was enlarged to protect more settlers. When the British lieutenant governor Henry Hamilton was captured in 1779 at Vincennes by George Rogers Clark and brought to Fort Harrod on the way to Williamsburg, he described it as composed "of about 20 houses, forming an irregular square."[9] He was referring to an L shape.[10]

Present Fort Harrod is a complete reconstruction, smaller in size than the original and built on adjoining land to the south. It was dedicated in 1927, two years before Van Cleve's manuscript was published. Most of the reconstruction was considered satisfactory, and only the schoolhouse was altered. Backs of the cabins serve in lieu of sections of the south palisade. The only gateway is in the east side. It was not recessed and is aligned to a formal approach from College Street. The stockade underwent more authentic rebuilding in 1989.

A counterpart of Fort Harrod was built simultaneously by Daniel Boone at Boonesborough on the Kentucky River. No town developed there, as at Harrodsburg and elsewhere.

THE FORT AT LEXINGTON. Acting on orders from Williamsburg in 1779 Robert Patterson led a party of twenty-five men from Fort Harrod to the site of Lexington, where they cleared about thirty acres and with the timbers built a blockhouse surrounded by a stockade. A rectangular enclosure containing rows of cabins followed. Several versions of it are reported.[11] The defeat of garrisons along the Licking River in 1780 prompted Colonel John Todd to construct a more substantial fort at Lexington. On 15 April 1781 he wrote to Governor Thomas Jefferson that it was to be "proof against Swivels and small Artilery," and he enclosed a plan scaled 20 feet to the inch.[12] The fort was a hollow square of 80 feet, with projecting bastions at the corners. It had walls of tamped earth, 7 feet thick at the base and 9 feet high. Four feet above ground level inside was a 2-foot ledge for riflemen, connected with platforms in the bastions. The outside was sheathed in upright timbers, with a picket rising 6 feet above the earthen wall as a protection

"against Small Arms." The fort was surrounded by a "Ditch 8 feet wide, and between 4 & 5 feet deep," and it was filled with water from nearby Town Fork of Elkhorn Creek. A gateway was centered on the east side of the fort, nearest the earlier blockhouse and a spring. Opposite was a "sally port" or postern. In the middle was built a powder magazine, 20-feet square, with a roof of "14 foot pitch" and perhaps a lookout platform on it (fig. 1.7). For a distance of 70 or 80 yards the adjacent land was cleared to expose those who approached the settlement in plain view. Construction of the fort was accomplished by sixty men and a few teams in about three weeks at a cost of 11,341 pounds, 10 shillings. Inasmuch as the fort was to be used only during attack, it made no provision for domestic accommodations.

The Lexington fortification was a medieval type which European colonists built in North America from the seventeenth century onward for protection from each other. Some examples along the Atlantic seaboard and Gulf Coast may have been known to inland settlers.[13] Among smaller but closer versions that may have served as prototypes for Lexington was Fort Loudoun, located on the Little Tennessee River, some twenty miles from Knoxville and almost directly south of Lexington. Designed by William Gerald de Brahm, it was built in 1757, following a rhombus plan, with large bastions at the acute angles and smaller ones at the obtuse angles.[14] Obviously, the forts along the Ohio, particularly at Pittsburgh, would have been familiar as well as those in the Illinois country, which had recently been captured by fellow Kentuckians.[15] Also on the Ohio (opposite Paducah) was Fort Massac, where George Rogers Clark began his overland march to the fort near St. Louis. Likewise built in 1757, it was "a Picqueted Fort with four Bastions," surrounded by a ditch and breastwork.[16]

An attack by British and Indian mercenaries on Bryan's Station in 1782 prompted the building of a second "cannon proof" fort at Lexington. It was located near the summit of the slope across Town Fork and southwest of its predecessor. The later fort contained one house, "which was occupied by old Mr. January, then 105 years of age, & lady, who were too frail to move in haste, in case of alarm."[17] The first fortification was demolished in 1787, and on the site (south side of Main, west of Mill Street) were built a market house and other commercial buildings. The second example, west of Broadway and north of

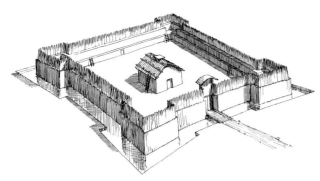

Fig. 1.7 Reconstruction of Col. John Todd's Fort (1781) at Lexington.

High Street, was replaced by residential expansion of the town and is now occupied by the Hyatt-Regency Hotel and Civic Center.

FORT NELSON. A pioneer-type fortification called Fort-on-Shore was built on the Ohio River at Louisville in 1778. Four years later Captain Richard Chenoweth at the head of "regular troops assisted by the militia from all the settled parts of the state" erected a more substantial defense.

This fort was situated between the present Sixth and Eighth streets, on the northern side of Main street, immediately on the bank of river; and it was called fort Nelson, in honor of the third republican governor of Virginia; Seventh street passed throught the fort gate opposite to the head quarters of Gen. Clark. The principal military defense in this part of the country, deserves a few more particulars. It contained about an acre of ground, was surrounded by a ditch eight feet deep and ten feet wide, intersected in the middle by a row of sharp pickets; this ditch was surmounted by a breast work of log pens filled with the earth obtained from the ditch, with pickets ten feet high planted on the top of the breast work. Next to the river pickets were deemed sufficient, aided by the long slope of the bank.

This account by Mann Butler, published in 1832 in *The Louisville Directory*, noted that "some of the pickets were this summer dug out, in excavating the cellar of Mr. John Love's stores, on Main street, just below Sixth street."[18] Evidently the description was the basis for a perspective drawing of Fort Nelson made for Colonel R.T. Durrett in 1885 (fig. 1.8).

The fort at Louisville was similar to but more ample than its precedessor at Lexington. Instead of the base being tamped earth, the easily erodible soil along the Ohio was retained in log pens with pickets projecting from the breastwork. The river side was protected only by pickets. The bastions were also of horizontal logs. A battered wall sheathed in horizontals, of course, could be mounted by an enemy, and it may explain the necessity for the alignments of "sharp pickets" in the moat.

Concerted Indian attacks in Kentucky concluded with that on Bryan's Station, near Lexington, on 15 August 1782, followed a few days later by the great loss at the engagement at Lower Blue Licks. Soon settlers began moving out of the forts and erecting houses on newly acquired land. These were meant to be permanent abodes and were constructed with

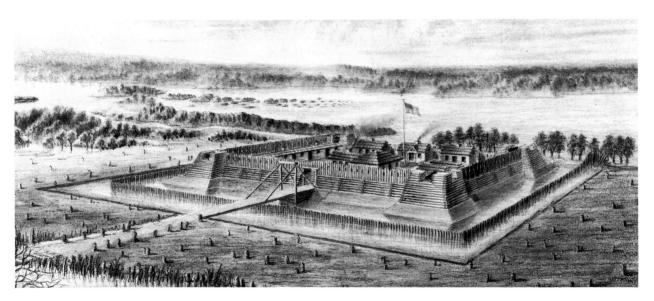

Fig. 1.8 Reconstruction of Fort Nelson (1782), Louisville. Sketch made in 1885 by Col. R.T. Durrett. Courtesy of the Filson Club.

more care. The chief innovations were taking the time and going to the trouble to season and square the timbers.

Several systems of corner notching appeared in squared-log buildings. The first was a carryover from the saddle joint, which seems to have been used universally in round-log construction. In the later phase it became angular. Here the end of a timber was hewn like a gable roof on which was fitted the shallow inverted V-shaped notch of another log (fig. 1.9). The weight of logs placed one upon another locked them in place. Examples of this type appear in Mercer County, in the Watts and Crenshaw cabins in Fayette, the Hutton House in Anderson, the Carroll House in Jessamine, the Cane Ridge Meeting House in Bourbon, and the barn at The Cedars in Harrison County.

A second system was termed dovetail or half-dovetail, depending on how the underside of the notch was cut. The notched end of the log was left protruding as a wedge form, often narrower on the outer side and widest on the outer end (fig. 1.9). Outwardly sloping planes were intended to drain off rainwater. The dovetail system, used in Scandinavia and Germany, was transplanted to Pennsylvania, where the saddle joint may also be found.[19] The two systems seem to have about equal distribution in Kentucky, although the earlier saddle variety dominates in numbers. Both required chinking in the spaces between the logs. The Rankin House in Lexington, the Bowman House in Fayette County, and Mefford's Fort in Mason County employ the dovetail method.

A third mode was the lapped joint, composed of neatly squared cuts formed perpendicular to one another. Timbers were fitted so closely that little filling was required between them. One wonders if dowels sometimes were inserted vertically through the ends

Fig. 1.10 Detail of logs tenoned into post in wing of log house off Vince Road, Jessamine County. Photo, 1973.

to keep the logs from slipping out of place. The one lapped-joint example known to the author is the superstructure of a small stone springhouse near the site of the Carroll House in Jessamine County.

A fourth system, equally unique, consisted of squared logs with ends fashioned into tenons that were fitted into slots in an upright post. It was similar to the locking method used in the house on Johnson Road in Mercer County (fig. 1.3). As there, it was for attaching an addition, except that at the connection the end tenons were fitted into a slot in an upright post. A hole was then drilled through both, and they were fastened together by a pin. The method permitted a fairly tight joint. This type figures in the rear ell of a four-level house off Vince Road near Nicholasville. The outer corners of both parts are saddle-notched, and mortised posts are placed at the lines of junction, the tenons of the extension logs fitted into them (fig. 1.10). The horizontal members are a good six inches thick, and some exceed a foot in height. The building, with a spring and cooking fireplace in the cellar, is in a ruinous condition. Another two-storied log house in Jessamine County on Indian

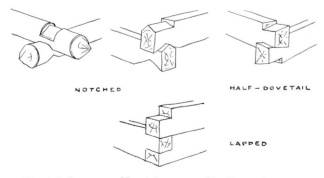

NOTCHED   HALF-DOVETAIL

LAPPED

Fig. 1.9 Systems of log joinery used in Kentucky.

Falls Road contains a wing with the same arrangement.[20] Elsewhere it employs the dovetail system. It also is dilapidated.

Other systems of log joinery are known to have existed in inland America and may have figured within the limits of the commonwealth.[21] Another mode of log construction relied on vertical timbers. Upright puncheons are thought to have been employed in the earliest shelters along the James River during the seventeenth century.[22] The French in the Mississippi River Valley sank logs deep in the ground (*poteaux en terre*) and later set them on wooden sills elevated on stone foundations (*poteaux sur sole*) for the walls of buildings. The dwelling later used as a courthouse (ca. 1737) at Cahokia, Illinois, makes use of the latter system.[23] A related example is on Royster Road, east of Lexington. It is a dogtrot house built of horizontal logs up to second-story windowsill level. From there up is a row of vertical logs, split in half, set adjacent to one another with the flat side out.[24] The exterior has been covered with clapboards; the inside is coated with plaster, though not so as to obliterate the corrugated forms of the log. This probably was an early method for heightening the second story, and raising the roof.

THE JOHN BOWMAN II HOUSE.   One of the oldest detached houses still in existence was on the land of John Bowman, whose tract of seven hundred acres lay north of James Harrod's preemption, northwest of Danville in Mercer County near the present Boyle County line. John Bowman II was granted permission to build a mill on Dick's (Dix) River in February of 1784, and it would seem that he abandoned his father's station and constructed his house near the

mill at this time.[25] It stood about three-quarters of a mile southeast of Bowman's Station. This was a large dwelling a bit short of a full second story, constructed predominantly of oak logs, saddle-notched at the corners. Oak chips figured prominently in the chinking between the logs, along wih stones and clay, and an occasional sapling. The building had a central dogtrot, or breezeway, open at both ends, on each level. The west pen had a root cellar beneath it, with walls of dry stones, and it was entered by stone steps on the south side of the chimney. Great bark-covered logs served as first-floor sleepers; and in the second story, small round logs functioned as roof rafters. The second floor, however, was carried on slender 7½-inch squared joists, beaded on the lower edges, indicating they were exposed. The two stone chim-

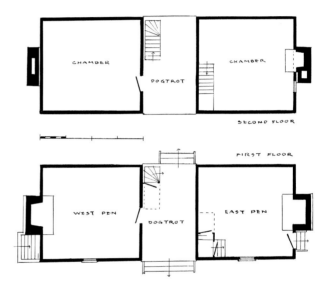

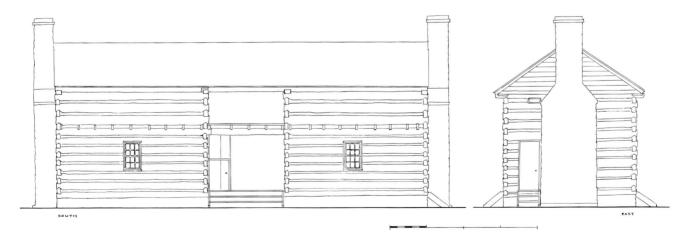

Fig. 1.11 Restored elevations and floor plans of the John Bowman II House (1784), Mercer County.

neys were of similar size, though that at the east end accommodated a fireplace on both floors, whereas its mate had one only on the first (fig. 1.11).

The only windows in the house were the single openings in the south wall of the two lower rooms. All three outside doors faced east. That to the easternmost room adjoined the chimney, those to the two west rooms opened onto the lower and upper dogtrots. The upper west chamber had only the door opening. The jambs of these openings, as well as those of the chimneys, were puncheons with pins driven into the ends of the logs. The upper east room had only a narrow slot, about 8 inches tall by 23 inches wide, between logs over the outside door below. It probably was furnished with a removable

board and served as a porthole. This room was reached by an enclosed stairway in the southwest corner of the pen. The stairway in the dogtrot was an enlargement of earlier stairs, as parts of the upper floor joists had been cut away for its passage. Unlike the original stairs in the east pen, it had winders at the base; its railing was modern.

The second-floor volume expanded into the roof structure. The round rafters were seated on cornice logs 8 inches high and 16 deep, pinned into the top wall logs and overhanging the outer plane 10 inches. Cornice logs and joist beams of the east pen continued across the dogtrot, their ends resting on short wood pieces projecting from the west pen (fig. 1.12). An odd feature was that the logs in the upper walls

Fig. 1.12 The John Bowman II House on its original site, from the southeast. Photo, 1982.

were larger than those below, indicating no regard for the hoisting problem.

Later, the dogtrot was enclosed, a lean-to was added across the south front, and the building was covered with clapboards. Various doors and windows were cut through the original walls, and the east entrance by the chimney was converted into a window. In 1987 the house was disassembled and moved to Boyle County.

THE CARROLL HOUSE.   Joseph B. Carroll settled on five hundred acres bordering the Kentucky River downstream from Clay's Ferry, in what is now Jessamine County, where he built his home. On a timber in the main room he incised his name and the year 1785. It was similar to the Bowman House in that its logs were saddle-notched and it was a dogtrot type with a three-quarters second story (fig. 1.13). There was a cellar under one pen and a separate, single-storied kitchen. The walls were of oak, and a single log sill spanned the entire width of the large pavilion (47 feet). The roof rafters and ridgepole were of cedar, and the roof was sheathed, pegged, and shingled with oak.[26] The three end chimneys and foundations were of limestone, the latter being of respectable proportions to counter the acclivity of the site overlooking the river. The dogtrot was reached by a stoop with stairs on either side, at least during the late years of its existence. Narrower cuttings under the sills of the first-story windows indicated original openings were smaller; and the upper fenestration was later. Unlike the Bowman House, the upper dogtrot may have been enclosed from the beginning. The lower dogtrot was filled in relatively recently.

The two principal rooms opened onto the breezeway between them, and a second door at the back of

Fig. 1.13 The Joseph B. Carroll House (1785), Jessamine County. Photo, before 1949, by J. Winston Coleman, Jr.

the east room was convenient to the kitchen (fig. 1.14).[27] Fireplaces were arched, and the east room had a remarkably large hearth, measuring over 5 by 7 feet. Stairways were placed similarly to those in the Bowman House, and both had winders at the base. The kitchen may have been detached originally, but the intervening space had been roofed over by this century. The 7-foot-deep porch across the back of the house was a later addition, and it subsequently was enclosed. A small wing appended to the kitchen was demolished during the early 1940s, and the logs were used to enclose part of the dogtrot. The Carroll House burned to its foundations on 7 March 1949.

Near the ruins is an 8-foot-square springhouse (fig. 1.15). It has limestone walls 2 feet thick, with a ledge opposite the window facing the river (fig. 1.16).

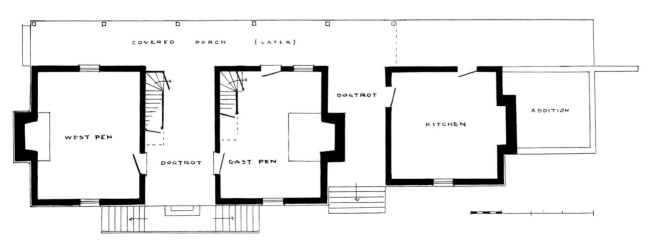

Fig. 1.14 Restored first-floor plan of the Carroll House.

Fig. 1.15 Springhouse at the Carroll House. Photo, 1964.

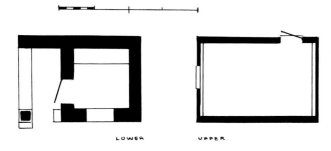

LOWER   UPPER

Fig. 1.16 Floor plans of springhouse at the Carroll House.

A storage room above is built of squared lapped logs with close joints, and there are horizontal planks on the gable ends.

THE ABRAHAM BOWMAN HOUSE. The log dwelling behind the Sowyel Woolfolk House on Bowman's Mill Road, a mile west of South Elkhorn in Fayette County, is thought to have been built by Abraham Bowman, who had established Bowman's Station in Mercer County with his brother, John.[28] Its dovetail construction suggests a later date than that for his nephew's house discussed above. The cellar and garret are reached from ground level by stairs sheltered by an overhanging gable (fig. 1.17). Pegs driven in this sheltered end served for hanging up provisions and equipment. A stone fireplace is in the southwest wall of the main room (fig. 1.18). A single small window (perhaps a later insertion) is in the gable end beside the chimney shaft. Several hundred feet southwest of the house stands a small barn of squared walnut logs, with a breezeway between two bins, or enclosures. On the creek at the foot of the hill Bowman later built a two-storied stone mill, with stone and frame additions, including a clerestory superstructure on the roof.[29]

THE HUTTON HOUSE. A larger house, with open galleries and an outside staircase relating it to the Abraham Bowman cabin, was built at about the same time by Samuel Hutton on what is now Clifton Road in Anderson County.[30] It stands over a spring, its stone basement serving as a springhouse. Two full stories of logs above are saddle-notched. The galleries, or porches, are on the front of the house, and the roof, with gable ends, covers the combined structure

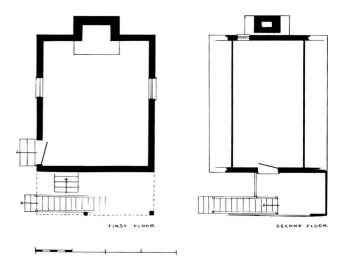

Fig. 1.17 Restored sketch of the Abraham Bowman House (late 1780s), Fayette County.

FIRST FLOOR   SECOND FLOOR

Fig. 1.18 Floor plans of the Abraham Bowman House.

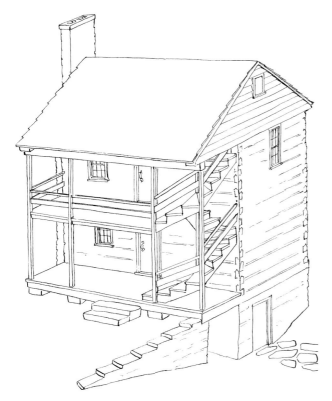

Fig. 1.19 Restored sketch of the Samuel Hutton House (after 1783), Anderson County.

(fig. 1.19). Gallery stairs under the roof swing around a newel post to the third floor. At the opposite end, the chimney is centered on the roof peak, putting fireplaces near the front corner of the first- and second-story rooms. A lean-to has been added at the back of the house, and much of the building is covered with clapboards.

Outside stairways reappear on later stone and brick buildings in Kentucky, such as on the kitchen of the John Smith House in Franklin County (chap. 3), outbuildings at Rose Hill on North Limestone Street in Lexington, and Grassland on Shelby Lane in Fayette County.

THE RANKIN HOUSE. Until recently, the oldest building in Lexington on its original site was the log house of the Rev. Adam Rankin, built on West High Street in 1784 (fig. 1.20). Considerably more sophisticated than its contemporary, the John Bowman II dogtrot house, it has a developed stair hall at one end, being a rudimentary townhouse plan, and its logs are dovetailed. An eight-foot-broad chimney, undoubtedly of stone, was on the west end. Windows, although small, are relatively plentiful, and batten doors are at front and rear of the stair hall (fig. 1.21). The staircase was open, with a closed string and square posts and banisters. A single large cham-

Fig. 1.20 The Rev. Adam Rankin House (1784, with addition before 1794) at 214 West High Street, Lexington. Photo, 1960s, courtesy of the *Lexington Herald-Leader.*

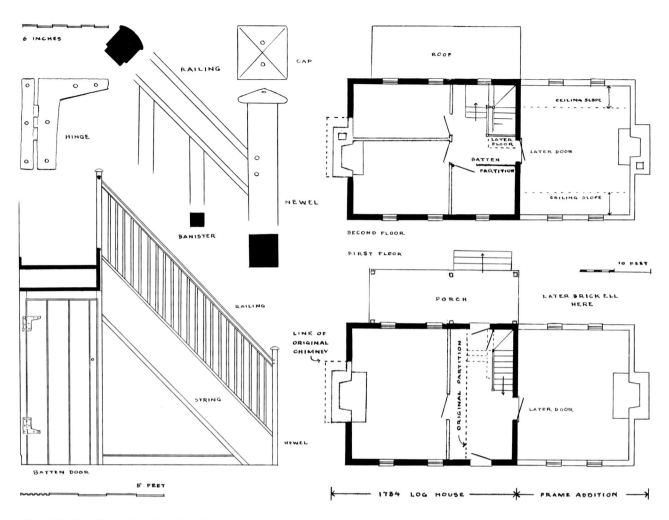

Fig. 1.21 The Rev. Adam Rankin House. *Left:* Elevation and details of staircase. *Right:* Floor plans after 1794. Surviving portions of original structure are shaded.

ber corresponded to the parlor, and a batten partition formed a small chamber at the front of the upper hall.

Within a decade a frame addition was built on the east end of the house, and undoubtedly changes to the log structure were made at that time. The outer walls were covered with clapboards to provide uniformity. The original chimney was replaced by a narrower one of brick, matching that constructed on the far flank. The new fireplaces being solely for heating would indicate provision for a kitchen in a detached building.[31] A back porch (its chamfered posts existed into the 1960s) was contemporary and may have continued across the addition. The lower hall was widened approximately two feet, the old narrowed parlor became the dining room, and the larger new room henceforth was the parlor. The original upper west room was divided, and the south side of the stairwell was shortened for access to the bedroom in

the east wing. Both floor levels of the addition are a few inches above the old, and the roof is lower, the later bedroom upstairs having a ceiling that slopes front and back. When Urban Renewal destroyed Lexington's most historic row on High Street in 1972, the Adam Rankin House was relocated at 317 South Mill Street by the Blue Grass Trust.[32]

THE CRENSHAW CABIN. On the old Berry farm below Lexington at the northeast intersection of Armstrong Mill Road and Squire's Road stood the David Crenshaw saddlebag log house of 1788.[33] The saddlebag plan, with chimney between pens and recesses front and rear, was used in Virginia, the Carolinas, Ohio, Tennessee, and the Deep South. The Crenshaw Cabin was of saddle-notch construction and contained two equal rooms, 16 feet square, connected by a 6-foot stone chimney (fig. 1.22). The spaces adjoining the chimney may have

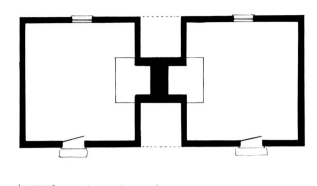

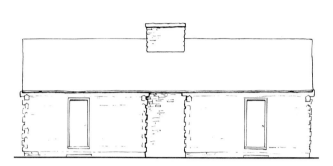

Fig. 1.22 Plan and elevation of the David Crenshaw Cabin (1785), Fayette County.

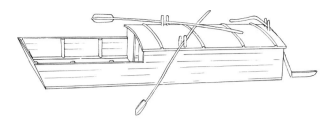

Fig. 1.23 Sketch of an Ohio River flatboat.

sheltered stock at night, and would have been provided with a gate. Another small log structure, about seventy-five feet to the northeast and presumably also built by Crenshaw, had dovetail joints.

Ruins of a saddlebag cabin were at the Col. John Smith stone house in Franklin County (chap. 3). One of the finest in existence is south of the Old Frankfort Pike, between U.S. Route 62 and Aiken Road in Woodford County. It has high stone foundations.

Another saddlebag is the remaining one of three log cabins built by William Christian at A'Sturgus Station along Beargrass Creek in Jefferson County east of Louisville in 1785. Christian was mortally wounded by Indians and buried in front of his cabin in the Bullitt family cemetery, now part of Oxmoor.

MEFFORD'S FORT. A regional type of dwelling, thought once to have been plentiful along the Ohio River, particularly around Limestone (Maysville), was the "flatboat" house. Early settlers coming by water procured bargelike flatboats that drifted with the current and were guided by two oars and a rudder (fig. 1.23). A water-powered sawmill had been built near Fort Pitt (Pittsburgh) in 1777, and it turned out planks that were used in making flatboats. They carried household furnishings, farming utensils, and

livestock, besides the settlers themselves, and when disassembled at their destination, the planks went into floors, partitions, stairs, and doors in log houses. The only known example originally stood on Mapleleaf Road above Maysville (fig. 1.24). Built in 1787 by George Mefford, and referred to as Mefford's Fort, it is believed to be the second house erected in Mason County.[34] It employs dovetail joinery. The enclosed stairway ascends from the larger east room to the west upper chamber (fig. 1.25). Lower rooms have exposed squared beams, and the rafters above are round logs, which support the sheathing for the roof shingles and are halved and pegged together at the apex. A lean-to was built much later on the north side of the house, a porch was added across the front, and the structure was covered with clapboards. Restoration was undertaken by the Mason County Historical Society in 1964. Five years later it was moved as a unit to Washington and the chimney was rebuilt.[35]

Fig. 1.24 Mefford's Fort or the George Mefford House (1787), Mason County. Photo, 1964.

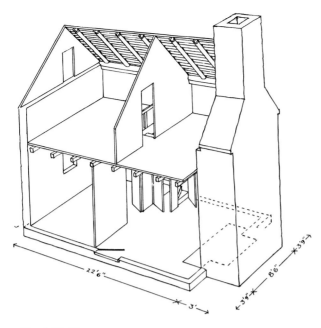

Fig. 1.25 Cutaway perspective sketch of Mefford's Fort.

THE BOARD HOUSE.   A compact, two-and-a-half-story log house was built in 1788-89 for Philip Board just west of the Dry Fork of Chaplain River near the south line of Mercer County.[36] It measured 32 by 21 feet and had a center door front and back and four windows all in the southeast front, facing the stream. Large stone chimneys had been built on each end, providing heat for rooms on both levels, but when first seen in 1980 the one on the right had been rebuilt smaller, and the left one had disappeared. The Board House was a classic of the hall-and-parlor type, with

rooms separated by a batten partition (fig. 1.26). The stairway situated in the parlor had a square landing, entered—two steps up—from both rooms. A closet was under the upper flight. The stairway emerged in the southwest chamber. An early partition upstairs roughly corresponded to that below, and a later wall closed off the stairs. These partitions consisted of overlapping beaded clapboards affixed to studs with square-cut nails, probably dating from the second or third decade of the nineteenth century. From a closet in front of the stairway 22-inch-wide ladderlike stairs ascended to the floored garret. Roof trusses included 3-by-3½-inch squared rafters connected by horizontal collar beams fifty inches above the floor. Light was limited to what seeped in between the weatherboards on each gabled end. First-floor joists were round logs, whereas those for the two upper floors were square and measured 4 by 8 inches with beaded lower edges. For interior finish, plaster was applied directly to the log walls, and the partitions and ceilings were painted. There may have been a separate kitchen. In a mound about 25 feet on axis with and beyond the rear door was a root cellar. The Board House was demolished in 1987.

THE WATTS HOUSE.   A two-story house with walls of saddle-joint construction and inside stairways was built by David Watts on extensive landholdings he acquired in the Boone Creek area, east of Cleveland Road and below Sulphur Well Road in Fayette County between 1790 and 1824.[37] The structure presumably was erected soon after his initial purchase of one hundred acres. The conspicuous external feature of the house was its stone chimney,

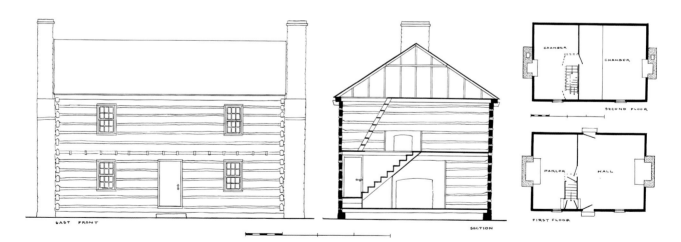

Fig. 1.26 Restored east elevation, section, and floor plans of the Philip Board House (1788-89), Mercer County.

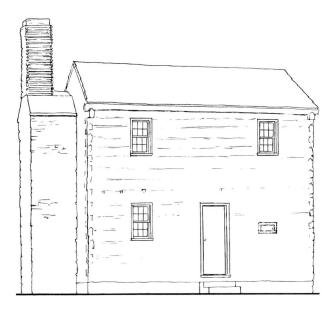

Fig. 1.27 Restored sketch of the David Watts House (ca. 1790), Fayette County.

over eight feet across and 4 feet deep. The chimney stack, later in brick, undoubtedly was originally of small logs well removed from the gable (fig. 1.27). As in the Rankin House, a single large room occupied most of the lower story, and its big fireplace, rectangular in plan, also accommodated cooking (fig. 1.28). In the southeast corner was a boxed-in double staircase with a press and closets beneath each one (fig. 1.29). The two sets of steps rose in opposite directions to separated upper chambers. The end openings on the upper level—like that below in the corner stairway—were lookout slots or portholes. A frame wing was added to the east flank and across the back early in the nineteenth century. When the house was examined in the 1950s it had not been lived in for several decades and the building (especially the frame section) had deteriorated.

THE BURTON HOUSE. Ambrose Burton purchased land a mile east of McAfee in Mercer County

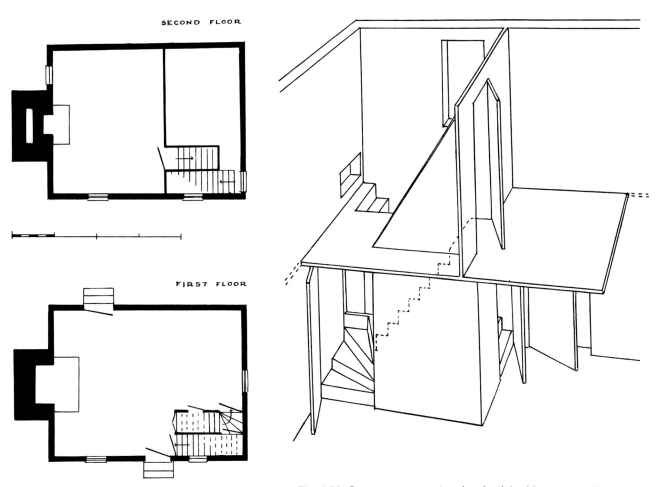

SECOND FLOOR

FIRST FLOOR

Fig. 1.28 Floor plans of the Watts House.

Fig. 1.29 Cutaway perspective sketch of double stairs in the southeast corner of the Watts House.

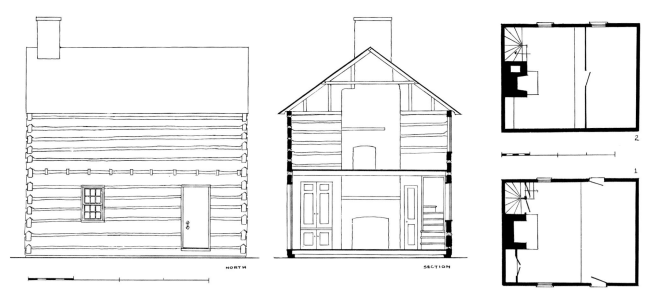

Figs. 1.30, 1.31 Restored north elevation, section, and floor plans of the Ambrose Burton House (1798), Mercer County.

in 1798 and shortly erected his house.[38] It is comparable in size to the Watts House, but it differs from examples so far considered in that its chimney was inside the log pen.[39] The stairway was situated in a recess on the south side of the chimney, and a press was set in the other (fig. 1.30). The first-story interior was neatly finished. Chair railing as well as baseboards encircled all but the fireplace end of the room, and hand-split laths were nailed to the walls and plastered over. The stone chimney breast, dominating the east end, had a wood mantel (now missing) whose nailing board is incised with the first owner's initials and a hex sign inscribed in a circle. Exposed joists were carefully squared and smoothed, and the undersides of the floor boards they carried have a fine bead mold at their junction. The wall of the stairwell was plastered to about a foot and a half above the upper-floor level; otherwise the second story was unfinished, its space rising to the rafters. Floorboards run east to west, and they are in two sections that come together in a straight line across the room (fig. 1.31).

Another feature of the Burton House not encountered before is that in place of a cornice log the plate logs are flush with the walls, and rafters extend as eaves; the seating notch continues as a concave cut visible in the under surface of the rafters from outside (fig. 1.30). Among other log dwellings using the motif is the Joseph Adams House on Van Arsdall Road in Mercer County. A mud-filled frame section was added to the west flank of the Burton House and a frame rear ell was later appended to it.

A LEAN-TO LOG HOUSE. Situated on Coopers Run in Bourbon County, on land that had been owned by Gen. Green Clay, stands a remarkable log house that is a result of additions probably made before 1790 (fig. 1.32). This building forms the nucleus (partly two-storied) of what is now a sophisticated residence with a Greek Revival recessed, square-piered gallery, facing south, flanked by framed end pavilions. The original house seems to have been two rooms of one story with chimneys at either end. A second story of similar plan was added—the upper east room alone with fireplace—and a lean-to at the back. The lean-to contains an enclosed stairway, two rooms below, divided by a batten partition like the rooms in front, and a storage space above. There is a high step from the upper level of the lean-to to the second floor of the front portion. Another enclosed stairway ascends from the smaller, west chamber to the garret over the main part of the house (fig. 1.33). A cellar underlays the lean-to section, entered by an outside hatch at the east end. Beams supporting second-floor joists throughout have beaded lower corners and attest to the early date of the enlargement. Logs of the addition walls are engaged to the principal structure by tenons fitted into the slots of upright posts pegged to the corners of the original house, in the manner described earlier as the fourth system of log joinery. The lean-to form

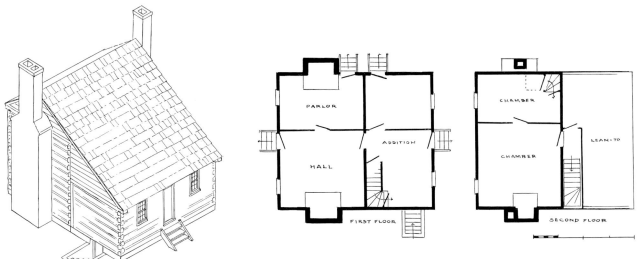

Figs. 1.32, 1.33 Restored sketch, floor plans of the lean-to log house (before 1790?) on Coopers Run, Bourbon County.

makes a unique contribution to Kentucky's assortment of pioneer log dwellings.

LA CHAUMIÈRE DES PRAIRIES.   Perhaps the most singular and extensive log house in Kentucky was built for David Meade II (1744-1929), a wealthy Virginian formerly residing at Maycox, an estate opposite William Byrd's Westover on the James River. In 1795 Meade purchased about 330 acres in Jessamine County, nine miles below Lexington, and the following year he built his house, called Chaumière des Prairies, meaning "thatched cottage on the plains." Well-educated, much-traveled, and something of an artist and connoisseur, Meade laid out his residence symmetrically in the English cottage-farm manner, all of it one-storied. As was customary on the Kentucky frontier, however, it was built mostly of logs. He sketched a plan of the residence and dependencies (scaled ⅟₁₆ inch to the foot) as existing in 1800, upon which the drawing presented here was based (fig. 1.34).[40] Such formality in an inland country seat was unusual for the eighteenth century. The house proper embodied a T plan, with an entrance hall (having benches on either side) and a crosswise passage leading to four chambers. Behind was a 20-foot-square dining room, wainscoted in black walnut and with wide windows and deep seats on both sides.[41] The section beyond the dining room was of frame construction, containing two bedrooms and entries before and to the rear. A covered way connected the frame section to the kitchen, which had cupboards on each side and a huge cooking fireplace and oven at the far end. Chaumière was remarkable for its closets in most of the rooms, including the kitchen. It was flanked by a matching dairy and a smokehouse, both frame. They formed the front corners of a square yard, whose other buildings were log. It was outlined on the east by hen houses and a whiskey house, opposite to which was the privy; and at the two back corners were servants' cabins (fig. 1.35). One assumes that the frame elements were constructed slightly later than those of log.

Meade added rooms to the house after 1800, including a brick pavilion containing a large octagonal parlor, and pleasure grounds of an exotic nature. The early layout has disappeared, but its existence has been verified through the excavation of foundations.[42]

CANE RIDGE MEETING HOUSE.   The earliest western migrants attended to practical matters before building houses of worship. The first churches in Kentucky were built by people with a transplanted communal affiliation, as in the case of Cane Ridge Meeting House, on Flat Rock Road east of Paris in Bourbon County. Constructed in 1791 by Presbyterians from North Carolina, it was the scene of a famous interdenominational revival in 1801. A crowd variously reported from 20,000 to 30,000 persons gathered for a week of prayer and sermons, with seven ministers preaching in the woods. Three years later the congregation of Cane Ridge, led by the Rev. Barton W. Stone, withdrew from the Presbyterian fellowship. When Stone was joined by the Rev.

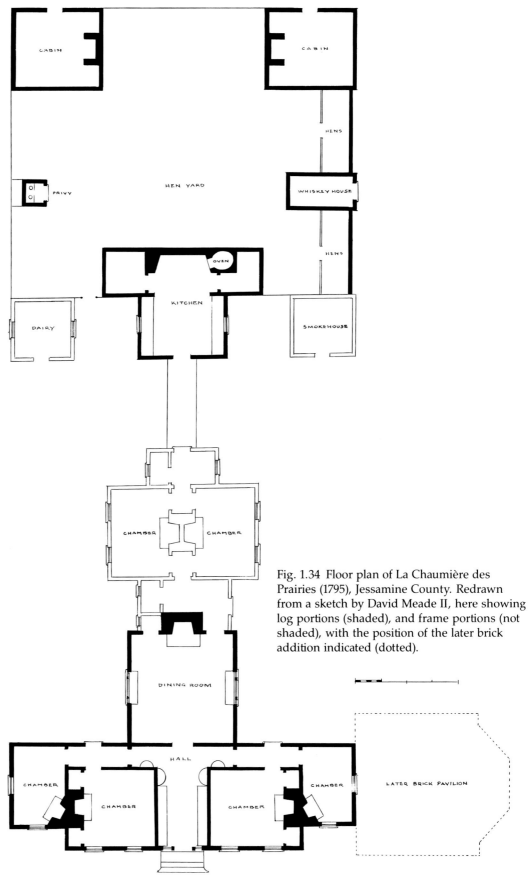

Fig. 1.34 Floor plan of La Chaumière des Prairies (1795), Jessamine County. Redrawn from a sketch by David Meade II, here showing log portions (shaded), and frame portions (not shaded), with the position of the later brick addition indicated (dotted).

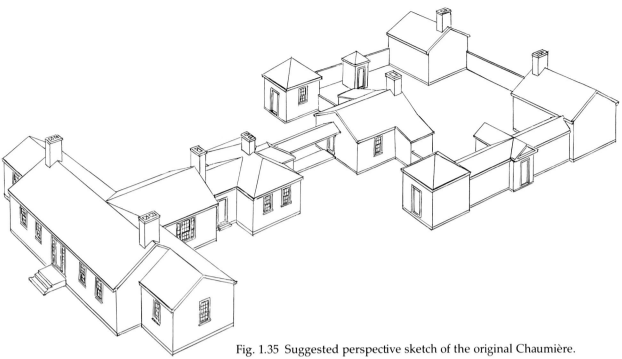

Fig. 1.35 Suggested perspective sketch of the original Chaumière.

Fig. 1.36 Cane Ridge Meeting House (1791), Bourbon County. Photo, 1940s, courtesy of the Library of Congress.

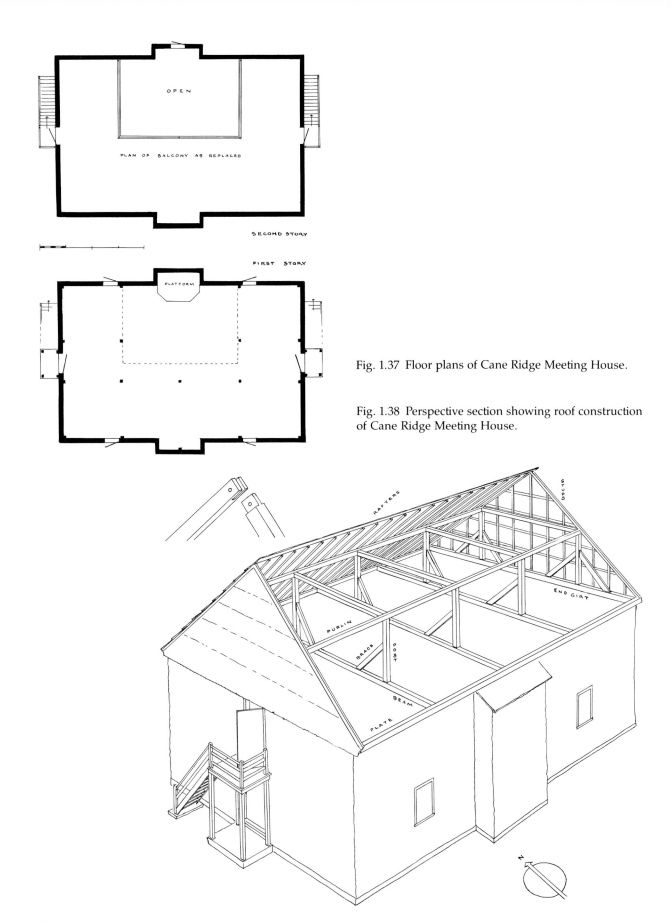

OPEN

PLAN OF BALCONY AS REPLACED

SECOND STORY

FIRST STORY

PLATFORM

Fig. 1.37 Floor plans of Cane Ridge Meeting House.

Fig. 1.38 Perspective section showing roof construction of Cane Ridge Meeting House.

RAFTERS

STUDS

END GIRT

PURLIN

BRACE

POST

BEAM

PLATE

N

Alexander Campbell in 1823, the independent church became known as the Disciples of Christ, a sect whose membership now ranks fifth in the commonwealth and has spread throughout the United States.[43]

Cane Ridge Meeting House measures 48½ by almost 30 feet. Its 16-foot-high walls on stone foundations are of saddle-notched, square-hewn ash logs, with mud and limestone chips for chinking (fig. 1.36). Shallow projections are centered on each of the longer sides, one accommodating the preacher's platform and containing a high window to light the pulpit. Windows and doors are batten and swing on strap hinges. Upper doors indicate a second-floor gallery, later removed. It was supported by posts independent of the walls and reached by outside stairways (fig. 1.37). The present replacement covers three-fourths of the area of the church.

The roof structure is set on three nearly foot-square oak beams, two end girts, and foot-square plates surmounting the side walls. These support a system of 6-inch-square posts holding up 7-by-9-inch purlins connected by 6-inch tie beams (fig. 1.38). Twenty-two pairs of approximately 3½-inch rafters, notched into the plates and over the purlins, are pegged together with mortise-and-tendon joints at the summit of the roof. Subsidiary in the gables is a grid of studs and boards onto which the shingles were nailed. Roof shingles are exposed about 30 inches.

Later the old building was clapboarded outside and plastered inside, and windows were enlarged. About 1940 it was stripped, the balcony was rebuilt, and new shingles were attached to the gables. Two decades later, the historic shrine was enclosed within a protective brick edifice.

Similar to Cane Ridge Meeting House is Old Mulkey Meeting House in the state park of that name near Tomkinsville, Monroe County. It was constructed in 1804 by Jiles Thompson and named for a Baptist congregation leader, Jonathan Mulkey. It has the projections on the north and south sides, the latter now pierced by a doorway, and a wider doorway once was on the west side. The building did not have a balcony.[44]

LAIR'S LOG BARN AT THE CEDARS. The several log farm buildings subsidiary to dwellings that have been noted were of limited size. Mathias Lair's log barn was a major Kentucky structure. Captain Lair sold his Virginia lands after the Revolution and brought his family and belongings down the Ohio River, settling near Cynthiana, where the Buffalo Trace meets the Licking River. He built a brick house in 1794 (enlarged by his son Charles in 1825) and called it The Cedars. Here he erected a huge log barn in 1811.[45] Built on two levels, it was what in Pennsylvania is called a "bank barn," having an earth ramp leading to the upper part. Frame lean-tos were added to either side at an early date (fig. 1.39).

The original superstructure consisted of two mows for the storage of hay, each about 25 feet square, separated by an interior space of about equal

Fig. 1.39 Capt. Mathias Lair's barn (1811) near Cynthiana, with lean-tos partly collapsed. Photo, 1967.

Fig. 1.40 Detail of the Lair barn showing revolving door and a corner of one of the log mows. Photo, 1936, courtesy of Mrs. Eugenie Lair Moss, Cynthiana.

dimensions, used for threshing and loading. The mows were built of giant timbers, fastened together by saddle joints, with center openings in the inner sides on two levels for filling from floor or wagon level (fig. 1.40). The roof structure spanned the entire form, as on a dogtrot house. The lean-tos doubled the size of the barn's second level. The door arrangement is unusual. Whereas Pennsylvania barns of this type normally have large double swinging doors on strap hinges, with a smaller door in one for easy access by persons, the barn at The Cedars has a great main door 16½ feet across, which pivots on a square vertical center post set with iron pins at top and botton. Narrower hinged doors are to right and left, measuring 4 feet 4 inches and 3 feet 6 inches across. When the center door is opened to a ninety-degree angle, a wagon can be driven in, unloaded, turned and driven out again.

The log barn is elevated on a dry stone foundation, and it has an 8-foot areaway under the lean-to on the south side. A series of doors and a few grilled windows open from the inner space, providing access to the stalls for horses and cows, and narrow feeding passages between. Grain bins in the corners connect with the upper level. When last visited in 1967 the stone foundations at the east end and the north appendage had collapsed. The big door, however, was still in good working order.

Felled trees supplied most of the building needs of Kentucky pioneers. This material went into forts and stockades, dwellings and meetinghouses, and barns. It was supplemented by other natural resources, cut stone and tamped earth. Round-log buildings are scarce because their unseasoned timbers degenerate rapidly. Their crudity prompted early replacement by a society self-conscious of its provinciality. Yet many structures of squared logs still serve as residences, though usually hidden behind clapboards and sometimes a veneer of masonry for a more genteel appearance. Pride in historic matters has been responsible for some preservation, such as the sheltering of Cane Ridge Meeting House; for restoration, such as the Rankin House and Mefford's Fort; and for reconstruction, such as Fort Harrod. But, even in ruins, original buildings are infinitely more valuable than reconstructions, in which inaccuracies are practically inevitable. In restorations, errors may occur, no matter how conscientious and knowledgeable the restorer.

2 FRAME CONSTRUCTION

HEWN FRAME HOUSES flourished in Kentucky during the last decades of the eighteenth century and into the nineteenth. In this period of rapid expansion, frame construction fit the tempo of the times. Lexington was described in John Bradford's local newspaper in the late 1780s as the "budding metropolis" made up of "about fifty houses, partly frame and hewn logs, with the chimneys outside."[1] Less than ten years later, according to the only extant contemporary statistical source, *Charless' Almanack for 1806*, Lexington had grown to "104 Brick, 10 Stone & 187 Frame and log Houses."[2] François Michaux, who visited Kentucky in 1802, reported that nearby Paris, which "in 1796 contained only eighteen houses, now has upwards of 150, nearly the half of which are of brick." One would expect the prosperous centers of the Bluegrass to favor brick construction, whereas other towns would resort more to wood. Thus, Michaux described Limestone (Maysville) as having developed within fifteen years and as being composed of "between thirty and forty houses constructed of planks." Also, Washington, four miles distant, was said to have "about two hundred houses all built of planks."[3] The Frenchman had a tendency to exaggerate numerically, but his observations on building materials were discerning. In the days before steamboats favored river towns with abundant commerce, structures in those landing places where travelers and immigrants arrived by flatboat were likely to be predominantly wood. This was as true for Louisville, at the falls of the Ohio, as for Maysville. Josiah Espy, who traversed Kentucky in 1805 and counted thirty brick houses under construction in Lexington, spoke of Louisville as "one of the oldest towns of the state," which had "about 200 dwelling houses, chiefly wooden."[4] The distribution of frame buildings in Kentucky was irregular and somewhat in reverse proportion to regional wealth. The popu-

larity of frame buildings began during the middle of the 1780s and gradually diminished with the coming of the revival styles. A few frame houses—as in Shaker communities—were built in the interim up to the Civil War. Afterward wood as a building material came into its own again, temporarily, as an economic expediency brought on by the impoverishing effect of the war.

Frame construction was introduced into Kentucky originally as a cultivated advance over the frontier practice of building with logs. Its introduction, however, was simultaneous with that of stone, and brick soon followed; being noncombustible and more enduring substances, the latter two were preferred, if they could be afforded. Although log and frame buildings are materially alike, their structural systems differ more than those of log and masonry, where walls are built tier upon tier in horizontal courses. Framing entails fashioning an articulated support, or skeleton, in which squared timbers encase each plane and are strengthened by parallel subsidiary members and diagonal braces forming rigid triangles. The whole is fitted together with mortise-and-tenon joints and locked with wood pins (fig. 2.1). Such a frame could be made flat on the ground and lifted onto stone foundations prepared for it. In the early days, the process known as house raising was participated in by friends and neighbors. When the framing for the various walls was erect and secured, sometimes the interstices were filled with mud and straw, or low-fired brick nogging—laid dry or with a clay binding. In the example illustrated, the spaces were filled with bricks tied together in alternating rows of headers and stretchers, known as English bond. The frame-building method came to the colonies from medieval Europe and especially England, where the practice was to fill the voids of the frame with wattle-and-daub, which then was

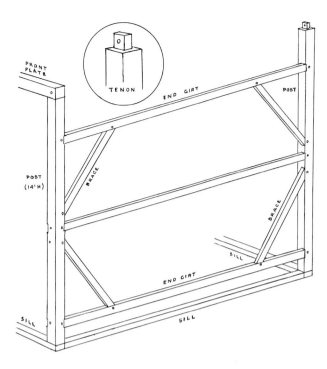

Fig. 2.1 Isometric sketch of end framing of small building west of Coopers' Shop, East Family, Pleasant Hill. In ruins in 1940.

plastered over. The exposed dark structural timbers and light intervening areas presented a decorative effect, and in England such houses were known as "black-and-white." In America, both in Massachusetts and Virginia, the climate demanded a covering, so weatherboards, then shingles (borrowed from the Dutch in the Hudson River region), and finally clapboards were affixed to the exterior. The result was a building of neat appearance, unlike exposed log structures. Inasmuch as log houses were modernized by a sheathing of clapboards as a rule, this probably accounts for the linking together of log and frame buildings in the descriptions of Lexington and Louisville cited above. Today there is a tendency to consider old clapboarded houses frame, whereas many are log underneath.

Although the main timbers for frame buildings were hewn, framing required a quantity of lesser lumber which was not practical to produce by hand methods. Frame construction, therefore, as indeed parts of other methods of construction, depended upon the output of sawmills. Water-powered sawmills had been common in Europe from the middle of the fifteenth century, and they became so in both New England and Virginia beginning in the mid-seventeenth century.[5] Interestingly, they appeared

in America before they were adopted in England, where they were suppressed to prevent unemployment. A diagram of a Virginia example, published in 1650, shows an improved gang-saw type, which consists of several parallel blades in a sash, capable of cutting out a number of boards at one time.[6] Inland sawmills, more than a century later, showed the same characteristics. The first beyond the Alleghenies was that started in 1777 fourteen miles above Fort Pitt on the Monongahela River, and which contributed to the construction of flatboats, as already mentioned.

It has also been noted that water mills appeared in Kentucky soon after the Revolution (like Bowman's, 1784). By the mid-1790s they were beginning to change hands, as advertisements in the *Kentucky Gazette* confirm for one at Hanging Fork on Dick's (Dix) River, a tributary of the Kentucky, in 1793; a combined grist and sawmill on Salt River, eight miles below Harrodsburg, in 1796; as well as similar combinations on Grier's Creek in Woodford County and Silver Creek in Madison County, in 1797.[7] Michaux mentioned that he witnessed in Lexington a machine for sawing wood and stone in 1802. It was probably that of John Jones (1758-1849), to whom George W. Ranck attributed a machine for sawing stone at that time.[8] One assumes it was powered by water like the earlier mills, or perhaps by horses. The use of steam power for such purposes was introduced into central Kentucky in 1806, when contracts were let for building a frame plant for the Lexington Steam Mill Company, with preference for the work "given to such persons as will take shares in the company, if in other respects their terms are equal."[9] In a description of the Bluegrass community, dated 4 March 1809, Fortesque Cuming mentions "a machine for the manufacture of flour to go by a steam engine recently erected, which promises to be of considerable importance."[10] Mills for grinding and sawing often were combined, and for steam to be applied to one would be only a step away from its application to the other. In his *Sketches of Louisville* (1819), Dr. Henry McMurtrie described the "Upper Steam Saw Mill . . . that drives two saws, and one pair of stones for the grinding of corn. . . . The building was erected in 1812."[11]

Companion to the use of boards were nails, which were produced in Kentucky simultaneously. In 1788, John Duncan advertised that his store, opposite the new courthouse in Lexington, had for sale dry goods, groceries, and "a quantity of Nails of different sizes, of his own manufacturing." According to the exchange practices of the times, he was prepared to dispose of these items "on as moderate terms as possible, for Cash, Indian Corn, Tobacco, Butter, Tallow, and Hogs lard."[12] In 1794 Thomas Hart and Son offered "a general assortment of Nails, Brads and Spriggs" of 10-, 12- and 20-penny sizes and flooring brads at 1 shilling, 4 pence per pound for 100 pounds or more, and 8-, 6- and 4-penny nails for progressively higher prices up to 2 shillings, 3 pence, including "spriggs," or wedges, for holding panes of glass in a sash. The same advertisement announced the need for "a number of Journeymen Nailers . . . to whom generous wages will be given in CASH."[13] Two other nail manufactories came into existence in Lexington within the next decade, the more important being that of George Norton in 1801.[14] Out-of-state nail factories bid for Kentucky trade through attractive pricing. Hughes and Fitzhugh of Hagerstown, Maryland, offered a general assortment "on reasonable terms" in 1797, and in 1802 Alexander Hawthorn of Morgantown, Virginia, listed a range of sizes from 12 penny at 11 pence per pound to 4 penny at 18 pence—about two-thirds the price listed locally by Thomas Hart and Sons.[15]

Edward West (1757-1827), Lexington's first watchmaker and a silversmith, inserted a notice in the *Kentucky Gazette* in 1802, to wit: "AS I have invented a *Machine* for the CUTTING OF NAILS, which will on a moderate calculation, cut one thousand pounds of Iron into Nails of any size, in twelve hours; and have shewn a model thereof, to a number of my friends and acquaintances; also, have taken the proper steps to obtain a patent for the same, I do hereby forwarn all persons from making use of said invention, under the penalty of what the law directs in such cases."[16] In all likelihood this was the invention Michaux saw demonstrated in Lexington the same year. "A citizen of this place," he reported "obtained a patent for a new machine for making nails, which was more complete than that employed in the prisons of New York and Philadelphia."[17] Thomas Harris Barlow (1789-1865), who settled in Lexington in 1825, invented a self-feeding nail and tack machine, "which was a success."[18]

Early nails wrought by blacksmiths had shafts tapered on all four sides. The first machine-made nails were square, split from a flat, somewhat wedge-shaped plate of iron. The early machine method resembled that of splitting shingles, and indeed Joseph Coppinger of Baltimore advertised in the *Kentucky Gazette* in 1809 for a Kentucky agent to handle his invention that could "alike be applied to the making of Shingles, Laths, Barrel Staves as also to the Cutting of Nails."[19] They were made in such a way that two corners of the nails were rounded and two burred, the similar corners being adjacent or opposite to one another depending on whether the nail was cut in one stroke or two. Like wrought-iron nails, the first machine-cut nails had hammered heads, which spread out on all sides. Later they had machine-stamped heads, which usually expanded only on one side.

The type of nail used may be the most reliable evidence for determining and dating wood construction, inasmuch as frame houses can be easily altered, openings made larger, trim changed, and additions made, without the telltale signs left in masonry buildings. Wrought-iron nails were the only ones available up to about 1795; cut nails with hammered heads date from then until about 1830, and cut nails with stamped heads came afterward. Round nails, such as persevere today, came into use toward the end of the nineteenth century.

Frame buildings, being the most vulnerable, were not erected until Indian raids had subsided. A well-aimed flaming arrow could transform a frame house into ashes. The last organized Indian attack was led by the British against Bryan's Station in the summer of 1782, and a few years of uninterrupted tranquillity were needed to assure settlers that a frame house could be erected and occupied without anxiety. Such buildings reflected well-established types in tidewater Virginia, whence many of the people had come.

OXMOOR. One of the oldest existing frame houses in Kentucky was built by Alexander Scott Bullitt (1761/2-1816). In 1787 he purchased 1,200 acres in Jefferson County on Beargrass Creek, nine miles east of Louisville, and called his place Oxmoor.[20] His story-and-a-half residence, completed about 1791, has stone foundations, clapboard walls, a nine-foot-broad brick chimney on each gabled end, and nine-over-nine-paned sash windows downstairs and six-over-six above (fig. 2.2). The first story is divided by a central transverse hall of two sections not on axis with one another. The staircase in the west portion is unusual in that its railing has a horizontal volute at the base but no projecting first step of similar shape under it, perhaps a later alteration. The four lower rooms are of various sizes, each with a corner fireplace and—originally—three outside openings (fig. 2.3). The smallest room has a door on the north side

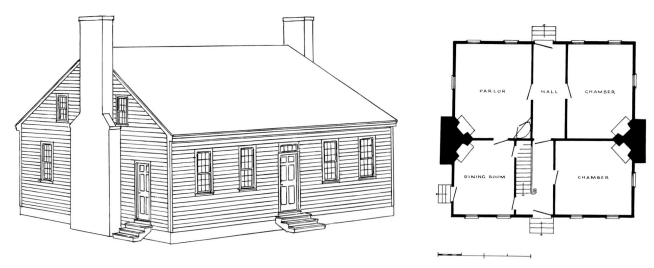

Figs. 2.2, 2.3 Restored sketch, first-floor plan of Oxmoor (ca. 1791), Jefferson County.

and a closet under the stairs, evidently for china, silver, and linens, indicating the room to have been for dining. A detached kitchen stands not far off. The room adjoining the dining room is the largest (about 16 by 20 feet) and served as a parlor. A cupboard in the southwest corner balances the fireplace. The two rooms on the south side of the house were chambers, as were the two on the second floor.

Except for the divided hall, the plan resembles that of Mount Vernon at Lawrence Washington's death in 1752, before it was enlarged to two full stories and extended. Dumfries, Bullitt's birthplace, was on the Potomac River fifteen miles from Mount Vernon. In plan the house on Beargrass Creek also relates to certain dwellings in Williamsburg, such as the Dr. Philip Barraud House (before 1796) on Francis Street, and the Archibald Blair House (probably third quarter of the eighteenth century) on Nicholson Street, the latter two-storied.[21] All three Virginia residences have nine-paned sashes in the first story, and Mount Vernon and the Barraud House have six-paned sashes above, like Oxmoor. The dormer windows of the Barraud House and those in the second story of the Blair House, however, have fifteen panes. The most provincial features of Oxmoor are the off-center chimneys on the flanks.

After Alexander Scott Bullitt died, his son, William C. Bullitt, in 1829 built in front of the house a story-and-a-half brick pavilion, which was connected to the back of the old frame structure by a hall.[22] A descendant, William Marshall Bullitt, added a kitchen wing in 1916, a second story over the pavilion in 1926, and an enormous library wing in 1927. His son continues to reside at Oxmoor.

SPRING HILL. Located on Colby Road in Clark County, Spring Hill was begun when the land was part of Fayette County, Virginia. As much as Oxmoor, the house belongs to the Old Dominion, and it is the only one in the commonwealth known to have had a curb roof (fig. 2.4). The owner, Hubbard Taylor, came from Caroline County, south of Fredericksburg, and in 1791 he purchased five hundred acres of Dr. Thomas Hinde's military tract, subsequently clearing a portion and erecting "some cabbins." Taylor brought his wife, two children, and a brother-in-law and his family down the Monongahela and Ohio rivers to Limestone, thence overland to the property. Upon arrival they found "the hall [hull?] of a house without a floor, chimney or door." It was completed as a frame structure, with brick fill, set upon a stone basement, with gambrel, or double-pitched, roof, and dormer windows front and back. Massive chimneys, laid in Flemish-bond brickwork (that on the left flank with glazed headers), stand on the gable ends. The five-bayed facade has double doors opening into a center stair hall flanked by parlor and dining room. Paneled mantels are plain, with dentils beneath the shelf and brick fireplace openings bridged by a segmental arch (fig. 2.5). Ceilings are ten feet high. The upper floor was portioned into three bedrooms, the smallest in the middle, alongside the enclosed staircase.

At an early date the house was enlarged at the back by a deep lean-to flanked by two smaller chimneys (fig. 2.6). An arch replaced the original rear doorway, which was moved about nine feet farther back. The staircase was lengthened, becoming quite easy of ascent. The addition provided first-story rooms with

Figs. 2.4, 2.5 Spring Hill (after 1791), Clark County. Photo, 1968, by J. Winston Coleman, Jr. Parlor mantel at Spring Hill. Photo, 1968.

ceilings considerably lower than those in the original house. The new dining room, adjoining the old one, has an off-center fireplace. Originally it had an entrance on the outer wall, and, opposite, a steep, narrow enclosed stairway to a little chamber above (fig. 2.7). A recess at the base of the stairs probably had a small serving door in the wall opening on the shallow back porch, and there was a trap door in the floor, an odd place for this as it was nearly over the

rear entrance to the basement kitchen. Two chambers, possibly for travelers, were superimposed on the other side of the lean-to, accessible from the rear gallery. Walls between the extended hall and these chambers are of thin battens.

Subsequent alterations in the nineteenth century included the building up of the box front evident in the photograph, the addition of a front porch, and a wide arch cut between the two dining rooms. The

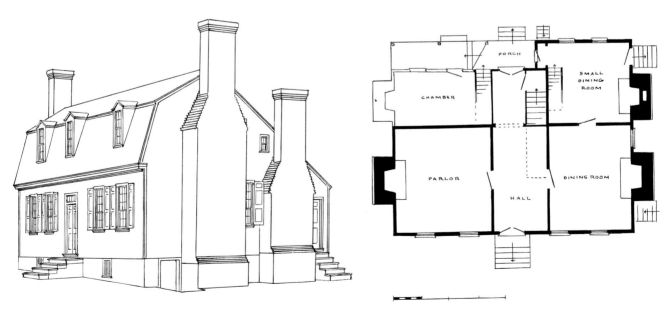

Figs. 2.6, 2.7 Restored sketch, first-floor plan of Spring Hill after addition of lean-to (ca. 1800).

house was renovated in 1967 by Mr. and Mrs. William Rogers Sphar II, and many of the original features were restored.[23] The roof was continued over a new rear ell and a porch. The stairs in the dining room were removed, and the nine-over-six-paned sashes of the first-story windows were reversed for installation of storm windows.

THE McCANN HOUSE. A survivor of a type that once had other adherents in central Kentucky is the original portion of an enlarged house on the south side of Todds Road, nine miles southeast of Lexington. It was built by Neal McCann probably about

1797.[24] The house was two full stories, and although less wide, its plan (fig. 2.8) resembled that of Spring Hill. The staircase in the center hall is of the simplest kind, having a crude column newel (perhaps a replacement) at the base of the railing and chamfered post at the upper end. There is no extension to the stairwell. In the upper hall an enclosed stairway leads to the garret.

Facilities for cooking were provided in the basement. A detached brick kitchen, dating from the first quarter of the nineteenth century, is located about thirty feet to the rear and a little beyond the plane of

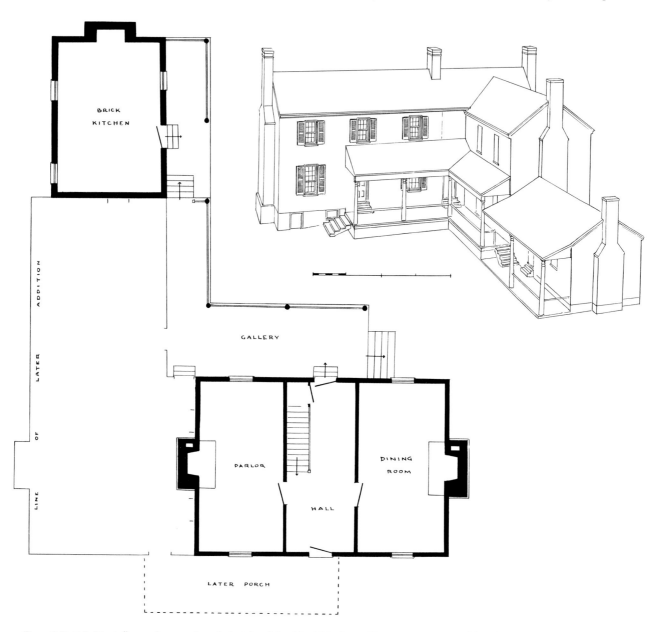

Figs. 2.8, 2.9 First-floor plan, restored sketch of the Neal McCann House (ca. 1797 and later), Fayette County.

the east wall (fig. 2.9). The two structures were connected by an L-shaped frame addition of two stories that seems to belong to the 1840s, though baluster posts suggest a prior date for the galleries. A single horizontal rail, waist high, between the posts, evidently served as a temporary rack for saddles, blankets, garments, tools, and other equipment, as well as a guard for the platform portion of the porch.

THE JOHNSTON HOUSE.   Dr. John Johnston came to Kentucky from Salisbury, Connecticut, in 1785 and settled in Washington.[25] He was the first physician in the town and built or acquired a two-storied frame house off Main Street facing the side of the stone courthouse (chap. 3). The dwelling would have been one of the "about two hundred houses" Michaux counted here in the early 1800s. A porch spans the west end (fig. 2.10). The residence follows a townhouse plan, with the hall east of the parlor and dining room, the interiors separated by thin batten partitions (fig. 2.11). Unusually deep chimneys allow for great thickness of brickwork between the fireplaces and clapboarded walls. Three chambers occupy the second story. The kitchen, in a detached building probably of brick, was connected to the house by a covered way.[26] The Confederate general Albert Sidney Johnston (1802-62), Dr. Johnston's son, was born in the house in 1802. Owned by Mason County, the building is maintained by the Limestone Chapter of the Daughters of the American Revolution and the

Washington Study Club, who restored and furnished it in 1956.

THE McDOWELL HOUSE.   The two-story frame house with brick attachments on South Second Street in Danville is best known for its occupancy by Dr. Ephraim McDowell (1771-1830). McDowell had come as a child to Kentucky from Augusta County, Virginia, and returned East to study medicine under Dr. Alexander Humphries at Staunton. He later matriculated at the University of Edinburgh but did not complete his course and came back to establish a medical practice at Danville in 1795. His fame rests on the world's first recorded ovariotomy, which he performed in this house in 1809 on a forty-five-year-old woman. He twice duplicated the feat and was awarded an honorary M.D. degree by the University of Maryland in 1825.

When McDowell returned from Edinburgh, he and Dr. Adam Rankin rented and in 1797 purchased a little brick building on Second Street for use as a doctor's office and apothecary shop. The doors, consisting of a series of narrow horizontal panels, are unusual, but other early buildings in the vicinity have them, and they may be original.

In 1802 Ephraim McDowell married Sarah Hart Shelby, the oldest daughter of Kentucky's first governor. He acquired the property next to his office and had William Crutchfield, a carpenter and house joiner, build a frame house (fig. 2.12).

Figs. 2.10, 2.11 The Dr. John Johnston House (mid-1790s), Washington. Restored sketch made from an old photograph lent by Mrs. Belle Boganz, Lafayette, Ind. First-floor plan of the Johnston House.

Fig. 2.12 The Dr. Ephraim McDowell House (before 1800 and later) and apothecary shop, Danville. Photo, 1964.

Fig. 2.13 First-floor plan of the McDowell House and adjoining apothecary shop and office.

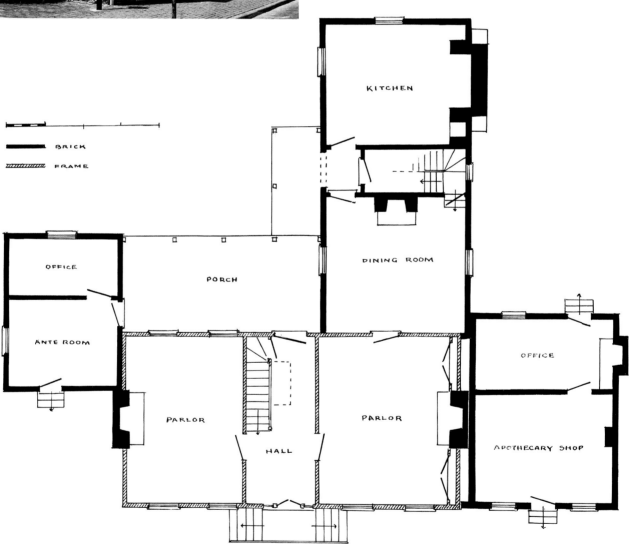

The building has a transverse stair hall between two rooms on the first floor, the larger with presses flanking the fireplace (fig. 2.13). Its mantel is rather plain, supported by fluted pilasters, the cornice-shelf projecting forward at its ends (fig. 2.14). Other early features include the wide batten door with strap hinges under the stair landing to the back porch, and twelve-over-twelve-paned windows.

Dr. McDowell may have incorporated part of an existing brick structure into a wing at the back, covered by a flounder roof, housing a new dining room and kitchen separated by a subsidiary stair hall. The chamber over the dining room is believed to be where the ovariotomy was performed. A storage space is above the kitchen. A second brick addition on the southwest corner of the frame house, connected by an open gallery across the back, contains his later office and anteroom.

The house's frontispiece has an elliptical fan and sidelights containing leaded glass; panel moldings are characteristic of the late 1820s or early 1830s. The present stoop is modern. The north parlor once had a door cut through a window in the front wall, and the back porch was enclosed in 1909.

The Ephraim McDowell House was purchased by the Kentucky State Medical Association in 1935 and was restored by the Commonwealth of Kentucky under the auspices of the Works Progress Administration, becoming a state shrine four years later. It was returned to the Kentucky State Medical Association in 1949, and the Women's Auxiliary of the association maintains it as a museum. A fireplace in the manner of Matthew Lowery (chap. 7) was installed in the south parlor. The little brick apothecary shop adjoining was rescued, restored, and refurnished, and became part of the museum in 1959.[27] The doorway restoration dates from the early 1980s.

OLD MUD MEETING HOUSE. Descendants of Dutch colonists in southern New Netherland and of their Huguenot associates began migrating westward from New Jersey into the region below the Susquehanna River about 1765. On Conewago Creek, near Gettysburg, they experienced repercussions of the American Revolution, crop failures, and Indian

Fig. 2.14 Fireplace wall of parlor, McDowell House. Photo, about 1936, courtesy of the Library of Congress.

raids. Consequently, families began moving on to Kentucky, settling in Mercer, Henry, and Shelby counties. On 22 December 1800, the "agents and overseers" of the Dutch Reformed Church purchased three acres "on the dry fork of Salt River in Mercer County" from David and Elizabeth Adams for "the sum of four pounds, ten shillings, Virginia currence." Here, about four miles southwest of Harrodsburg, they built the first Dutch meetinghouse west of the Alleghenies (fig. 2.15). The first pastor, or dominie, was Thomas Kyle, who had migrated from Pennsylvania, like most of his parishioners, and had been living in Washington County.[28]

Fig. 2.15 Old Mud Meeting House (1810) from the southeast, Mercer County. Photo, 1990.

Their building is of half-timber construction with clay filling, related to the last Pennsylvania survivor, the Moravian Meeting House (built 1743-45)) near Reading, and to a few buildings still standing in Missouri and Wisconsin of the 1840-60 period.[29] Whether from intention or not, the Mercer County example stood for many years with exposed walls and began to be called Old Mud Meeting House. The building is 34 by 46 feet. Floor joists are tusk-tenoned into front and rear sills at upward of 40-inch intervals, which necessitates flooring of 2-inch thickness. Posts 14 feet tall, on limestone foundations, are spaced about 4 feet apart front and back, and less than 3 feet apart on the ends, with wind braces here, as originally there were no openings below girt level (fig. 2.16). Vertical mortises were incised in the sides of the posts, into which were fitted horizontal staves or wattles for holding the straw-impregnated clay in place. The method of cutting the mortises or grooves was to bore a series of 1-inch holes, 3 to 7 inches apart, and chisel out the intervening spaces. The building is covered by a roof upheld by sixteen trusses spanning the plates, and resting on a great center beam supported by four piers, with branching braces. Each pier is a foot square and 22 feet tall, the two centermost rising from the middle of the floor. There also were four tie beams, linking alternate pairs of posts on the long side at a height of 12 feet. The complexity of the structural system, with vertical and horizontal timbers breaking up the volume, must have created a rather confused interior.

By contrast, the outer form of the building was

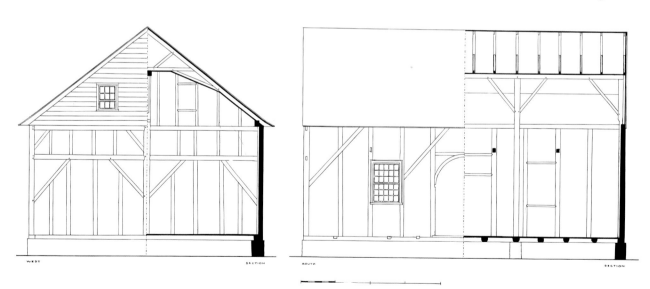

Fig. 2.16 Elevations and sections of Old Mud Meeting House.

relatively simple, especially if surfaces had been coated with stucco, which must have been the intention. The most "Dutch" feature would have been the flanks, with perfectly plain lower walls, the gables shingled and pierced by two small, nearly square windows, and the roof flaring out at the base. Four windows, 4 feet up from the floor and 6 feet tall, provided the main source of light. In addition, two high single sashes pierced the two middle bays in the north wall to light the pulpit. Directly opposite was the wide arched doorway with double doors.

Dominie Kyle quit the Reformed Church and joined the Methodist, and within a little more than a decade the Old Mud Meeting House was without a regular pastor. For a while Presbyterians conducted services in the building. On 27 April 1849 they passed a resolution to "weatherboard and paint the outside of the house; lower the windows; make and hang shutters; erect a suitable pulpit in the east end of the house; cut two doors fronting the branch, and one in the west next to the graveyard; change the pews so as to form two aisles running east and west through the house; and lath and plaster overhead with two coats, and also repair the roof." A sum of $300 was raised for the improvements, and Cornelius Scomp was chosen to oversee them.[30] These changes, although leaving intact its size and shape, greatly altered the appearance of the building. The new ceiling precluded the gable windows. At a later date a shallow balcony was installed at the west end, and the great freestanding posts were exchanged for others erected a few feet away. Abandoned in 1928, the building and adjoining cemetery were deeded to the Harrodsburg Historical Society, and in 1933 federal aid was acquired to repair the building and refurbish the graveyard. The meetinghouse was remodeled and used as a Baptist church. In 1972 the congregation moved elsewhere, and the building was stripped down to the framework; restoration was undertaken by the Harrodsburg Historical Society, following a study made by Milton L. Grigg, an architect from Charlottesville, Virginia.

Several dwellings in the area employ a similar system of construction. They were built by members of the Dutch colony who had, apparently, worked on the meetinghouse itself. The groove-in-post system of Old Mud is replaced in the domestic examples by vertical strips affixed against the inner corners of the posts to hold the wattles. The walls of all the residences seem to have been covered with clapboards at the time of their construction.

THE BANTA HOUSE.   Located about a mile southwest of the meetinghouse, on the west branch of Salt River, the Peter C. Banta dwelling (ca. 1807) of not quite two full stories resembled houses of more than a hundred years earlier in the Middle Colonies.[31] When examined by the author in 1981 the building had been stripped down to the early framework. The house featured a large living-hall with a fireplace in the eight-foot-broad stone chimney (fig. 2.17). An enclosed stairway, supplanting a smaller original, was in the southwest corner of the room. The difference between this plan and that of contemporary log and stone houses in the area is that the balance of the first floor here was not a parlor but two small chambers. In the local manner, first-floor joists were round logs, and second-floor joists were squared timbers, but instead of the latter being exposed, with lower corners beaded, the first story had a ceiling of poplar planks. The second story was divided by batten partitions into a transverse passage and two chambers. The partitions were old, but whether they were original or not could not be determined. The only windows upstairs would have been in the gables.

As in the meetinghouse, corner posts of the Banta house were L-shaped in plan, and they and the center posts in the long sides were substantial timbers from which others branch. This frame was almost two-storied with descending braces in the lower and ascending braces in the upper parts. Roof trusses were simpler, befitting the smaller size of the building. Rafters were spliced together at the top and held rigid by collar beams some eight feet above the upper floor level. They were seated on plates projecting beyond the front and rear wall planes, being in fact, cornice logs, such as are found in the log house of John Bowman II, for example. Fenestration adhered to six-over-six-paned sashes of 8-by-10 glass. Apparently the lower story had windows in the front and rear walls, and there may have been such openings originally in the first-story flanks. There were doors at the base of the stairs and to a closet under the lower part; lintel notches for the adjoining doors to the chambers were present in the studs. No further corresponding provision for doors was visible; but on the outside of the north wall, on the third and fourth posts from the northeast corner, mortises with dowel holes about seven feet up from the sill may be interpreted as belonging to a hood over an outside doorway. The exposed frame of the Banta House was blown down by a storm in the spring of 1988.

SOUTH EAST

CHAMBER

HALL

CHAMBER

Fig. 2.17 Restored elevations and first-floor plan of the Peter C. Banta House (ca. 1807), Mercer County.

THE COZINE HOUSE. Another Dutch dwelling was built for John Cozine, a blacksmith. He was the son of Cornelius Cozine II, and grandson of Cornelius, the dominie to the Conewago colony in Pennsylvania. The house is about a mile southeast of Old Mud and on a branch that empties into the Dry Fork of Salt River above the meetinghouse. A Civil War skirmish, related to the Battle of Perryville (8 October 1862), took place in the meadow in front of the Cozine House, and a cannon ball reportedly knocked down part of the west chimney. The stonework was rebuilt, but whether in the exact shape of its predecessor is questionable. It extends out farther and is not as wide as its companion, and its shoulders are stepped, rather than sloping (fig. 2.18). The masonry around its single fireplace in the principal rooms seems not to have been disturbed, whereas much of the outside shows later repointing. A signature

stone, set in the south side above the shoulder, either survived or was added and bears a weathered inscription that seems to read "Io [John] Cozine / OCT 8 1806." The year has been supplied by those who remember it in better condition. The "OCT 8" is provocative, as it coincides with the event in 1862 that prompted the rebuilding. Still, the date rings true for completion of a house on the 240-acre farm purchased on 25 November 1805.[32]

Although similar in size and construction, the Cozine House is more sophisticated than the Banta House was. It is more nearly square, has a more complex plan, and more fireplaces and openings, including two doors and four windows in the south wall, the latter having been fifteen rather than twelve-paned. The first story contains four rooms, each of a different size and shape, and a separate stair hall (fig. 2.19). The largest room was the parlor, with

Fig. 2.18 The John Cozine House (ca. 1806), Mercer County. Photo, 1981.

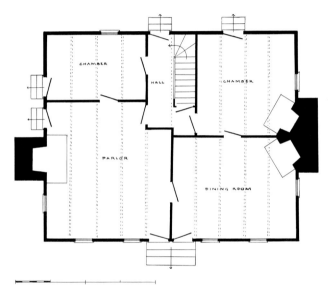

Fig. 2.19 First-floor plan of the Cozine House.

a fireplace nearly centered in the flank wall. One of the two rooms with a corner fireplace may have served for dining; the others were chambers. Overhead are exposed joists with beaded lower corners. They measure 3 by 10 inches, and are 30 feet long. Evenly spaced, they constitute a regular bay system that determines the placing of the interior elements, such as the stairwell, angles of the partitions, and the doors and windows. The earliest doors in the house are batten with iron latches and butt hinges. The staircase has a square newel post, chamfered and with lamb's-tongue stops, around which three winders ascend to a straight flight of fourteen steps with

open string. A closet and a passage to the northeast room occupy the space under the string, here arched. The second story is an open loft in which the stairwell is encircled only by a banistered railing. The original windows in the gable ends were removable casements.

WATERING PLACES. Many early Kentucky watering places or hotels at springs were of frame construction. Wealthy southern planters and city dwellers flocked to them with families and retainers to escape the heat and, sometimes, epidemics that plagued them at home. The curative properties of mineral water, in an age when hydropathy was an accepted remedy for many organic disorders, offered an incentive and later an excuse for social gatherings in the summer. Following a period of modest beginnings—a simple log house by a mud lick—the hostelries developed into respectable establishments modeled on earlier spas in Virginia. One of the first of note was Olympian Springs, fifteen miles east of Mount Sterling, where Col. Thomas Hart, father-in-law of Henry Clay, built an inn. Beginning in 1803, the first regular stagecoach service in the commonwealth left Lexington every Thursday morning at four o'clock for Olympian Springs.[33]

Buildings at the watering places developed a distinctive character. They were narrow, elongated structures, one, two, or three stories high, sheathed in clapboards, their fronts overspread with long, open galleries, supported by slender posts with railings. These porches provided promenades and shaded lounging places for enjoying fresh air and the view. In 1809 a new building was constructed at Greenville Springs, site of Beaumont Inn, Harrodsburg, with a porch 112 feet long.[34] Twenty years later, Greenville Springs was combined with Harrodsburg Springs, becoming Graham Springs.

BLUE LICKS SPRINGS. A popular watering place was Blue Licks Springs, in Nicholas County at the horseshoe bend of the Licking River, site of a bloody Indian battle in August 1782. The property, consisting of thirty-three acres, included the old battleground, which had become a cedar grove sown in bluegrass, affording "a delightful retreat to visitors in the hot months" and featuring two salt wells, one on each side of the river, with a white-sulphur spring on the west bank. Already provided with a tavern—a brick building containing eighteen guest rooms—fourteen comfortable cottages, and numerous dependencies, the setting "was improved and beautifully adorned," and a colossal frame structure was

Fig. 2.20 Blue Lick Springs (early 1840s), Nicholas County. From Lewis Collins, *Historical Sketches of Kentucky* (Cincinnati, 1847), facing p. 480.

added when taken over by J.H. and L.P. Holliday in the early 1840s. This, the "main hotel," was "six hundred and seventy feet in length, three stories high, and surrounded by large and airy galleries, eighteen hundred feet in extent" (fig. 2.20). It also had "a large and commodious dining room, ball room, and three elegantly furnished parlors."[35] In its heyday, up to six hundred guests were registered.

Inasmuch as the extensive structure was built in the 1840s, its details probably would have been Greek Revival, although the frailty of the porch posts refutes the Greek ideal. In any case, detailing on a structure of seasonal occupancy would have been minor, so the hotel can be considered to belong more to the frame tradition than to any particular style. During 1850-51 the premises were leased to the Western Military Institute, founded in Georgetown, Kentucky, in 1847. Blue Licks reverted to its intended role the following year. Balls and the display drill of Morgan's Rifles were counted among its later special events to attract patronage.

The main hotel building was destroyed by fire on 7 April 1862.[36] Its successor, the Arlington Hotel, met a similar fate in 1889, and although another building,

the La Rue House, persevered for a time, it was forced to close when the celebrated springs dried up five years later. Today the site is the Blue Licks Battlefield State Park, landscaped by Olmsted Brothers.

THE CYNTHIANA COVERED BRIDGE. Fortesque Cuming, during his tour of the western country in 1807, tells of coming "to the north fork of Licking river, which . . . [was] crossed by a wooden bridge supported by four piers of hammered limestone, with a transverse sleeper of timber on each which supports the sill." Cuming described the bridge as "seventy-seven yrds long, and only wants abutments to be very complete." He met a man who shared his interest in the structure. "A wagoner had stopped his wagon on it to measure its proportions. He told me that he had contracted to build a similar bridge on the south fork of Licking at Cynthiana, forty miles from here."[37]

The bridge constructed at Cynthiana was slightly larger, the covered portion 258 feet long, the graded approach on the northeast side 54 feet and that on the southwest 44 feet. The 16-foot-broad structure consisted of three spans over the Licking River, which is about 250 feet wide there. The spans were supported

Fig. 2.21 Covered bridge at Cynthiana (ca. 1810). Photo, 1930, by Theodore Webb, courtesy of the Library of Congress.

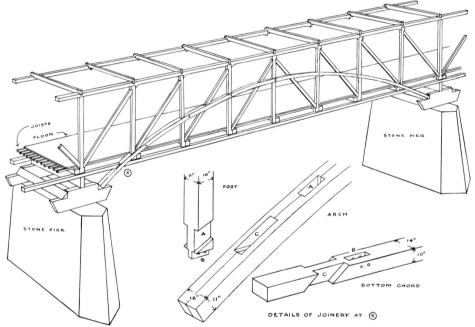

Fig. 2.22 Sketch of structural members of one span of the Cynthiana bridge with typical joinery details.

on stone piers and abutments that rose about 17 feet above water level (fig. 2.21). The two piers, which stood in three feet of water, measured 9 by 24 feet at the base and were battered in about 1½ feet on each side. They had a splayed projection on the southeast or upstream side, and they were capped by an impost of oak, adding 4 feet to the height and providing a bearing surface 10 feet across (fig. 2.22). From these sprang the 11-by-15-inch rib arches that supported the main weight of the bridge. The arches were of four lengths of timbers, doubled, the joints staggered, and each halved at the junction with the

members of the truss. The floor of the bridge was approximately 3 feet above the 10-by-14-inch bottom chords, on which were set alignments of 10-by-11-inch vertical posts, 13 feet high, flanking the roadway. These were tied together at the top by plates and cross beams, and there was a diagonal brace in each bay slanted in toward the center of the span. Most of the timbers were hand-hewn, and they were neatly jointed and held together by wood pins, except for the braces, which were fastened with hand-wrought iron spikes. The bridge was sheltered by a low-pitched roof, composed of beams and diagonal wooden tie poles (bent around one another rather than notched at the crossing), and the sides were sheathed in foot-broad vertical boards, with a narrow space left open below the eaves for light and ventilation. The Cynthiana bridge was demolished in 1946.

The culmination of wooden-bridge building was reached in the Kentucky River bridge between Jessamine and Garrard counties at Camp Nelson. It was designed and constructed by Lewis Wernwag (1769-1843), a German carpenter and mechanic, who settled in the vicinity of Philadelphia. In 1812 he built the famous Colossus over the Schuylkill River at Fairmount Park, a single-span bridge 340 feet in length, the load of which was carried on five parallel laminated arch ribs, each 3 feet 6 inches deep, and two double diagonal trusses. It burned in 1838, the year Wernwag launched his Kentucky enterprise. The bridge at Camp Nelson was a 240-foot span having three parallel trusses supporting two separate 12-foot roadways. Age and heavier loads required it to be strengthened in 1928, and after a few more years it was replaced.[38]

A variation of the arch-and-truss bridge was the lattice-truss system, which was patented in 1820 by Ithiel Town (1784-1844), a native of Thompson, Connecticut, and a resident architect of New Haven and New York City. The design consisted of a system of diagonal timbers crisscrossing at regular intervals so as to transfer loads from one to the others. The spans could be longer than in an arch-and-truss bridge, and the simplicity of the design kept the costs lower.[39] Town planned at least fifty wooden bridges of this type; one of them was to cross the Ohio River at Louisville, but it did not materialize. In its place, an iron trestle bridge of some twenty sections on stone piers was constructed at the same location by Albert Fine during 1868-70.[40] It included two "channel spans" (with trusses above the railroad bed—other spans had them below) to allow for the passage of steamboats beneath. No plans or contract are known to exist, but Town's partner, A.J. Davis, noted in 1837 or 1838 that Town was "interested in" such a construction "one mile long, 60 ft. above low water, 25 above high water 240 feet between the piers, 20 feet high in side truss. 50 feet wide, 4 [railroad] tracks." It was to cost $420,000. John Stirewalt, who went to Louisville under Davis's employ and later became a builder of Gothic Revival churches, mentioned in a

letter to the home office on 2 March 1842 that Town had left an unfavorable impression and "creditors" there, adding, "I expect He has given up his Bridge case."[41]

An iron bridge of some note was put up over the Kentucky River at Shaker Landing, where the gorge is 1,200 feet wide and 275 feet deep. A wire suspension bridge had been begun here in 1853 by John A. Roebling for the Lexington and Danville Railroad Company. Roebling was the engineer responsible for the vehicular and railroad bridge over the Niagara River near the falls, and later for the suspension bridges connecting Covington and Cincinnati (1866) and Brooklyn and Manhattan (1869-83). Abandonment of the Kentucky River project left twin stone towers on either side. They became abutments for a subsequent railroad bridge known as High Bridge. That project was undertaken by Charles Shaler Smith and L.F.G. Bonscaren for the Cincinnati Southern Railroad. Two lattice piers on stone foundations supported three fixed-end deck trusses and cantilevers of wrought iron, each 375-foot spans. The structure was replaced in 1911 by a bridge of steel that followed closely the form of its predecessor. These iron and steel bridges are the direct descendants of those of wood framing, but they have taken us far afield.

There are fewer remaining examples of early frame than of log buildings in Kentucky, indicating that the former was an interim system filling the gap between pioneer shelters and subsequent masonry architecture. Frame houses enjoyed a boom in communities that mushroomed after the frontier became more peaceful. But these centers either were to dwindle (like Washington) or experience later population and economic escalation (like Louisville) that swept away old structures to provide sites for larger buildings less susceptible to fire. In either case frame examples became obsolete and disappeared. The surviving frame houses reflect the wooden tradition of the Atlantic Coast, whence their builders came. Besides residences, frame construction lent itself to mass accommodations at early-nineteenth-century watering places. These hostelries also flourished and then vanished as suddenly as they had appeared. Wooden bridges were as short-lived, being replaced by those of more durable iron and steel. Other examples of frame construction of the antebellum period belong to the Shakers and will be taken up later.

3 STONE CONSTRUCTION

KENTUCKY'S RESOURCES included building stone as well as wood. In a sense stone was used before timbers, inasmuch as stone foundations were laid preliminary to constructing log walls, as in the first cabin built by the Walker party near Barbourville. Surface stones are easily attainable, and they require no seasoning prior to building. Irregularities of form and size, however, make them difficult to lay without cushioning with mortar, which was scarce—if not unavailable—in the early days, though clay was substituted. Examples of dry stone walls of chest height still exist along back roads and are among the most pleasant constructions in Kentucky. Quarried stone necessitated equipment that attended a settled society. Houses, then, of squared logs with great chimneys and often a full basement story of stone, as well as buildings with walls entirely of stone, began to appear in the early 1780s, soon after the advent of the second phase of log construction.

In the eastern highlands of Kentucky—between the Cumberland National Forest and the Virginias—the predominant building stone is sandstone, which consists of grains of sand held together by a binding material. Some limestone has been used in Carter County in the north near Ashland and in Laurel County and Harlan County in the southeast. It abounds throughout central Kentucky. Limestone consists essentially of calcium carbonate ($CaCO_3$) which has been separated from water, rendered insoluble, and accumulated by the action of living organisms, the remains of which are often found in it in fossil form.

The variety of limestone called marble is a metamorphosed limestone, distinguished by its crystallization, coarser grain, greater compactness, and purer color. Among the best building stone in America is the marble on the Kentucky River at Tyrone in Anderson County. The walls of the old State House

(1827-29) at Frankfort are built of it. The blocks were quarried at Tyrone and barged down the river to the state penitentiary, where they were sawed and polished by convict labor. The columns of the old statehouse are of marble from the Grimes Mill quarry on Boone Creek at the Kentucky River in southeast Fayette County. A third source of good Kentucky River marble was tapped by the Shakers for building the fine stone buildings at Pleasant Hill between 1809 and the mid-1840s. Kentucky provides limestone also throughout its southern and western sections as far as the Jackson Purchase, where it becomes fairly scarce.[1]

When the Louisville and Portland Canal was begun at the falls of the Ohio River in 1826, it was found that the limestone removed from the channel, when burned, ground, and mixed with sand, produced a superior hydraulic cement. Louisville cement became known nationally, although it is sometimes confused with the English cement from the Portland Peninsula in Dorsetshire.

QUARTERS AT CLERMONT. The smallest and simplest stone houses in Kentucky hardly excelled the poorest log cabins. A single-room type is exemplified in the older section of the surviving quarters at Clermont, the Green Clay place in Madison County, where a two-story brick house replaced an earlier log dwelling in 1798-99 (chap. 4). The old stone cabin at Clermont has an earth (perhaps once brick) floor, a single door, and a window at front and back (fig. 3.1). The room measures 12 by 13 feet, and walls are 2 feet thick. One end is devoted to a cooking fireplace, 3 feet deep and 10 feet across (fig. 3.2). The ample size of the fireplace suggests that this little building may have been the detached kitchen for the log residence. A stone addition to the west end is nearly twice as large as the first section. It also has a single door, but it has two windows front and back and its fireplace is

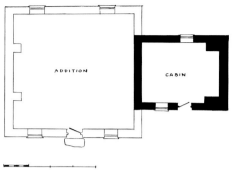

Figs. 3.1, 3.2 The stone cabin or kitchen (1790s) with addition at Clermont, Madison County. Photo, 1967. Floor plan of the cabin (shaded) with addition (unshaded).

slightly smaller. After construction of the brick house and its own kitchens, this building probably continued to be used by the blacks for cooking.

THE McGEE HOUSE.   John McGee of Botetourt County, Virginia, came to Kentucky with the McAfee company (associates of James Harrod) in 1775. He built a cabin on a 500-acre tract on the Salt River, four miles north of Harrodsburg. In 1790 he constructed a stone house, which resembled the Philip Board log house, also in Mercer County.[2] Both houses sat close to the ground, were two-storied hall-and-parlor types with end chimneys, and enclosed stairways, including steps ascending to the garret. The features, however, were treated differently.

In the McGee House the great size of the fireplace in the hall, with evidence of its having had a trammel, or sliding crane, indicates its use for cooking. A closet occupies the space between this fireplace and the east wall, and the staircase (resembling that in the Ambrose Burton log house, about 2½ miles away) is in the enclosure jutting forward on the west side (fig. 3.3). Batten partitions separated the rooms on both floor levels. The lower doors are six-paneled, the upper are four-paneled; the front and back doors have wrought-iron strap hinges, the other H-L or butt hinges. The parlor chamber is without fireplace. Only the parlor has as many as two windows, its second window and the hall door being the only openings in the west wall. The house faces east. Each of its four windows had fifteen panes of 7-by-9 inch glass (presently restored).

The sill of the front door is of limestone and has ribbing on its top side. There are neat stone voussoirs over the lower windows and door, but the walls are of

Fig. 3.3 Restored east elevation, section, and floor plans of the John McGee House (1790), Mercer County.

46 TECHNIQUES AND MATERIALS

rubble. Perhaps they were meant to be covered with stucco. There were no cornices, only a soffit, as in the Old Mud Meeting House, and not unlike the Ambrose Burton House. One-storied frame structures were added to the north and west sides of the McGee House. That at the rear still exists. It has reeded door and window frames inside and out, with rosettes carved in the corner blocks. A root cellar is located about ten yards northeast of the building.

CAVE SPRING. In 1784 Robert Boggs settled a tract about eight miles southeast of Lexington, now reached from the Athens-Walnut Hill Road.[3] He completed his stone house in 1792. The masonry resembles that of the McGee House, but there are cornices. Called Cave Spring, from a nearby feature, the two-story residence was a hall-and-parlor type with a one-and-a-half storied detached kitchen (fig. 3.4). Unusual for early Kentucky, the chamber over the kitchen is lighted by a dormer window at front and back. Windows in the first story of the main house are nine-over-six-paned, whereas all others are six-over-six. Square porches sheltered the doors to the hall. The one toward the river has been replaced by a full-length open gallery, which necessitated moving the outside cellar steps to the front. The porches have chamfered posts five inches square, with banistered railings. Seven-paned transoms are over the nine-paneled outside doors to the hall. Other doors are six-paneled, except that under the parlor stairs, which is four-paneled. The hall and parlor are more nearly square than in the McGee House. Stairways, with railings, are in the outer front corners of the rooms (fig. 3.5). Stairs in the hall chamber rise to the garret. A press occupies the space between the parlor chimney breast and rear wall.

Due to the site slope, the kitchen is six steps lower than the first floor of the residence proper. The space

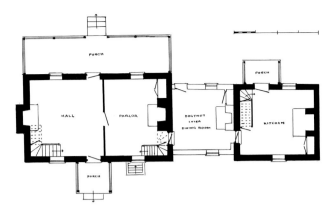

Fig. 3.5 First-floor plan of Cave Spring.

between was filled in later to make a dining room, with fireplace, at a halfway level. The kitchen stairway consists of four winders and an enclosed straight flight ascending to the upper chamber.

The present owner is Samuel M. Cassidy, a great-great-great-grandson of Robert Boggs. He says that family tradition attributes the construction of the house to an Irish stonemason named Devore, who lived in the house below the junction of Richmond Pike and Grimes Mill Road, two miles below Cave Spring. Mr. Cassidy has restored the kitchen fireplace wall, had the partition between the two principal rooms removed, and has added a one-story wing on the north flank of the house.

THE MORGAN HOUSE. Perched on the highest knoll within miles and commanding a magnificent vista in all directions over Montgomery County is the stone house of Ralph Morgan, a grandson of Welsh immigrants to Virginia and a nephew of Gen. Daniel Morgan. In 1789 Ralph Morgan established Morgan's Station at a spring on Slate Creek, about six miles west of Mount Sterling, near the present Harper's Ridge Road. It consisted of five or six log cabins and, at diagonally opposite corners of a stockade, two blockhouses. The station was last attacked by Indians in 1793. About three years later Morgan built his tall stone house on the same site.[4] The stone came from a quarry about a mile east of the house. The limestone contains iron, and its oxidation has turned the exposed wall surfaces a warm brown. Facing south, and the spring, the house has three-bays, with center doors, front and back. Great external chimneys are at each end, flanked by small garret windows in the gables (fig. 3.6). Setbacks are at two levels of the chimneys, there being a fireplace in the east room upstairs but none in the west. Refinements in wall

Fig. 3.4 Restored sketch of Cave Spring (1792) with enclosed dog trot, Fayette County.

Fig. 3.6 Restored sketch of the Ralph Morgan House (ca. 1791), Montgomery County.

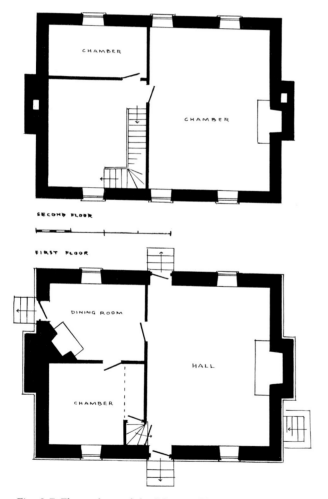

Fig. 3.7 Floor plans of the Morgan House.

construction include horizontal courses of long blocks level with lintels over the openings, and the use of larger stones at the corners, all flush with the wall plane.

The house contains three rooms on each floor, a garret, and a full cellar under the principal room. Steps down to the cellar's outside entrance are on the east flank. The hall, with fireplace five feet across, occupies more than half of the first story. The balance is divided into a parlor or dining room with corner fireplace and a chamber in back of an enclosed stairway (fig. 3.7). The dining room has an outside door adjoining the fireplace, indicating that a detached kitchen—perhaps one of the surviving cabins of the station—originally stood west of the residence. Interior woodwork consists of paneled dado and doorway frames with "ears" at the top and overdoors, most of them having three impost blocks supporting breakfront cornices. A small primitive pediment is set over the stairway door, and a much larger and more elaborate one is over the fireplace in the main room (fig. 3.8). The mantel in the dining room has a pair of short dangling pilasters in the frieze and modillions under the shelf. Mantels are carved of cherry wood, and other fittings are of black walnut and pine. The stairway, enclosed below, ascends into an open hall, and a stairway above leads to the garret. In the bedroom over the living hall was a chimneypiece that had fluted pilasters to either side of the segmental arched opening, an exceedingly high frieze with center panel, and dentils with other moldings under the shelf. It is now in the parlor of the Arthur Stevens House, on Howard's Mill Road. In the Morgan House a small chamber is over part of the dining room. Partitions are of brick-filled framing.

A frame addition has been built on the south front of the house and a porch added on the north, the foundations of which are of the same stone as the walls. Windows contain later inner frames with double sashes, once of two panes each, but replaced in 1967 by others containing six panes. Figure 3.6 shows the house from the southeast as it would have looked originally, its windows with nine-paned sashes. Also in 1967, the woodwork was removed, scraped, and put back in place, and the floors, interior walls and ceilings were restored.

THE DePUY HOUSE. Contemporary with the Boggs House in Fayette County is the stone dwelling of Joel DuPuy in Woodford County on Grier's Creek, about five miles southwest of Versailles and near the site of DuPuy's mill. Built of Kentucky River marble

Fig. 3.8 Detail of pedimented hall mantel in the Morgan House. The bracketed shelf is a later addition. Photo, 1980.

Fig. 3.9 The Joel DuPuy House (ca. 1790) on Grier's Creek, Woodford County. Photo, 1964.

laid in even courses, the two-storied pavilion is four bays across and ten feet wider than the main block of Cave Spring (fig. 3.9). The square porch has a wavy-edge vergeboard pendant from the horizontal cornice, and four posts across the front, but otherwise its details are like those of the Boggs House, including fully shaped supports against the masonry wall. Splash stones, or paving, extending out two feet

from the foundations at grade, front and back, indicate the original absence of eaves gutters.

The main rooms are of about equal size (approximately 16 by 17 feet), and each has a staircase ascending to the chamber above (fig. 3.10). The stairways are built between partitions separating the rooms. That from the dining room begins under that from the parlor, and an upper stairway from the parlor

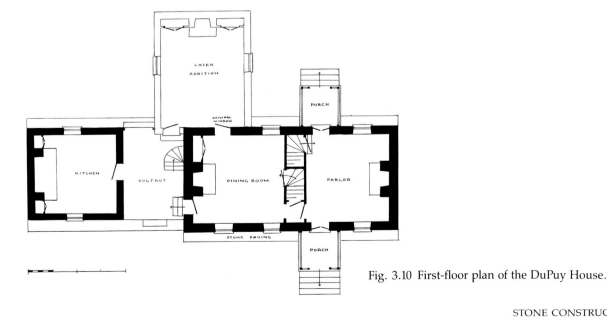

Fig. 3.10 First-floor plan of the DuPuy House.

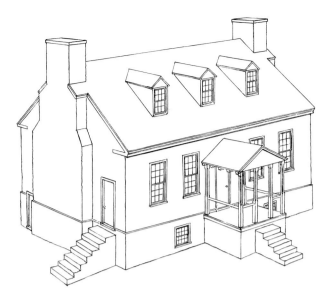

Fig. 3.11 Restored sketch of the John Two-Nine Scott House (ca. 1787), Jessamine County.

chamber leads to the garret. The lower stair arrangement is peculiar but similar to that in two other houses in the neighborhood—the stone house of Col. William Steele and the 1794 brick residence of Edward Trabue, both on the Kentucky River.[5] Beyond the open dogtrot in the Joel DuPuy House is a one-storied stone kitchen with its large (7 feet 4 inches broad and 6 feet high) cooking fireplace. Another stone wing containing a single room was added behind the dining room, and a door to it was cut through a former window. An original door opens onto the dogtrot, from which a hatch-type stairway descends to the basement. The dogtrot has been enclosed, the kitchen converted into a study, a new frame kitchen has been added along with modern conveniences, and the rear porch has been removed.[6] West of the house stands the outbuilding of round logs illustrated in figure 1.4.

THE SCOTT HOUSE. Four miles south of Nicholasville on Route 27 stood until 1987 a story-and-a-half stone house on a high basement. It was the home of John Two-Nine Scott, an Irish Presbyterian, who came to America in 1775 with two shillings and nine pence in his pocket.[7] After settling along the border between Pennsylvania and Maryland, he came to Kentucky and in 1787 purchased from Lewis Craig and James Power(s) the land presumably on which he built his house sometimes called Stoney Lonesome.[8] Scott would represent Jessamine County in the legislative session of 1800.[9]

The striking features of the Scott House were its

gigantic chimneys, that on the south flank (16 feet across) accommodating two fireplaces on the main floor, and the other (14 feet across) containing a recessed press alongside the parlor fireplace (fig. 3.11). These chimneys recall early brick forms in Virginia, Georgia, and especially southern Maryland, although those chimney stacks usually were paired and slender.[10] The unique aspect of these in Kentucky was the roof projecting over the upper setback or shoulder. The extreme breadth of the chimneys precluded second-story windows in the gable ends. Light and ventilation were provided by dormers in each slope of the roof. The enormous chimneys were quite medieval, as were the two square porches, which, however, may not have been original. They were virtually independent structures, composed of stone foundations and six chamfered posts connected only by a rail and supporting a system of beams and rafters (fig. 3.12).

The house had five bays across the front, and the main door led into the great room or hall (fig. 3.13). The dining room was to the south, sharing a closet with the hall, and having a door in the fireplace wall opening on a steep flight of outside steps for bringing food from the basement kitchen. An entry was centered at the rear of the house, a little window lighting the adjoining enclosed stairway. To either side was a

Fig. 3.12 Detail of east porch, Scott House. Photo, 1964.

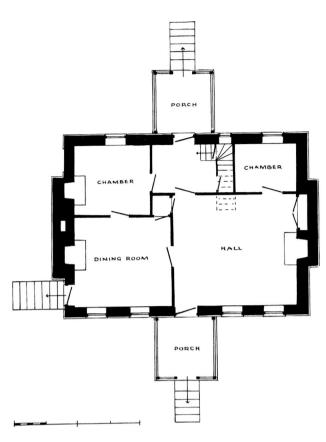

Fig. 3.13 First-floor plan of the Scott House.

tiny bedroom, each with a single window in the west wall. There were two chambers upstairs, only one provided with a fireplace. Interior details of walnut were plain.

THE MCKEE HOUSE. Situated conspicuously on the west side of old Limestone Trail, also called the National or Cumberland Road, now Route 68, in Millersburg is a long, two-story building of stone. Its masonry resembles the work of John Metcalfe, who may have built it with the help of his younger brother, Thomas "Stonehammer" Metcalfe, later governor of Kentucky. The house was constructed for James McKee presumably in 1798, when Millersburg was laid out. In 1837 it was purchased for Jefferson Thomas Vimont, and his seventh child, Elizabeth Jane Hendricks Vimont, resided here until her death in 1930.[11] Thus it is sometimes referred to as the Vimont House.

The original building has six-bays across the front, with a two-bay addition on the north end (fig. 3.14). The third opening from the south end is the main doorway, the upper facing of which displays primitive leaf-on-branch motifs aligned to the pilasters and alongside the arch, and peculiar triglyphs alternating with pierced metope lozenges in the frieze beneath the pediment (fig. 3.15). The treatment is as provin-

Fig. 3.14 The James McKee House (ca. 1798), Millersburg. Photo, 1940.

Fig. 3.15 Detail of the principal doorway and cornice, McKee House. Photo, 1940.

cial as the overmantel in the Ralph Morgan House (fig. 3.8) and relates to two frontispieces on Front Street houses in Augusta. The door itself is later and the fanlight is a restoration. The entrance opens into a transverse stair hall, with parlor and dining room on one side and two long shops or schoolrooms opposite (fig. 3.16). Each of the four rooms has a fireplace, and only that in the back dining room is centered. Flues feed into a single chimney stack at either end of the building. The parlor mantel, displaying the same sort of workmanship as the doorway, contains a seven-pointed star on the center block, a candle on each end block, and swags between (fig. 3.17). A motif of three leaf-bearing branches in a narrow-waisted vase is centered on the overmantel panel, which, like the stone fireplace itself, is flanked by pilasters, only those below have a sunken panel in the shaft and those above are reeded. Except for the candles, which are convex, the decorative motifs are flat cutouts. Second-story chambers follow a plan similar to the rooms of the first floor. The house has four-bays at the back, with doors from the hall and stores or schoolroom opening onto a porch; and another door to this back room was at the side prior to the construction of the bank addition. The present decor of the shops or schoolrooms is of the 1840s period and postdates the building itself.

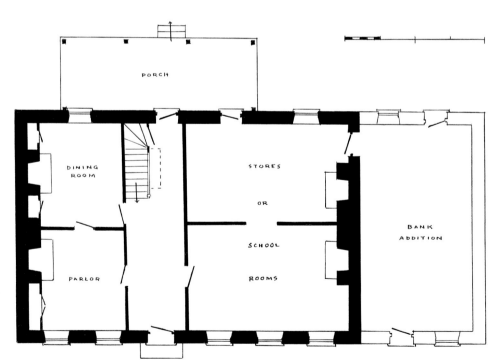

Fig. 3.16 First-floor plan of the McKee House.

Fig. 3.17 Parlor mantel in the McKee House. Photo, 1940.

THE SMITH HOUSE. About 1795 Col. John Smith emigrated from Virginia, acquired a large tract on Elkhorn Creek in Franklin County, seven miles east of Frankfort and north of the Lexington-Leestown Pike, and first built a saddlebag cabin of squared logs (mentioned in chap. 1). He then proceeded to construct a stone house of ample proportions and refined details.[12] The two-story residence with ell and dependencies probably was completed about 1814. The main block was over 60 feet broad and 25 feet deep, and it had a Federal-style frontispiece of double doors and sidelights, 92 inches across, spanned by an elliptical fanlight filled with leaded glass (fig. 3.18). Cellar windows in front were not aligned to openings above. This part of the basement contained two fireplaces.

The principal hall had a staircase ascending around an open well to the third floor, with a railing of delicate proportions. The first flight was boxed beneath with paneling (fig. 3.19). The parlor on the south side had niches flanking the broad mantel with breakfront shelf. Chair railing encircled the room at windowsill level, including inside the niches. The room of similar size across the hall had presses on either side of the fireplace, and a door led to the north gallery on the story-and-a-half wing. A second gallery ran along the south flank. The wing contained a service stair hall and dining room, and a later extension housed a chamber. The upper service hall was lighted by a dormer on the north side, and the chamber over the dining room had a window in the gable end. Attached to the north gallery and parallel to the creek was a dependency; a kitchen in the near end had a servants' room above reached by an external stairway. The early saddlebag cabin was on axis with this stone structure, twenty-six feet away. Beyond was a springhouse recessed in the creek embankment.

Fig. 3.18 Restored sketch of the Col. John Smith House (ca. 1814), Franklin County.

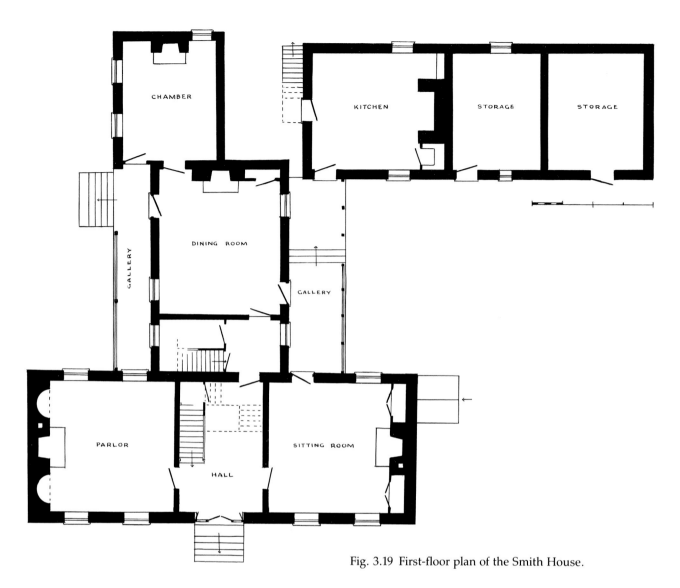

CHAMBER

KITCHEN

STORAGE

STORAGE

GALLERY

DINING ROOM

GALLERY

PARLOR

SITTING ROOM

HALL

Fig. 3.19 First-floor plan of the Smith House.

In 1831 Smith sold the farm to Joel Scott II, who added a two-story front portico with square piers, heavy railings, and lateral benches on the lower level (fig. 3.20). The upper level had to be reached by climbing through the hall window, which remained unchanged. The early stone front steps were moved forward ten feet to accommodate the new porch. The building burned in 1961.

THE HEAD HOUSE. Looking up from the bypass of the Louisville-Shelbyville Road, the Capt. Benjamin Head House at Middletown looks enormous. The illusion is due largely to the extra elevation afforded by the slope of the lot toward the back, permitting entrance to the basement at ground level under the kitchen and north end of the hall. From the front, the house with its thick stone walls gives the impression of solidarity but not exceptional size (fig. 3.21).

The house was built by Captain Head about 1815. The remarkable facade feature is the fanlighted doorway, which originally had paired colonnettes as slender as stair-rail banisters between the doors and sidelights and at the outer supports. The fanlight is elliptical, or three-centered, which is normal, whereas the lines of the voussoirs bridging it radiate from a single point. The doorsill across the 104-inch opening served as a landing; the steps in front were narrower and less deep, the bottom stone extended into voluted ends. Windows were nine-over-nine-paned downstairs and nine-over-six-paned above.

The plan is that of a townhouse, with the stair hall at one side of the principal rooms (fig. 3.22). The arrangement also reflects that of stone houses in western Pennsylvania, notable the Joseph Dorsey House (ca. 1787) near Brownsville, or the John

Fig. 3.20 Facade of the Smith House with portico added after 1831 by Joel Scott, Jr. Photo, 1954.

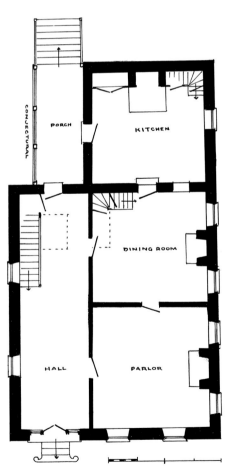

Fig. 3.21 The Capt. Benjamin Head House (ca. 1815), Middletown. Overhanging eaves and rear pent are later additions. Old photo courtesy of the *Courier-Journal*, Louisville.

Fig. 3.22 Restored first-floor plan of the Head House.

Roberts House at Canonsburg.[13] The Head House forms a link to smaller versions in Kentucky, such as in Nicholas County.[14] Simplicity and ample proportions are characteristics inside the Middletown house. The hall is 12 feet broad and 40 feet long; the parlor is 20½ feet square, and the dining room only slightly less deep. The kitchen in the wing is two steps lower and originally had a serving window to the dining room. Both of these rooms contained secondary stairways. The kitchen and main hall opened onto a back porch, which later was exchanged for a shingled addition. On the second floor are two large chambers, corresponding to the parlor and dining room, and a smaller bedroom, 13 feet deep, at the front of the hall. A stairway ascended to the single large room and storage spaces in the garret. Northeast of the house are several old dependencies, one a brick cottage with a fireplace.

Mantels, chair railing, and the stairs in the dining room were removed long ago. A stairway was cut to the basement in the southwest corner of the kitchen, the east kitchen window was enlarged to a broad opening, and a porch was added on the left flank off the dining room. Eaves were extended on the gable ends and elaborated with Gothic pinnacles at the apex and tracery at the bases, but these were re-moved along with a metal roof in a mid-1970s restoration by the Charles R. Matthews family.

WHITE HALL.   This house in Jessamine County near Troy seems to belong to two distinct periods—the first, very early, as indicated by the simplicity of its plan, and the second, later, by the sophistication of its form. Family tradition states that Robert Steele had the foundations laid before he went away to participate in the American Revolution and that he completed the building in 1791.[15] If construction were begun as early as claimed, then the house was meant to be two-storied; but it was not finished as such, and its present features are not eighteenth-century in character. Its floor plan is primitive, consisting of four rooms of equal size disposed in pairs on either side of a transverse hall (fig. 3.23). An odd feature is that the doors swing open into the hall rather than into the rooms. Fireplaces are centered on the outside walls. That in the parlor has great elegance, with paired colonnettes, carved sunbursts on imposts and center block, and a serpentine shelf (fig. 3.24). An enclosed stairway is within the dining room. The kitchen was in a separate pavilion across a dogtrot.

There are cellars only under the front half of the house, consisting of two separate rooms. The larger, beneath the dining room and part of the hall, is

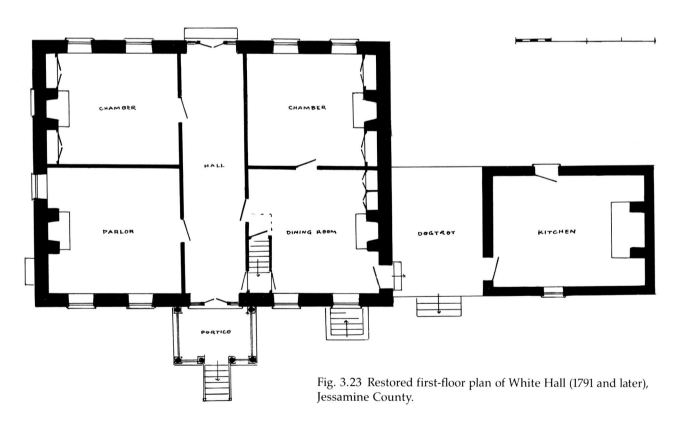

Fig. 3.23 Restored first-floor plan of White Hall (1791 and later), Jessamine County.

Figs. 3.24, 3.25 Detail of parlor mantel in White Hall and view of front. Photos, 1967.

entered by a door with outside stairs under the window nearest the dogtrot, and the smaller cellar under the parlor is reached from the far side. The former existence of chair railing points to the enclosing of two-thirds of the dogtrot (leaving a narrow runway from kitchen to dining room) at an early date. The intermediary room was given a fireplace and adjoining press, and it must have been used for dining or as an office.

Above the regularly coursed basement level, walls of the main part of the house are built of rubble coated with stucco. These stuccoed, single-storied walls, the hip roof, fanlighted doorway, Palladian window, and colonnetted mantel are characteristics of the 1810-35 period (fig. 3.25). Elderly neighbors remember a railing around the upper deck of the portico and another around the roof top which was truncated before being extended to the present ridge.[16] The same roof treatment was on the William Morton House (1810) in Lexington, and Elmwood Hall (1818-21) in Ludlow, both buildings having stucco over brick walls (chap. 8). White Hall makes better use of the upper area than either of the others, with a center hall lighted by a Palladian window (now a door) in the gable over the porch, and opening to three chambers.

The columns of the classic portico are rather thick, indicative of the late Federal or transitional period.

Porticoes were seldom set in front of fanlighted doorways in central Kentucky. This one was added, as the front cornice of the house continues straight across rather than being mitered into the portico cornice. The porch has two full-round supports adjacent to the wall, in addition to the four across the front, as have the example of other stone houses with chamfered posts. The portico and developed form of White Hall must date from the regime of Robert Steele's son, Samuel Campbell Steele.

In the mid-twentieth century the end of the kitchen was rebuilt so that a broad window replaced the fireplace, and the rear wall of the dogtrot room was moved back for a spacious new kitchen. The house was extended again in the 1980s.

THE HOLLOWAY HOUSE.   The pristine dwelling on settler Ezra Hamon's tract in Woodford County was a two-story log structure built at the end of the eighteenth century and dismembered in the mid-twentieth. William Barry Holloway bought the land in 1820.[17] The white limestone bed of Clear Creek running through the property breaks into rectangular blocks, and Holloway utilized it in building his home. The house resembles the DuPuy House on Grier's Creek. The principal block has two-stories, four-bays, and nine-over-six-paned sashes in the lower windows and six-over-six above. Two front doors open onto a centered porch with heavy, cham-

Fig. 3.26 The William Barry Holloway House (ca. 1820s), Woodford County, rear view from the northwest. Photo, 1970.

fered posts. This and the integral story-and-a-half ell at the back indicate a later construction date than the DuPuy House (fig. 3.26). The mantel with its full-round colonnettes and other woodwork in the parlor is characteristic of the third decade of the nineteenth century. The house on Clear Creek may be considered a further development of that on Grier's Creek. The two stairways are separated. The primary one is enclosed between the main rooms and ascends from a point adjoining the front entrances; the secondary stairway is in a corner of the dining room and rises to a chamber in the half-story wing that is lighted by a dormer and provided with heat by a small fireplace (fig. 3.27). It will be noted that the bedroom at the west end of the two-story block, originally accessible only from the back stairs, has no provision for heat. The room over the kitchen has only a tiny single sash window, oddly placed structurally between the stonework and boards at the end of the gallery. The floor of the two ell rooms extends part way over the open gallery.

After being leased for many years and then left empty for a while, the house was renovated in 1970. Presses were removed from either side of the fire-

Fig. 3.27 Restored floor plans of the Holloway House.

place in the kitchen, and the original ceiling was removed, leaving the joists exposed in a manner inappropriate to a house of this vintage. Victorian brackets were left attached to the posts of the front porch, and railings were not restored.[18]

DUNCAN TAVERN. Early hostelries functioned very much as residences, only for transients instead of family. They were of a similar appearance, though usually larger. Major Joseph Duncan built a tavern of stone in Paris on the hill (High Street) facing the public square about 1790, when other buildings there, including the Bourbon County Courthouse, were of log. Paris was a small community then, Michaux reporting that in 1796 it contained eighteen houses.[19] The imposing limestone inn is five bays across, two rooms deep, and two-and-a-half stories high. Rooms at the top are lighted by windows in the gable ends, by dormers, and—presumably original—a pediment with fanlight centered on the front (fig. 3.28). The front wall most likely was stuccoed, at least by mid-century. Duncan Tavern initially had windows of twelve-over-twelve panes in the first story and twelve-over-eight in the second and in the dormers.

On the first floor the two rooms to the south of the transverse stair hall are known traditionally as the assembly rooms, leading one to suppose that they were connected by a wide doorway (fig. 3.29). A parlor and dining room are on the north side. Kitchens were in the basement under these rooms, and food was brought up the stairs at the back of the hall.

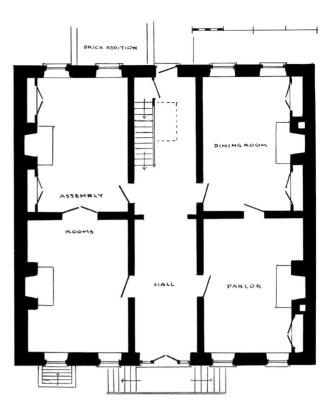

Fig. 3.29 Restored first-floor plan of Duncan Tavern.

Fig. 3.28 Duncan Tavern (ca. 1790), Paris. Photo showing its mid-nineteenth-century appearance. From William Rotch Ware, *The Georgian Period* (New York, 1923), vol. 2, p. 261.

Chambers are on the upper floors. A brick addition was attached to the rear of the building before 1815, and afterward it was extended.

The front windows later were enlarged and given hood molds, and the doorway was recessed. By 1940, Duncan Tavern had deteriorated considerably when the city of Paris purchased it and bestowed it upon the Kentucky Society of the Daughters of the American Revolution, which renovated and furnished it and maintains it as a museum. Changes in the facade openings were retained. Grilles in the basement windows, the Palladian window, and sashes in the dormers were replaced, but not in the form of the originals. Woodwork from other houses was installed inside, and some of the mantels indigenous to the building were shifted to other rooms. The adjoining early 1800s frame house of Duncan's widow was incorporated into the museum complex in 1950, and unfortunately it was faced with stone. Duncan Tavern is badly in need of a reappraisal of its miscellaneous interior fittings and an intelligent restoration.

THE FIRST STATE HOUSE. John Melish of Glasgow, Scotland, described Frankfort in 1811 as "neatly laid out, the streets crossing one another at right angles, and . . . mostly all paved. It consists of about 150 houses, the most of them handsomely built of brick, and contains 1099 inhabitants. The public buildings are the state-house and penitentiary . . . and a bank. A theatre and church are building." He stated that the penitentiary supported itself by the industry of its thirty-four inmates "mostly employed in sawing marble in the yard."[20] Fortesque Cuming, who had visited the capital four years before, reported that while most houses were of brick, some were built of a "good marble of a dusky cream color, veined with both blue and red, and capable of a good polish." The first statehouse, which both viewed, was constructed within a year or two after Kentucky attained statehood in 1792. An engraving published in 1796, depicted it as having three stories, with a center pavilion of three bays, two bays on each side, and an arched open belfry on the roof (fig. 3.30).

As Cuming described it: "The state-house of rough marble, is about sixty-six feet front, by fifty-four deep. It is an oblong square with a square roof, and a cupola containing a bell rising from the centre. The house is plain, but roomy and commodious. On the first floor are the treasurer's, register's, auditor's, and printing offices. On the second, the rooms for the representatives of the state, and the federal court of appeals, and on the third are the senate chamber, the general court and a school room."[21]

Combining this information with that gleaned from the elevation illustrated, one concludes the building had a center hallway and four rooms about

Fig. 3.30 The first Kentucky Statehouse (1793-94), Frankfort. From the *New York Magazine or Literary Repository*, July 1796.

twenty-five feet square with fireplaces on the flank walls in the first story; whereas above, the interior spaces were thrown together to make the larger assembly rooms. The first statehouse was destroyed by fire on 25 November 1813.

Its prototype may have been one of three similar, smaller buildings, built a few years earlier as courthouses for Nelson, Fayette, and Jefferson counties.

THE NELSON, FAYETTE, AND JEFFERSON COUNTY COURTHOUSES. Capt. John Cape made a specialty of building stone courthouses in Kentucky during the late 1780s. Nelson County records contain a contract signed by him in 1785 to erect a two-story structure of 40 by 23 feet, pedimented and three-bayed, with a chimney at each end, twenty-paned windows in the first story and sixteen-paned above.[22] The early Nelson County Courthouse built at Bardstown was two-storied, five-bayed, and square, its roof surmounted by a cupola; it bore a resemblance to the Fayette and Jefferson county buildings built by Cape, but was strikingly different from the building specified in the Nelson County contract.[23] The stone courthouse at Bardstown stood until 1891.

In 1780, a square was set aside in the center of Lexington for the Fayette County courthouse. The first courthouse was located on the northwest corner of Main and Main Cross (Broadway) streets, however, several blocks away. When this log building became inadequate in 1788, it was proposed to build a new courthouse on the ground initially allotted for it.[24] A contract was made with John Cape, who constructed it of limestone. It was the first of four to stand on the site. Only its immediate successor was of brick (chap. 7). The first stone courthouse was two-storied, having a hall and four rooms on each level. It also contained an underground vault, 5 by 7 feet and 7 feet high, which was discovered when the brick building succeeding it was demolished in 1883.[25]

Captain Cape also built another stone courthouse in 1788. This one was in Louisville for Jefferson County. Square, two-storied and three-bayed, it was covered by a hip roof with a cupola or belfry. An elevation of the building is shown on a prison-bounds plan of 1798. A sketchy delineation of it also appears on a view of Louisville seen from across the river, a vignette on a map of the falls area by Jared Brooks that was published by John Goodman of Frankfort in 1806 (fig. 3.31).[26]

THE MASON COUNTY COURTHOUSE. When Fortesque Cuming visited Washington in 1807 he noted that it contained ninety-six houses and three out-

Fig. 3.31 "View of Louisville from near Clarkesville," showing outline of the Jefferson County Courthouse (1788) at right. Insert from a map of the falls area by Jared Brooks, 1806. Courtesy of the Jefferson County Archives.

standing buildings: "a good stone court-house with a small belfry, a [Presbyterian] church of brick . . . , and another [Baptist] of wood."[27] Four years later, John Melish recorded: "The public buildings are a court-house, jail, and academy."[28] The courthouse was built by Lewis Craig, one of the leaders of the Traveling Church, a Baptist congregation, which migrated from Spottsylvania County, Virginia, in 1781 to central Kentucky. They established Craig's Station in the Lancaster-Crab Orchard vicinity and later moved to South Elkhorn, five miles below Lexington. In 1792 Lewis Craig went to Mason County, where he was a preacher and builder until his death in 1825.[29] He carved his initials and the date, 1794, over the main doorway of the courthouse.[30] Among other buildings he constructed was a brick church at Minerva, where he was buried.

The Mason County Courthouse stood far back from the main street in Washington, opposite the Johnston House (chap. 2). It was two-storied, without a basement, measuring a little more than 40 feet across and 20 feet from front to back. There were single chimneys and gables at each end, and from the center rose a tower of two stories, about 10 feet square, surmounted by an octagonal cupola with a campaniform roof, and a spar with a gilded ball and weathervane at the top (fig. 3.32). The building had a central stair hall with court rooms to either side, a simple plan not unlike that of the old State House

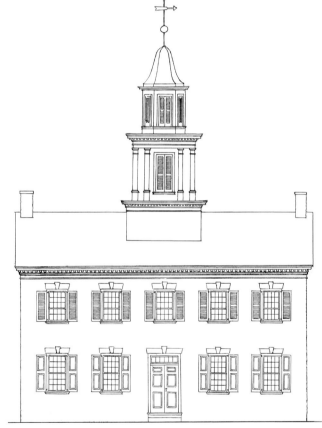

Fig. 3.32 Facade elevation of the Mason County Courthouse (1794), Washington. Drawing based on old photos lent by courtesy of Mrs. Belle Boganz of Lafayette, Indiana, and Mrs. Andrew C. Duke of Maysville.

(Independence Hall) in Philadelphia, before a new stair tower was built during the 1750s.

The seat of Mason County was moved to Maysville in 1848, but the old stone building in Washington remained until 13 August 1909, when it was struck by lightning and burned. A frame house was erected on its foundations.

THE WINERY.   The town of Augusta, fifteen miles below Maysville on the Ohio River, has been called Piedmont because of its location. Directly behind it at the base a of a steep hill a great stone structure was built, reportedly by William White and presumably during the decade prior to the Civil War. It was used for the making and storing of wine, and nearby hillsides were terraced for the cultivation of grapes. The winery consists of three levels. The uppermost, used for storage, is entered through the west gable from high ground nearest the road leading to town. The middle level opens out onto a fairly level plateau on the south side. The west half of it was left open for a work area; the east half was enclosed for living quarters. Below is the wine-storage chamber itself, entered through an arched doorway at the base of the building (fig. 3.33). Walls are four feet thick and support a vault that penetrates the mountain. The interior is rounded, apsidal fashion, at the far end. The wine could be kept at a fairly constant temperature the year around. A seam in the vault indicates that the 100-by-40-foot cavern was built in two nearly equal sections. An interesting feature is an aperture in the wall on the slope to the north, which opens into the space above the vault, where one can see the irregularities of the extrados stonework. Tales of soldiers being hidden here from their enemies during the Civil War expectedly persist. Like other attempts to grow grapes in Kentucky (and farther south), the crop did not flourish, and the winery at Augusta served its purpose but briefly.

Stone building in Kentucky was first manifested in structures as plain and primitive as the earliest log cabins, and it progressed to large and substantial buildings serving public needs. Stone was used for simple houses without hallways (Cave Spring and the DuPuy House), for complex forms from the Atlantic Coast (the Scott House), and for buildings

Fig. 3.33 The Winery (ca. 1850s), near Augusta. Photo, 1989, by Samuel W. Thomas.

showing such evolved Federal features as arched niches and broad fanlighted doorways (the Smith House). Durability and flexibility were great advantages of stone over wood construction. As well, buildings of dressed stonework could receive all the architectural detailing proper to brick construction, whose simplest examples will be seen in the following chapter. Further use of early stone building, by the Shakers, will be shown in chapter 5. It must not be forgotten that marble traditionally is the material for walls of the most noble edifices, and the state and county buildings discussed here were forerunners to the sophisticated specimens in the revival styles presented in Part 3.

4 BRICK BUILDING

THE BRICK BUILDING tradition predominant in Kentucky stems from Virginia. Bricks were manufactured at Jamestown (founded 1607) practically from the beginning. They were used for chimneys and nogging in frame houses; however, it is uncertain when the brick-walled building first appeared. The town of Henrico, about forty miles up the James River, was described in 1611 as having "competent and decent houses, the first storie all of bricks," and foundations had been laid for an ambitious church of brick.[1] The earliest brick structure in Virginia of which any part (foundations) survives is the First State House at Jamestown, a group of three row houses, two of which were erected before 1635. The three similar units had walls of English-bond brickwork two-and-a-half stories high, each with a central chimney, pantiled roof, and gables front and back. Each was three bays wide with a narrow transverse passage at the side, off which was a stairway in a recess alongside the massive chimney containing fireplaces serving the two rooms.[2] An adaptation with variations of the English medieval townhouse became the standard plan of the row house in America. The old brick church at Jamestown followed four frame predecessors. It was built between 1639 and 1644, with additions in 1680. The building was allowed to fall into ruin after it was closed in the mid-eighteenth century, and a replica was constructed on the site for the Jamestown Tercentenary in 1907. Bricks were made for chimneys in New England within the decade after the landing on Plymouth Rock in 1620. Since clay soil and lime were scarce, and since frame houses seem to have been preferred, not many brick houses were built during the early period in the northern colonies. In the South, where clay soil was more prevalent and lime was made from oyster shells, a goodly percentage of seventeenth- and eighteenth-century buildings were constructed of brick, in remote sections as well as in towns.

More than in the eastern part of the Old Dominion and elsewhere along the southern tidewater, the local clays of Kentucky are even better suited for making a good quality brick. Occasionally in the country near an early house one finds an old pit that furnished material for the bricks.[3] Undoubtedly at times the soil dug for the foundations was baked and used for the walls, so that the building grew literally out of the ground. As a rule, bricks have a deep red color, contrasting harmoniously with the ubiquitous green of the Kentucky landscape. The tonality of the brick is an indication of its quality—the darker the harder—resulting from the intensity of heat achieved in the firing process.

A front-page notice of the *Kentucky Gazette* for 31 March 1791 announced that the subscriber wished "To employ a Brick-maker, to make a number of bricks." Bricks also were procurable from brickyards, such as that of John Bob, who solicited additional hands, promising "good treatment and generous wages," and Walker Baylor, who wanted "*A good journeyman Brick Maker*, To whom liberal wages will be given."[4] John Bob's yard was located in Lexington, Walker Baylor's three miles outside of town. In the same year a Lexington merchant bearing the architectural name of Laurence Lintel offered for sale "A QUANTITY OF Excellent Lime, WHICH was burnt in this town at the corner of Cross [Broadway] and Water Street. Price for slacked [plaster] lime, six pence per bushel, and for stone lime nine pence per bushel."[5] Bricks were laid with thin joints of mortar composed of lime and a binder of fine "pike dust," gathered from the roads where the metal rims of wagon wheels scraped and pulverized the crushed limestone paving, giving the mortar a subtle hue of iron rust. Generally the mortar line was "grapevined" (scored) and "penciled" (the score painted with a fine white line), which separated each brick.

Masonry walls, several bricks in thickness, were

keyed together by a system of bonding. Three types apply to Kentucky building, as elsewhere, during the early period. The first we have seen was used as nogging in frame buildings. Soft-burned bricks not to be exposed to the weather were aligned dry or with a sand and clay mortar in alternating rows of stretchers (placed lengthwise) and headers (ends exposed) known as English bond (fig. 4.1). Apparently this arrangement was not applied to weight-bearing walls

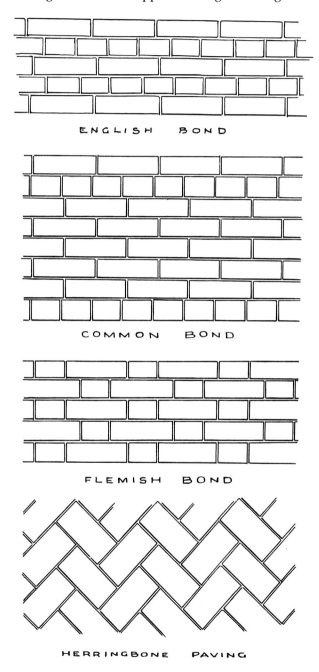

ENGLISH BOND

COMMON BOND

FLEMISH BOND

HERRINGBONE PAVING

Fig. 4.1 Principal patterns of early bricklaying.

in Kentucky. The usual type of brickwork, called American or common bond, consisted of approximately five rows of stretchers bonded by every sixth row of headers. For walls of greater visual elegance, a pattern of alternating stretchers and headers, horizontally and vertically, was used. It was known as Flemish bond, after the country of its origin. Usually it was reserved for the front facade, with common bond on the sides and back. But especially fine buildings often had Flemish-bond brickwork on all four sides. This refined type continued into the Greek Revival era. In rare early instances it was enriched with patterns of dark or glazed headers. When bricks were used to pave walks, terraces, and porches, they generally were laid diagonally in a zigzag design known as herringbone. Bricks were also in standard use for fireplace hearths, and sometimes they were molded to form water tables and cornices. They were not used for steps or door- and windowsills until the bungalow period, beginning about 1900.

The average size of early Kentucky bricks is 2¼ by 4 by 8¼ inches, but variations occur, although they seldom exceed more than a half-inch. Bricks of different dimensions may be employed in separate parts of a single building, but of course, it would be impossible to mix bricks of inconstant sizes in the same wall. White Hall, the home of Cassius Marcellus Clay near Richmond in Madison County, makes a good illustration. The nucleus of the Italianate house is Clermont, the residence of Cassius Clay's father, Gen. Green Clay, built in 1798-99, discussed later in this chapter. The two-story main block is constructed of bricks measuring 2½ by 3¾ by 7¾ inches, laid in Flemish bond with glazed headers in one wall. The south wall of the wing on the west flank, added probably soon after 1800, is composed of bricks of 2¾ by 4 by 8 inches (fig. 4.2). The bricks at the northwest corner are 2¼ by 4 by 8 inches, and the pier supporting the arch beyond has 2¼-by-4-by-8¼-inch bricks of a noticeably darker, purple color. It seems likely that this section was added by Thomas Lewinski, who designed the enlarged villa for Cassius during the 1860s (chap. 12). The later structure is of bricks measuring 2 by 3¾ by 7¾ inches.

Bricks provided fireproof walls that meant greater security, particularly for crowded town dwellers. Whereas in early forts, like Harrodsburg, a ten-foot safety space had been left between neighboring houses of wood, in towns, row houses came into being with adjoining dwellings sharing a wall between them. Often the party wall would rise above

Fig. 4.2 Detail of junction of west wing with south facade of Clermont, Madison County. Photo, 1964.

paneled dado. Some fireplace walls were paneled, and paneling adorned the space under the first flight of the hall staircase.

Improved tools made possible more efficient and better workmanship in house building and detailing. By 1788, Alexander and James Parker's store "two doors below the court-house" in Lexington stocked such carpenter's tools as "chisels and gouges . . . Turners tools & Wheelirons, Files & plane bitts . . .

Fig. 4.3 An early-nineteenth-century row house with crowstepped parapets on Second Street in Maysville. Photo, 1940.

the roofline, forming a slanting parapet (as in Lexington) or crowsteps or corbiesteps (as in Maysville—fig. 4.3). The projecting wall hindered the spread of fire to an adjoining roof. Also it allowed the owner of one house to add an extra story without disturbing the roof next door. As in the example illustrated, the need for light in houses that could have fenestration only in front and rear walls was indicated by the windows being greater in breadth than intervening wall sections, causing shutters to overlap in the open position.

In brick buildings, as with log and frame, stone was often used for foundations. It also served for stoops, copings, chimney caps, date corbels, sometimes for belt courses, water tables, and windowsills (as in the house of Green Clay, Clermont), articulated keystones, and exterior steps (fig. 4.4). Stone sills and steps had a projecting torus corresponding to the rounded nosing of the tread of wooden stairs inside, and the riser curved outward to a narrow fillet at the top. Vertical surfaces were tooled with shallow reeding. Also, as in developed log, frame, and stone buildings, the horizontal and sloping frame members of brick houses, as well as floors, inside stairways, and roofs were constructed of wood. Chair railing was employed generally, some surmounting

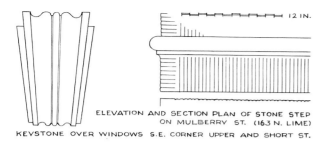

ELEVATION AND SECTION PLAN OF STONE STEP
ON MULBERRY ST. (163 N. LIME)

KEYSTONE OVER WINDOWS S.E. CORNER UPPER AND SHORT ST.

Fig. 4.4 Stone details of early Lexington houses.

[and] Saws assorted," as well as bolts, screws, brads and nails. The same year, Peter January and Son provided "Carpenters compasses, Cross-cut & hand saw, files . . . Hammers [and] Plain Irons," also nails, staples, and tacks. Two years later Teagarden and M'Cullough—next door to the Parkers—included "Chisels and Gimblets, Table butts and Wood Screws." In 1804 William Leavy offered a selection of saws classified as "Mill, Pit, cross-cut, Hand, Tenon, Dove tail, and Compass."[6] These merchants also carried hardware, the Parker brothers having "Nob and pad locks . . . H & HL hinges," and cupboard and chest locks and hinges. Probably these items were imported. Judging from the lion and unicorn seals on early door locks (as at Stoneleigh on the Greendale Road near Lexington), some came from England. On the other hand, James Lowry, who settled in Lexington, advertised in the early 1790s that in his Upper Street shop he made and repaired all sorts of things from guns to "Door Locks and Locks of all kinds."[7] Likewise, Woodruff and Company conducted a brass foundry at Lexington in 1811, keeping "on hand, and for sale, a general assortment of BRASS ANDIRONS, SHOVELS & TONGS, DOOR KNOCKERS, &c. &c."[8] The earliest iron furnace in Kentucky, begun on Slate Creek in Bath County in 1791, became known as the Bourbon Furnace, turning out bar iron and castings of kettles and stoves.[9] Some bar iron was forged into decorative ironwork for buildings by the whitesmith, the artistic counterpart of the blacksmith. Thomas Studman, a newcomer to Lexington, opening his place of buisness at the corner of Limestone and Water streets, advertised in 1809 that he engaged in "WHITSMITH'S WORK," including the making of "all sorts of plain and ornamental Railings, Grates . . . and smith's work in general, executed with neatness and dispatch, on the most reasonable terms."[10] Wrought-iron work had to be made to order. It preceded cast-iron work, which required heavier and more complex equip-

ment and did not come into its own until the middle of the nineteeth century.

Window glass was the one material for early buildings that invariably was imported from the eastern states—just as it had been imported there from England. Glassmaking did not become a commercial success in America until after the Revolution. In 1792 the firm of Elliot and Williams in Lexington announced the arrival of a shipment of "WINDOW-GLASS 8 by 10." No source of the glass was given, but a glassworks was advertised at New Geneva in southern Pennsylvania in 1800 and in Pittsburgh in 1804. By that date, glass for windowpanes could be purchased in the following sizes: 7 by 9, 8 by 10, 9 by 11, and 10 by 12 inches.[11] In rare instances early houses contained larger panes. In Liberty Hall at Frankfort, they measure 12 by 18 inches and were ordered specially for the building (chap. 7). Panes were set in sashes usually three across and two or three deep, sometimes four across and in three—possibly four or more—vertical rows.

Visitors to Kentucky during the early nineteenth century were impressed by the civilized amenities of the towns. Fortesque Cuming seeing Lexington in 1807 wrote:[12]

On entering the town we were struck with the fine roomy scale on which every thing appeared to be planned. Spacious streets, and large houses chiefly of brick, . . . since the year 1795, have been rapidly taking the place of the original wooden ones, several of which however yet remain. . . . [The town] contains three hundred and sixty-six dwelling houses, besides barns, stables and other offices. . . . There are societies of Presbyterians, Seceders, Episcopalians, Anabaptists and Roman Catholicks, each of which has a church, no way remarkable, except the Episcopalians, which is very neat and convenient. . . . The court house now finished, is a good plain brick building. . . . The number of inhabitants in Lexington, in 1806, was 1655 free white . . . 1165 negro slaves, in all 2820. . . . There are three nail manufacties . . . ten blacksmith shops . . . two copper and tin manufactures . . . four cabinet-maker's shops . . . one excellent umbrella manufactory . . . seven brick yards which employ sixty hands, and make annually two million five hundred thousand bricks; and there are fifty bricklayers, and as many attendants, who have built between thirty and forty good brick houses each of the last three years.

The Scottish traveler John Melish compared Lexington of 1811 to Philadephia: "The streets are wide and airy . . . and the buildings, being mostly of brick, the whole is as handsome, as far as it extends, as

Philadelphia; and the country round is much handsomer than that round the latter city."[13]

The examples discussed below reflect the characteristics of earlier eastern colonial buildings. Both groups are of the Georgian style. The selection included here are the simpler or more provincial versions. Those showing greater sophistication are discussed in chaper 7 and illustrate the first phase of the Federal period. The choice is somewhat arbitrary, however, there being no clear demarcation between the provincial type and later styles.

THE LAKE HOUSE. A typical early brick town dwelling is the Isabella Lake House on Mulberry Street (currently 173 North Limestone) in Lexington, built about 1800.[14] Although situated on a lot 33 feet wide, the house measures only 21 feet across the front, the right flank adjacent to the south boundary. Originally the windows contained nine-over-six-paned sashes, and the front door had a transom but was without elaboration (fig. 4.5). The profile of the front steps was shown in figure 4.4. Resemblances to the individual buildings of the First State House in Jamestown include the three-bayed facade and narrow passage at the side of the two rooms, increasing in breadth for the stairway (fig. 4.6). The gables and fireplaces are at the side, however, and the staircase occupies the rear half of the hall rather than an alcove alongside the chimney. The dual-leaf doors between parlor and smaller dining room remain centered in both rooms due to presses flanking the rear fireplace that balance the offset of the hall. The original kitchen was in the basement under the dining room, and flues from the fireplaces come together in a single chimney centered on the north gable. Both the base-

ment and second floors have a small room occupying the area of the front hall: a wine cellar below stairs and a small chamber above.

An extension was added at the back in two stages. The kitchen-smokehouse was probably built first, detached from the house. It was later connected via a new dining room.[15] An outside stairway alongside the smokehouse rose to the chamber over the kitchen. A wall of double thickness separates the wing from the original building. The extension antedates the ell of the neighboring house on the south, which was constructed against the lot line, leaving only a foot between the two structures. A gallery extending along the north side had a nearly flat roof

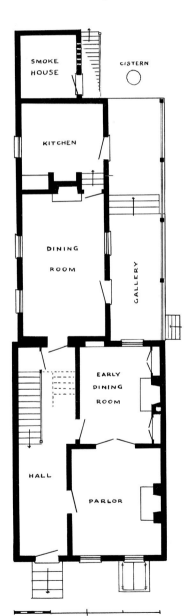

Figs. 4.5, 4.6 Restored sketch, first-floor plan of the Isabella Lake House (ca. 1800), Lexington.

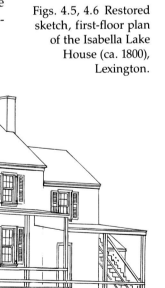

supported on square posts, with horizontal boards serving as railings. The fenestration in the main block has been enlarged and the front door replaced; the smokehouse, porch, and outside stairway have been demolished.

Although built singly, the Isabella Lake House is a common type of row house, originally having no windows on the sides, with the exception of one to the garret on the right flank. Brick row houses were not built in Kentucky towns until after 1800. The first of the four units of Morgan Row, in back of the courthouse in Harrodsburg, is thought to have been built by Joseph Morgan in 1814, and the last, Chiles Tavern, was added in the 1830s (figs. 4.38 and 4.39).

SPORTSMAN'S HILL. William Whitley and his wife, Esther (Fuller), came from Augusta County, Virginia, in 1775, establishing a station a few miles

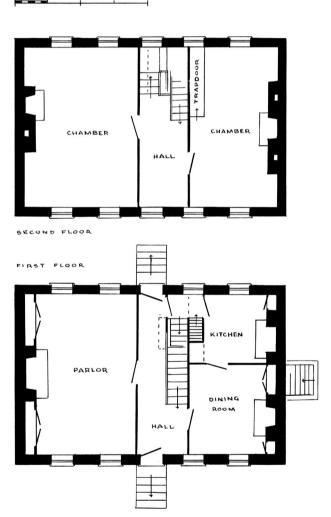

Fig. 4.7 Restored floor plans of Sportsman's Hill (before 1794), Lincoln County.

west of Crab Orchard in what is now Lincoln County. Whitley spent a portion of the next few years in the service of his country. He was with George Rogers Clark at the capture of Kaskaskia in 1778 and figured in the raid of Clark and Logan against Indian towns on the Big Miami in 1782. During this period the Whitleys lived in a log structure, last mentioned in their correspondence as a "station" in 1787. Then they built a brick house, Sportsman's Hill, identified as being their place of residence in 1794.[16] When it was being restored in 1938 as "an historic shrine," it was touted as the oldest brick house west of the Alleghenies, and in several respects it is the most unusual. At least two characteristics are archaistic, seldom found in the region other than in log and occasionally in frame and stone buildings. They are the use of batten partitions dividing rooms and halls, and the location of the kitchen on the first floor in the main block of the house (fig. 4.7). The high windowsills are another pioneer feature, such as in the John Two-Nine Scott House in Jessamine County.

Outwardly Sportsman's Hill presents a sophisticated appearance. The two-storied form, measuring more than 25 by 40 feet, has walls of beautifully laid Flemish-bond brickwork in the front and back with glazed dark headers forming the initials of the owners, "WW" and "EW," over the front and back doors (fig. 4.8). In a modified Flemish bond, a lattice pattern embellishes the flanks. Lozenge designs in brickwork are prevalent among houses on the Atlantic Coast but unusual this far inland. Openings in the five-bayed front and rear facades are quite plain. Center doors are eight-paneled outside and have diagonal sheathing inside, with a transom above, and all windows are fifteen-paned with low-arched headings. Crowning the front and back walls are handsome horizontal modillioned cornices.

A number of peculiarities figure inside the house. The thin partitions between halls and rooms intersect windows in the dining room and chamber above. The staircase has a console-type newel and two turned banisters per step, the steps symbolically numbering thirteen in the first flight, an argument in favor of a date for the house prior to 1791, when the fourteenth state was admitted to the Union (fig. 4.9). Carvings on the ends of the steps represent an eagle's head with an olive branch in its beak. The wall space beneath is divided into panels, the surface of which is flush with that of the stiles and rails. Turnip-shaped drops hang below the square newel posts of the upper flight. Partition walls are of random-width

Fig. 4.8 Sportsman's Hill. Photo, 1940s, by J. Winston Coleman, Jr.

vertical boards with beaded edges. Inside doors are six-paneled. Hardware, such as latches and H-L hinges, are of handcrafted iron. Woodwork in the parlor includes fluted pilasters flanking cupboard doors to either side of the arched fireplace, and a triglyph treatment over the mantel shelf with thirteen carved S shapes in metopes, and a central panel above with reentrant angles at the corners of the frame—a suitable place for a portrait (fig. 4.10). The dining room has similar paneling. These embellishments are said to have been executed by the German-born Swope brothers, whose descendants still live in Lincoln County.[17]

The parlor has an 11-foot ceiling; the smaller din-ing room and kitchen across the hall had only a 9-foot ceiling height. Over this portion of the first story was a 2-foot crawl space, or entresol, entered from the side of the steep, ladderlike secondary stairway adjoining the kitchen (fig. 4.11). It provided a hiding or storage place. The narrow stairs with grip slots (as reconstructed) connected with the basement steps under the main staircase. The basement extends under only a little more than half of the house. Flues from the dining room and kitchen fireplaces converge into a single chimney at second-floor level. The chimney breast in the northwest chamber is exceedingly broad. The fireplace, with the plainest enframement and narrow shelf over it, is centered. This

Fig. 4.9 Base of staircase, Sportsman's Hill. Photo, 1930s, courtesy of the Library of Congress.

Fig. 4.10 Fireplace wall in parlor, Sportsman's Hill. Photo, 1942.

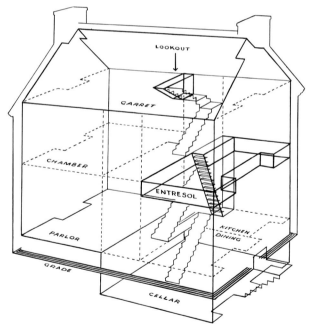

Fig. 4.11 Cutaway perspective sketch of Sportsman's Hill, showing secret stairs, entresol, and garret lookout.

room has a trap door in the floor to the secondary stairway. The parlor chamber has a fireplace equally stark, and it is at the southwest end of the chimney projection. A narrow staircase ascending from the second-floor hall has boards of cut-out design between railing and closed stringer of a type found in this country among the Germans of Pennsylvania, suggesting the workmanship of the Swope brothers. The stairs lead to the garret, which was used for quilting and other such pursuits. Adjoining the stairway and sharing the upper part of the middle rear window is a hideaway or lookout below the level of the third floor. Rafters are approximately 4 by 5 inches and 16 feet long, halved together at the apex, spaced about a foot apart, and the roof framing includes queen posts and collar beams.

A brick lean-to was added to the back, blocking up the rear windows of the original house; a columned opening was cut between the parlor and hall; the dining room and kitchen were made into a single interior entered by double doors from the hall, and the entresol and secondary stairway were removed. A colossal distyle portico was appended to the front, and the center upper window cut down to form a door; later a dogtrot and ell room were added to the left flank of the lean-to.[18] The extra rooms have remained, the dogtrot has been enclosed, and, except for the entresol and questionable front steps, the building has been restored. It is maintained by the Kentucky Department of Parks.

At age sixty-four, Whitley enlisted in the army to fight in the War of 1812. He was killed at the Battle of the Thames, and his flintlock musket, powder horn, and beaded belt were returned to Sportsman's Hill.[19]

ELLERSLIE. Thoroughly brick in concept, Ellerslie, the home of Levi Todd, was built about 1787 a few miles southeast of Lexington on the north side of the Richmond Pike. Perhaps the first brick house in Kentucky, it forms a link between the architecture of the tidewater and the western country just entering its second decade. The original residence measured 22 by 63 feet and contained three nearly square divisions on the first floor, the centermost a hall with a staircase rising in two equal flights in the northeast corner. Flanking it were a parlor and a dining room, each with two windows in front and two openings behind (fig. 4.12). The stairs ascended to a T-shaped hall leading to four chambers and a stairway to the garret. The second story was six-bayed across the back.

The house was doubled in size, probably in 1792,

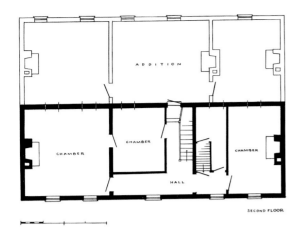

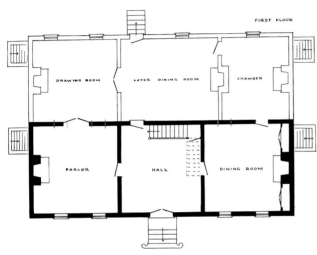

Fig. 4.12 Floor plans indicating the two building stages of Ellerslie (ca. 1787, shaded; early 1800s, unshaded) near Lexington.

when Levi inherited a hundred acres from the estate of his brother, John, who was killed at the Battle of Blue Licks. The large room on the first floor in the middle of the extension became the new dining room, with double doors opening from it into the drawing room, which was similarly connected with the parlor. Cooking was performed in a detached

Fig. 4.13 Restored sketch of Ellerslie after enlargement.

kitchen. The third room in the addition on this level was probably used as a chamber. Upstairs, the addition was entered across a platform bridging the topmost steps of the first flight. It seems curious that no service stairway was included in the new part. Except for the placement of the chimneys, the completed arrangement resembles the plan of Prestwould (ca. 1770) in Mecklenburg County, Virginia, but whose fireplaces are between rooms rather than on outside walls.[20] The enlargement of Ellerslie obscured the rear windows of the early house, leaving the two small second-floor rooms without light.

Outside, no less than inside, Ellerslie was a link between the eastern Virginia mid-eighteenth-century style and the late-eighteenth-century manner in the West. The house had stone foundations to the tops of the basement windows, and a foot or so above the stone line the brickwork at front and rear stepped in by means of a molded string or water table (fig. 4.13). A belt course at second-floor level spanned the front and right side. The upper windows were considerably smaller than those below, and all openings had a stone keystone centered on flat arches of brick. The horizontal cornices were plain, and flat raking boards were on the gable ends, cut short of the chimneys. One might expect larger windows to have been inserted in the gable ends to light the garret with the construction of the addition, but the small openings of the original structure were duplicated. Basement steps were at each end of both sections.

Levi Todd was the first clerk of Fayette County, and he kept the county records in a small stone house in the yard. It burned on 31 January 1802, destroying many documents and damaging others. Copies made from the remnants and of lost deeds solicited are referred to as the "Burnt Records." The clerk died soon afterward, and Ellerslie passed to his niece, who married Robert Wickliffe. At the time of the Civil War it was owned by Mrs. Margaret Preston. Front windows were enlarged, the doorway changed, and an entrance porch affixed. After years of abandonment, the house was razed in 1947. The small building indicated at the left of the residence in figure 4.13 was a brick dependency.

LOCUST GROVE. William Croghan emigrated from Dublin to Philadelphia in 1768 at sixteen, became involved in his uncle's landholdings in western Pennsylvania, and fought in the Revolutionary War. The major came to Louisville in the spring of 1784 with George Rogers Clark to survey for military land

Fig. 4.14 Locust Grove (ca. 1790), near Louisville. Photo, 1965, courtesy of Historic Homes Foundation, Inc.

grants. He obtained 387 acres on Beargrass Creek and the Ohio River from Hancock Lee in 1790, and added 300 acres in 1792 and 1811. Meanwhile, in 1789, he married Lucy Clark, sister of his surveying partner. About 1790 he built his country seat, which he called Locust Grove.[21] The two-story house has symmetrical, five-bayed facades of Flemish-bond brickwork front and back, the form of the building resembling that of Ellerslie, with the exception of having a belt course on both fronts, but not on the sides, broader windows (twelve-over-eight-paned sashes upstairs and twelve-over-twelve in the first story), narrower entrances (also with transoms), and ample fenestration on the flanks, especially on the west end (fig. 4.14). The treatment of the belt at the second-floor level is rare in Kentucky; it consists of two single projecting courses of brick two rows apart, a type that may be found on mid-eighteenth-century houses in Society Hill, Philadelphia, the historic district adjoining and to the south and east of Independence Hall. The modillioned cornice is a conjectural restoration of the 1960s.

Locust Grove has a transverse hall ten feet wide, although broader at the back because of the staircase in the northwest corner. The staircase has four winders at the base rotating around a turned newel post. The four rooms on the main floor are of similar size, those in the southeast and northwest corners having presses flanking the chimney breasts. A subsidiary

Fig. 4.15 Fireplace end of second-floor ballroom, Locust Grove. Photo, 1964, by Samuel W. Thomas.

stairway rises in the northeast room, which was the family dining room. On the right side of the fireplace is an outside door, through which meals were served from the detached kitchen. The largest room in the house is the ballroom upstairs in the southwest corner, measuring nearly 31 by 19 feet. The fireplace in the paneled chimney breast is off-center to allow for the passage of the parlor fireplace flue on the north side (fig. 4.15). Later the ballroom was divided into a bedroom and hall. Upon the removal of the partitions during restoration in the early 1960s, strips of French wallpaper by Reveillon were discovered and identified as having been executed by Cietti about 1786. The design was duplicated and replaced on the walls. The garret contains a central hall and four chambers, each with a single window and one with a fireplace. These were the children's rooms.

Dependencies near the house included a kitchen, stone barn, stable, smokehouse, icehouse, springhouse, and servants' quarters. A mill was built in a bend of the Muddy Fork of Beargrass Creek.

Locust Grove accrues historical interest through having been the sanctuary of the valetudinarian Gen. George Rogers Clark, who came to live with his sister in 1809 and remained until his death in 1818. William Croghan died in 1822, and the house stayed in the family until 1878. It reverted in 1883 to a farmhouse until 1961. In that year the residence and fifty-five acres were purchased by the commonwealth and Jefferson County. Restoration proceeded during the next few years by Historic Homes Foundation, Inc., under the direction of the architect Walter M. Macomber of Washington, D.C.

HURRICANE HALL. A house notable for its provincial, atypical characteristics and showing expansion to suit the needs of a growing family over a half century is Hurricane Hall, six miles north of Lexington on the west side of the Georgetown Pike. The original block, two-and-a-half storied and approximately 32 feet square, with 190 acres of land was purchased by Roger Quarles from David Laughed (or Laughead, or Lawhead) in 1805.[22] The house has four bays and Flemish-bond brickwork in front, common-bond brickwork elsewhere, and three-bays in the rear. A modillioned cornice follows the roofline on all four sides. Wood nailing blocks embedded in the brickwork indicate the intention of having horizontal members to the end pediments. Two chimneys rise above the east gable, and a single one was originally centered on the west end. The windows are twenty-four-paned downstairs and fifteen-paned above. The use of smaller windows for chambers aligned over the larger windows of the living quarters was an old Virginia practice, as at Westover on the James River, Elsing Green in King William County, and the Wythe House in Williamsburg, but in the eastern examples the dimensions of the windowpanes were decreased rather than their number.[23] A partition almost in the middle of the square house of David Laughed divided a hall on the west

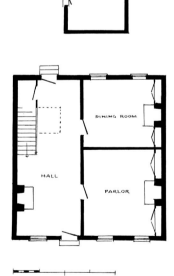

Fig. 4.16 Front elevation and first-floor plan of the original Hurricane Hall (ca. 1800), Fayette County.

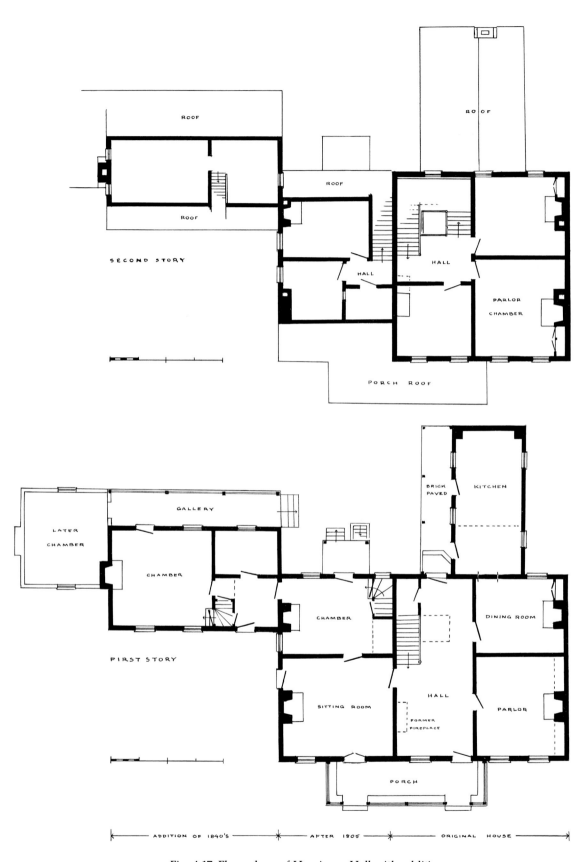

Fig. 4.17 Floor plans of Hurricane Hall with additions.

side from a parlor and dining room; the hall had a fireplace in the front half on the outside wall and a staircase at the back (fig. 4.16). The landing of the hall stairway is six feet deep. The parlor initially had presses level with the chimney breast. The kitchen, a detached brick structure, featured a broad cooking fireplace, nine feet across. The second floor of the house contained three bedrooms, each with a fireplace (fig. 4.17). The parlor chamber has presses between the chimney breast and front wall, with dangling pilasters alongside the paneled doors and a series of drawers beneath, including a pull-out writing shelf at chair-rail level (fig. 4.18).

Shortly after Roger Quarles acquired the house, a story-and-a-half extension was attached to the west flank and a front porch appended (fig. 4.19). Windows in the new wing were only three panes wide. The 28-foot porch was an interesting structure which, instead of lending impressiveness to the entrance, gave the front of the house an intimate look. The roof came down low and was upheld by square posts that were chamfered, with horizontal plank rails pegged into the posts and benches facing inward. A small porch sheltering the rear door has a scalloped pendant cresting, resembling that on the DuPuy stone house in Woodford County, with a cutout tulip motif in each lobe (fig. 4.20). The addition included a larger gathering room for the family, one that was less formal than the parlor, and a chamber on the first floor, this back room having a stairway to the two small

Fig. 4.19 Hurricane Hall. Photo of the late 1800s, courtesy of Mrs. James Benjamin Stevenson, Fayette County.

Fig. 4.20 Rear of Hurricane Hall. Photo, 1952.

chambers and closet above. The old parlor was hung with a French scenic wallpaper to celebrate the wedding of Sarah Jane Quarles to William Z. Thompson in 1817 (fig. 4.21). At that time the presses were removed from either side of the mantel and, because the wallpaper ran short, the section cut out for the hall doorway was pasted on the outside wall adjacent to the chimney, of course out of context with the adjoining panorama. The cornice over the former presses was left in place and the paper border brought down below the soffit line in the recesses. More will be said about the identity of the paper in chapter 6.

Dependencies of this period include a large brick

Fig. 4.18 Elevation of fireplace and presses in chamber over parlor, Hurricane Hall.

Fig. 4.21 Northeast corner of parlor, Hurricane Hall. Photo, 1964.

smokehouse, 16 by 22 feet, and a schoolhouse behind the house (fig. 4.22). Traces of the foundations of a row of slave cabins may be found beyond.

Later an ell was extended from the northwest corner of the house, set back so as not to obstruct both chamber windows; and it allowed for a window in the near gable of the ell. It includes an entry and two rooms on the first floor and a stairway ascending to two garret rooms. Moldings and tall panels in the doors indicate an 1840s construction. An open gallery ran across the back, and a porch was added later to the front of this section. Another extension was similarly placed against the second, probably during the 1850s, but it no longer exists. The entrance porch with the benches was replaced during the late nineteenth century by a three-bayed shelter centered on the hall door, and the replacement was removed in 1963.

CLERMONT. Green Clay of Powhatan County, Virginia, immigrated west in 1780, learned surveying, and rapidly acquired choice lands in Kentucky. He settled on some two thousand acres in Madison County and built the "first hewn log-house in the county." The brick residence constructed in 1798-99 to replace it "was also the first of that class." Clay's son, Cassius Marcellus, likewise described the permanent house as "a well-built brick structure; with heavy range work of Kentucky marble and grey limestone, and of the Grecian style, having three por-

ticoes of imperfect Corinthian and Doric columns," [24] "Grecian style," of course, is an ambiguous term and only means that the house had porticoes with some pretense of classicism. Its period warranted the source of inspiration as Renaissance—Roman at best—and not in any way Greek. Cassius added that his father's house was "after the English manner," an interesting remark though puzzling as to its exact import. The house was referred to earlier in discussing size variation of brick (fig. 4.2). The "range work of Kentucky marble and grey limestone" is in evidence as foundations, belt course at second-floor level, windowsills in the main pavilion (those shown in fig. 4.2 are later), and lintels in both sections of the house. The use of stone for these elements above basement level is unusual. [25]

The house was called Clermont. Its walls were laid in Flemish-bond brickwork with some glazed headers, most consistently employed in the north facade, presumably considered the front. It faced the Kentucky River, two or three miles distant. There were two front and two back doors, side by side, and pairs of windows on either side, with nine-over-nine-paned sashes. Windows above had nine-over-six paned sashes. The house, measuring about 30 by 40 feet, was divided by a partition down the middle, and one half of the first floor was further divided into two

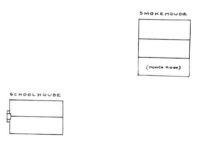

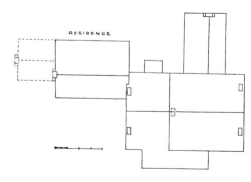

Fig. 4.22 Roof plan of house and nearby dependencies, Hurricane Hall.

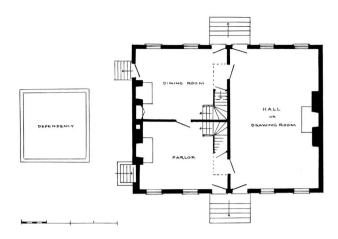

Fig. 4.23 First-floor plan of the original Clermont (1798-99), Madison County.

rooms (fig. 4.23). The big room was the hall, or drawing room, and the two smaller ones were the parlor and dining room. Staircases rose against the inside wall of the two small rooms toward the center of the house, turned in opposite directions and continued toward the front and rear walls, giving access to four chambers.

The downstairs rooms have paneled dadoes, and stone windowsills are continuous with and have profiles identical to the chair railing. The drawing room has an additional range of panels over the railing, the only other instance of such panels known to the author being in the stair hall at Marmion, an early-eighteenth-century house in King George County, Virginia.[26] The exceptionally broad chimney breast at Clermont is paneled from floor to ceiling, the outermost panels flanked by slender pilasters, reeded above fireplace level.[27] The fireplace is framed in marble and had no shelf until an inappropriate Federal-style mantel was added to it in 1970. The wide chimney breast supports those in the two chambers above. The fireplace in the parlor has a mantel with interlaced strapwork design in the frieze, reminiscent of a plate in William Pain's *The Builder's Pocket Treasure*, published in London in 1763 and republished in Boston in 1794 (fig. 6.1). This mantelpiece, at least, justifies Cassius's claim that the house is "after the English manner." The paneled dado between the fireplace and the south wall has a ten-inch hollow space behind it open to the basement, left over from the closing up of the early outside entrance to the cellar. A pilaster on the south wall has a crudely carved acanthus capital reflecting the descriptions of the "imperfect Corinthian," refer-

ring to the porticoes, of which only the stone podium and semicircular steps of that on the south facade have survived. Similarly curved steps, of wood, lead up to the side door of the dining room, but these steps may not have been the earliest.

The kitchen initially occupied the west half of the basement, and it was reached from outside by a bulkhead stairs on the west flank near the front corner of the building. Inside access was under the staircase in the dining room. Foundations of a 15-foot-square detached dependency (probably a summer kitchen), beginning 9 feet from this end of the house, have been incorporated into the north and west walls of a later two-story service wing. It must have been added soon after 1800, and it abuts the exposed brick wall of the original house. A porch (the third "portico" referred to) was on the north side, and the upper chamber of the wing was reached by a stairway opening from this shelter. A new basement entrance was made through the nearest cellar window facing north. It would seem that with the addition of the kitchen ell, the south facade became the main front of the house. We can assume the third, and most elaborate, portico dates from that time (figs. 4.24 and 4.25).

An odd feature of the second story is that there was a single window centered over the twin doorways on the south side but none on the north. Could it be that the steeply pitched roof of a pedimented portico precluded a center window on the original front, as at Cave Spring, the Robert Boggs stone house between Clermont and Lexington? A jog in the wall, making a little hall to one side at the head of the stairs, prevented the bisecting partition from dividing the middle south window. A stairway to the garret rose over this flight, and it was entered from the two north chambers. The chamber fireplaces are close together because their flues converge to a single chimney stack at each end, as in the contemporary stone house in Millersburg (chap. 3). The existing mantel in the southeast chamber of Clermont is a rude version of a mid-Georgian Virginia fireplace, with three panels over the opening flanked by pilasters, only these rest on the protruding corners or crossettes of the fireplace enframement, an element more properly belonging to an overmantel enframement for a painting. Except for the removal of the staircases and accompanying adjustments, most of the important features of Clermont were retained in its enlargement into White Hall after 1861 (chap. 12).

Fig. 4.24 Restored sketch of Clermont after addition of west wing (early 1800s).

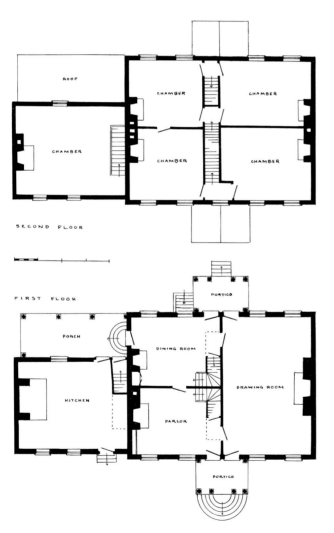

SECOND FLOOR

FIRST FLOOR

Fig. 4.25 Floor plans of the second stage of Clermont.

WOODSTOCK. Although the examples of brick houses already discussed were two full stories and not small, each was realistically planned to give domestic needs primary consideration, and except for modillioned cornices on two of them and "porticoes" on a third, they were practically without embellishments. The beginning phase of brick building in Kentucky also included smaller dwellings, one-storied or with a loft upstairs, like the first pioneer cabins. Dormer windows were rare in this region, particularly in brick houses, and rooms under sloping roofs, lighted and ventilated solely by small windows in the gable ends, were particularly uncomfortable in summer. A developed version of the small house is Woodstock, about six miles east and somewhat south of Lexington at the intersection of the Todds and Cleveland roads. The pristine residence of William Hayes constituted a story-and-a-half unit with a one-story service wing on its right flank. A brick in the chimney is inscribed with the owner's initial and date of construction, "H 1812."

The front of the main pavilion has three large windows containing twelve-paned sashes (fig. 4.26). The front door with a transom over it opens into the parlor. The two main rooms are equisized, and there are three small divisions at the back, a stair hall between chambers (fig. 4.27). Each of the four rooms has a fireplace. The layout and the stairway arrangement resemble those of the Scott House in Jessamine County and no doubt stem from elements in houses of Maryland, whence William Hayes came. Both buildings have outside walls of a single masonry substance from ground up. Six-paneled doors in the

Fig. 4.26 Restored sketch of Woodstock (1812, 1820), Fayette County.

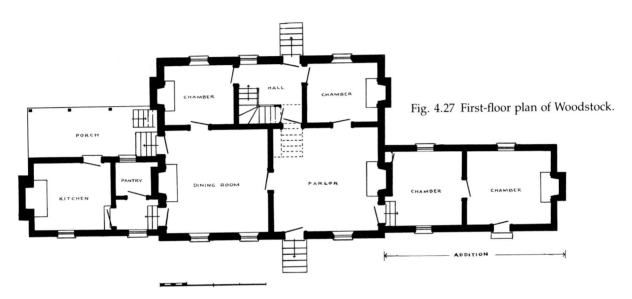

Fig. 4.27 First-floor plan of Woodstock.

main part of the Hayes house are unusual in having the panel surfaces level with the rails and stiles, outlined by a bead, a feature more proper to front doors, as at Liberty Hall and Federal Hill. Two chambers are upstairs. The service wing has a pantry between the dining room and kitchen, its floor being considerably lower than in the living quarters. A wing providing two chambers was added on the west flank, a brick in the end chimney here is incised "H 1820." An old gate at Woodstock, equipped with wrought-iron strap hinges and hook, has orbiculated tops on the end posts and slender square vertical bars, the peaks of which describe a low convex arc (fig. 4.28). An entrance porch with octagonal posts, added in the middle of the nineteenth century, was removed during renovations in 1942-43, and the parlor mantel was restored from an outline preserved in the plaster. But the work also included installation of wood cornices in the rooms, moving the stairway to the southeast corner of the hall, setting four dormers

in the rear slope of the roof, and rebuilding the wings on a modified plan.

OAKLAND. Oakland is similar to and farther out the Todds Road from Woodstock, west of Combs Ferry Road. It may have been constructed about the same time and by the same builders. Oakland is on land owned by Joseph Graves, whose estate was acquired by Samuel Coleman in 1830.[28] Coleman undoubtedly added the square-pierced portico which lends focus and attractiveness to the massing,

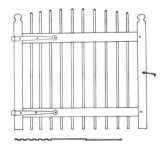

Fig. 4.28 Elevation of an old gate at Woodstock.

Fig. 4.29 Oakland (early 1800s), Fayette County. Photo, late 1800s, courtesy of E.I. Thompson, Lexington.

and probably extended the ell (fig. 4.29). Oakland consists of two 18-foot-square rooms (parlor and dining room), two 14-foot-square chambers at either end, and an 18-foot-square kitchen with bedroom over it (fig. 4.30). Each room, including the upper one, has a fireplace, as does the basement under the dining room. The mantel in the parlor is exceptionally fine for Fayette County, resembling the carved work of Matthew P. Lowery of Mercer County (chap. 6). It has paneled pilasters at the sides, a sunburst on the center block of the frieze, and a band of carving under the breakfront shelf (fig. 4.31). High ceilings and broad windows give a sense of spaciousness that

belies the small size of the house. Stairways at both Woodstock and Oakland have an element of afterthought about them. Although the stairs at Woodstock rise in a hallway provided for them, the upper flight cuts into the ceiling of the parlor and over a foot farther into the room than is necessary for the width of the steps themselves. At Oakland, the stairway to the little room over the kitchen is entered from a door in the dining room, necessitating precipitous winders at the base. Having the entrance originate there, rather than in the kitchen, gave the upper chamber family social status. After being abandoned for many years, Oakland was purchased and restored in 1972.

Figs. 4.30, 4.31 Oakland. Restored first-floor plan. Parlor mantel. Photo, 1972.

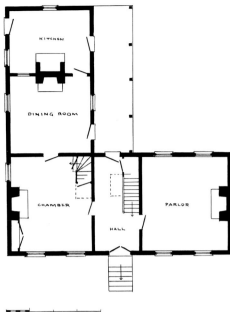

Figs. 4.32, 4.33 Woodsland (after 1809), Harrodsburg. Photo, 1972, and restored first-floor plan.

A frame wing replaced the defunct early addition, showing at the back in figure 4.29, and once more the house is being enjoyed as a home.

WOODSLAND. Once situated on a tract of four acres with brick cabins and other dependencies clustered around it, but now restricted to a town lot on the corner of East Street and Woodsland Drive in Harrodsburg, this little brick house seems to belong to eighteenth-century Virginia. It is an L-shaped, story-and-a-half house of dark brick and is especially Virginian in having two dormers piercing the roof (fig. 4.32). Attention has been lavished on excellence of proportions and craftsmanship, whereas achitectural details have been kept plain. The house was built for Archibald Woods, who acquired the land in 1809.[29] The building has no cellar, but the brick walls sit on stone foundations and vent slots for the crawl space are left in the brickwork. The four rooms on the main floor are connected by stair hall and open gallery (fig. 4.33). In the hall is a simple banister staircase with open string, rising to a landing at the back and continuing around an open well to the second story. The parlor on the south side is eighteen feet square. The smaller room across the hall was a bedroom, making the porch essential for access to the dining room and kitchen, which have a serving window between them. Because of the rather steep pitch of the roof, the two upstairs chambers are more spacious than one would expect; and with fireplaces and

small windows in the gable ends as well as the front dormers, they are functionally equal to first-story rooms. Except for the installation of a bathroom in the gallery behind the hall, the closing up of the fireplace and serving window in the kitchen, the removal of the chair railing and replacement of baseboards in parlor and hall, and the exchange of the six-paneled front doors with ones of three panels, the house has remained intact. The Woods family still owns and lives in the house.

BIG SPRING MEETING HOUSE. The early church on Rose Hill in Versailles is in the tradition of plain eighteenth-century houses of worship in rural Virginia. It was built by the Baptists in 1819.[30] Measuring 47 by 32 feet, the building has five bays on the long sides and three on the other two and is covered by a hipped roof (fig. 4.34). The south and east sides are of Flemish-bond brickwork, with jack arches over the windows. On the other two sides, continuing directly over the openings, common-bond was used. Dual-leaf doors with transoms are centered on the east facade ad north end, with similar entrances flanking a center window on the south side. Windows, in two tiers, contain nine-over-six-paned sashes in the first story and six-over-six-paned sashes above, with a fifteen-paned window between the two levels in the middle of the west wall, behind and over the minister's platform.

An upper gallery, 11½ feet deep on the north, east,

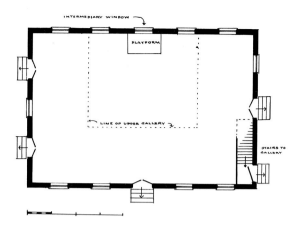

Figs. 4.34, 4.35 Big Spring Meeting House (1819), Versailles. Photo, 1978, and restored first-floor plan.

and south sides of the auditorium, is open above the pulpit (fig. 4.35). Enclosed stairs to the gallery are in the northeast corner of the building, with a single door at the side. There is no lower window in this area.

Big Spring Meeting House suffered two major vicissitudes. The first was about 1830, when it changed hands and served as a church for the Disciples of Christ, and the second was after 1854, when it became a residence. The first may have been responsible for the cavernous entrance once centered on the south front, which would have meant that the two original doorways in this wall were closed up. The mid-century renovation was more drastic. It included the addition of a steep bracketed gable in the center, a new entrance with sidelights and triple window above to one side, and the enlarging and replacing of windows elsewhere in the south front. Three windows were filled in on the east side, and four on the west, including the one on the intermediary level. A new opening was cut on this side, and three windows were obliterated and a new door opened on the back. The interior was made two-storied throughout, and it was partitioned into a stair hall and rooms. Chimneys for fireplaces were run up through the roof. In 1970, funds were raised for purchasing the building, and restoration was carried out over the next few years by the Woodford County Historical Society.

THE METHODIST EPISCOPAL CHAPEL. Fortesque Cuming's description of Lexington in 1807 noted that there were five Christian sects with churches, and "also a society of Methodists, which has not yet any regular house of worship."[31] The congregation was to wait thirteen years to be suitably sheltered. The Methodist Episcopal Chapel was built on the north side of Church Street between Upper and Mulberry (Limestone) streets. McCabe's *Directory* of 1838-39 described it as "a plain, well finished brick building, measuring 60 by 50 feet, and contains 75 pews on the ground floor, with a spacious gallery above. This place of worship was erected in the year 1822, at the cost of $5,000, and was dedicated by the late Bishop [Enoch] George."[32] Accurately, it measured 56 by 47 feet, was built without a cellar on low stone foundations, and had five bays across the front, presumably with three portals on Church Street.[33] The flanks had four bays each, those nearest the back on the first floor being doors (fig. 4.36). Windows were twenty-four paned, and a glazed arched opening was in the front gable. A parapet crowning the facade constituted the only suggestion of decorative finish, and

Fig. 4.36 Restored sketch of the Methodist Episcopal Chapel (1822), Lexington.

it projected at the sides on stone brackets at cornice level. The feature set the chapel apart from residences. Inside, facing the entrances, stood the pulpit, with low windows at either side and an arched window centered higher in the back wall (fig. 4.37). A gallery nine feet deep ran along the west, south, and east sides, supported on nine square reeded posts. Stairways were in each of the front corners. It is to be noted that, whereas in the Versailles meetinghouse the balcony faced the pulpit on the long wall, in the

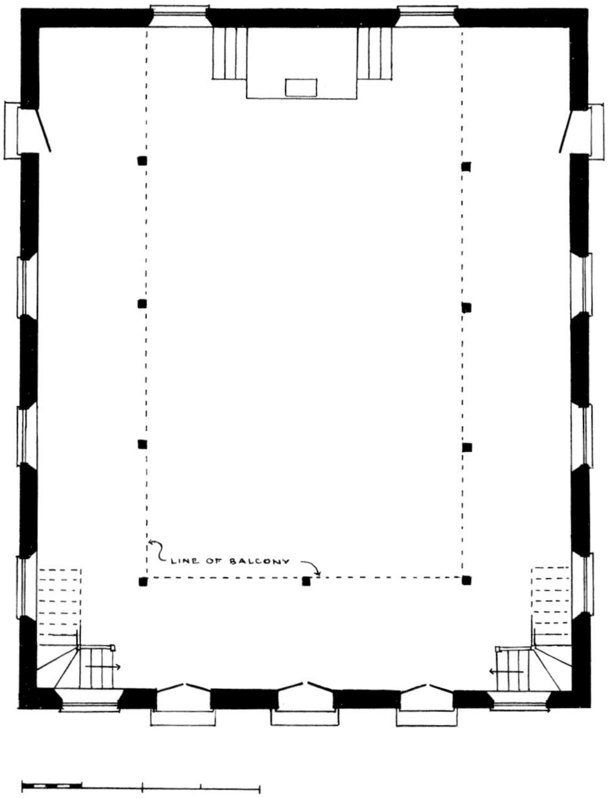

Fig. 4.37 First-floor plan of the Methodist Episcopal Chapel.

Lexington chapel it opened on the shorter side. Neither had a sloping balcony floor.

After the congregation moved to High Street in 1841, the building served as a theater, city hall, and a lodge hall. During the Civil War it was known as Independence Hall, a place for public meetings. Afterward it became successively a black church, a dance hall, and a tire market. Prior to its destruction in 1958, it was the oldest existing church in Lexington and the only one retaining an early meetinghouse form.

MORGAN ROW TAVERNS. About 1814, Joseph Morgan built a brick inn of two and one-half stories in

Harrodsburg on Broad Street (now Chiles Street), directly behind the Mercer County Courthouse (fig. 4.38).[34] The inn has five bays across the front, three of which are doors two steps above walk level. The centermost door opens into a hall with enclosed staircase, and the door to the south leads into the taproom (fig. 4.39). Arches in the upper part of the back wall connect with the 52-foot-long tavern room occupying the rear half of the first story. A surviving mantel from fireplaces located at each end of the

Fig. 4.38 Morgan's and Chiles' taverns (ca. 1814, 1833), Harrodsburg. Photo, 1990.

room and other original woodwork are plain, with reeding in the openings. Doorways that alternate with windows lead down into the backyard. As the ground slopes downward from the street at the rear of the building, a high basement story is entered at grade. Rooms here have fireplaces and were for the coach drivers, grooms, and other tavern personnel.

The second floor contains guest rooms. From the northeast chamber a stairway ascends to the third floor, where a supper room and large ballroom with sloping ceilings are lighted by dormer windows front and back.

Several three-bayed row-house units extend

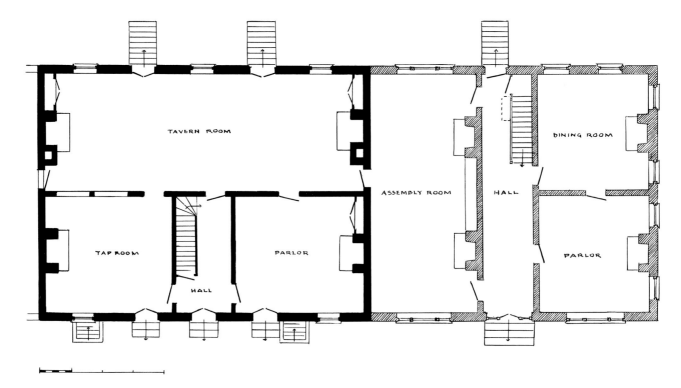

Fig. 4.39 First-floor plan of Morgan's and Chiles' taverns.

Fig. 4.40 Fireplaces and buffet in the assembly room of Chiles' Tavern. Photo, 1983.

southward from Morgan's Tavern. They are brick and continue the cornice line, with fire walls rising above the roof.

Morgan's son-in-law, John G. Chiles, extended the row northward by building his own tavern. The date 1833 and a pomegranate in relief embellish the original leader head at the south end of the building (its mate is a 1964 replacement). Chiles' Tavern is of the same height and depth as its neighbor, but its facade is eight feet shorter. Its stair hall traverses the building, and along the south side is the long assembly room with pilastered mantels on projecting chimney breasts, between which spans a built-in buffet (fig. 4.40). A door opposite opened into Morgan's tavern room. Each end of the assembly room is lit by a nine-foot-broad window of three lights. They resemble those of the brick courthouse that had been built across the street in 1818. The courthouse windows had pilasters and abbreviated-entablature enframements modeled on some in the Main Building (1816) at Transylvania University in Lexington, whereas the tavern openings have reeding and corner blocks. This feature may be said to place the building in the geometric phase of Federal architecture (chap. 8). Iron pintles only in the outermost uprights indicate that the shutters were hinged and opened back against the brick wall, as on the later Trustees' Office at Pleasant Hill (chap. 5). The north rooms were well lighted and ventilated, with windows flanking the fireplaces. The staircase in the transverse hall has an open string, square banisters, and colonnette newels. A door under the landing leads to the backyard. The garrett space was not lighted.

Both buildings are owned by the Harrodsburg Historical Society, which restored them in the 1960s. Chiles' Tavern serves as the society's headquarters.

THE LEXINGTON AND OHIO RAILROAD STATION. Railroads came into being as a public conveyance simultaneously in 1830 at Manchester, England, and Baltimore, Maryland. The Mount Clare Station, a two-story semi-octagonal brick building, was built adjoining the site of the present Baltimore and Ohio Transportation Museum.[35] About then Joseph Bruen made and ran a locomotive in his iron foundry in Lexington that was to pull a car between there and Frankfort. The Bruen locomotive was modeled after one by Thomas W. Barlow, a facsimile of which has been preserved by Transylvania University. In 1830, the Lexington and Ohio Railroad also offered stock in its company.[36] Within the next two years, grading was accomplished for four miles of track to be laid. The first train west of the Alleghenies was put into regular operation and a timetable issued in September 1832. The road was extended to six miles the following year, ending at Lindsey's Spring, or the Villa House, a resort providing an "excellent bar, saloon for dancing in, handsome fishing boat, and large stables."[37] It will be recalled that almost thirty years earlier, the first stagecoach in Kentucky operated between Lexington and such a watering place, Olympian Springs. Horses initially pulled the rail passenger car but were replaced by a steam locomotive in 1835, when the route was lengthened to Frankfort. The run took four hours each way, leaving Lexington at 6:00 A.M. and returning at 6:00 P.M.[38] The rails were of wrought iron, about 3 inches broad and 1½ inch thick, made in 14-foot lengths and fastened to stone sills by spikes set in lead-filled holes drilled in the stone. A section unearthed a few miles west of Lexington was reassembled and put on display in front of Mechanical Hall on the campus of the University of Kentucky.

On the improved map of Lexington published by Luke Munsell in 1835, the railroad tracks on Water Street end short of Mill Street, and apparently the market house occupying the block on Vine Street between Mill Street and Main Cross Street (Broad-way) first served as a depot. In the following year the Lexington and Ohio Railroad Station was built at the west end of the block across Mill Street by John McMurtry (1812-90), a native of Fayette County. He later designed and constructed many edifices and villas in the romantic styles, some of which will be discussed later (chaps. 10, 11, and 12).[39] His depot was a two-story brick building 40 feet across and 100 feet long. Ten-bayed on the flanks, the voids were arranged in three sets of pairs, plus four that were evenly spaced. Lower openings were equipped with double doors to allow for an even flow of passengers and porters in and out of the long building, showing a far greater understanding of the problem of loading and unloading trains than at the compact Mount Clare Station in Baltimore, modeled on a turnpike toll booth. Offices of the company were located upstairs.

A bridge was built over the Kentucky River at Frankfort in 1851, and the line was completed to Louisville in the following year. During this period a third story was added to the Lexington station, the new windows showing splayed frames typical of mid-century (fig. 4.41). Funnels forming heads to the downspouts, shown in the illustration, were common accessories to cornice gutters, especially on buildings adjacent to streets in towns, as at Chiles' Tavern, from the beginning of the nineteenth century through the Greek Revival period.

The Louisville and Nashville Railroad took over the Lexington-Louisville stretch in 1881, and in 1895 a deed was made between this company and the

Fig. 4.41 The Lexington and Ohio Railroad Station (1836, 1850s), Lexington. From the *Mechanical and Electrical Engineering Record* (Lexington), October 1908, p. 24.

Chesapeake and Ohio whereby they would use the tracks jointly. The old station continued to serve Lexington until the erection of the yellow-brick, triumphal-arch Union Depot adjoining the viaduct in 1908, when it became a storehouse. In 1959 the Lexington and Ohio Railroad Station was razed for a parking lot; and not long afterward Union Depot also was destroyed for the identical purpose, train service having been shifted to a suburban-type platform at Rose Street.[40] It, too, was abandoned in 1968, and the tracks were taken up from downtown Lexington.[41]

Examples selected for discussion in this chapter have construction dates ranging over fifty years. In a region undergoing such rapid growth as Kentucky during the late eighteenth and early nineteenth centuries, the tenor of building changed drastically. The earliest examples, Sportsman's Hill, Ellerslie, and Clermont, came into being among primitive log and stone structures, whereas, by the time the Lexington and Ohio Railroad Station was built the Federal style had nearly run its course and the first Greek Revival

building in the West had been serving as the Kentucky capitol for six years. Comparisons have been made between a number of houses here and specimens in the Old Dominion, and undoubtedly in most instances these similarities were a thoroughly conscious procedure. Some of the Kentucky features were of medieval origin from England, still being employed in rural districts there and transplanted to America. Included were parapet walls between units in row houses and on gables (as in Lexington and Maysville), casual planning that reached an extreme wherein division walls abutted openings in the outer shell, the use of decorative brickwork (both figuring in the Whitley house), brick water tables and belt courses (at Ellerslie and Locust Grove), chamfered posts and pendant crestings on porches in lieu of orthodox porticoes, a fireplace in the hall (this and the porch features at Hurricane Hall), external chimneys of complex form (at Woodstock and Oakland), and the lack of architectural embellishment around openings (in the domestic, religious, and railroad buildings).

INTERLUDE
SHAKER COMMUNITIES

5 PLEASANT HILL AND SOUTH UNION

NORTH AMERICA was colonized largely by religious groups from England and northern Europe. The Reformation, which launched a successful separation of the Protestants from the Catholic church, begot a variety of discordant sects. The New World offered asylum to abused minority groups. Thus the Pilgrims (Puritans) came to Massachusetts, the Quakers (Society of Friends) to Pennsylvania, the Anglicans to Virginia, and Huguenots and other Protestants farther south. By the end of the eighteenth century sectarian groups began moving inland. The three principal groups to come into Kentucky were the Traveling Church, the Trappists, and the Shakers. The Traveling Church created little of architectural significance, unless one counts the buildings, such as the Mason County Courthouse in Washington, erected by the Rev. Lewis Craig, working independently as a stone and brick mason. The first Trappists arrived in Casey County in 1806 and built a log monastery. It burned eight years later, whereupon the monks moved to Illinois and later returned to France. The permanent Trappist establishment in Kentucky, the Abbey of Our Lady of Gethsemani, was erected after 1850 by a group from Melleray in France. That complex of Gothic Revival buildings will be discussed in chapter 11. The Shakers were already in Kentucky when the first Trappist monks arrived, and they developed two thriving communities, each containing more than two hundred structures.

Shakerism originated in England. Its official title was the United Society of Believers in Christ's Second Appearing. The society grew out of the injustices, ignorance, and depression of the Industrial Revolution, its founders being illiterate workers in the textile industry centered at Manchester. They were sparked by the Quakers and then by the Camisards, French Prophets who had been exiled because of their armed resistance to Catholicism, and who performed emotional exhibitions among the English, predicting the Second Coming of Christ. The Shakers adopted the prediction, only perceiving it to manifest in the female, specifically in a strange young matron, Ann Lee Standerin, whose unnatural aversion to men prompted an order in which both sexes were to live together in "family" houses yet maintain strict celibacy. Ann was addressed as "Mother." Frequently jailed because of their rowdy meetings, ten members accompanied Mother Ann to America in 1774-75. Conversions led to the forming of two communities in upper New York State, and before 1800 nine others were in existence in Connecticut, Massachusetts, New Hampshire, and Maine. Having become a successful venture, the time had come to expand westward. Seven communities were to materialize in Ohio, Indiana, and Kentucky.[1]

In 1805 the headquarters church at New Lebanon sent three representatives to attend the revivals that had been smoldering in Logan County since 1798 and at Cane Run since 1801. In Kentucky their testimony was indifferently received. They continued on to Ohio, then returned to Kentucky several months later, where they formed the community of Pleasant Hill and, two years later, that of South Union.

The first proselyte in Kentucky was Elisha Thomas of Mercer County, who offered his 140-acre farm on Shawnee Run for a community. He was joined by several members of the Dutch (Friesian) Banta family and others. They acquired adjoining land called Pleasant Hill, which they took for the name of their settlement, a high and fertile site near the Kentucky

River, seven miles northeast of Harrodsburg. Between 1806 and 1812 the communitarians acquired 3,000 acres of land (later increased by almost half) and inaugurated a building program. Pleasant Hill reached its peak during the second quarter of the nineteenth century, with a maximum population of 500. Its decline began after the Civil War, but the community managed to survive until 1910. During its existence of over a century, some 1,200 persons resided at Pleasant Hill.[2]

BUILDINGS AT PLEASANT HILL

The first Shakers on Shawnee Run lived in log houses already on the Thomas farm, and those who united with them later built similar cabins. In 1808 they constructed a sawmill on the stream, and erected a "meeting house or rather a stand," an uncovered platform on which they held their boisterous meetings.[3] By this time they had begun to expand to newly acquired higher ground to the east. Two log houses were erected at the center of the proposed village in 1808 for members and in anticipation of the ruling ministry. The first Shaker document to record the name "Pleasant Hill" was the Society Covenant dated 12 March 1810.

FIRST CENTRE FAMILY HOUSE. The first permanent building erected at Pleasant Hill stands at the northeast intersection of the old roads from Danville to Lexington and Harrodsburg to Lexington. It was built in 1809 as an improved stone residence for the first ruling ministry, composed of two elders and two eldresses, who had been trained at New Lebanon and had interned at Union Village, Ohio.[4] One of the two log cabins served as a detached kitchen. The 25-by-36-foot building has two-and-a-half stories, three-bays in front and rear, and nine-over-six-paned window sashes in the first story and six-over-six in the second. Doors with transoms are centered in the east and west halls, chimneys rise from the two gabled ends, and there is a small pent over the cellar stairs on the south flank (fig. 5.1). The walls are of roughly squared blocks of limestone laid in uniform courses of slightly varying height. Horizontal cornices are without bed or crown moldings, raking boards taper, and door and window frames are plain.

Both outside entrances opened into narrow vestibules with doors left and right, that on the east side leading to a straight flight of steps to the second floor (fig. 5.2). In all likelihood, as in the earliest Shaker houses in New York State, the men lived downstairs

Fig. 5.1 The first Centre Family House (1809), Pleasant Hill. Photo, 1973.

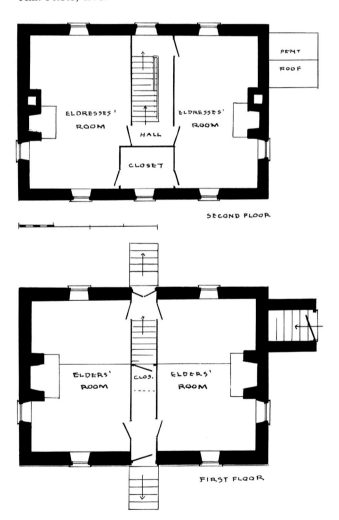

Fig. 5.2 Floor plans of the first Centre Family House.

and the women above. Two large rooms on the second story and a closet at the front are divided from the stairs and narrow passageway. All interior walls are vertical-board partitions. Under the soffit of the garret stairs, at the head of the lower flight, are two sliding panels to small overhead compartments. The Shakers provided themselves with ample closets and took advantage of odd nooks for smaller storage spaces.

A similar stone dwelling was built a hundred yards to the west in 1811, facing south. It was the first West Family House. Both early stone buildings were sup-

Fig. 5.3 The second Centre Family House (1812-15), Pleasant Hill. Photo, ca. 1902, by A.B. Rue, courtesy of the University of Louisville.

planted by larger residence halls and would serve other purposes.

A two-story stone meetinghouse was built to the north of the two residences in 1810-12. It was damaged by earthquakes in 1812-13 and was succeeded by the present frame meetinghouse of 1820 on a different site. Thereafter it mostly served as a workshop until its destruction by fire in 1839.[5] The early meetinghouse was supplemented by a ministry's shop built directly north of it in 1812. Here, members of the ministry, like lay members, produced marketable goods for the support of the colony. The frame two-story shop has a large brick chimney on the north gable end.

THE SECOND CENTRE FAMILY HOUSE. Directly across from the stone meetinghouse was the first sizable building at Pleasant Hill, built also of stone between 1812 and 1815. Its plans originated in Kentucky and were sent to New Lebanon for approval, where Mother Lucy Wright had Brother Nicholas redraw them according to her wishes. Porches were eliminated, a third story was added to the main pavilion, and a proposed separate kitchen was attached.[6] The building followed a T plan and showed the separation of the sexes on each floor, having a center hall containing twin stairways to the sleeping rooms in the main part, and a dining room, assembly hall, kitchen, and smaller rooms in the ell. Its unique

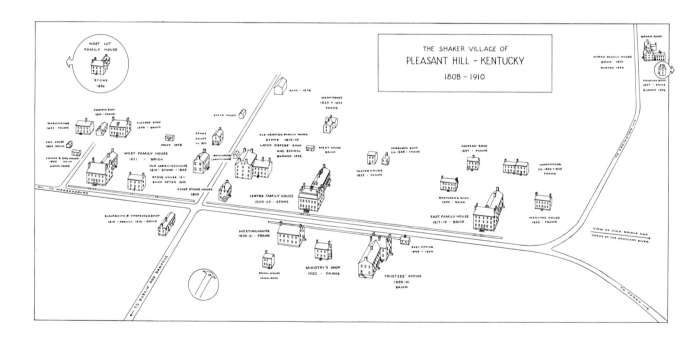

Fig. 5.4 Sketch of the principal buildings at the Shaker village of Pleasant Hill.

feature was the two front doors to the stair hall (fig. 5.3). The Shakers had used twin doors to meetinghouses and two staircases in the same hall, one for men and the other for women, but the second Centre Family House at Pleasant Hill was the first dwelling to feature double outside entrances to a hallway. It established the form of later "family" residences at Pleasant Hill. The building burned in 1932.[7]

The first use of brick was for the blacksmiths' and wagonmakers' shop, built in 1815 at the southwest corner of the crossroads. A second innovation dating from this time was a change in the village's principal orientation. The stone meetinghouse and two Centre Family houses were laid out on a north-south axis, but henceforth the east-west Lexington-Harrodsburg Pike would constitute the main street (fig. 5.4). Also a master builder had appeared who was to bestow architectural refinement on future undertakings. Micajah Burnett (1791-1879) was born in Virginia and entered the community in 1809 as the oldest child in a family of eight. Micajah testified to working on the framing of the first stone house. Shaker journals credit him with a major role in all building and engineering operations at Pleasant Hill beginning with the construction of the East Family House.

THE EAST AND WEST FAMILY HOUSES. The residence for the East Family was built at the Lexington end of the new axis during 1817-19. It reflected the second stone Centre Family House in size, shape, general appearance, and plan (fig. 5.5). But its walls were of brick, and its trim was more detailed, having bed and crown moldings on the cornices, and backbands on door and window frames (fig. 5.6). The present wide stone steps in front are later replacements, probably of wood originals.

The East Family House was balanced at the other end of the axis by a brick West Family House built in 1821. The two dwelling houses resemble one another, except that the main pavilion of the latter had

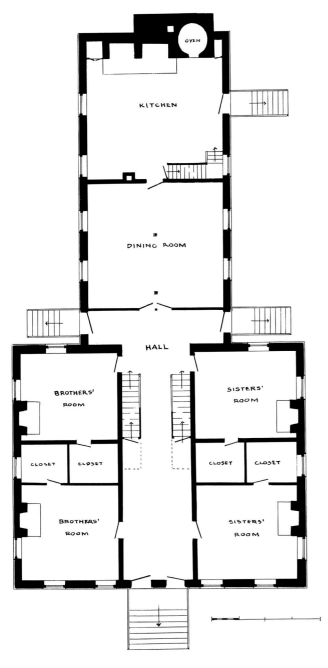

Fig. 5.5 First-floor plan of the East Family House (1817-19), Pleasant Hill.

Fig. 5.6 The East Family House from the southwest. Photo, 1973.

only two and a half stories, as it accommodated elderly people, who would find it difficult to climb stairs. Also, the West Family House contained more and smaller rooms in the main block and more ample kitchen facilities. The family houses were linked by wood fences along the roadside, picket immediately before the buildings and post-and-rail between them. Stone-paved walks inside the fences were for the Shaker women. Shaker men walked in the road.

THE MEETING HOUSE. The frame meetinghouse of 1820-21 was sited at the later center of the theocratic village. The building is a facsimile of the meetinghouse at Union Village, Ohio, built in 1818.[8] The timber framing is filled with brick nogging. The clapboards are painted white, which Shaker protocol reserved for religious buildings, other frame structures being painted brown, yellow, or red. The 60-foot-wide facade has five bays, the second and fourth lower openings being doorways (fig. 5.7). Narrower doors at each end open to enclosed stairs ascending to the second floor. Small windows at the summit of the first flights look down into the meeting room, so that an elder or eldress could scrutinize participants' behavior. With the exception of the stairs, two chimneys, and adjoining closets, the entire first floor is devoted to the assembly space. Its ceiling is suspended by a system of uprights attached to the roof trusses (fig. 5.8). In the garret, twelve posts are divided into four sets of three each, of which half penetrate

Fig. 5.8 View in the garret of the Meeting House showing trusses and suspended posts. Photo, 1972, by Jim Blue, courtesy of Shakertown at Pleasant Hill.

the second story to sustain the first-story ceiling beams. The principal members are the center posts in the outermost groups, and the outer posts in the innermost groups. The heavy center uprights are hung from the rafters to support braces that help hold up the flanking pair. The arrangement coincides with partitions in the second story, where the elders and eldresses had chambers. Four similar rooms are located next to the chimneys, for stove flues, and outside-type windows are provided opposite the front fenestration lighting the stairways (fig. 5.9). Walls between the pairs of end chambers are sufficiently deep to accommodate the posts hanging from the trusses, and the same is true for the inner wall of the center room on this floor.

The Meeting House is set on heavy limestone foundations, which are under the main beams as well as the sills of the outer walls. The building is braced to withstand any strain that might be inflicted upon it. Preaching services were tame, but the ritual dances, with participants stomping in unison, created intense vibrations, as did "Indian Jubilees," when disincarnate spirits would obsess the Shakers and cause them to leap and jerk wildly for hours at a session. After the Shaker regime the meetinghouse served as a Baptist church from 1952 to 1965, then it became part of the restored village. Next door to the meet-

Fig. 5.7 The Meeting House (1820-21), Pleasant Hill. Photo, 1980.

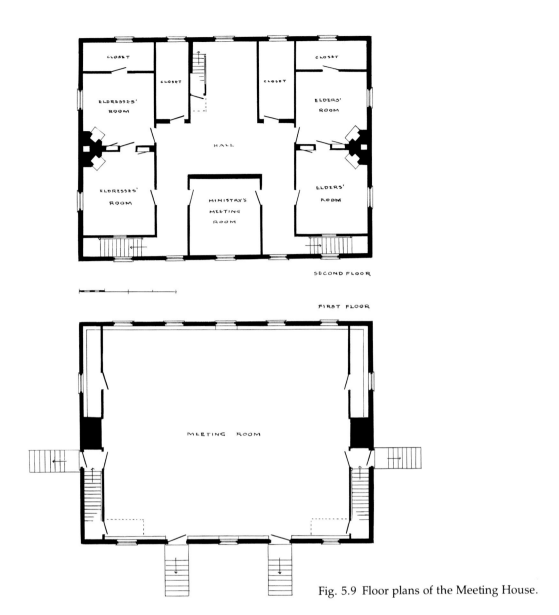

SECOND FLOOR

FIRST FLOOR

Fig. 5.9 Floor plans of the Meeting House.

inghouse on the east is the ministry's Work Shop, built at the same time. The small frame shop has two and a half stories, with a center stair hall.

THE THIRD CENTRE FAMILY HOUSE. The most impressive edifice at Pleasant Hill is across from the meetinghouse and midway between the two brick family residences. Although dates inscribed in a plaque on the upper wall state that it was begun in 1824 and finished in 1825, this was not the case, as dissension within the colony delayed its completion until 1834.[9] Like the residences on the old north-–south axis, this Centre Family House is built of stone. The facade has six-bays, and its dimensions match those of the meetinghouse, but because of a jerkinhead gambrel roof the building has a full three

stories, and the main block is three rooms deep (fig. 5.10). Low parapets between the chimneys mask the upper part of the roof, and a balustrade connects the first two chimneys at the break in the front roof. This ornamental feature seems ostentatious for a sect professing simplicity, but no more so than the fancy picket fence before the building (fig. 5.11).

The third Centre Family House surpasses the others in complexity and breadth of proportions, as may be perceived in the floor plans (fig. 5.12). The transverse hall is wider, and it affords a direct route to the dining room, beyond which are the kitchen and bakery. Four of the six chambers on this level have large closets adjoining them. The building also provides a variety of built-in presses and storage spaces. They

Fig. 5.10 West flank of the third Centre Family House (1824-34), Pleasant Hill. Photo, 1979.

were supplemented by Shaker cupboards, chests, desks, and other pieces of furniture. A distinctive Shaker device is the pegboard, or pinrail, which girded halls and rooms at eye level. It was used for hanging clothes, mirrors, candle sconces (the height could be adjusted), and chairs (when cleaning the floor). No open fireplaces are to be seen, as by this time the Shakers were heating by stoves, mainly of their own manufacture. They were of two kinds: one was long and low and had a stovepipe at the back, and the other, designed for maximum radiation, was shorter, with a second heat chamber bent over the top, the flue rising from near the front end. The black stoves became the principal accent in the white-walled rooms. Woodwork in the house is a dark blue-

gray, except for the baseboard, whose deep red brick color is carried across the lower part of doors. Floors are natural ash, oak, or poplar. Ceilings are twelve-feet high in the first story, and arches and vaults rise above some of the passages, the form culminating in the curved ceiling of the assembly room upstairs (fig. 5.13). It may have been inspired by the vaulted meetinghouse (1824) at New Lebanon, or, along with the roof balustrade (chap. 7), by halls in Matthew Kennedy's Main Building (1816) for Transylvania University in Lexington. The dark paneled dado, doors, and window recesses give stability to the volume, and the slender line of the pinrail calls attention to the airiness of the upper part of the assembly room. The building is a paragon of good design, simplicity, and excellence of craftsmanship. It testifies to the proposition that a thorough understanding of building processes is more vital than design theory for good architectural results.

THE TRUSTEES' OFFICE.   East of the meetinghouse and ministry's shop is the second finest of Micajah Burnett's buildings, built of brick in 1839-41. The Trustees' Office, which also served as a tavern and guest house, differs from the other large buildings in having a single doorway, permissible here because it was not a family house. The builder's acquired taste for grace through curved members is apparent in the elliptical fan of the doorway, bridging double paneled doors and sidelights (fig. 5.14). The date is late for a fanlighted doorway, although Bucknore, near Paris, built in 1841, also has one. Transitional elements include wood muntins, rather than lead dividers,

Fig. 5.11 The third Centre Family House. Photo, 1979.

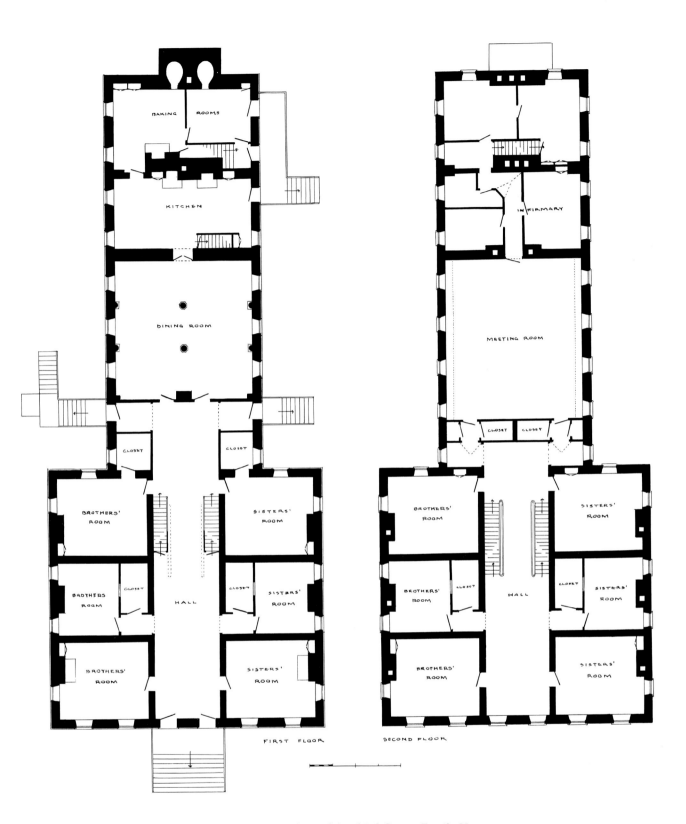

Fig. 5.12 Floor plans of the third Centre Family House.

Fig. 5.13 Assembly room on the second floor of the third Centre Family House. Photo, 1973.

larger panes limited to wedge shapes, and a lighter frame showing the splayed profile used in the Greek Revival style. Consistent with the doorway are wide windows of three lights, with double-hinged shutters, such as appeared on Chiles' Tavern in Harrodsburg (fig. 4.38).

The outstanding feature inside the Trustees' Office is a pair of circular staircases (fig. 5.15). The stairs on either side of the hall spiral in opposite directions around five-foot open wells up to the third floor, where the curves are echoed in the concave shapes of the ceiling (fig. 5.16). The narrow elliptical dome at the top relates to a characteristic Shaker form appearing on the family houses in the village, a double-faced dormer astride the roof ridge, serving as both a lookout and a cupola. Returning to the first floor, the center hall opens onto an arcaded porch on the east side of the rear ell (fig. 5.17). The five openings are provided with louvered shutters. Two are accessible to outside stone steps, and a stairway at the end ascends to the second story, making the porch an important circulation element of the tavern. The Trustees' Office was sold with 766 acres in 1898 to

Fig. 5.14 The Trustees' Office and Guest House (1839-41), Pleasant Hill. Photo, 1968.

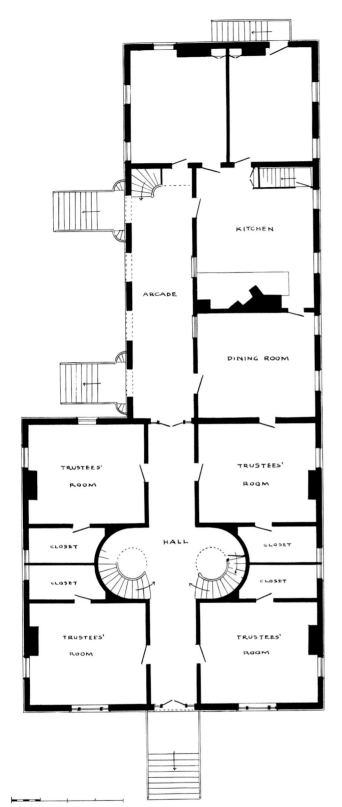

Fig. 5.15 First-floor plan of the Trustees' Office.

Fig. 5.16 Looking up west stairs at the ceiling forms in the Trustees' Office. Photo, 1968.

Fig. 5.17 Arcaded porch of the Trustees' Office. Photo, 1978.

become a private dwelling and horse farm. Afterward it reverted to a hostelry. The building, with an acre of land, was the first property acquired by Shakertown, Inc., in 1962.

Two satellite residence complexes supplemented the village (fig. 5.18). The first North Lot Family House was a preexisting frame house standing on property purchased by Samuel Banta for the community in 1807. To accommodate converts, it was moved to a site a mile toward Lexington on the Harrodsburg Pike in 1816, where rooms were added and other alterations made.[10] A second and much larger brick North Lot Family House was built south of it in 1831. It resembled the West Family House, though it had a single doorway and a semicircular fan arched over sidelights. It burned in 1946. A mile west of the village, toward Harrodsburg, downstream from Elisha Thomas's land on Shawnee Run, young believers built a stone West Lot Family House in 1826 for their own accommodation. Smaller than the village residences and built on a slope, the dining room and kitchen are in the basement. It has a single front door with transom, but two straight flights of stairs in the main hall. The first North Lot Family House and the West Lot Family House were restored during the 1980s and early 1990s.

In addition to the major buildings, Micajah Burnett built a number of utilitarian structures. Of special interest is the water house (1833), northeast of the third stone Centre Family House. It is a small, square, two-story frame shell containing a round cypress tank perched on high stone piers. Gravity caused the water to flow through iron pipes to residence kitchens and washhouses. A floating gauge extending up through the roof could be seen at the Tanyard spring, so when the water level was low, the horse-powered pump could be started to fill the tank. This was one of the earliest water-supply systems in the West. Two-story washhouses and shops accompanied all the major family houses, and there were smaller outbuildings. Burnett and Tyler Baldwin built a large stone and frame grist mill (1816-17) on Shawnee Run, whose spills turned two overhead wheels. Burnett, who sometimes traveled to other Shaker villages to solve their engineering problems, projected and supervised the building of the road to the Kentucky River.[11]

Pleasant Hill was not greatly misused or de-

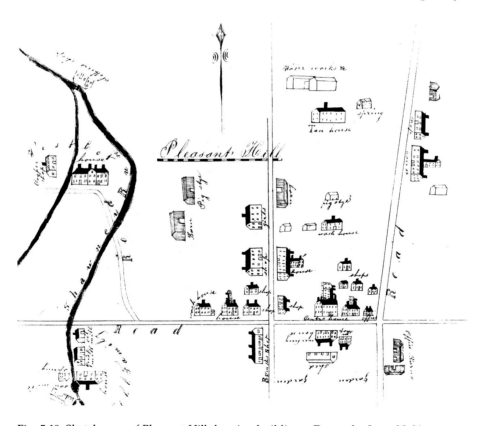

Fig. 5.18 Sketch map of Pleasant Hill, locating buildings. Drawn by Isaac N. Youngs, 1834; printed by George Kendall, 1835. Courtesy of Shakertown at South Union.

veloped, and its architectural merits invited restoration of the village. The prime mover was Earl D. Wallace, who in 1961 founded Shakertown at Pleasant Hill, Kentucky, Inc., a nonprofit, educational institution, and the restoration was directed by James L. Cogar. Various properties that had fallen into private hands were purchased, and restoration of the buildings was begun, financed by private donations and a long-term loan from the U.S. Department of Commerce. The task of converting the village into an extensive museum representative of the Shaker way of life was performed with diligence and care. Pleasant Hill was opened to the public in 1968. The Lexington-Harrodsburg Pike subsequently was rerouted around the village, thus eliminating the most disturbing modern encroachment upon the peaceful setting. Some of the buildings serve as overnight guest houses, and the Trustees' Office continues as an inn. Two smaller buildings function as gift shops, and several other buildings are used to demonstrate Shaker crafts. The Meeting House and Centre Family House are wholly museums, provided with lectures by costumed guides. In 1972 Pleasant Hill was designated a National Historic Landmark.

BUILDINGS AT SOUTH UNION

The second Shaker community in Kentucky was founded in 1807 at the headwaters of Gasper River midway on the road from Bowling Green to Russellville in Logan County. Its name, South Union, was derived from the inland Shaker center, Union Village in Ohio. Plans of Pleasant Hill and South Union made by Isaac N. Youngs in 1834 show that the layouts of the two villages were similar, and they had a comparable array of buildings (figs. 5.18, 5.19). Both were known for the quality of their industries, bottling honey and preserves, canning vegetables, packaging seeds, making brooms, and raising silkworms and weaving silk. South Union also manufactured stoves.

THE FIRST CENTRE FAMILY HOUSE. The oldest known building at South Union was a small house of 1810 that was a clapboarded frame counterpart of the first stone Centre Family House at Pleasant Hill (fig. 5.20). Its details were as simple; the chimneystacks were brick. It stood northwest of the crossroads and served as a shop and later a schoolhouse before disappearing. The church group grew up around it to the east.

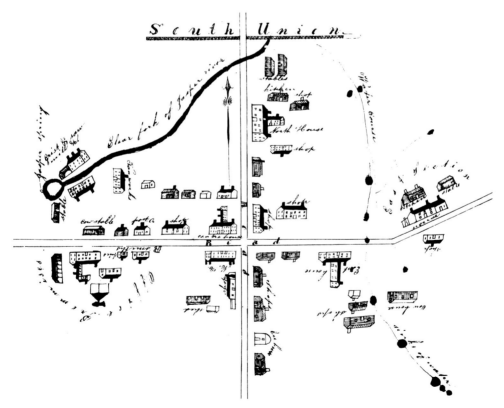

Fig. 5.19 Sketch map of South Union, locating buildings. Drawn by Isaac N. Youngs, 1834; printed by George Kendall, 1835. Courtesy of Shakertown at South Union.

Fig. 5.20 A frame dwelling or shop (1810), South Union. Photo, ca. late 1800s, courtesy of Shakertown at South Union, Museum Collection.

THE MEETING HOUSE. Across U.S. Route 68 (coincidentally the same road which passed through Pleasant Hill) was the meetinghouse, the center of all Shaker communities. South Union's was unusual in being built of brick, which material contributed to its being the handsomest of its kind.[12] The Meeting House was begun in 1813, with excavation for the foundations and assembling materials, and it was completed in 1820. As in Pleasant Hill brick buildings, the foundations are of a fine quality limestone. Although the masonry buildings at South Union are predominantly brick, more use of stone was made in their trim than at the sister village, as in labels over the windows and doors, copings, and roof cornice gutters, or "troughs," on the principal buildings. The Meeting House lintels were splayed at the sides, like brick jack arches, whereas on later South Union buildings they were rectangular. The pattern of doors and windows in the facade was similar to that of the Union Village and Pleasant Hill meetinghouse design, whereas the rear of the building had six bays, with narrow half-windows constituting the two center openings. The sides of the Meeting House had three bays, with parapets rising over the roofline and connecting twin chimney stacks (fig. 5.21). Stone lintels and narrow windows were features seen in New England Shaker villages, and they and closely spaced end chimneys were to be the hallmarks of South Union architecture. The Meeting House was demolished after the community disbanded in 1922, and the masonry was salvaged for constructing a

house on the site. Accompanying the meetinghouse was a brick ministry's shop, built in 1846 to replace a "temporary" predecessor of about 1815 (fig. 5.22).[13]

THE SECOND CENTRE FAMILY HOUSE. The foremost surviving building at South Union is the second Centre Family House, begun in 1823 and completed in 1833, and thus a contemporary of the big stone house at Pleasant hill. Its facade matched in size, shape, and materials that of the meetinghouse directly across the road, and their main masses coincided in form and magnitude as well (fig. 5.23). Narrow windows flank the single front door of the brick residence hall. Steps to the right and left of the stoop connect to two crosswalks to the meetinghouse. A sizable ell is at the rear. Most interior features are normal to the Shakers. Twin straight flights of steps rise in the main hall, at the back of which is the meeting room on the first floor (fig. 5.24). The dining room is below, with kitchen and bake house behind. The second story of the ell is divided into small rooms in much the same way as the Trustees' Office at Pleasant Hill. The unusual aspect of the plan is the chimney arrangement in the main block of the building. Great masonry shafts between the three sets of rooms on each side of the hall serve fireplaces in the north or south walls, whereas chimneys rise above the east and west walls

Fig. 5.21 Rear of the Meeting House (1816-20), South Union. Photo, ca. late 1800s, courtesy of Shakertown at South Union, Museum Collection.

Fig. 5.22 The Ministry's Shop (1846), South Union. Photo, ca. late 1800s, courtesy of Shakertown at South Union, Museum Collection.

Fig. 5.23 The Centre Family House (1822-33), South Union. Photo, ca. late 1800s, courtesy of Shakertown at South Union, Museum Collection.

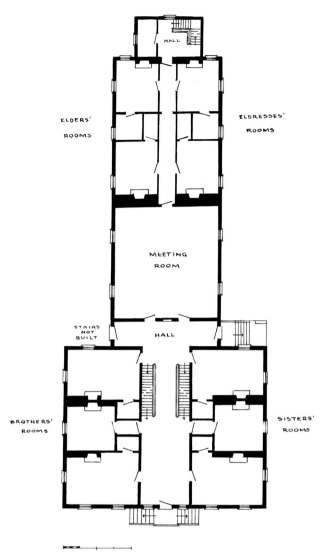

Fig. 5.24 First-floor plan of the Centre Family House.

of the building, so the flues have to be directed outward. This is accomplished by sloping masonry ducts protruding in the garret chambers. The sleeping apartments throughout are amply supplied with closets. Pinrails and chair rails, as well as the door and window frames, were painted a mustard color; baseboards and some doors were painted a brick red.

THE EAST FAMILY HOUSE. A larger version of the foregoing building replaced an East Family House of

1826. It bore the date stone of 1847. The principal mass was three and one-half stories, and in the grouped windows at the center the outermost openings were three instead of two panes wide (fig. 5.25). The sides were similar, only there were raking boards level with the roof instead of standing parapets. The brickwork, rather than Flemish bond as in the building's predecessors, consisted only of stretchers. The house showed no awareness on the part of its builders of the Greek Revival style raging in Kentucky at the time of its erection.

THE OFFICE. On the south side of the east-west road through South Union, Isaac N. Young's 1834 map showed a group of buildings which he labeled "Office Premmises." In the center of the group was a

Fig. 5.25 The second East Family House (1847), South Union. Photo, ca. late 1800s, courtesy of Shakertown at South Union, Museum Collection.

brick tavern built between 1825 and 1828. A frame office was built to the east of the tavern in 1841 (fig. 5.26). It had two and one-half stories and repeated most of the traits of the brick buildings of this size in the village.

THE CENTRE FAMILY SISTERS' WORKSHOP AND WASHHOUSE. To the rear and west of the Centre Family House is the Sisters' Workshop and Washhouse, with the date 1854 incised in the stone lintel of the middle second-story window. The brick structure is the largest of the Shaker shops built in Kentucky. It has three stories and nine bays, and its three doors give it the appearance of a tenement house (fig. 5.27). In this aspect the Sisters' Workshop seems to belong more to the eastern communities, where Shaker settlements appear more like factory towns than religious orders. Certainly Pleasant Hill and South Union escaped that look, except for this one construction. Most of the buildings have dignity and charm and are a credit to their settings. They are notable illustrations that utilitarianism can achieve a beauty in its simplicity. But this one example shows how too much repetition, without a sense of proportion, can be monotonous.

THE SOUTH UNION TAVERN. The tavern in the

"Office Premmises" group, west of the Centre Family House, burned during the Civil War. Its replacement was situated a mile from the village adjacent to the Memphis branch tracks of the Louisville and Nashville Railroad. It was completed in 1869, and although it excels the time limit of this study, the building represents one facet of the Shakers better

Fig. 5.26 The South Union Office (1841), South Union. Photo, ca. late 1800s, courtesy of Shakertown at South Union, Museum Collection.

Fig. 5.27 The Centre Family Sisters' Workshop and Wash House (1854), South Union. Photo, 1989, by Edith S. Bingham.

than any other. This was their concession to worldly endeavors where making money was concerned. The tavern was their bid to recoup financial losses suffered during the war. The building was outfitted with store-bought furniture and leased to a non-Shaker proprietor. Its architecture is remarkable for a Shaker building, in that it sports an up-to-date Italianate facade, with a pedimented portico of six colossal square brick piers supporting arches, the outward thrust of which is checked by iron tie rods at springing level (fig. 5.28). Under the arcade a long balcony projects even with the second floor. Doorway and windows are capped with segmental-arched hood-drip molds. The fore part of the building is only one room deep, and whereas the portico presents a bold and ostentatious front to those alighting from the trains, it looks cumbersome from the side. Although gaining some reputation for its hospitality and cuisine, the tavern was not wholly a success.

During the nineteenth century the South Union Shakers kept apace with the Pleasant Hill communitarians with running water in kitchens and washhouses. Both kept abreast of the times by installing lightning rods, and they used the latest labor-saving

Fig. 5.28 The South Union Tavern (1869). Photo, 1989, by Edith S. Bingham.

devices, such as corn shellers and sewing machines. While the Mercer County group was declining early in the twentieth century, the Logan County believers were forging ahead, installing telephones and bathrooms, acquiring an automobile, and having one of the first gasoline pumps in the area. A store and post office were built across the road from the tavern in 1917. South Union came to a halt in 1922, the last survivor of the seven western Shaker societies.

In 1971 the Centre Family House and Preservatory, where jams and jellies were made, were purchased from Saint Mark's monastery, which remained the neighbor on the west, and under the direction of Mrs. Curry C. Hall, former president of the Shaker Museum in Auburn, the first story of the main building was restored, partly furnished, and opened as a museum the following summer. The collection that had been displayed in an Auburn church for a decade was moved to the more appropriate quarters. Also for a decade a Shaker festival had been held yearly during mid-July in the nearby town, and it too came to South Union after the acquisition. Featured is a drama entitled "Shakertown Revisited." It relates to the presentation of Shaker songs and dances given from time to time in the meetinghouse at Pleasant Hill.

PART TWO

EVOLVING A
REGIONAL
ARCHITECTURE

6 THE FEDERAL PERIOD

PRACTICALLY SIMULTANEOUS with the first purely functional brick buildings in Kentucky was the appearance of sophisticated architectonic form—an artistic ideal that went beyond mere fulfillment of the need for shelter and was endowed with overtones of a refined sense of space concepts and attractive decorative details. The source of inspiration had come from the established culture on the Atlantic seaboard and was traceable back to the Renaissance movement in England and continental Europe. In Kentucky the manifestation never attained High Renaissance conformity, but it gained in having regional originality, ethnic appeal, and down-to-earth human scale. It was an inland version of the American Federal style, whose more orthodox application was championed by Samuel McIntire of Salem, Massachusetts; Charles Bulfinch of Boston; John McComb II of New York; Dr. William Thornton of Washington, D.C.; Thomas Jefferson of Virginia; and Gabriel Manigault of Charleston, South Carolina. Kentucky, likewise, experienced the awakening of the aesthetic consciousness and the development and patronage of skilled local crafts. The Bluegrass and beyond attained something worthy of the name of architecture. The Federal style in Kentucky displayed a high degree of sectional and individual characteristics, while paving the way for the more nationalistic revivals that followed.

The advent of the Federal signaled the surcease of the pioneer period. It required the support of a settled agrarian and mercantile society of some opulence. Strict utilitarianism was passé for the growing class of people of sufficient knowledge, taste, and wealth to desire something greater. Their sponsorship of the arts was fundamental, inasmuch as it beautified their permanent environment and gave them lasting pleasure and a sense of self-esteem. Because of this close connection with their lives, they spared no effort and brought into play all the means at their disposal to attain a gracious setting. The labors of creating buildings to their liking were divided among specialists: the carpenter or joiner; perhaps a separate stairbuilder; the mason; the carver of mantels, doorways, arches, chair railings and other woodwork; and the glazier, plasterer, and painter. These men plied their trades from fixed quarters, or went about as itinerants, living on the premises of current endeavors, often for months at a time. The many artisans who devoted their time and talents to the realization of the fine Federal buildings were workmen worthy of their hire. Their work acquired a certain personality and unity due to a timely virility and pride of craftsmanship shared among them, and the buildings of this era are among the treasures of Kentucky's architectural heritage.

Builders' handbooks were principally responsible for standardizing Federal architecture. The first published in America were reprints of guides of the English carpenter-architect Abraham Swan, whose *The British Architect* and *A Collection of Designs in Architecture* were issued at Philadelphia in 1775. The first had appeared initially at London in 1745 and the second in 1757. *The British Architect* also was reprinted at Boston in 1794. It is significant that the earliest listing of books on architecture available at a local store in the *Kentucky Gazette* includes "Swan's Architecture." It is one of the three titles offered at John Bradford's bookshop, "near the Public Spring, on Main Street, Lexington," in 1795.[1] Which of the Swan books is referred to is a question, but it probably was one of the American editions. Equally ambiguous is the notice of "Swan's Architecture" found in a bulletin of goods advertised for sale by MacBean, Poyzer and Company at Main and Cross (Broadway) streets in 1798.[2] *The British Architect* was a typical English publication of the period, primarily devoted to engraved plates giving correct Georgian details and meant as a guide for the carver and decorator rather than the builder. Out of sixty plates, twenty-six illustrate the orders, six show moldings, fourteen give staircase details, ten are of rococo designs for mantels and miscellaneous ornaments, one contains a house plan, and two are of roof trusses. *A Collection of Designs in Architecture* is a thin volume of ten house plans and facade elevations. Each is more academic than any house that materialized in Kentucky.

Another book obtainable at Bradford's bookstore was listed as "Paine's Architecture," which could be any of a number of books by William Pain. Very likely it was either *The Builder's Pocket-Treasure*, published in London in 1763 and in Boston in 1794, or *Practical Builder*, which appeared in London in 1774 and in Boston in 1792 (a reprint of the fourth London edition of 1787), as these were the only two available through American publishers in 1795. The bookstore of Johnson and Warner, at Main and Mill streets, Lexington, advertised in 1810 "The Builder's Pocket Treasure, with 15 plates—price 2 dols." The notation, "15 plates," perhaps is a typographic error, as the book contained fifty-five plates.[3] The last engraving in the *Pocket-Treasure* includes a fireplace design with a frieze combining two units of a Greek key flanked by interlaced strapwork, and the ends finished with slender console forms (fig. 6.1). This unusual pattern has been related to the parlor fireplace in Clermont (chap. 4), and it served as the basis for a mantel in Waveland, a two-story brick house of about 1800 on the outskirts of Danville. There, however, the frieze is contained between impost blocks carved with elliptical sunbursts and supported on pilasters (fig. 6.2). A similar interlacing strapwork alone is shown in detail on plate 52. Another appears on plate 32 of

Fig. 6.2 Detail of fireplace wall in parlor of Waveland, Danville. Photo, 1964.

The Practical Builder, and plate 47 is presumably the source of inspiration of the applied fret in the entablature of the Waveland room. The Ionic order with rosette on the echinus may have come from plates 18 or 21 in the same volume. The name of the Danville artisan is unknown, but local tradition says he was from Philadelphia.

The third item in Bradford's 1795 advertisement is "Town & Country Builder." John Norman's *The Town and Country Builder's Assistant*, printed at Boston about 1786, was the first book of its kind compiled in America. In addition to having architectural delineations showing treatment of special features, this book contains designs for stairs in various polygons, and diagrams for building odd-shaped roofs. Plates 46 and 53 suggest the bonnets on the corner flankers of Woodlands (fig. 8.15).

Johnson and Warner's bookstore in Lexington announced in 1810 that it had copies of "Biddles Architecture."[4] Owen Biddle's *The Young Carpenter's Assistant* was first printed and sold by Benjamin Johnson of Philadelphia in 1805. The edition issued in 1810 is inscribed as being "sold at [Johnson and Warner's] bookstores in Philadelphia; Richmond, Virginia; and Lexington, Kentucky." Biddle, who died the year after the original publication, was a carpenter and teacher of architectural drawing. He made clear in the subtitle of the book that it was "adapted to the

Fig. 6.1 "Entablature for Chimney-piece." From William Pain, *The Builder's Pocket-Treasure* (London, 1763), detail of pl. 55.

style of building in the United States," and as this suggests, the designs look similar to architectural details used during the second and third decades of the nineteenth century, although it is difficult to relate them to executed features. Doorways with half-moon transoms in the *Carpenter's Assistant*, however, resemble those at Vaucluse, Coolavin, and Ashland in the Lexington vicinity.[5] In 1813 Daniel Bradford listed the "Carpenter's Assistant" among his "new Books."[6] Johnson and Warner brought out a third edition in 1815, Benjamin Warner a fourth in 1817, and other publishers issued four more between 1833 and 1858.

Ownership of a specific builder's guide by an early Kentucky builder is confirmed by signatures in an existing copy of Asher Benjamin's *The Builder's Assistant* (1800), which is a third edition of *The Country Builder's Assistant* (1797). Both were published in Greenfield, Massachusetts. The book originally belonged to Mathias Shryock of Lexington and later passed to his son, Gideon, and was obtained by the late Louisville architect Frederic L. Morgan.[7] Among designs for architectural features presented in the handbook is plate 12, for a frontispiece or doorway, with a fanlight remarkably like that of the William A. Warner cottage, which stood on Main Street, Lexington (fig. 6.3; compare with fig. 9.12). The enframement of the Benjamin design resembles those

Fig. 6.4 Doorway of Clay Hill, Harrodsburg. Photo, 1941.

of Vaucluse and Coolavin, mentioned above. Plate 29, representing the facade of a two-story house with a belt course and a Palladian doorway, suggests the entrances of the Main Building (1816) of Transylvania University (fig. 7.14). It also relates to the door of Winton (1823), north of Lexington on Newtown Pike.[8] Plates 31 and 32 give the plans of a house with octagonal end pavilions, each with its own chimney, as at Plancentia and Woodlands (figs. 8.13, 8.16). In the Benjamin design, however, the octagons are attached by hemicycles and contain circular rooms covered by low-pitched roofs instead of bonnets.

Close parallels between imported design and Kentucky execution are the exception rather than the rule, as applied woodwork was usually fashioned according to the taste and manner of local craftsmen. The most distinguished was Matthew P. Lowery,

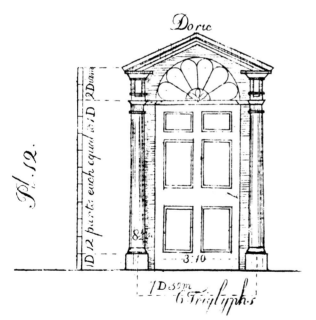

Fig. 6.3 Design for a frontispiece. From Asher Benjamin, *The Builder's Assistant* (Greenfield, Mass., 1800), detail of pl. 12.

who moved from Madison County to Mercer County about 1800 and produced carved wood fittings in the Bluegrass during the balance of the Federal period.[9] He is said to have carved the decorative features of Clay Hill, built about 1812 for Beriah Magoffin in the south end of Harrodsburg. The paneled front door has an elliptical fanlight under an articulated archivolt and is enframed by engaged Tuscan colonnettes on pedestals supporting an entablature (fig. 6.4). Panels in the pedestals (like the colonnette shafts) are reeded, and the frieze displays five sunbursts of three different patterns—unknown in such context on antecedent monuments. Reportedly, Lowery also executed the woodwork in the Lambert Brewer residence near McAfee in Mercer County during the early 1800s. The story-and-a-half house has staircases in the corners of the parlor and the dining room, and mantels of engaging charm (fig. 6.5). The pilaster shafts are composed of convex panels of reeding encased in beaded moldings, and the imposts are ornamented with circular rosettes. In the center frieze panel is an elliptical sunburst, and a typical gouged banding forms a dentil course under the breakfront cornice. These motifs have evolved from the most expedient way of using their creator's tools. They are abstractions, as opposed to the traditional nymphs and garland swags of the sophisticated English classic Adam school. Lowery's motifs are simple, effective, decorative, and appropriate to the buildings in which they occur. The mantel in the adjoining dining room of the Brewer House contains rectangular reeded panel insets in the frieze and pilaster shafts. A Lowery-type mantel was noted in the parlor of Oakland in Fayette County (chap. 4). A very elaborate version was in the Ezekiel Fields House, on Main Street in Richmond, which was incorporated into Gibson Hospital. The building resembled Rose Hill, Lexington, in plan, and the mantel in question was in the long drawing room at the back. The chimneypiece had colonnettes and a serpentine shelf, with rosettes, sunbursts and carved horizontal bandings resembling Lowery's work (fig. 6.6). Other examples of fine carving in Madison County were in Woodlawn (1822, razed mid-1940s; fig. 6.7), and Castlewood (ca. 1825).[10] The parlor mantel in Woodlawn must have been produced by the same hand responsible for that in the Fields House. These fittings were carved from pieces of poplar, cherry, or walnut wood, and assembled. Contemporary figure and leaf ornaments were cast in white metal or modeled in some kind of "composition" and applied. An example of this species is the mantel in the Barker House on Cleveland Road in Fayette County, originally in the parlor of a house standing on East Main Street near Ransom Avenue in Lexington (fig. 6.8).

Fig. 6.5 Parlor-detail in the Lambert Brewer House, Mercer County. Photo, 1964.

Fig. 6.6 Drawing-room mantel in the former Ezekiel Fields House, Richmond. Photo, 1940.

The formal Federal-style mantel usually was accompanied by an equally new manner of wood trim around doors and windows. Unlike the typical Georgian casing that was like a picture frame, with the most elaborate molding, or backband, around the outer side, the innovative Federal version was symmetrical in profile, with various types of reeding in a recessed panel and elaborate corner blocks. These blocks were often a little larger than the vertical and horizontal members and normally contained a cir-

cular motif, either with diameter profile matching that of the adjoining casing, as at Mount Airy (fig. 9.11), or else a carved star or round sunburst resembling those on mantels, as at Warwick in Mercer County (chap. 9). Enlarged, it survived into the Greek Revival period.

Stone artisans bid for some of the carved-mantel trade. In 1802 PETER PAUL & SON, STONE CUTTERS from London, . . . living on the Woodford road, Lexington," informed the "public at large" that they could supply all sorts of stone work, including "Polished MARBLE CHIMNEY PIECES, and FREESTONE ditto."[11] The only surviving marble mantels of the period known to the author are in the William Morton House (1810), to be discussed in chapter 8. They are plain; a cove molding around the fireplace supports a cornicelike shelf with vertical grooves in sets of five, interspersed with dogwood motifs, and there is another cove serving as crown mold. The Pauls may have produced them, as well as the exterior stone detailing of Lexington houses mentioned in chapter 4 (fig. 4.4).

In 1815 Robert H. Armstrong, a newcomer to the Bluegrass from Charleston, South Carolina, professed to execute "Stucco-work, plain Plastering; cornices, plain or ornamented; centre pieces, plain or ornamented"; and he tinted "walls in various water colors."[12] If Armstrong's "stucco-work" in any way

Fig. 6.7 Parlor in Woodlawn, Madison County. From Elizabeth Patterson Thomas, *Old Kentucky Homes and Gardens* (Louisville, 1939), p. 78.

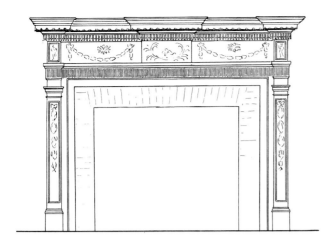

Fig. 6.8 Parlor mantel in the Barker House, near Athens; originally in a Lexington residence. Drawing from a photo taken in 1953.

measured up to that of other Charleston artisans, such as Ezra Waite, who executed the exquisite reliefs in the Miles Brewton House (1769), he could have contributed to the beauty of early houses in central Kentucky. His address was given as "Mr. William Clark's Hotel," signifying that he was not settled. His name does not appear in the 1818 city directory, and one suspects that he did not long remain. Except for the exterior frieze on the William Morton House in Lexington, the notable Kentucky stucco work of that period is in Elmwood Hall (1818) at Ludlow. The square entrance hall has four pendentives connecting tympanum arches set on columns stationed at the corners of the room. The continuous frieze at springing level, the soffit of the arches, a border around the flat, circular ceiling, and a shell-on-console motif in each spandrel are of plaster produced in molds (fig. 8.38). The artisan is unknown. He may have been an itinerant, perhaps engaged from the seaboard especially for this job.

The availability of wallpaper and hangers can also be ascertained from advertisements in Bradford's *Kentucky Gazette.* As early as 1793, wallpaper was sold at the emporium of Joseph Hudson on Main Street, Lexington, "next door to the Sign of the Buffaloe." Listed with various kinds of hardware and paints was "Stampt paper for rooms."[13] In 1805, the art and decorating concern of F. Downing and Company, which besides cutting profile likenesses with the "physiognotrace," engaging in gilding and japanning, and restoring and repairing old looking glasses, as well as house and sign painting, offered its services in "*Papering,* and decorating apartments in

the most finished style."[14] George Ruth likewise advertised in 1809 that he performed "PAINTING, GLAZING AND PAPER HANGING . . . in all its various branches, on the lowest terms."[15]

An interesting list of wallpaper design subjects appeared in the *Kentucky Gazette* in 1816. They were available in the stock of Downing and Grant, which firm the 1818 directory identifies as "Painters and Grocers, Short Street." They announced receipt of "an elegant assortment of *French and American Paper Hangings.* . . . Among them are a few sets of the Monuments of Paris, Views of the City and Bay of Naples, with an elegant representation of Mount Vesuvius, Captain Cook's voyage in the Pacific Ocean, and a representation of his death by the Owybee nation, a view of the chase, Paul and Virginia, and some views in India."[16] One is tempted to relate the "views of the City and Bay of Naples" to wallpaper in the parlor at Hurricane Hall, five miles north of Lexington. The subject is an Italian pastoral panorama with Roman ruins in the background, and figures and domesticated animals scattered about, but there is no "elegant representation of Mount Vesuvius." The Hurricane Hall specimen is identified as "Paysages d'Italie" (fig. 4.21). The designer and atelier are unknown, but it is thought to have been issued shortly before it was applied in 1817.[17] Its colors remain natural and remarkably fresh.

The scene designated "a view of the chase" may have been that of the paper in the parlor of Woodlawn in Madison County (fig. 6.7). Although the house was not built until 1822, the paper is said to date from 1814. It bears the mark of Jacquemort and Bénard, the successors of Reveillon, the outstanding French wallpaper manufacturer of the late eighteenth century.[18] The amusing story is told in connection with Woodlawn that its walls were too tall for the wallpaper, and the paperhanger had to wait the better part of a year for "more clouds" to be sent from Paris. The paper was sold and removed from the house in 1929.

A paper by the Reveillon studio was on the walls of the ballroom at Locust Grove (ca. 1790) outside Louisville. Rather than a scene, the design by Cietti of about 1786 presents a repeat pattern of nymphs, putti, and floral sprays in blues, rose, and brown on a background of light green. Fragments of the original were found when a later partition was removed. The full design was obtained and copied, and a reproduction now graces the walls (fig. 4.15).

Painted murals also figured in decorating early Kentucky interiors. Three houses in Woodford

County display landscapes in their parlors and in the adjoining stair hall of one of these as well. The paintings are in oil colors applied directly on the plaster. They were done about 1830 by Alfred Cohen, a native of Bordeaux, France. Alfred and his brothers, John and Henry, immigrated to central Kentucky probably in the mid-1820s.[19] Alfred Cohen was a primitive artist, without knowledge of linear perspective. His forms are simplified, often angular, relating to one another mostly by spacing; and his colors are predominantly greens, browns, and gray blues, toned down by the addition of black. Tradition links the scenes with Kentucky history, but the scarcity of figures, their casual and diverted attitudes, and the character of buildings and plants represented are decidedly reminiscent of southern France.

One house containing Cohen murals is Airy Mount, off the Mortonsville Road, between two and three miles from Versailles, purchased by Willis Field in 1813 and serving as his home from 1816 until his death in 1837.[20] The parlor is about eighteen-feet square with a ten-foot ceiling height. It has a door and fireplace centered on opposite walls, a second

door alongside the chimney breast, and pairs of windows in the front and back walls. The landscape covers the intervening spaces between chair rail and ceiling (fig. 6.9). A horizon line is maintained around the room slightly above seated eye level. Architectural accents in the scene include a three- or four-story building with projecting end pavilions connected by an arcade, a domed temple with pedimented portico, a three-span stone bridge leading to an ancient town, and a basilicalike church with a square keep or tower. In the hall, the painting over the staircase contains a sloping horizon, parallel to the railing, which gives a peculiar distortion to a row of houses with vertical walls, looking as if they are about to slide down the incline. One is reminded of the fresco over the stairway in the Colburn House in Westwood, Massachusetts, where the rocky peaks of an island are on a similar slant and the coastline sweeps rakishly upward.[21]

A second parlor mural is in the Gen. James Mc-Connell House on the Mortonsville Road a mile beyond Airy Mount. The room is about twenty feet square and has two windows and a door in the wall

Fig. 6.9 Parlor of Airy Mount, Woodford County. Photo, ca. 1938, by Lafayette Studio, Lexington.

Fig. 6.10 Fireplace wall in parlor of the Gen. James McConnell House, Woodford County. The mantel is a replacement. Photo, 1948.

facing the road, similar openings opposite, a single door on the inside wall, and a fireplace on the chimney breast across from it. The ceiling height is about the same as in Airy Mount, but in a foot-deep band of gray at the top of the wall is painted a red-fringed drapery caught up in a series of festoons alternating with tassels (fig. 6.10). Also, the dado is enriched with marbleized panels. The horizon level is as at Airy Mount, except on the front of the chimney breast, where it is elevated to divide equally the space between the mantel shelf and festooned border. The inside wall provides the largest uninterrupted area in the three houses, being fourteen feet in length (fig. 6.11). In the center is a pond in which are a sailboat and rowboat. Vehicles in front and on the road to the right include a two-wheeled cart carrying a keg and drawn by a single horse, and a couple in a gig pulled by a pair of horses. Beyond the water are two houses and a churchlike building that has four vanes attached windmill-fashion to its spire. Except for a few great trees, the terrain is relatively barren.

The third example is in Pleasant Lawn, situated between Midway and Versailles, built for Daniel Jackson Williams in 1829. The house is also architecturally noteworthy and will be discussed later. The parlor has walls fourteen feet high, and being a later house, is without chair railing. The mural rises from the baseboard, and a low horizon is maintained around the room, so that fully half of the wall area is sky. As in the McConnell House, there is a drapery frieze (fig. 6.12). The fireplace end presented unusual problems because the mantel rises higher than the horizon of the painting and because the fireplace is not centered; one of the arched recesses is adjacent to the mantel whereas the other has a space in between. Cohen responded by lifting the skyline over the mantel, and he strengthened the position of this feature as a focus by painting a domed pavilion viewed between two similar palm trees on axis (fig. 6.13). The Mediterranean landscape was most appropriate to this house, where the parlor windows open on an arcade resembling the architecture depicted in Cohen's work. The murals in Pleasant Lawn had been repainted when they were destroyed by fire on 19 December 1964. The house has been rebuilt and the murals have been replaced by facsimiles on canvas.

Alfred Cohen had a contemporary competitor in Lexington. Horace E. Dimick, proprietor of the Great Western Manufactory, makers of furniture, Venetian blinds, mattresses, feather beds, and other such items, at 15 Hunt's Row (Water Street between Mill and Upper), filled orders for "*Landscape Painting* on walls or fire boards, in oil or distemper colors," as well as any other kind of "ORNAMENTAL PAINTING as may be wanted."[22] No known specimen of work from Dimick's manufactory has come to light.

Two frieze panels on which have been painted stiff allegorical figures in dark landscape exist on the dining-room mantel at Vaucluse a few miles from Lex-

Fig. 6.11 Mural on partition wall in parlor of the McConnell House. Photo, 1948.

Fig. 6.12 Mural on parlor wall adjoining stairhall in Pleasant Lawn, Woodford County. Photo, 1948.

ington on the Georgetown Pike. Just before the Civil War, the house, then called Eothan, was owned by Oliver Frazer, one of Kentucky's leading portrait painters, and the mantel decorations are thought to have been conceived by his daughter, Bessie (1841-1910).[23]

Even less sophisticated in concept is the painting on an enclosed stairway in the earliest room of what became a large dogtrot house with frame lean-to on Van Arsdall Road in Mercer County. The house was built by Joseph Adams about 1795. The staircase is enclosed by vertical planks, providing a closet under the steps and a rectangular surface on the outside. The mural is in the space above chair-rail height (denoted by a thin black horizontal line). Below is blue-gray, and on a tan background above is depicted a seven-bayed white building with pedimented center pavilion, red chimneys at the outer corners of a red hipped roof crowned by a cupola. The image resembles the first Kentucky statehouse, except for being only two instead of three stories high (fig. 3.30). The building is flanked by two large trees, and several smaller trees are scattered around on a light green lawn. A black valance is gathered aside above.

In the same room of the Adams House are remarkable repeat patterns painted on vertical sheathing around the walls. The background color matches that through stencils, whereas some elements, like the foliage of the trees, were sponge stippled. The painted patterns in the James Coleman House were discovered under wallpaper in 1987 and await restoration. The Coleman House resembles Locust Grove, whose ballroom was decorated with wallpaper.

The majority of early Kentucky interior walls were glorified by neither murals nor wallpaper. Some were left plaster white or were whitewashed and offset by painted woodwork. Probably most walls were painted in flat colors. Much use was made of pale

Fig. 6.13 Mural on fireplace wall of Pleasant Lawn. Photo, 1948.

Fig. 6.14 Wall decorations in the Joseph Adams House, Mercer County. Photo, 1981.

of the mural. Dado level presents blue-gray sponged chevrons, evidently to represent marbleizing, and above a thick black line are crude ellipses of green, black, and red that might be interpreted as being either longitudinal watermelon slices or rag rugs. The sponge-application technique suggests either seeds or multicolored strips of cloth (fig. 6.14).

The chaos of freehand sketches of repeated motifs can be avoided by the stencil. Apparently Alfred Cohen made use of it in laying out frieze festoons. Certainly stencils were employed in outlining similar festoons and tassels on the upper walls of the hall at Warwick in Mercer County, unfortunately now painted over. Stencils were used extensively for wall decorations in the second-story ballroom of the James Coleman House (ca. 1812) northwest of Cynthiana. The work probably predates that of Cohen. A border adjoins the baseboard and carries over the two fireplace mantels. The walls are organized by an evenly spaced serpentine vine motif with heart-shaped leaves in the concave curves right and left, which divides the surfaces into vertical panels in which there are alternating flower-spray and bird-in-tree vignettes. The basic scheme was executed colors, with the trim and paneling given darker tones. The original paint on some mantels and baseboards—as in the intended ballroom at Liberty Hall, Frankfort—was black.[24] The range of colors available can be ascertained from contemporary advertisements. Although many of the tinting materials were imported, Edward Howe's Lexington mill was pressing linseed and flaxseed oil in 1793.[25] In the same year Joseph Hudson listed a stock of "Prussian blue, Rose pink, Patent yellow, Red and White Lead, Litharge, Spanish whiting, [and] Verdigrease."[26] Prussian blue is a strong, cold blue; patent yellow is Turner's yellow (patented in England by James Turner in 1781), a warm yellow of temporary duration, eventually turning black; litharge is lead oxide, a yellowish, earthy substance; Spanish white is an obsolete, bismuth white; and verdigris is a green or blue copper acetate. Robert Holmes, in 1795, carried all but the last color, and in addition had "Yellow Ochre . . . Spanish Brown, [and] Lamp-Black."[27] Spanish brown is a warm burnt umber. During the second decade of the nineteenth century other Lexington merchants increased the list: "French Verdigrise, Chinese Vermilion" (S. Woodruff); "Terra de Sienna" (W. Mentelle); "MINERAL GREEN, TURKEY OMBRE, BLOOD LAKE" (Daniel Bradford); "Stone Ocher, Dutch Pink . . . King's Yellow . . . and Ivory Black" (John Wainwright); and "Cromic Yellow" (James Garrison).[28] Chinese vermilion is a brilliant red made from cinnabar; raw sienna is a brown-tinted yellow ocher; mineral green is a copper carbonate; "turkey ombre" was evidently raw umber, *terre d'ombre*, a cold brown; blood lake is a rose madder or alizarin crimson; Dutch pink and king's yellow are pigments not of the highest quality, and if used a century and a half ago probably have retained little of their pristine chromatic value; ivory black is a purer and deeper black than lampblack; and chrome yellow is a warm, canary yellow. The Lexington White Lead Manufactory, beginning operation in 1815, claimed its "Dry White Lead . . . superior to any imported from Europe." It produced "White Lead ground in Oil, Red Lead, Litharge, Patent Yellow, and Sugar of Lead."[29] Sugar of lead is lead acetate, white crystals that form when acetic acid comes in contact with lead. Generally it is considered undesirable because it is highly toxic and has a tendency to turn brown and effloresce. Most paintbrushes in Kentucky were probably imported. Still, James C. Ramsey advertised in 1802 that he would pay "Eighteen Pence per pound . . . for COMBED HOGS' BRISTLES" to go into the

making of brushes, admonishing his compatriots "to encourage manufactures in their own country."[30] Hog bristles are the traditional material used in brushes for oil paint.

The Lexington Oil Floor Cloth Factory operated a mill that in 1810 could "grind above an hundred weight of paint a day," and the concern would "execute House and sign painting, gilding, glazing, paper hanging &c," as well. The proprietors, Messrs. Levett and Smith, claimed to have "prepared a most curious and useful article as covers for waggons, (by a process invented by Mr. Levett; and known only to him, and to Mr. Smith) it is light, pliant, and unimpenetrable to rain; and is highly worthy the attention of all those concerned in the carriage of goods."[31] One assumes that the product related to the oil floor cloth that gave title to the factory. During the early nineteenth century oil floor cloth was widely used in hallways and family dining rooms. Cloth impregnated with oil or rubber as a water resistant has an obscure history. Rubber became known in the United States about 1790, but its incorporation in floor coverings is much later. A preparation of Indian rubber masticated with ground cork and rolled out into sheets between heavy, steam-heated rollers was patented by Elijah Galloway, an Englishman, in 1844.[32] It usually had a canvas backing and was called kamptulicon. Levett did not take out a patent on his "curious and useful article," and the extent of its use on vehicles is uncertain.

The men directly responsible for Federal-style buildings, the architects who drew the plans and the housewrights or builders who constructed them, may be divided into two categories. The first were easterners of considerable reputation, who designed buildings in Kentucky though they never came here; and the second were immigrant builders, some of whom became full-fledged architects. Two notable absentee designers in the Federal style left their imprint upon Kentucky. The first was Thomas Jefferson (1743-1826), third president of the United States, who was born and educated in Virginia. He conceived the four-range scheme of the University of Virginia (1817-26); designed with Charles-Louis Clérisseau the capitol (1785) at Richmond, the first temple-type building of modern times; and planned or acted as adviser on a number of residences for himself and others. Jefferson was what was known as a gentleman architect, innocent of formal training, having derived his knowledge of architecture from books by or about the sixteenth-century Italian, Andrea Palladio, and from the British volumes by James Gibbs, Abraham Swan, and especially Robert Morris.[33] Jefferson conceived a house design for Senator John Brown of Frankfort, but it was received after Brown had settled on another plan and building had commenced; and he devised the plan of Farmington, the John Speed residence in Louisville, which materialized in altered form, as will be seen. Thomas Jefferson adhered to the classical ideal, whether Italian, French, or American.

The second eastern architect to contribute to Kentucky was Benjamin Henry Latrobe (1764-1820), born and trained in England, who practiced in the United States for a quarter of a century following his coming to Norfolk in 1796. Latrobe designed residences and public buildings, and introduced two styles to America. His Bank of Pennsylvania (1798-1800) in Philadelphia was the first in the Greek Revival style, and Sedgely (1799-1800), the house of William Crammond on the Schuylkill River, was the first Gothic Revival building. Latrobe was in complete charge of the construction of the Capitol in Washington from 1808 to 1812, and again from 1815 to 1817. He planned the John Pope House and wings for Henry Clay's Ashland, both in Lexington, discussed below.[34] Devoting his full time to architecture, Latrobe was the better rounded and the more innovative of the two designers.

Foremost of foreign-born architects to reside and leave notable monuments in Kentucky was John Rogers (1785-1836), who was born in Ireland and reared by a Presbyterian uncle, Sir Arthur Rogers. In 1804 he emigrated to Baltimore, reconverted to his mother's Catholic faith, and became associated with the Sulpician Order at Saint Mary's Seminary and College. In 1814 Benedict Flaget, the first bishop west of the Alleghenies, called John Rogers to Kentucky to complete a small Gothic chapel begun at Saint Thomas Seminary four miles south of Bardstown. Rogers designed and built a cathedral for Bardstown that was consecrated in 1819 and known as Saint Joseph's Cathedral. He is assumed to have planned and built an adjoining college, begun in 1825, now called Spalding Hall. Rogers also had a hand in Wickland (Chap. 8). It is said that the mantelpiece from his home at 212 South Third Street, Bardstown, was taken to the World's Columbian Exposition of 1892-93 in Chicago and exhibited in the Kentucky pavilion.[35] In 1835 he went to Louisville to superintend the construction of James Dakin's Bank of Louisville, but he died the following year without completing the project.

Matthew Kennedy (1781-1853) was born in Augusta County, Virginia. He was in Kentucky by 1796 and in 1811 married Jane C. Smith of Versailles. The next year he announced in the *Kentucky Gazette*: "The subscriber informs his friends that he has returned to Lexington, where he intends to co-partnership with James W. BRAND, to pursue his profession of *House Carpenter & Joiner* in all its branches, if liberally encouraged."[36] Kennedy soon began to work independently, and during the summer of 1814 he inserted a notice in the *Gazette* stating a need for "TWO or THREE boys as apprentices, to learn the Carpenter's Trade."[37] In 1814 Matthew Kennedy began the second Kentucky statehouse, and in 1816 the Main Building for Transylvania University. He designed the Grand Masonic Hall, built in 1824 on the north side of Main Street in the middle of the block west of Broadway; but his scheme was abridged, and when the building was dedicated on 25 October 1825, Samuel Cawden was listed as the "Principal Architect."[38] For Transylvania, Kennedy also designed the Medical Hall, built in 1827. About 1816 he erected his own home at Limestone and Constitution streets in Lexington, and very likely he built other residences of this type throughout central Kentucky. In the mid-1840s, Kennedy moved to Louisville, where he died in 1853.[39] His major buildings are considered in chapter 9.

The best-known surname in Kentucky architecture is Shryock—originally Dutch, van Schrieck—belonging to three men who distinguished themselves as builders. The founder of the family in Lexington was Mathias Shryock (1774-1833). He came from Frederick County, Maryland, and in 1809 built his home at 149 North Broadway, between Short and Second streets, a two-story brick house that was demolished in 1901 or 1902.[40] He constructed a house on North Limestone, where Lexington Junior High School now stands.[41] His name is listed as having worked on the old Transylvania Company college building.[42] He helped construct the David Fork Baptist Church (1801), antecedent of the present Greek Revival building on the Cleveland Road, as well as the Episcopal church (1814) on Market Street, predecessor to the Gothic Revival Christ Church now on the site.[43] He died during the cholera epidemic in June 1833, and his body was interred in the Episcopal cemetery on East Third Street. A miniature Greek temple, designed and erected by his son, Gideon, marks his grave. Gideon Shryock and a younger brother, Cincinnatus, followed their father's calling.

The builder Michael Gaugh (1778-1855) was closely associated with Mathias Shryock, both professionally and through marriage. They worked together on the Episcopal church in Lexington, the David Fork church, and the Transylvania building; and Shryock married Gaugh's sister. Gaugh lived in the same block on North Broadway, and his carpenter shop was at the back of the lot. He built a house for his son, Jerry, on the north side of Shryock's house, and he constructed another for a second son, Perry, on the same side of Broadway two doors beyond Third Street.[44] Neither son entered the building profession. Like Mathias Shryock, Michael Gaugh was buried in the Episcopal cemetery on East Third Street.

Early Lexington directories give us the names of many men engaged in building. Among some 273 listings in the first, *Charless' Almanack for 1806*, are to be found those of eight house joiners or carpenters, and eleven stone or brick layers, in addition to several nailers and other laborers who may have been engaged in construction work. The subsequent directory, Worsley and Smith's of 1818, with 575 listings, contains the names of 46 house joiners and 14 masons. With few exceptions, we do not know what buildings these men constructed. David Sutton designed the 1806 Fayette County Courthouse, built by Hallett M. Winslow and Luther Stephens; Asa Wilgus built the John Pope House (1811-14) after Latrobe's design; and Samuel Long constructed the Thomas Bodley House, each of which will be dealt with more fully. We have existing plans by Jefferson and Latrobe for their Kentucky undertakings, and Kennedy drawings for the Transylvania Main Building, but to what extent prepared drafts were used by the average local builder remains an open question. Of interest in this regard is a notice in a *Kentucky Gazette* of 1804: "DRAWING, Ground plans, elevations, and sections for buildings of any description, in the most plain and elegant style; also Bills of material, and estimate of expenses, to execute such plans, as will be given, may be had at a small expense by applying to O.P. ROBERTS, at Mr. John Keiser's, Lexington."[45] Inasmuch as Roberts' name does not appear in the 1806 directory, he likely had moved. Keiser was an innkeeper. In all probability few local builders could or did provide clients with such complete data. They usually contracted for the job with a written description and estimate of costs, concluding with the reassuring generality, "all to be executed in a neat and workmanlike manner," which in those days was backed up by the workman's honor or the court.

The Federal style appeared in Kentucky during the early 1790s and flourished until the 1840s. During the 1830s it began to be superseded by the Greek Revival. As has been said, it was distinguished by the advent of forms of an aesthetic nature and by the introduction of architecture per se. Federal architecture had three distinct phases, which existed simultaneously. It should be emphasized that some brick buildings discussed in part 1, and even a few stone and frame examples, display style references that might justify their inclusion under one or another of the Federal-style categories given below. As noted earlier, Morgan and Chiles taverns in Harrodsburg could be included under the geometric phase of Federal architecture. Hurricane Hall contains Georgian features in both its interior and exterior, the main cornice of the house resembling that of Liberty Hall. But the floor plan of the original Hurricane Hall—also of Clermont—is essentially a primitive hall-and-parlor type (with an extra room on the first floor), and it falls short of the more gracious and sophisticated arrangements of Liberty Hall, Federal Hill, and Ashland. Also it is evident that the last three houses belong to the same period and thus could have been put with other early Kentucky brick buildings in chapter 4. Further, it must not be overlooked that buildings considered under a particular Federal substyle often do not entirely belong there. The John Wesley Hunt House, for instance, is characteristically geometric both inside and out, distinguished by an unsurpassed fanlighted doorway centered in the facade, and yet the office entrance on the side is wholly Georgian in style. In this book, examples have been distributed according to how they best relate to the topic under discussion, whether to the progress made in the use of materials and techniques, or as an expression of one or another of the three types of Kentucky Federal-style architecture.

Type 1. The first is colonial or Georgian survival. It employs those pre-Revolution architectural features such as came from the early British and American builder's handbooks—Swan, Pain, and Norman (the last actually dates from three years after the Treaty of Paris, ending the Revolution)—and their immediate successors in this country—Biddle and Benjamin—discussed earlier. The primary motifs were half-round arches, semicircular fanlights, attenuated colonnettes, and broken-pediment enframements to doors and windows. These are properly eighteenth-century embellishments and expected accompaniments to molded-brick strings, belt courses, prominent chimneys, and heavy, pegged, opening enframements. They are to be found less often after 1816, as by that time classic details had shifted from Georgian-manner manifestations to Classic Revival—type 3 below.

Type 2. The greatest number of Federal houses of merit and those most characteristic of the region belong to the second type. It tends to shun foreign academic influences and attains a sophistication based upon simple, abstract forms. For this reason it may be referred to as the geometric phase. House plans became more complex, with circular and polygonal elements. Also included in this category is the one-storied, spreading cottage of three or five pavilions, laid out on a symmetrical scheme. Roofs often were hipped rather than gabled and, in some instances, domed or bonneted. The geometric character filtered down to details, as in carved woodwork of the Lowery type, mentioned above, where relief or intaglio shapes were derived from the carvers' tools. The outstanding feature was the broad fanlight doorway, differing from the Georgian in having a three-centered instead of a single-centered or half-round arch, and in having a flat, slightly sunken, reeded or fluted casing in place of an applied enframement of orders. Enframements around openings were generally symmetrical, rather than backbanded. The archaic masonry elements of brick strings, belt courses, and overt chimney articulation recede from this phase, though Georgian-classic elements may be included, as in the case of the pedimented office entrance to the Hunt House in Lexington, or colonnetted mantels in Wickland at Bardstown. More appropriate are the severely plain chimneypieces in the Morton House at Lexington, or those elaborated in a creative manner, as in Elmwood

Hall at Ludlow. The geometric phase belongs mostly to the second decade of the nineteenth century, although it persisted through the 1830s.

Type 3. The third type is termed the classic phase, being most indebted to the Classic Revival as it was variously practiced in Europe, England, and the eastern states. In Kentucky, however, it was to have a decided local, even provincial, flavor. The colossal-order portico, the hallmark of the style abroad and along the Atlantic appeared on only a couple of Kentucky public buildings, and on no known residence. A unique instance of superimposed orders does distinguish the two-story portico of the Gano House in Covington. But small porticoes were not uncommon, and there was even one example of a prostyle or temple-form dwelling, the Warner Cottage in Lexington. More numerous were those buildings, both public and domestic, that had two-story pilasters applied to the facade and integrated with a pediment. Also, there were several notable masonry arcades; in two dwellings (White Cottage and Pleasant Lawn) they were featured as facades with Palladian windows in wide pediments above. These and the large pilastered pavilions partake of the same regional tendency toward simplification found in type 2. Colonnetted mantels, not un-Georgian, are to be found in Kentucky classic-phase buildings. The Gano residence with the portico of superimposed orders likewise makes use of colonnetted doorways (both inside and outside) at the main entrance. The classic phase, as distinct from the Georgian survival, seems to have started prior to 1810, before the debut of the geometric, and it continued until replaced by the Greek Revival. Bucknore, a house in Bourbon County with pilasters embracing a two-story facade, appears to be the last example and bears the date 1841 over its arched doorway. As a matter of fact, Bucknore seems to have sounded the swan's song of Federal architecture in any of its ramifications in Kentucky.

7 THE GEORGIAN SURVIVAL STYLE

THE SIGNATURE OF Georgian architecture in Kentucky was the frontispiece flanked by slender colonnettes with a lunette over the door. In some instances it was the only external feature of the house that partook of style. This condition stemmed from the practice of division of labor, whereby a carver was engaged to dress up the entrance, along with fireplaces and other elements inside. The simplest doorway form had a horizontal entablature atop the fanlight. Examples include the Marshall Key House (ca. 1815) in Washington, and Clay Hill (ca. 1812) in Harrodsburg (fig. 6.4). Others, to be discussed adorn Liberty Hall, Federal Hill, and Ashland. A primitive variation contains flat, reeded pilasters in place of round colonnettes, as in Augusta on one of the row houses facing the Ohio River. Pilasters, though much thicker (practically Greek Revival in character), flank the doorways of Vaucluse, the house near Taylorsville occupied by Knox Brown (John Brown's great-grandson), and the Richardson House (1831), which stood at 129 West High Street in Lexington.[1]

A second basic type of Georgian doorway found in Kentucky is pedimented, with the entablature limited to impost blocks over the colonnettes, and the fanlight thrust up into the tympanum area. Vaucluse, about a mile north of Lexington, built for the Rev. James Moore during the late 1790s, has such a doorway; and the John Leiby House (1805), which adjoined the Richardson House on High Street, must have had one too. A fine example graces the Dr. Joseph Scott House (ca. 1800) at the corner of Main and Washington streets in Frankfort.[2] The muntins in its fan are modern and copied after those in Liberty Hall. Cottage Grove, near Bardstown (fig. 7.9), and Coolavin, formerly in Lexington (fig. 8.30), had similar doorways. Three of the type were on the unused design of 1815 for the Transylvania University building (fig. 7.13), but the one built the following year had twin doorways of this category. Their excessive width was accommodated by four colonnettes but created a problem for the raking cornices, which according to Jouett's drawing did not bridge the entire span of the doorway (fig. 7.14).

LIBERTY HALL. The Kentucky building most thoroughly Georgian in style is Liberty Hall. It was built for one of Kentucky's first U.S. senators, John Brown (1757-1837), from Augusta County, Virginia. He purchased the land on Wilkinson Street, Frankfort, backing up to the river, early in 1796. A plan with explanation from Thomas Jefferson, sent on 5 April 1797, arrived too late to be considered, as construction already was under way, as mentioned earlier.[3] The Jefferson design was for a low, spreading house of the geometric type, whereas that undertaken followed the pattern of an East Coast urban residence of the colonial period. Its massing and details of the facade bear affinities to those of the main block of the Matthias Hammond House in Annapolis, Maryland, the work of the architect-carver William Buckland during 1773-74.[4] Both have a pedimented central pavilion three bays across and a single bay right and left beyond, both are of Flemish-bond brickwork, with molded string at the first-floor level and belt course at the second. Both have modillioned cornices, round or half-round lights in the pediment, and colonneted doorways (frontispiece and fig. 7.1). The Annapolis doorway is more elaborate and pedimented, the window above is not Palladian, and the roof is hipped rather than gabled on the ends. Also, the Hammond House has symmetrical

Fig. 7.1 Facade of Liberty Hall (1796-1804), Frankfort. Photo, 1982.

wings which terminate in two-storied polygons, whereas Liberty Hall has a service ell at the rear. The chimney stacks of the Frankfort house are larger and more heavily capped, like those of the mid-eighteenth century in Williamsburg, as on the George Wythe House.[5] Cornices of its gabled ends are simpler than those in front, lacking the articulated parts (fig. 7.2). Windowpanes measuring 12 by 18 inches are unusually large for a house of this period so far inland. Ordered initially from Pittsburgh, they finally were procured from the Geneva Glass Works in

1802, delaying completion of the house until 1803.[6] Fenestration in the ell is considerably smaller, consisting of nine-over-six-paned sashes below, and six-over-six above, with 8-by-10-inch glass, as in the garret windows.

A central transverse hall divides two pairs of rooms of slightly different sizes on the first floor (fig. 7.3). An archway across the middle has square, paneled pilasters and a decorative keystone (fig. 7.4). The staircase in the rear portion has turned banisters carrying a railing with ramps at the upper newels, and the railing applied against the wall follows the same contours. All door frames have ears at the top. Hall and front dining-room doors make unique use of a keystone (like that to the hall arch) centered on the horizontal lintel. The hall doorway in the drawing room has an overdoor with advanced corner blocks to the frieze. Chair railing runs at windowsill level throughout the house.

A single-story gallery with chamfered posts across the rear of Liberty Hall expands to a service porch, with arched openings on the garden side downstairs, on the near half of the two-story ell. A service stairway occupies the corner of the wall adjoining the dining room. The kitchen at the back originally was a detached pavilion of one and one-half stories that later was connected to the house and expanded to a full two stories. The second story of the house proper originally was to have contained a ballroom, 25 by 44

Fig. 7.2 Restored sketch
of Liberty Hall.

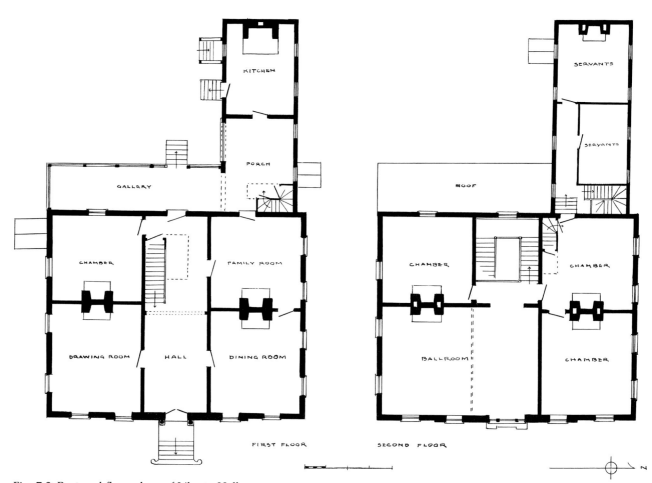

FIRST FLOOR   SECOND FLOOR

Fig. 7.3 Restored floor plans of Liberty Hall.

Fig. 7.4 Hall arch and staircase,
Liberty Hall. Photo, 1988.

feet in size, in the southeast corner, entered from the stair hall (fig. 7.3). There were such upstairs ballrooms in the Miles Brewton (1765-69) and Hayward-Washington (ca. 1750) houses in Charleston, South Carolina, and in Locust Grove, Louisville. But, perhaps because of John Brown's marriage to straitlaced Margaretta Mason, the room did not get more than the base coat of plaster. After the house was inherited by Mason Brown in 1837, the space was partitioned into a study (over the front hall) and a bedroom. He also added a stairway to the garret in the center portion and a railing across the Palladian window, both of which have been removed. Some mantels belonging to the later period still survive.

The property was purchased by the Liberty Hall Association in 1937, and since then the residence has been open as a museum. It was taken over by the Colonial Dames in 1956 and designated a National Historic Landmark in 1972. About that time the garret stairs were rebuilt in the north bedroom, and in 1979-80 the entire back of the house and various interior features also were restored.

FEDERAL HILL. The residence of John Rowan (1774-1853), west of Bardstown, has been immortalized as "My Old Kentucky Home." Here Rowan's cousin, Stephen Collins Foster, visited, and although the first name for his famous melody "Poor Old Uncle Tom, Goodnight" derived from Harriet Beecher Stowe's novel *Uncle Tom's Cabin*, the lyrics and title had taken their present form before publication in 1853.

John Rowan acquired fifteen hundred acres here in 1795. The rear ell on the west side is said to have been the first section of the house built, and the family resided in it until completion of the whole about 1818. Federal Hill has Flemish-bond brickwork on all sides. A molded brick course at first-floor level extends along the north front and east flank. The only ornamental exterior feature is the colonnetted and fanlighted front doorway with swags incised in the frieze (fig. 7.5). The facade is unusual in including seven bays; the windows immediately to the right and left of the doorway are narrow, and similar fenestration is above. The arrangement may be found in a number of eighteenth-century houses in England and the eastern United States, like Swan House (1711), Chichester; the former Mannsfield (ca. 1760s), Fredericksburg, Virginia; Stenton (1728, with two normal windows above the three center openings), Philadelphia; the Gen. Philip Schuyler House (1762), Albany; and Johnson Hall (1763), Johnstown, New York.[7] The form of Federal Hill was even more unique, the hall and east side being two rooms deep, and the west but one, covered by only the front plane of the roof. Thus there was a full gable on the right flank but only a half gable on the outer left flank (fig. 7.6).

Fig. 7.5 Federal Hill (completed ca. 1818), near Bardstown. Photo dated 1882 in State File, courtesy of the Commonwealth of Kentucky.

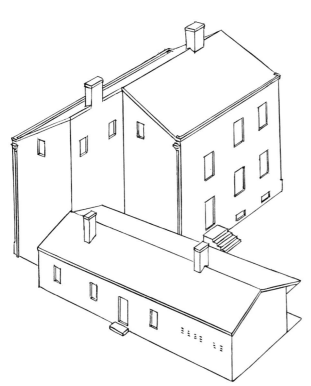

Fig. 7.6 Sketch showing the original form of Federal Hill from the southwest.

With the wide stair hall lighted by two half windows as well as the fanlight in the doorway in front and a window on the landing at the back, and with each of the two east rooms having four generous windows, the interior of the main block is light and airy (fig. 7.7). An arch spans the hall, and the stairs ascend around a large open well to the third floor. The principal mantels are colonnetted, supporting impost blocks with elliptical recesses in the frieze and a breakfront shelf (fig. 7.8). Service rooms cluster around the court behind the dining room, and a covered walk runs along the east side of the ell.

Federal Hill was damaged by fire in 1840, and John Rowan signed a contract with Alexander Moore to restore "the flight of stairs, Doors, Window frames, facings, Mantles, washbroads, etc." Moore was to add presses in some of the rooms, and he was to rebuild the roof, lowering the tall rear wall of the west wing and making a symmetrical gable on the end. The agreement states that Moore was "to cut down the south wall of the Ell or western wing to a level with the front of the same and roof & shingle it after the Manner of the Main Building."[8] In crawl spaces off the garret of the house one can see the 1840 roof, with a later roof structure beginning a couple of feet

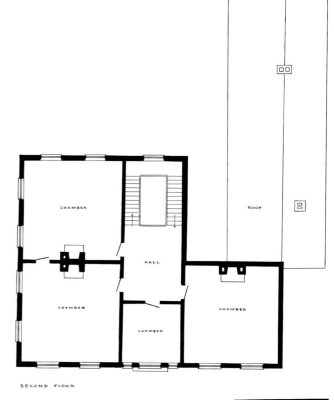

SECOND FLOOR

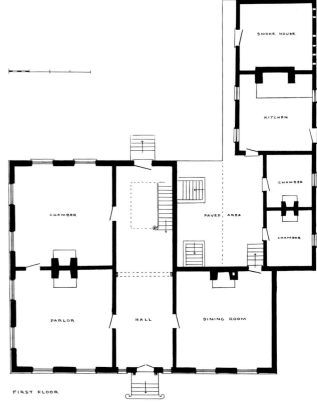

FIRST FLOOR

Fig. 7.7 Floor plans of Federal Hill.

Fig. 7.8 Parlor mantel, Federal Hill. Photo, 1964.

above it on the outer walls, rising to a superimposed ridge. Pre-1930s photographs show a brick coping instead of a cornice in front, which may or may not have been original. Whatever the treatment, it is certain that the present heavy wood cornice replacements are inappropriate. Federal Hill was taken over by the commonwealth in 1922 and opened as a house museum by the Department of Parks. Extensive renovation was carried out in 1950. The grounds include the family burial lot and Judge Rowan's log office rebuilt over the stone springhouse.

COTTAGE GROVE.   Not far from Federal Hill,

Thomas Speed built an interesting little house about 1810 (fig. 7.9). Its water table across the front, Flemish-bond brickwork on all sides, and Georgian doorway flanked by narrow windows resemble features of the later Federal Hill. But Cottage Grove was a story-and-a-half building, having twin gables front and back connected by a crosswise roof, with a stretch of horizontal cornice over the doorways at either end of a transverse hall. The main entrance is of the pedimented variety; its semicircular lunette has interlaced muntins, and flanking windows immediately adjoin the square piers. Half-round windows in the upper story were directly above the nine-over-nine-paned fenestration in the facade gables; the second level was further lighted by two dormers on each side and a nine-over-six-paned window in each rear gable. In the Nelson County manner (as at Wickland, fig. 8.1), the window frames are quite narrow.

A stairway at the back of the central hallway has been somewhat altered. Rooms lie front and back of the chimneys. That at the rear, to the left of the hall, was used for dining; a similar room at the front on the right was the parlor, and the corresponding space behind was divided into two narrow chambers.

Family legend ascribes the designs of Cottage Grove to an "English architect," but, except for the gables, its physical characteristics indicate a builder no more exotic than that employed at Federal Hill. A mansard roof has replaced the front gables and the first pair of dormers. Except for the door itself and window sashes, the frontispiece remains intact under a later porch.

Fig. 7.9 Cottage Grove (1810), near Bardstown. Photo, ca. 1889, by Thomas Speed, courtesy of the Filson Club.

ASHLAND. The largest and most complex house with a colonial-manner doorway was the home of the Hon. Henry Clay (1777-1852). His holdings were described in 1847 by Lewis Collins as

comprising the house, grounds and park . . . situated a mile and a half south-east of the court-house in Lexington, on the south-west side of the turnpike leading to Richmond. The whole estate of Ashland consists of five or six hundred acres of the best land in Kentucky. Ashland proper was projected for an elegant country seat. The house is a spacious brick mansion, without much architectural pretensions, surrounded by lawns and pleasure grounds. The grounds are interspersed with walks and groves, and planted with almost every variety of American shrubbery and forest trees. As the domicile of the great American statesman, Ashland is one of the household words of the American people.[9]

Contemporary prints (fig. 7.10) substantiate the rural magnificence of the setting, but it is not surprising that the "spacious brick mansion" was adjudged "without architectural pretensions," as the statement was published at the height of the Greek Revival period, when colossal-order porticoes were prevalent on country houses, and by comparison a delicately detailed Georgian doorway was a commonplace entrance. It was of the rectangular type, and like that of Liberty Hall had a Palladian window above; but the great difference was in its presentation. The doorway was set in a projecting polygonal vestibule, with tall three-sash windows in the splayed sides. Above, the Palladian opened onto a balcony having an encircling guardrail. The Gwathmey House (ca. 1810) on Sixth Street in Louis-

ville showed a similar arrangement, only on a raised basement. At Ashland, these forms precede a pedimented central pavilion projecting from the two-storied main mass. Single-story connectors join wings that step forward in equal balance. Each front plane of the extensions included a window of three lights. The arrangement suggests that of the Matthias Hammond House in Annapolis, the octagonalism of its outermost pavilions transferred to the projecting portal bay at Ashland.

The design of Ashland, at least of the wings, may be attributed to Benjamin Henry Latrobe. A letter from Latrobe to Henry Clay, dated 15 August 1814, indicates that the extension housing chambers and the nursery were under construction, and one assumes the main block had been completed.[10] Latrobe's accompanying plan is sketchy and shows little familiarity with the building (fig. 7.11; compare fig. 12.20). The architect submitted another plan on September 5, which may have been the one followed.

Ashland was declared unsound after Henry Clay's death, and it was rebuilt between 1854 and 1856. Elements such as the general form, placing of chimneys, openings, and the character of the doorway and Palladian window were followed in the later work, leading one to assume that the layout corresponded to that of the original building. In addition to the entrance hall, the dining room and library were octagonal, the last having a cloister-vaulted ceiling with skylight at the apex. Several other rooms had fireplaces in the corner, and the stair hall was elliptical and covered by a dome. These unusual

Fig. 7.10 Ashland (ca. 1813-15), Lexington. Courtesy of the Filson Club.

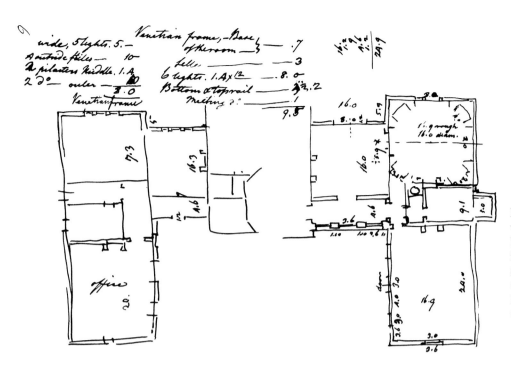

Fig. 7.11 Sketch plan for wings of Ashland, by Benjamin Henry Latrobe, in a letter to Henry Clay, 8 September 1813. Courtesy of the Mrs. Ferdinand C. Latrobe Collection, Baltimore.

shapes, coupled with the spreading plan, relate Ashland to the ideals of the geometric phase of Federal-style architecture.

THE THIRD FAYETTE COUNTY COURTHOUSE. Kentucky was divided into three counties in 1780. Lexington was declared the county seat of Fayette, and the first log courthouse was built two years later. In 1788 it was replaced by one of stone, which served for eighteen years (chap. 3). Growth through immigration continued, and a larger courthouse was needed. In 1806 notices were inserted in the local newspaper that bids would be received and contracts assigned. The desired design was described: "60 by 50 feet, the foundation to be of stone, 3½ feet below the surface and 1 foot above the surface, three stories high; the first story to be 14 feet high of brick, and 3 brick thick; the second story 12 feet high and 2½ brick thick; the third story 10 feet high and two brick thick, with two offices in the first story, each 16 by 20 feet, to be arched over with brick, to be fire proof—the fronts of said house to be of stock or sound brick, laid with lime and sand mortar." Also included was a schedule of the carpentry work, the girders to be "9 by 15 inches, principal joists 7 by 14 inches, joists 3½ by 15 inches . . . all of which timbers to be of white oak, with the window and door frames to be of such wood as is usually put in good brick buildings, with a pavillion roof, and good poplar shingles 18 inches long and 1 inch thick at the lower part." A plan of the building drawn by David Sutton was to be shown "by

the commissioners at the same time of the contract."[11] The contract was awarded to Hallet M. Winslow and Luther Stephens. Georgian elements included the pedimented central pavilion in front, encircling belt courses at the upper floor levels, and chimneys rising above the "pavillion" (hipped) roof on the flanks. Doors and windows were rectangular and unadorned.

The feature that gave the building architectural pretensions is not mentioned in the specifications and must have been an afterthought. This was the superstructure, consisting of a square clock tower, octagonal belfry capped by a campaniform roof, and an attenuated spire finished in a ball and weathervane. The height of the building was doubled and it became the tallest construction in town (fig. 7.12). Special provision inside the building for supporting the impressive tower was described in 1810 by the Scottish ornithologist Alexander Wilson. "It was found necessary to erect, from the floor, a number of large, circular, and unplastered brick pillars, in a new order of architecture (the thick end uppermost), which, while they serve to impress the spectators with the perpetual dread that they will tumble about their ears, constitute also, by their number and bulk, to shut out the light, and to spread around a reverential gloom, producing a melancholy and chilling effect; a very good disposition of mind, certainly, for a man to enter a court of justice in."[12] The town clock was installed in its appropriate section in 1814, and a

Fig. 7.12 The third Fayette County Courthouse (1806), Lexington. Photo, ca. 1870s, courtesy of J. Winston Coleman, Jr., Lexington.

300-pound bell followed in 1817. About 1840, two smaller buildings, each of two stories and with low wings, for sheriff's and clerk's offices, were built to the east and west of the main building. This ensemble served the county until 1883, when a stone edifice in the eclectic Renaissance style replaced them on the site.[13]

TRANSYLVANIA UNIVERSITY MAIN BUILDING (1816). Transylvania Seminary, the first institution of higher learning west of the Allegheny Mountains, opened near present Danville in 1785. Four years later the school moved to Lexington, where in 1792 it was housed in a two-story brick building situated on a three-acre lot bounded by Market, Mill, Second, and Third streets. In 1799 it united with Kentucky Academy, which had been operating at Pisgah for several years, and became Transylvania University. In 1812 the trustees launched a movement to provide new and larger quarters. A note appears in the minutes regarding payment of postage for plans by Ben-

jamin Henry Latrobe, but nothing further about them is recorded. A local architect, Matthew Kennedy, was asked to prepare designs. His estimates were within the university's budget of $20,000, but proposals from builders exceeded the amount, and the trustees decided to postpone the venture and repair the old structure.[14]

A renewed need for a larger building in 1815 brought forth four known schemes. The first is a wash rendering, consisting of an elevation and two floor plans for a three-story brick building, inscribed "Lexington——15," the numbers signifying the year. The scheme follows the style of eighteenth-century college architecture—such as Hollis Hall (1762-63) at Harvard University, University Hall (1770-71) at Brown, Dartmouth Hall (1784-91), and Nassau Hall (1754-56) at Princeton—being multistoried, its walls

Fig. 7.13 Elevation and plans for a Transylvania University Building, Lexington, 1815. Courtesy of Transylvania University Library.

Fig. 7.14 Transylvania University Main Building (1816), Lexington. Engraving by E.G. Gridley after a drawing by M.H. Jouett. From Charles Caldwell, *A Discourse on the Genius and Character of the Rev. Horace Holley . . .* (Boston, 1828), facing p. 190.

pierced by evenly spaced rows of windows, having a pedimented center pavilion, and an open belfry on the roof (fig. 7.13).[15] One notes especially the three identical pedimented doorways with archaic stairs spilling out the front and sides. A parapet over the cornice, punctuated by urns on pedestals, is an extra refinement. The design was not executed, though elements may have been borrowed for the Fayette Hospital, begun the following year.

Two neoclassic renderings were made at about the same time and will be discussed later (figs. 9.30,

9.31). The fourth design was signed by Matthew Kennedy, who would build the new Main Building in 1816. It was Georgian in manner but followed the floor plan that accompanied the columned facade. The only existing contemporary delineation of the building is an engraving made by E.G. Gridley after an elevation drawing by the portrait painter Matthew Harris Jouett (fig. 7.14). The pedimented pavillion was broader than that of the 1815 proposal, its doorways wider and four-columned, reflecting the form of a central Palladian window. Other fenestration varied from arched to flat-topped and triple windows; a great fanlight pierced the pediment, and a fully developed balustrade surmounted the cornices. Its crowning glory was a cupola in the baroque manner, having a square base, octagonal belvedere with arched windows between corner columns, urns atop the broken entablature, and a curvilinear bonnet supporting a slender vane with an elaborate finial. The building had a 56-by-36 foot chapel in the center, transverse passages, and stair halls on a cross axis between lecture rooms in the four outer corners of the first story. Above these were "thirty airy, warm, and well lighted rooms."[16] The building cost $30,000 to construct and stood in front of the old seminary in the center of the lot, now Gratz Park, facing south. Between the buildings, near the east and west boundaries, were built two long, low brick dependencies.

On Saturday evening, 9 May 1829, the Kennedy building burned. About three-fourths of the library

Fig. 7.15 Transylvania University and environs, 1816-29.

TRANSYLVANIA UNIVERSITY AND ENVIRONS 1816-1829
LEXINGTON - KENTUCKY

and "Philosophical apparatus" were removed to safety, but the centerpiece of that grand layout was a total loss.[17] The east dependency is the only part of the old university group in the park that survives.

The university complex, with its broad sweep of lawn down to Second Street, surrounded by some of Lexington's finest residences, constituted a model of early urban grouping (fig. 7.15). Across from the lower green were the balanced facades of the John Wesley Hunt and Thomas Bodley houses, dating from 1814. In the foreground stood the Col. Thomas Hart House (1798; demolished 1955), and up Mill Street beyond the Hunt House was Mount Hope (ca. 1819), built by Gen. John M. McCalla and later occupied by Benjamin Gratz. Across Second Street from the Bodley House, which had been built for Thomas Pindell, was that of Dr. Frederick Ridgely (mid-1790s; not shown in fig. 7.15), and north of the Bodley House on Market Street are those of Alexander Moore (1836), Peter Paul II (1816), and John Stark (1813).

FAYETTE HOSPITAL / THE LUNATIC ASYLUM. The largest building of this era in Lexington was begun in 1816 as the Fayette Hospital, a privately sponsored institution. The project defaulted, and the partially built hospital remained in limbo until taken over by the commonwealth in 1822, to be completed and opened as the Lunatic Asylum two years later. It was located on a seventeen-acre tract above the junction of Newton Pike and Fourth Street. The building had three stories, covered by a hipped roof with a skylight. The doorway was arched and fanlighted, and was in a three-bayed pedimented central pavilion, with two bays on either side. There were two wings of two stories and six bays (fig. 7.16). Each appendage to the 66-foot-square main block was 62 by 44 feet. The main block resembled Saint Joseph College (ca. 1820) behind the cathedral in Bardstown, and the entire edifice the 1815 Transylvania rendering (fig. 7.13). By the mid-1840s, pavilions of three stories, pedimented in front, had been added to each end of the asylum.

Fig. 7.16 The Lunatic Asylum (1816-20s), Lexington. The main pavilion as seen through gateway. Photo, late 1800s, by I.C. Jenks, courtesy of Transylvania University Library.

The early core of twenty-five rooms contained housing for the superintendent and his family and the resident physicians, a surgical room (on the top floor under the skylight), and "dayrooms and refectories for the male and female patients." Each of the early wing sections included six rooms per floor, and the later end pavilions probably more. A report of 1829 stated that all the rooms outside the main block were "supplied with heat through flues, passing from the basement story so as to avoid entirely any danger from fire."[18]

The building has suffered many changes. The outermost additions have been demolished, and the remaining portions have been completely rebuilt inside, changing the story heights and consequently the fenestration pattern of the facade. A rear ell was built on axis in 1847, and a somewhat similar building was erected to the west in 1867. Other constructions have gone up farther afield, including the present administration building, which postdates 1900.

8 THE GEOMETRIC PHASE

THE GEOMETRIC PHASE of Federal architecture produced some of the finest and most distinctive specimens of Kentucky building design. That it was primarily a provincial manifestation is indicated by its private patronage of domestic examples; whereas group and institutional endeavors more often veered to the other two nationally (and internationally) accepted types, the backward-looking Georgian and forward-looking neoclassic. In a sense the geometric was an advanced order of early styleless brick construction, a step beyond mere functionalism, embracing new and innovative forms with a flair. As has been said, its signature was the plain fanlighted doorway, and its salient feature, the graceful overarching curve.

WICKLAND.   Wickland was built about 1825 on a tract of eight hundred acres near Federal Hill for Charles A. Wickliffe, later governor of Kentucky. Its plan and execution are attributed to John Rogers and James Marshall Browne, respected as architect and builder in Bardstown.[1] Wickland is straightforward and somewhat archaic for its day. Flemish-bond brick walls rise flush above limestone foundations. Recalling Rowan's house, windows are of generous size; their frames are unduly narrow. Sidelights are incorporated under the wide fanlight of its two severe frontispieces (fig. 8.1). Brick cornices run across the rear of the house and horizontally along the wing, but the present front cornice is of wood with string-of-pearls decoration under consoles, and lozenge motifs affixed to the soffit. Old photographs show a balustrade above. There are thin raking boards on the gables. The south flank of the building faces the road, and west of the secondary fanlighted doorway to the side hall are four blind windows consisting of closed shutters set in recesses in the masonry, a device that recurs frequently in this period of Kentucky architecture. The lower ell on the east end

bears an affinity to the service wing of Liberty Hall, having traditional door and fenestration on the south side, whereas the gallery, now enclosed by clapboards, was open toward the yard.[2]

The main block of Wickland has twin parlors on the north side of a transverse stair hall, with smaller rooms divided by the passageway to the side door opposite. The staircase resembles that of Federal Hill, but there is no hall arch. The parlors have enormous hinged paneled doors between them, permitting an ample combined space. Twin mantels further integrate these rooms. The mantels combine small columns using Tower of the Winds Corinthian capitals, like those in the nave of the Bardstown cathedral (chap. 9), with Adamesque cast pewter sunbursts and swags in relief in the frieze (fig. 8.2). Their elaboration, like the details of the soffit of the front cornice, contrast notably with the general plainness of the building, though they suggest a Baltimore origin. Wickland is owned privately, but it may be visited as a house museum.

THE HUNT HOUSE.   The home of John Wesley Hunt (1773-1840) was built on a lot about two hundred feet square, purchased in 1814, located on the corner west of the lower Transylvania University grounds in Lexington.[3] Hunt had come from Trenton, New Jersey, and he became the first millionaire in the Bluegrass Region. His residence embodies an elegance that far surpasses its size. Its facade is pedimented and features the finest doorway of its type in the commonwealth, with a Palladian and arched window above (fig. 8.3). The building was set back from Mill Street, and the front yard was enclosed by a handsome Greek Revival iron fence of a date later than the house. The south flank is adjacent to Second Street. A door to Hunt's office, already described as Georgian, matches the pedimented entrance to the court under the upstairs gallery; a six-foot-high brick

Fig. 8.1 Wickland (ca. 1825), near Bardstown. Photo, 1964.　Fig. 8.2 Mantel in rear parlor, Wickland. Photo, 1964.

Fig. 8.3 Restored
sketch of the
John Wesley Hunt
House (1814),
Lexington.

Fig. 8.4 Gateway to the service court, Hunt House. Photo, 1941.

room. Cooking was done in the cellar. The second-story arrangement resembles that of the first, except a passage through the middle of the house links the service stair hall with the front.

The only early mantels remaining in the house are in an upstairs chamber of the wing and the bedroom over the dining room. In this last, reeded frames and circular motifs in the cornerblocks, reflecting the lower woodwork, are surmounted by a breakfront

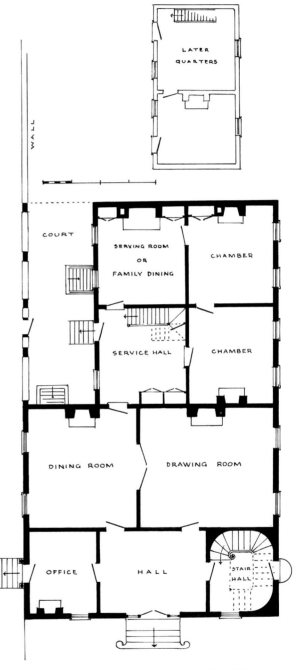

Fig. 8.5 Restored first-floor plan of the Hunt House.

wall runs back to the former carriage gates, beyond which is the stable (fig. 8.4). The north side of the house faces a garden, originally more extensive than at present.

The front doorway opens into an entrance hall centered between the office and stair hall (fig. 8.5). The staircase ascends around a rectangular well from the first to third floor. Its plan is similar to that on the last plate of Pain's *British Palladio*, published at London in 1788. Confining the staircase to its own compartment helps conserve heat which would otherwise escape up the open well in wintertime. The drawing room has tall windows (probably originally with triple sashes) close to ground level, which together with the door under the stairway, provide ready access to the garden. The dining room connects with the quadrant of the ell containing the service stairs. Two of the other wing divisions may have been chambers, and the fourth, in the southwest corner, was a food-warming, or informal, eating frieze and serpentine shelf. About the middle of the nineteenth century, marble mantels replaced those in the drawing and dining rooms, plaster center-pieces were added to their ceilings and that in the front hall, and chair railings were removed. Also, a detached two-story servants' house containing four rooms was built at the rear of the wing.

After 1891 the division wall in the first story of the wing was taken out to make a new long dining room of the north half, and large sliding doors were in-stalled between the original dining-room wall and a new partition on the drawing-room side. Exterior changes included erecting a huge, double-decker porch on the front, as well as a small portico at the stair-hall door, and a two-storied bow window in place of the office doorway. Most of the windows were cut lower in the facade and north walls, case-ments replaced sashes in the upper-level Palladian window, and the plain cornice was exchanged for a deeper version carried on consoles. An insignificant iron fence replaced the Greek Revival paling and its stone coping in front. The old brick carriage house– stable behind was enlarged by a frame addition at the back, and a louvered cupola was set on the roof.

John Wesley Hunt's daughter, Henrietta, married Calvin C. Morgan and for a while lived in the house with her son, John Hunt Morgan, later a general in the Confederate army. Another distinguished resi-dent of the house was Dr. Thomas Hunt Morgan, a winner of the Nobel Prize in 1933 for his work in biology. In 1955 the house was purchased by and made the headquarters of the Blue Grass Trust. The appended front porch by then had fortunately disap-peared. The Trust removed the little portico on the north side, and later took out the centerpieces and marble mantels, substituting colonnetted wood chimneypieces attributed to Matthew P. Lowery, ac-companied by new chair railing of appropriate de-sign. In 1979 the bow window was removed and replaced by a facsimile of the original office doorway, the cornice brackets were taken off, modern bathroom windows were bricked up, and many coats of paint were removed from the brick walls.

THE BODLEY HOUSE. Thomas H. Pindell engaged Samuel Long to build the house at the northeast corner of Market and Second streets that he sold to Thomas Bodley for $10,000 in 1814.[4] The site is di-rectly opposite the John Wesley Hunt House, across the open green of Transylvania University. The Bodley House balanced the new Hunt residence, and like it, had a gable at the front but no horizontal

cornice forming a pediment (fig. 7.15, extreme right). The Palladian motif over the arched doorway was not set low (as in the Hunt House) but on a level with the other second-story fenestration, its arch precluding the horizontal member of the pediment. The fan and sidelights of the Palladian window are blind, as are the outermost openings on this level in the five-bayed facade, and the northernmost one below. The garret window is arched.

The plan of the Bodley House is similar to that of its neighbor, though inverted, but the hall spanned the entire front and had subsidiary entrances at each end. The outstanding feature of the house is the elliptical staircase connecting the three floor levels. The upward sweep is graceful and the treatment of details is restrained and delicate (fig. 8.6). Beyond the parlor, the wing extending along Second Street is a separate house, whereas the service ell runs along the east side of the property, adjacent to an alley called The Byway.

Changes were made to the house during the Greek Revival period. The fan of the Palladian win-dow was obliterated by the completion of the pedi-ment; the fanlighted front doorway was squared off and sheltered by a Doric portico matching that of the Robert Wickliffe house (1841) diagonally across the street intersection; the south end of the hall became a small room; the south door was made into a window, and a colossal-order portico was attached to the north flank of the main house. A wrought-iron fence was added around the front yard, similar to its contempo-rary formerly at the Hunt house. Later, the windows acquired sashes of single panes. In modern times a brick wall was built to enclose the garden along Mar-ket Street.

THE POPE HOUSE. The home of John Pope (1770-1845), lawyer, state and U.S. legislator, U.S. senator, and territorial governor of Arkansas, was built during 1811-14 on a tract southeast of the cross-ing of Rose and High streets in Lexington, the house now facing Grosvenor Avenue.[5] The architect was Benjamin Henry Latrobe, who wrote the local builder Asa Wilgus in 1811: "As I shall probably never see Mr. Pope's house, it is necessary that my house on paper & yours in solid work should go up exactly alike." Wilgus had received an apprenticeship to be taught carpentry in 1806, and in 1814 he bought a lot on Main Street from John Pope. After 1818 he went to St. Louis, where he died in 1889.[6] Comparison of Latrobe's drawings with the house before its devas-tating fire in 1987 showed that although the main

Fig. 8.6 First, second, and third flights of the staircase in the Thomas Bodley House (ca. 1815), Lexington. Photos, 1964.

block corresponded in scale, shape, and general disposition of rooms, there were differences, and the question arises as to how much they may be attributed to original deviations from the design and how much to later changes.

Latrobe conceived the building with an English basement practically at grade, the main or first story being above. His drawings present an alternative, having a third level (fig. 8.7). Both front elevations show a portico with Doric columns set between arched forms. The facade windows of the upper level, composed of single windows flanking one of three lights over the doorway, are considerably larger than those below. The plan, however, indicates Latrobe intended triple windows for all three upper openings, and examination of the brickwork confirms that the larger openings were realized (fig. 8.8). The plan shows that the front doorway was to be recessed, but no indication of its treatment appears on the elevation. The house is crowned by a truncated hipped roof having a railing around the top. Basement rooms are square, separated by intersecting halls. An office and parlor are in the front corners, complemented by kitchen and servants' rooms at the back, with a wash and bake house between. Three of the rear rooms are at a lower level. Main and service stairways are in the

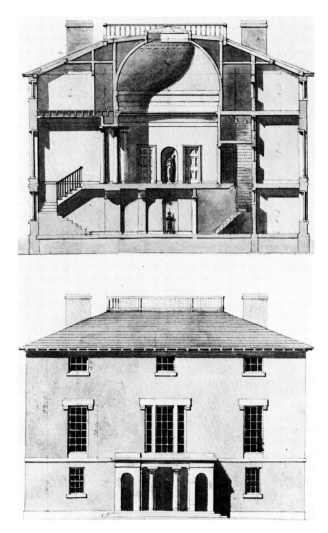

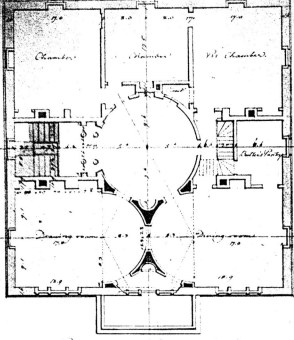

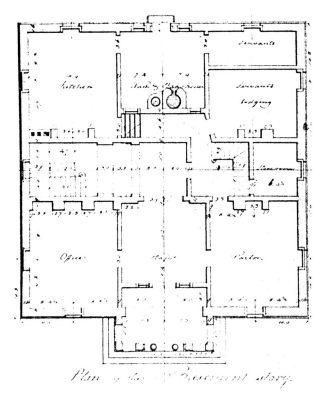

Fig. 8.7 Cross section and front elevation of a house design by Benjamin Henry Latrobe, presumably for John Pope of Lexington, ca. 1811. Courtesy of the Library of Congress.

middle. The principal staircase ascends to an upper hall that had double columns opening into the circular rotunda. Its dome is lighted by a skylight. Responding to the round shape are curved ends of the drawing and dining rooms at the front. A similar arrangement was repeated by Latrobe three years later in the first-floor plan of the commandant's house at the Pittsburgh arsenal, but the rotunda was replaced by the semicircular end of a hall.[7] A nearly identical arrangement was used by Robert Mills in the Ainsley Hall residence at Columbia, South Carolina, begun in 1823; but following the death of the owner the house was not completed exactly as planned.[8]

The house built for John Pope has 10-foot ceilings

Fig. 8.8 Ground and principal floor plans for the Latrobe house design. Courtesy of the Library of Congress.

Fig. 8.9 Detail of upper part of niche in the drawing room of the John Pope House (1811), Lexington. Photo, 1942.

in the basement story and 12-foot-8-inch ceilings in the principal story. Its plan is not notably different from the Latrobe design, except that the main staircase rises from the opposite side of the middle hall.[9] Woodwork was typically Kentucky in character, making use of bead moldings, reeding, keystones, and gouged work (fig. 8.9). The residence must have rivaled the Morton and Hunt houses for elegance in Lexington. Here the leaseholder Maj. William S. Dallam entertained President James Monroe during his western tour in 1819.[10] John Pope was absent during his tenure (1829-35) as territorial governor of Arkansas, then in 1836 he sold the house to Catherine Barry and moved to Springfield, Kentucky.

J.T. Palmatary's bird's-eye view of Lexington shows major changes having occurred in the house by 1857. The roof had been made pyramidal and had an octagonal cupola on the apex replacing the old skylight. At the rear a long service ell contained the cooking and washing facilities, which left their former spaces inside the main block free for other purposes. Existing photographs of the dependency reveal Greek Revival details, thus postdating Pope's occupancy.

The building was purchased by Joseph Sowyel Woolfolk and remodeled by Thomas Lewinski in

1865. It was modernized into a romantic villa, given gables, with deeper eaves set on coupled brackets. The facade fenestration was changed into narrow multiple-arched windows at both levels. Colonnetted bay windows were added to the flanks. An elaborate iron porch spanned most of the front (fig. 8.10). Except for an addition on the south end of the west flank, the removal of the service stairway, and probably the installation of wide doorways in the east and north walls of the lower back hall at this time, the plan remained about the same as in the 1850s (fig. 8.11). The room nearest the ell was the dining room. The upper front rooms were henceforth called the ballrooms.[11]

In the twentieth century, the building was converted into apartments. The service ell was razed, and a shorter wing of two stories was erected on part of its site. Brick-piered porches of two stories were added on the front, using iron railings from the Lewinski gallery. Inside, the stairway was removed, and a new straight flight opposite the front door ascended within the rotunda. The building was severely damaged by fire in October 1987. The Blue Grass Trust acquired the house in January 1988 and began its restoration.

THE AYRES HOUSE. In 1833 Dr. David J. Ayres purchased at auction four adjoining lots on Broadway in Danville amounting to four acres, on which shortly afterward he had a residence built.[12] The building bears a resemblance to the Thomas January House in Lexington (enlarged into the Tobias Gibson mansion) and Spring Station, built by Norborne Beall in Louisville. The latter has a more attenuated plan and will be discussed shortly. The January House had a pedimented two-story center pavilion with one-

Fig. 8.10 The Pope House as remodeled for Joseph Sowyel Woolfolk in 1865. Photo, late 1800s, courtesy of Miss Mamie Woolfolk of Memphis, Tennessee.

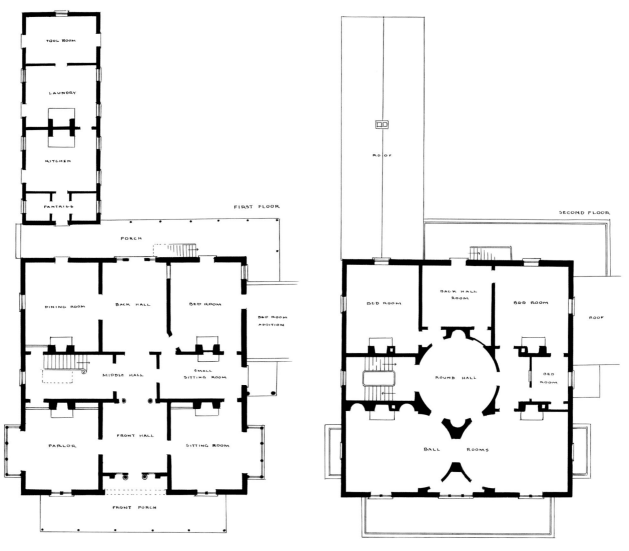

Fig. 8.11 Floor plans of the Pope House after remodeling in 1865 with room designations used by the Woolfolk Family.

story wings having gables on the ends (fig. 10.47). The prototype is the house, then about twenty years old, acquired in 1800 by James Semple on Francis Street in Williamsburg, Virginia.[13] The form may have derived from plate 37 in Robert Morris's *Rural Architecture*, London, 1750. It was manifested in clapboarded examples along the Atlantic Coast, notable in Virginia and North Carolina.[14] The Kentucky houses cited are of brick.

Like specimens of the type in North Carolina, the home of David Ayres has a considerably larger main pavilion than the Semple House, where the wings are less than two-thirds the width of the center block. The main mass of the Ayres House is a bit over twice as wide as either wing. The facade has broader win-

dows, being the only one of the group mentioned that has twelve-paned sashes, and a triple window over the entrance (fig. 8.12). The late date of its construction permits a fanlight over the doorway and a similarly treated lunette in the pediment. Fortunately, despite later alterations to the house, including some to the fenestration, both glazed half-ellipses survived until its present acquisition. The doors proper have been restored. The use of horizontal panels (as in McDowell's apothecary shop, chap. 3) was a local early architectural characteristic, which often changed to square panels in dual-leaf doors or other special instances. This rule was followed in the restoration here.

The floor plan included a hall 14 feet deep across

Fig. 8.12 The Dr. David Ayers House (ca. 1835), Danville. Photo, 1980.

the front of the main pavilion, with doors to the wing rooms centered at each end, and doors to the parlor and dining room behind opposite the facade windows. All four rooms have fireplaces opposite the hall doors, and the two at the back have great double doors connecting them. The present twin staircases, in the rear corners of the hall, are turn-of-the-century replacements. New flooring and plastering preclude investigation for signs of the original stairs, but probably they were in the front corners, the steps rising under the windows.

Toward mid-century Dr. Ayres moved to Lexington, selling the Danville house to Nancy Gill. It was later acquired by the Weisigers, who made extensive Romanesque-colonial alterations toward the turn of the century.[15] Much of this style was removed during the 1980 restoration.

PLANCENTIA.   The partially constructed residence of Col. Lewis Sanders, one and one-half miles from Lexington on the east side of the Georgetown Pike, overlooked an eighty-four-acre estate that included woodland and garden. To meet the owner's need for cash, it was offered for sale in 1815; by that time nine years of meticulous industry and care had gone into the creation of a fine orchard of apple, peach, pear, plum, and quince trees, grapes, and the choicest shrubbery and flowers. There were three wells with pumps, a root house, a stone stable, a carriage and cow house, a stone house for a gardener, two log houses, and a number of sheds. The principal improvement was the "intended Dwelling House, calculated for a large family." This news-

paper statement was modified by an explanation that the house was unfinished, but all materials had been procured, "and it could be completely finished in 4 months." The included description read: "It faces the Georgetown road—an oval room in the center, 26 by 30 feet, with a dome ceiling—two octagonal rooms, connected with the oval room by saloons; back, and adjoining which, is a two story Brick House, 55 by 58, with a 10 foot passage, having six rooms on each floor. The basement of the brick building is of stone, nearly the whole of which is above ground, with several convenient rooms, and passage as above; also cellars under the whole of the front."[16]

Col. James Morrison purchased the property, telling the builder he might reside in the house as long as he wished. Sanders remained until 1823, then moved to Sanders, Kentucky, near Carrollton.[17] The "two story Brick House, 55 by 58," has survived, but not the oval and octagonal rooms and connecting "saloons" in front, which may have been built of wood, or proved too costly to complete. The cubic form is crowned by a double-pitched hipped roof, which held a reservoir. Chimneys are not equally balanced. Two pairs of triple windows are set in the south wall; the lower ones are each spanned by a lunette with leaded glass identical to that in the John Hunt House doorway. They light the parlor and dining room, which have fireplaces back to back (fig. 8.13). Originally the back hall at the southeast corner of the building held a stairway. Three rooms are aligned along the north side of the center hall.

One can only conjecture about the appearance of the front structure. Probably its width spanned the front wall of the greater mass. After Elijah Noble established The Sign of the Golden Eagle tavern here in 1825, a front portico replaced the one-storied section. It was pedimented and had brick end walls flush with the flanks, perhaps making use of existing foundations (fig. 8.14). Also a porch was added on the rear and part way along a newly built brick ell, which extended forty-eight feet back from the northeast corner of the original block. The portico has been removed and windows have been cut in the front wall. The building currently serves as a private residence. A new staircase was installed in the transverse passageway, and the old stairs were removed, the lower area becoming a kitchen. Cupboards have been built alongside the mantel in the adjoining dining room, and closets added in the bedrooms.

WOODLANDS.   In 1794 George Trotter II acquired land on the original mile-radius city limits of Lex-

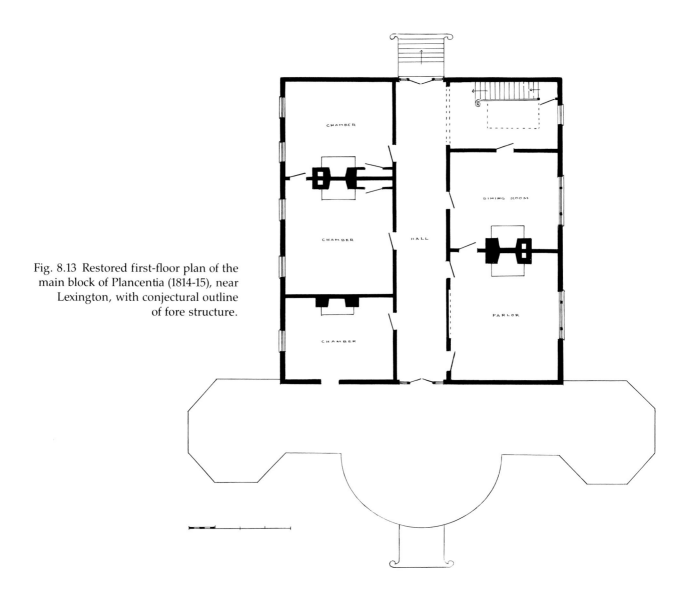

Fig. 8.13 Restored first-floor plan of the main block of Plancentia (1814-15), near Lexington, with conjectural outline of fore structure.

CHAMBER

CHAMBER

CHAMBER

HALL

DINING ROOM

PARLOR

Fig. 8.14 The Sign of the Golden Eagle tavern, formerly Plancentia. Photo, late 1800s, courtesy of Dr. W.O. Bullock, Lexington.

ington, south and a bit east of the Fayette courthouse center. He built a two-and-a-half-story brick house with gabled ends. In 1829 it was purchased by Elijah Warner, who sold it two years later to Henry Clay's son-in-law, James Erwin.[18] The new owner came from Louisiana and added a complex of low pavilions on the front and *garçonnières* at the four corners. Additions to the facade consisted of an elliptical entrance hall, with a fanlighted doorway and a single window in the curved wall at either side, connectors with three-light windows set in a segmental arch, and outer octagonal wings (fig. 8.15). A balustrade masked the low-pitched roof over the three center units, and the flankers were capped by bonnets. If the projecting center motif recalls the polygonal reception hall of Henry Clay's Ashland (adjoining which was an elliptical stair hall, fig. 7.10), the entire addition reflects the same sequence of forms we have just considered at Plancentia. The ellipse and four octagons were longer left to right than front to back, and the wings had blind windows on the outer walls, with fireplaces inside and chimneys above. Lower rooms in the main body of the house were lighted only on the sides, whereas those above had windows at front or rear. Upper windows in the facade were of three lights under a segmental arch, like those in the connectors, and probably were contemporary replacements of earlier plain fenestration. The entrance hall at Woodlands was only a little over two-thirds the size of that at Plancentia, and it was not covered by a dome. One wonders whether the bonnets sheltered more than flat ceilings in the corner pavilions. No measured drawings are known to have been made of the house. The conjectural first-floor plan presented here was derived from the placement of chimneys and openings and was scaled by counting bricks in two extant photographs (fig. 8.16).[19]

Woodlands housed the Kentucky Agricultural and Mechanical College from 1868 to 1880. Soon afterward the grounds became a public park, and the house served for balls and other entertainments. It was razed early in the twentieth century. One of its mantels was installed in the residence at 1605 Fairway Drive in Lexington.

LA CHAUMIÈRE DES PRAIRIES. The formal log-and-frame farmhouse group in Jessamine County begun by David Meade II in 1796 was discussed in chapter 1. Meade spent ample time and resources lavishly improving his premises. The place is said to have had a stone parlor's lodge and stone gateway through which one entered a meadow of one hun-

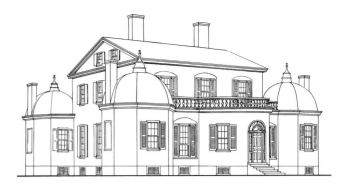

Fig. 8.15 Restored sketch of Woodlands (1790s, 1830s), Lexington.

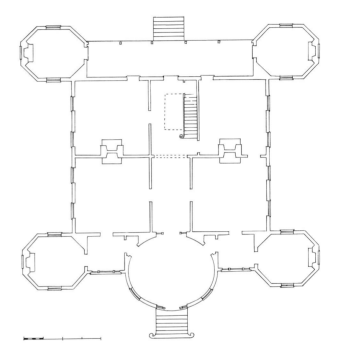

Fig. 8.16 Conjectural restored first-floor plan of Woodlands.

dred acres seeded in bluegrass and enclosed by a low stone wall masked by honeysuckle and climbing roses. The house was enlarged into what the owner referred to as "the first lordly home in Kentucky." It was described by Colonel Meade's granddaughter:

The house was what might be called a villa,—covering a great deal of ground, built in an irregular style, of various materials—wood, stone, brick,—and one *mud* room, which, by the way, was quite a pretty tasteful spare bedroom. The part composed of brick was a large octagonal drawing-room, the only really handsome room of the establishment. . . . There was one large square hall, and numerous passageways, lobbies, areas, etc. The grounds were quite extensive. . . . in a secluded nook [was] a most beautiful, tasteful Chinese pavilion. The bird-cage walk was one cut through a dense plum thicket excluding the sun; it led to a dell where was a large spring . . . by the mouth of . . . [a] cave. . . . At this point was the terminus of a lake, at which, after a hard rain, there was quite a waterfall. . . . From the shore to the island there was a pretty little bridge.[20]

Dr. Horace Holley described the footbridge as "a white bridge of one arch."[21] Anna Maria Von Phul, a frequent visitor to La Chaumière, painted a watercolor of this scene about 1815, showing the railing of the bridge to contain a Chinese lattice design (fig. 8.17).

From these glimpses we gather that the grounds were laid out in the manner of an English park, no doubt resulting from Meade's having gone to school in Britain. The English park or natural landscape garden, called on the Continent the *jardin anglo-chinois*, was an influence from the Far East, and counter to the geometric style of European gardens. Chinese ornaments abounded in these settings, such as the famous 163-foot-tall pagoda (1761-62) by William Chambers in Kew Gardens near London. The Chinese pavilion and bridge at Chaumière were exotic structures appropriate to the landscape. All the landscape improvements have disappeared.

Only one wing of the house that David Meade II knew stands. It was built on the east end of the old

log building and contains the octagonal drawing room and anterooms (fig. 8.18). William Leavy wrote that this room was built in the latter part of the proprietor's life, which would date it in the 1820s or 1830s.[22] Exterior details are quite Jeffersonian. The eight-sided interior is a regular shape twenty feet in diameter, with a fireplace and a deep, paneled window on axis, and three windows in the bay. It has (and always has had) a flat ceiling.

David Meade willed his estate to his childen, who sold Chaumière in 1832. The new owner turned stock in to graze on the lawn, pulled down parts of the house, and stored grain in others. Edward Carter bought Chaumière in 1838, and on the site of the old front structure, adjacent to the drawing-room pavilion, he built a two-story Greek Revival residence of brick. The house remains a dwelling.[23]

The type of house Thomas Jefferson recommended to John Brown, when he was about to build Liberty Hall in 1797, was a low symmetrical building of a single story with wings. A similar plan was drawn for Jefferson's Albemarle County neighbor, Norborne Beall, when he departed for Kentucky. This design was followed in building Beall's home, Spring Station, near the intersection of Lexington Road and Cannons Lane in Louisville, mentioned before in connection with the Ayres House.[24] Beall's

Fig. 8.17 The Chinese bridge at La Chaumière des Prairies, Jessamine County. Watercolor (ca. 1815) by Anna Maria Von Phul, courtesy of the Missouri Historical Society, St. Louis.

Fig. 8.18 Existing wing of Chaumière (late 1820-30s) with plan superimposed. Later Greek Revival addition is beyond. Photo, 1941.

house, however, has a two-story center pavilion, although the wings are low, consisting of connectors to advanced end sections, the last pedimented like the central mass. Spring Station dates from ca. 1805. A one-story version in Kentucky already existed.

LEWIS MANOR.   Perhaps the earliest low spreading brick residence, at least in central Kentucky, was Lewis Manor, on Viley Road three miles west of

Lexington. Col. Thomas Lewis acquired the land in 1788, but building probably did not begin until about 1800.[25] The outer pavilions are later, or were attached to the main house later. The west unit originally was separate, and it was joined by extending the front wall and the roof. The location of the kitchen, at the far end, required carrying food some distance to the dining room. For meals to have been brought inside, the carrier would have had to pass through a bedroom as at Chaumière (chap. 1). The gabled east wing was a subsequent addition and could be reached only by going outside. Except for the outermost extensions, the building is covered by hipped roofs (fig. 8.19).

In the main part of the house window sashes originally may have contained twelve panes, which would have been more readily obtainable and in better scale with the lights in the lunettes over the doors and the fenestration in the wings than the present six-paned sashes. The frontispiece has a semicircular fanlight over double doors, but without colonnettes, entablature, or pedimented hood. It is an intermediary between the Georgian type and a doorway with elliptical fanlight and sidelights, as in the John Hunt and David Ayres houses. The portico of Lewis Manor is probably an afterthought, but nevertheless of early construction, showing primitive features. Full-round columns are against the

Fig. 8.19 Restored sketch of Lewis Manor (ca. 1800), near Lexington.

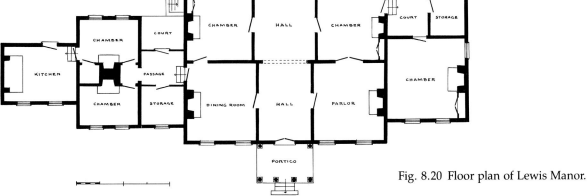

Fig. 8.20 Floor plan of Lewis Manor.

THE GEOMETRIC PHASE 143

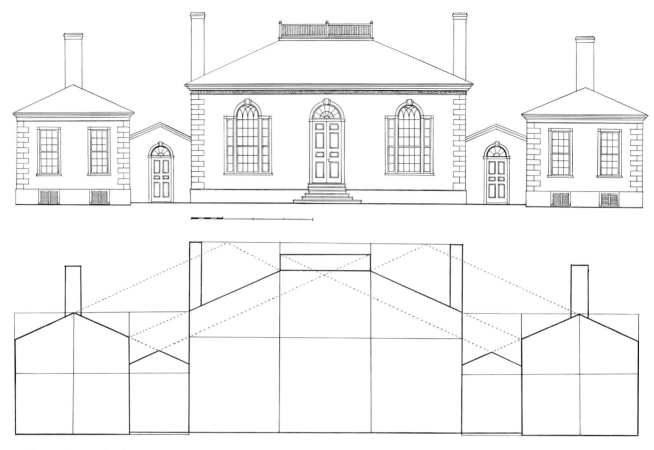

Fig. 8.21 Facade elevation (restored) and design analysis of the William Morton House,
Lexington. Forms (in heavy lines) are based on simple configurations of squares (in thin lines).
Dotted lines relate the intangible elements of the design, achieving optical unity.

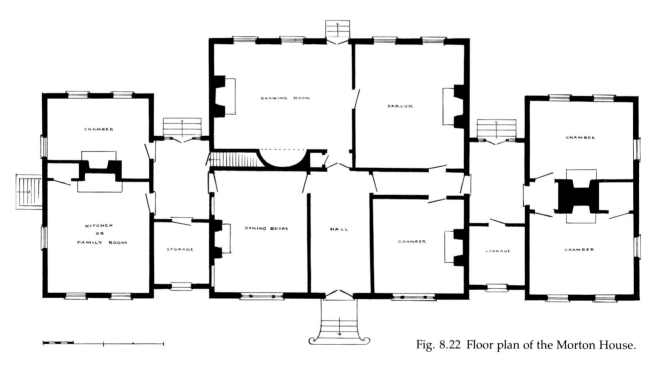

Fig. 8.22 Floor plan of the Morton House.

wall. They have double entases, with banding at windowsill level. The lower swelling substitutes for a pedestal, and a double abacus is at the top.

The center hall of Lewis Manor is divided by an arch set on coupled colonnettes; the rear portion is wider, and there are two rooms on either side (fig. 8.20). Lewis Manor was renamed Kilmore in 1915.

THE MORTON HOUSE. The most elegant house of the type in central Kentucky is that of William "Lord" Morton, built on the five-acre outlot #76 at the northeast corner of Mulberry (Limestone) and Fifth streets in Lexington. In the frieze under the front cornice at the north end of the principal block is the date "1810." The building is composed of three hipped-roof sections and two connectors. The main pavilion had a railing (now replaced) around the truncated top, and the connectors with low-pitched roofs are slightly recessed behind the plane established by the other three units. The large scale of the house eludes one from a distance, lacking reference to the nearly 10-foot height of the front dual-leaf doors and 8-foot width of the Palladian windows. The parapeted connectors had paneled false doors and pierced fans which provided light for the service rooms inside. The facade, in its proportions and details, was carefully conceived for visual effect, suggesting derivation from a two-dimensional elevation drawing (fig. 8.21). The facade is stuccoed and the surface scored to resemble stonework; raised quoins accent the front corners. Cornices have brick cores. The frieze of the center pavilion contains dogwood blossoms in a meander of circular reliefs, and this motif is repeated on the enframements of the doorway and Palladian windows. These windows had inside shutters, a rarity then in Kentucky, and the same rooms have dogwood flowers incised in marble mantelpieces, which are the only fireplaces surviving in the main block.

In spite of the symmetry of exterior forms, no strict sense of balance in layout or in individual rooms prevails inside the Morton House (fig. 8.22). The entrance hall is not centered on the front doorway or the door opposite. The door at the rear opens into the drawing room through a shallow vestibule. Three openings (one a doorway) in the back wall are evenly spaced but not centered. Opposite them is an 8-foot-wide niche, perhaps meant for a curved sofa. The adjoining parlor (or perhaps bedroom) is three feet deeper, and if there had been a door between them, it could not have been on axis with both rooms (the present double doors are late). A passageway con-

nects the entrance hall with the south wing, whereas on the north side, the dining room occupies the entire area from the front wall to that behind the drawing-room niche. Arched recesses flank the dining-room fireplace. It is curious that the floors in the wing rooms are level with that of the main pavilion, whereas those of the connectors are a step lower. The chimney indicates that the front room in the north end was a kitchen, probably only for winter use. The connectors once may have been open at the rear. An enclosed stairway ascends from the north connector over the niche in the drawing room to the space under the main roof. It is plastered and finished, but can be lighted and ventilated only by opening a hatch. The cellar is under the north-wing pavilion and is without a fireplace. Mid-nineteenth-century maps of Lexington show that a number of outbuildings existed behind the Morton residence, and it is likely that one of them was a detached summer kitchen.

Cassius Marcellus Clay purchased the house for $18,000 in 1839, two years after the builder's decease, and twelve years later it passed to Lloyd Warfield.[26] The property came into the possession of the Duncan family in 1873. Changes made then consisted of replacing the mantels in the drawing room and parlor and cutting a large doorway between, adding coarse woodwork around openings inside the center block, enlarging the wings with extensions and bay windows, and installing a porch at the back. The land was acquired by the city in 1913 and became Duncan Park. The residence has served various purposes. Some restoration and renovation work occurred in 1967, 1979, and 1988.

ROSE HILL. Diagonally across the intersection of Limestone and Fifth streets from the Morton House is Rose Hill, built for John Brand a few years after he purchased the five acre outlot #60 in 1811.[27] The house stands nearer to Fifth Street, as the south half of the property was used for ropewalks and other commercial purposes. In massing and plan Rose Hill is indebted to its neighbor, although smaller, more straightforward, and in some respects more appealing. It is composed of three instead of five sections, the lower wings projecting forward from the plane of the main block without intermediary links (fig. 8.23). The frontispiece has a wide, leaded fanlight spanning doors and sidelights, with rococo-Gothic clustered colonnettes separating the voids. The Greek Ionic portico dates from at least a quarter of a century later; and though it detracts from the full impact of

Fig. 8.23 Restored facade elevation of Rose Hill (ca. 1815), Lexington.

the doorway, it is in perfect harmony with all elements of the building. Of the same period are the fine gates and cage posts of cast and wrought iron at the steps to the front walk on Limestone Street (fig. 8.24).

The disposition of rooms in Rose Hill is basically

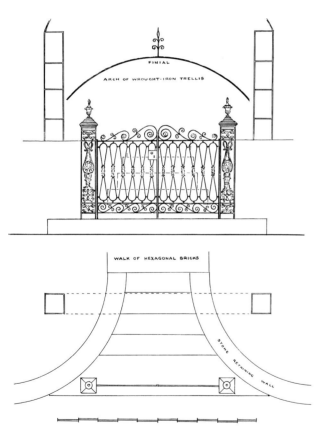

Fig. 8.24 Elevation and plan of the front gateway and steps to Rose Hill.

an inversion of the Morton House plan, except the side passages are contained in the end pavilions (fig. 8.25). As if they were courtyards, these passages have unplastered brick walls and are lighted by large transoms over the wide doorways opening to the rear terrace. At the upper side of the terrace are a two-storied kitchen and quarters for the house servants (fig. 8.26). A large smokehouse survives nearby; and at one time a brick privy and stable were situated west of the quarters. An icehouse was south of the right wing of the residence. Slave cabins occupied the west end of the yard.

Rose Hill has not been seriously modified. Kitchen and bathrooms have been installed inside the house, a bay window was added on the south flank, and larger lights replaced small-paned windows—including the leaded glass around the front doors. In 1978 some of these features were restored. Dormer windows at each end of the main roof were removed; they were contemporary with the front portico, which was left intact.

Extant houses of the same type include The Grange, built in 1818 for Edward Stone four miles north of Paris on the Maysville Pike. Like Rose Hill it has the addition of a Greek Revival portico. Forest Hill, the house of Rev. Samuel K. Nelson, two-and-a-half miles from Danville on the Lexington Pike, was built about 1815.[28] In Richmond the John Speed Smith House on North Street was built in 1818, and the Ezekiel Fields House on Main Street was constructed about 1820. The drawing-room mantel of the Fields House was shown earlier (fig. 6.6). The latter two houses were razed in 1957. Another of the type was Sugar Grove, the Daniel B. Price residence at the

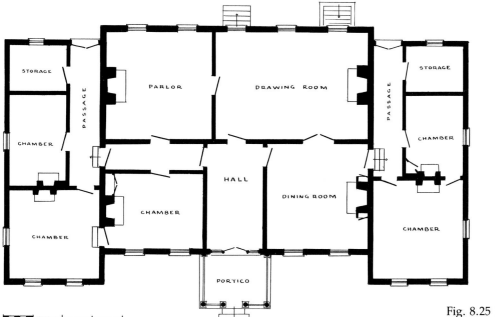

Fig. 8.25 Floor plan of Rose Hill.

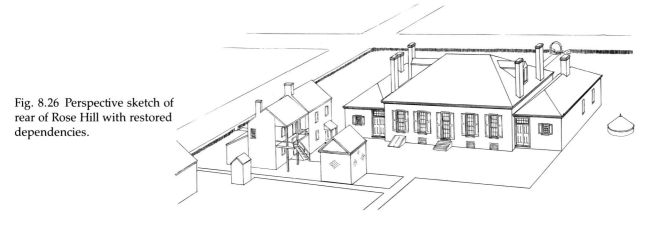

Fig. 8.26 Perspective sketch of rear of Rose Hill with restored dependencies.

edge of Nicholasville on the Sulphur Well Road. It was torn down in 1969.[29]

RIDGEWAY. Located at Saint Matthews, just east of Louisville, Ridgeway was built for Col. Henry Massie after he obtained clear title to a four-hundred-acre tract in 1816.[30] Ridgeway is a well-developed example of the type being considered and is characterized by an integral portico, elliptical interior arches, the use of closets, and large-size windowpanes (13 x 20 inches). The massing very much resembles that of the Morton House, and there must have been a railing around the flat top of the hipped roof (one has been restored), as well as peaked parapets over the false doors in the connectors, now pierced by modern windows (fig. 8.27).[31] There was also a retractable cupola on the roof at Ridgeway. The overall widths of

the two houses are identical, though the center pavilion of Massie's house is slightly greater than Morton's. The principal differences are the exposed brick walls and, of course, the projecting portico with half-round responds against the wall. The wall of the portico which is partly recessed is plastered in the Jeffersonian manner and in general reflects the portico at Farmington, built some years earlier on Bardstown Road in Louisville (fig. 9.7). A similar portico was contracted for in 1829 by Massie's brother-in-law William C. Bullitt at nearby Oxmoor.

The layout of Ridgeway was derived by a methodical and thorough mind. It is as though someone took the plan of the Morton House, studied it, and recreated the scheme, arriving at its logical conclusion. The entrance is a spacious hall, with a wide arch at

Fig. 8.27 Restored front elevation of Ridgeway (after 1816), St. Matthews.

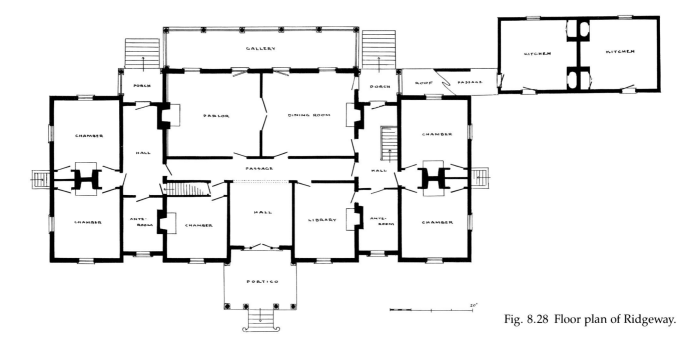

Fig. 8.28 Floor plan of Ridgeway.

the back, opening to a crosswise passage (fig. 8.28). Opposite are arched doors to the drawing and dining rooms, which are connected by a wide fanlighted doorway (fig. 8.29). Windows look out onto a rear porch or gallery. The innermost windows also function as doors, their lower "sashes" being hinged with the recessed paneled apron beneath. With such strict regularity as the house exhibits elsewhere, one is surprised to find that the fireplaces in the east rooms of the main pavilion are flush with the wall, whereas those on the west side have projecting chimney breasts. Mantels are colonnetted and rather restrained. The floor is on a single level throughout the house. Its passage system permits access to any room without going through another. Rooms at front and sides are chambers, and all except the one in front of the dining room have special entries or vestibules, with two sets of doors acting as noise barriers against

the rest of the house. The exception may have been intended as an office or library rather than a sleeping room. The front room across the hall contributes a narrow strip to basement and garret stairs. Various storage places were handy for a country domestic establishment.

From the rear, the rooflines of the porch are rather awkward, and there is a claim to its being a later construction, but the window-doors to the two main rooms refute it. A French publication of the 1940s, *Residences et plantations dans les vallées de l'Ohio et du Mississipi au début de 19e siècle*, presents a rear elevation drawing with the porch nearly covered by an extension of the main roof; but this is as much fantasy as the floor plan shown on the preceding page.[32]

The kitchen, containing two rooms with a chimney between, was a separate building. Its dimensions duplicate those of the wings of the house, only

Fig. 8.29 View from drawing room into dining room, Ridgeway. Photo, 1927, by Tebbs and Knell, courtesy of the Library of Congress.

it is oriented at right angles, is set low to the ground, and has a gable roof. At some point there were changes in the openings of the kitchen. A lean-to runway was constructed to connect it to the cellar under the east passage, which contained service stairs to the main floor. The rear bedroom currently serves as a kitchen.

Thrice widowed, Helen Scott Bullitt (Massie, Mar-

tin, Key) died childless in 1871. Except for a farmer living in part of it for a while, the house was abandoned. Ridgeway was extensively renovated in 1931. It underwent careful restoration in 1985.

COOLAVIN. Akin to Ridgeway in having a portico, presumably original, was a residence north of present Sixth Street at Bellaire Avenue in Lexington, built before 1820 by James B. January or Judge Thomas M. Hickey, who listed the place in the 1838 city directory as Coolavin.[33] The colonnetted front door was crowned by a pediment whose horizontal cornice was broken for a half-round fanlight. The entrance was flanked by narrow windows lighting a transverse hall, reminiscent of Federal Hill (fig. 8.30). The portico had slender colonnettes matching those of the frontispiece but set on pedestals with railings between. The front massing was in perfect balance, and an ell extended at the back and turned inward, creating a rear court (fig. 8.31). The entire house was covered by low-pitched roofs with gabled ends, and it produced an effect not unlike Lewis Manor. Coolavin was renamed Locust Grove after the Civil War, when it was acquired by Daniel Webster Price. By World War II only a remnant of the rear extension of the house had survived as part of a little dwelling west of Price Avenue, and its doorway embellished the entrance of an antique shop on West Short Street.

THE GIST AND SINGLETON HOUSES. Levi I. Gist bought a lot at the southeast corner of Mill and Maxwell streets, Lexington, in 1816, and he built his home facing Mill Street.[34] The facade of the small dwelling was divided into three nearly equal sections (fig. 8.32). Walls were of Flemish-bond brickwork

Fig. 8.30 Coolavin (1813), Lexington. Photo, late 1800s, courtesy of Dr. W.O. Bullock, Lexington.

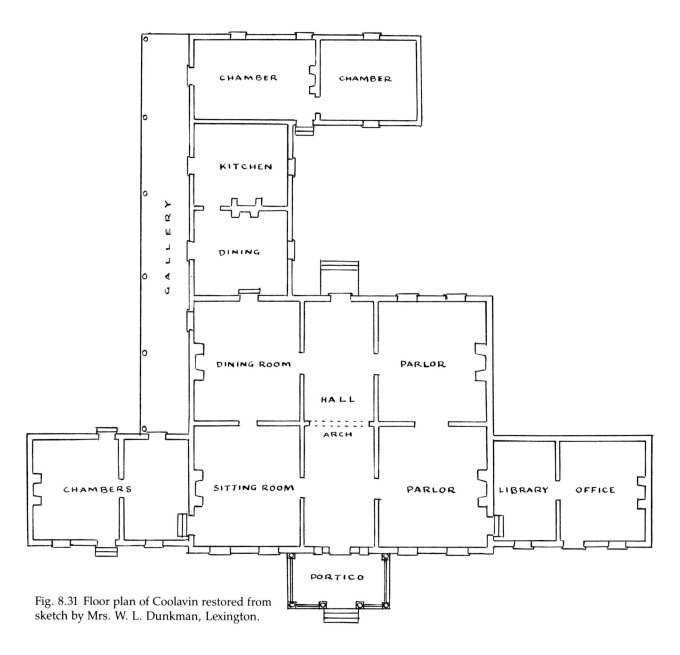

Fig. 8.31 Floor plan of Coolavin restored from sketch by Mrs. W. L. Dunkman, Lexington.

from the ground up, and the outermost units had triple windows with reeded frames set in applied arches. As noted earlier, such triple windows were first used by Matthew Kennedy in the Transylvania building, and one was to appear in his own home built at this time (fig. 9.22). The recessed middle section of the Gist House was stuccoed and contained a handsome fanlighted doorway. Its sheltering porch had a cornice below those on either side, and it was supported by four exceedingly thin colonnettes, unusual in that the space between columns at the center was less than in the outer bays. Delicate railings encompassed the stairs and connected the posts

beyond. The proportions of the masses, the importance given to roof and chimney forms, the attenuation and spacing of members of the porch, and the treatment of details in general depart from classical proprieties, yet they combine into an engaging and harmonious little edifice. It is a tiny version of Stratford (ca. 1725), the home of the Lees in Westmoreland County, Virginia.[35]

On the Hewitts' topographical map of central Kentucky counties (1861), which includes a layout of Lexington, the Gist House has indentations at front and back (signifying two porches), and the southeast arm is extended into a long wing, which would have

Fig. 8.32 Levi I. Gist House (ca. 1816), Lexington. Photo, late 1800s, courtesy of Charles R. Staples, Lexington.

contained the kitchen and services. The house was razed to make way for the Maxwell Street Christian Church completed in 1910.

A sister house to the Gist cottage is that of Jackoniah Singleton on the Lexington-Harrodsburg Pike in Jessamine County, not far from Chaumière. Jackoniah Singleton participated in the War of 1812, and he must have built his home a few years after his

return. He died in 1836.[36] The building is low to the ground and has stone foundations. Arches over the front door and to window recesses are flatter than in the Gist House, and the cornice of the porch seems always to have been level with that on the side. The pair of outer posts remaining seem of unlikely connection to the original supports, whose spacing is conjectural (fig. 8.33). The plan is basically the same

Fig. 8.33 The Jackoniah Singleton House (ca. 1816-20), Jessamine County. Photo, 1941.

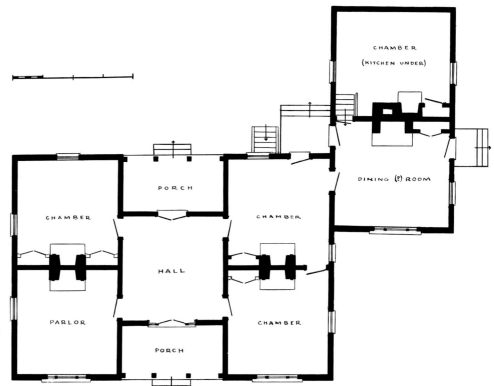

Fig. 8.34 Floor plan of the Singleton House.

as that of the Gist House, only the ell is stepped out to the side (fig. 8.34). All rooms are square and on the same floor, except at the rear where a bedroom over the kitchen takes on a split-level arrangement. The only gable on the house is here at the back. The main room in the wing has the same triple window in front as in the facade of the main block, and it has two outside doors, one of them accessible to the kitchen. A door adjoining opens to a short flight of steps ascending to the upper chamber. Panes of glass in the front triple windows are exceptionally large, their four-pane height being greater than that of five panes (nine-over-six sashes of 10-by-12-inch glass) in the side windows of the same rooms.

A large brick and stone residence was built almost directly in front of the Singleton House toward the end of the nineteenth century, and the little building was used for storing grain.

ELMWOOD HALL.   In the spring of 1827, William Bullock, the enterprising proprietor of Egyptian Hall, Piccadilly, London, and his wife, while traveling in the New World, reached New Orleans and embarked on a voyage up the Mississippi River and its principal eastern tributary, the Ohio.[37] He spent a morning in Cincinnati inspecting the marketplace and then accompanied several gentlemen on an excursion of the

environs. The highlight of their ramble was a visit to the finest house—or "villa," as Bullock termed it—in the vicinity. It was across the river in Kentucky, situated on what locally was called a farm, consisting of about a thousand acres, with a waterfront of two-and-a-half miles. The owner was Thomas D. Carneal, and his domicile was called Elmwood Hall. Bullock described its site as "a gentle acclivity, about 150 yards from the river, with beautiful pleasure grounds in front, laid out with taste, and decorated with varieties of magnificent plants and flowers, to which we [English] are as yet strangers; it commands a full view of the river, and all that passes on it." "Mr. Carneal," he continued, "selected this desirable spot for his abode, and, at considerable expense, about six years since, erected the elegant mansion he now resides in. It is considered the completest residence in the country, and built of stone and brick, after his own designs, with three handsome fronts. The lofty apartments, which it contains, in point of beauty or convenience, are surpassed by few, even in the Atlantic cities, as no expense was spared for its completion. It is surrounded by every requisite for a gentleman's country-house, domestics' houses, barns, stables, coach-house, dairy, &c."[38]

The Bullocks remained as guests for two weeks

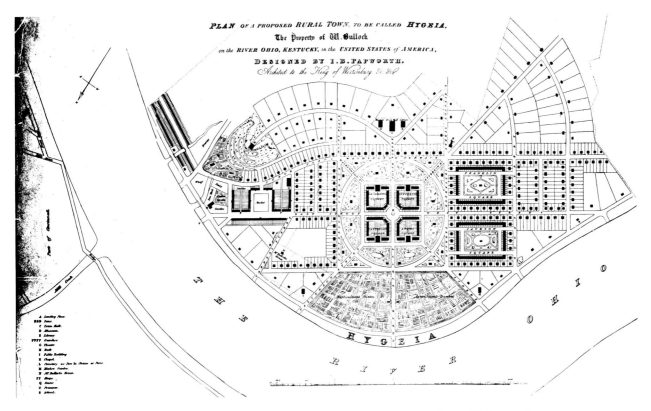

Fig. 8.35 "Plan of a Proposed Rural Town," designed by John B. Papworth. From William Bullock, *Sketch of a Journey through the Western States . . .* (London, 1827).

and were so taken by the merits of Elmwood Hall that they purchased the estate. Bullock's intention was not to continue enjoying its rural delights, however. He visualized a model residential community of squares and avenues, a civic center, market, horticultural and agricultural gardens, parks, and a cemetery on the acreage. The proposed town, called Hygeia, later was delineated by John Buonarroti Papworth, who identified himself as "Architect to the King of Wirtemburg." Bullock had the plan printed and then publicized the project. He even brought his favorite art treasures over from England and set up residence in the house to await colonizers. Incredible as it seems, a row of duplex houses was proposed in front of the villa, destroying the "beautiful pleasure grounds" and obstructing the view of the river (fig. 8.35).

The construction date usually assigned to Elmwood Hall is 1818, rather than Bullock's contention of about 1821. A sundial on the premises is inscribed "Thomas Carneal 1820." Undoubtedly the house was under construction for several years, and all these dates could apply. The house is one-storied, raised on a high basement, covered by a hipped roof once with a railing around a truncated deck (fig. 8.36). The main block is approximately 60 feet square, and to it was attached an open gallery across the back and to a service wing. The front entrance with a span of 10 feet 6 inches may be the widest fanlighted doorway to a Federal house in the United States. The twenty-four paned, double-sash windows are 4 feet 10 inches across. There are recessed porticoes in each flank, their cornices supported on six closely spaced round posts. Blind windows north of each portico exist for visual balance. The rear appendages were of lesser height, their roofs rising only to the soffit of the main cornice (fig. 8.37). The walls, like those of the Morton house, are stuccoed.

The fanlighted doorway opens into an 18-foot-square hall. In each corner stands a column from which springs connecting arches joined by pendentives framing a flat circular ceiling. The upper part of the interior is ornamented by restrained decorative plasterwork (fig. 8.38). The hall leads to chambers on either side and twin parlors behind, the latter divided by sliding doors (fig. 8.39). Windows to the side

THE GEOMETRIC PHASE 153

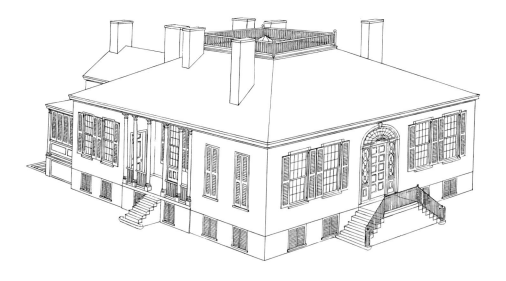

Fig. 8.36 (*top*) Restored sketch of Elmwood Hall (ca. 1818-21), Ludlow.

Fig. 8.37 Rear view of Elmwood Hall. From a colored postcard (ca. early 1900s).

Fig. 8.38 (*left*) Detail of entrance hall, Elmwood Hall, showing pendentive in west corner. Photo, 1954.

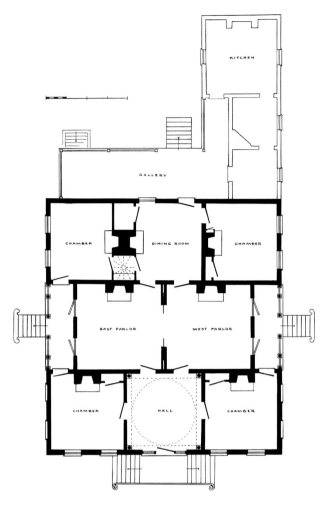

Fig. 8.39 Floor plan of Elmwood Hall.

porches have hinged panels that swing outward beneath the sashes. The dining room, centered at the back, is flanked by chambers. Between it and the east chamber is an anteroom-closet surmounted by a winding staircase ascending to the garret, the first step of which is reached by means of a detachable ladder. Like Ridgeway and the Morton House, the garret was lit through the roof. The mantel that was originally in the west parlor (now in the southeast bedroom) displays a handsome combination of pure forms—urns, sunbursts, panels, and moldings—carved from wood (fig. 8.40). For artistry and harmony, these motifs are equal to those of plaster in the front hall. The well-ordered, symmetrical arrangement of Elmwood Hall, with its square rooms and indented porticoes, suggests villas in northern Italy designed by Andrea Palladio and published in his *Second Book of Architecture*, such as the Villa Ragona or Villa Angerano at or near Vicenza. Perhaps Thomas Carneal had a copy before him when he planned Elmwood Hall. If so, he automatically thrust himself into the society of Thomas Jefferson, Dr. William Thornton, and other American gentleman-architects of the eighteenth and early nineteenth centuries. It is noteworthy that Palladio's villas usually were built of brick coated with stucco. The simplified, sculpturesque details, the space-defining forms of arches and pendentives, and the portioning of the floor plan render Elmwood Hall the apex of the geometric phase of Federal domestic architecture in Kentucky.

William Bullock occupied the house about four years, during which time it became apparent that the

Fig. 8.40 Detail of mantel originally in west parlor of Elmwood Hall. Photo, 1954.

model-town project had failed. In 1831 he sold the residence and some seven hundred acres to Israel L. Ludlow for $21,300, and eventually disposed of the remainder to him for $30,000. Ludlow's father, Israel Ludlow, laid out Cincinnati in 1788, and the town that grew up around Elmwood Hall took the Ludlow name. Ludlow sold the house and thirty-two acres in 1840.[39] The villa was divided into two dwellings, and some time afterward the back wing was destroyed. In 1920 it became Mrs. Thomas' Candy Kitchen. Currently it is a duplex residence designated 244 Forest Avenue, Ludlow.

AUGUSTA COLLEGE. The town of Augusta is on the Ohio River between Covington and Maysville. The college was founded in 1822 as a merger of Bracken Academy (established in 1798) with conferences of the Methodist Church of Ohio and Kentucky, becoming the first Methodist college in the world.[40] The college building erected in 1825 had two stories and measured 80 by 40 feet (fig. 8.41). The seven-bayed facade had a doorway with fanlight and sidelights, a Palladian window above, an extremely broad lunette in the pediment, and an open cupola. Dormers were on either side, and end chimneys were linked by parapets. These features place the building in the geometric phase of the Federal style. Though appropriate, early nineteenth century college buildings in America generally adhered to one or the other phase of the Federal style, like the Kennedy designs for the Main Building of Transylvania University. That built, as we have seen, was Georgian in style, whereas the rejected scheme as we shall see, was classic. Most large public buildings of the Federal period in which architectural exuberance was desired resorted to either of those two styles in preference to

Fig. 8.41 The main building of Augusta College (1825), Augusta. From Lewis Collins, *Historical Sketches of Kentucky* (Cincinnati, 1847), facing p. 209.

the geometric. Augusta College, except for its arched openings, might have been placed among the early brick examples in chapter 4.

True to the human-rights background of Methodism, Augusta College became the center of the antislavery movement in Kentucky. Its charter was repealed by the state legislature in 1849. Fire damaged the hall in 1852 and completely destroyed it in 1856. From 1868 to 1896 the Augusta Male and Female College occupied the site. At present it is the location of Augusta High School.

9 CLASSICISM

THE CLASSIC REVIVAL, or neoclassic, architecture of Europe and England was a reaffirmation of Renaissance ideals of the fifteenth and sixteenth centuries in Italy and of a somewhat later era in northern and western Europe and the British Isles. Between the Renaissance and Classic Revival styles throughout Europe as well as to some extent in the colonies were the baroque and rococo of the seventeenth and eighteenth centuries. The Classic Revival came out in full force during the early Republic period in the United States. As this was also the time when Kentucky was being settled, it awaited a stage of some maturity before putting in an appearance here. This phase of Federal architecture took up where the Georgian survival left off. The Classic Revival's hallmark was the sophisticated columned portico, which replaced the colonial colonnetted doorway and the porch with chamfered posts. We have already seen examples of porticoes on the Lewis, January, Massie, and Carneal residences, but they either were not well developed or were at least partially recessed. The Classic Revival portico went beyond the function of shelter. It lent dignity and distinction to the entrance of a building. It usually had a triangular pediment, which in ancient temples signified the dwelling place of a deity.

WARWICK. The most provincial or primitive portico in Kentucky is on Warwick, the home of Moses Jones (1773-1842). He migrated westward with his family, was captured by the Chickasaw in Tennessee at the age of seven, and after living with them for nine years, he rejoined his father at the landing of Warwick on the Kentucky River, eleven miles north of Harrodsburg. With his patrimony, he purchased sizable tracts in the neighborhood. He married Mary Henderson in 1804. Jones mortgaged his land to Alexander Henderson in 1809 and redeemed it in 1811.[1] Very likely the residence was built during this interim. The story-and-a-half house is located on a slope with the cellar at ground level in the rear; the walls are entirely of Flemish-bond brickwork (fig. 9.1). Porticoes precede both front and rear doors, and they have full supports against the masonry walls, like the porches on the DuPuy and Scott stone houses discussed in chapter 3 (figs. 3.9, 3.12). Supports at Warwick are square up to pedestal height and are joined by banister railings, the banisters being miniature replicas of the supports. The upper part of the posts are round colonnettes with exaggerated entases, resembling enlongated urns, having Doric capitals. They recall posts on the gallery of the Jean Pascal House (after 1726) in New Orleans.[2] The Kentucky house features a meander-dentil motif at the base of the cornice that carries around all horizontal roof lines.

Warwick has a hall-and-parlor plan, with two enclosed stairways between the rooms. The steps rise from opposite outer walls and turn toward their respective chambers over a corbel-arched recess in the east parlor, which has Georgian-type woodwork, and there is a delicately modeled keystone at the apex of the opening (fig. 9.2). Both rooms have classical mantels. That in the hall is exceptionally fine, having coupled colonnettes, sunbursts on the imposts and center block, strapwork in the frieze between, and a serpentine shelf whose edge is embellished with basketworklike design suggesting native influence (fig. 9.3). Window and door trim in this room is Federal, with running moldings and corner blocks containing carved radial stars. Doors have a double head, bringing them up to window height. A drapery-tassel frieze was painted around the walls at the ceiling line. Although features of the woodwork resemble those of Matthew P. Lowery and the painted swags those of Alfred Cohen (figs. 6.5, 6.6, 6.10, 6.11, 6.12, 6.13), family tradition assigns them, as well as the making and laying of the bricks in the walls, to Moses Jones.

Figs. 9.1, 9.2 Warwick (1809-11), Mercer County. Front. Photo, 1967. Recess under stairways in parlor. Photo, 1988.

Fig. 9.3 Mantel in hall, Warwick. Photo, 1978.

He also made some of the furniture for the house. Four pieces that are or were in Harrodsburg include three tables (one a Hepplewhite gateleg for dining) and a narrow cabinet with a gooseneck pediment, an eighteenth-century feature like the strapwork on the hall mantel. A secretary or bureau with roping and baluster turnings, and a scroll-headed bed with incised decorations and posts are in Versailles. A plain

square cherry chest of drawers has been returned to the house. The inventory of Moses Jones's effects lists a wooden clock (perhaps referring only to the case) made by him.[3]

The house originally had a separate log kitchen, and later an attached frame kitchen, entered off an open gallery on the east flank. It had been missing for several decades when a stone and frame wing took its place in 1979. The rear portico was restored at that time. Warwick as a riverport community has long since ceased to exist, but the name perseveres as the address of the house of Moses Jones.

FARMINGTON.   John Speed built his home, Farmington, a few miles from Louisville on Bardstown Road on a 554-acre tract he took possession of in 1809. He had married Lucy Gilmer Fry in 1808. Both John and Lucy had been brought to Kentucky as children, the Speeds having come from Surry County and the Frys from Albemarle County, Virginia. The Frys were friends of the Jeffersons, and the connection brought about the drawing of the basic plan for John Speed's house by the Sage of Monticello. Jefferson evidently conceived it as a one-story house measuring 50 by 60 feet, with central hall, and octagonal projections on two sides with porticoes beyond, in the manner of the terrace facade of Monticello (fig. 9.4).[4] The two eight-sided rooms were meant to be parlor and dining room; the rooms in the four corners, chambers. Three of the latter are provided with French bed alcoves, typical of Jefferson's planning,

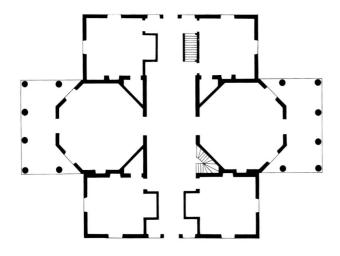

Fig. 9.4 Floor plan for a one-story house by Thomas Jefferson, prototype for Farmington. Redrawn from the pencil original in the Coolidge Collection, Massachusetts Historical Society, Boston.

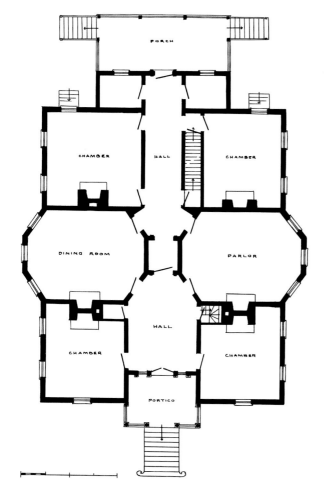

Fig. 9.5 Floor plan of Farmington (ca. 1809-10), near Louisville.

the space of the fourth accommodating a stairway. A second stairway is fitted rather awkwardly in a triangular space adjoining one of the octagons. Corresponding triangles were closets. Fireplaces are between rooms. Probably the kitchen was meant to be in the cellar. The lack of outside stairs on the drawing gives us no clue as to the intended elevation of the first story.

Farmington embodied most of the elements indicated in Jefferson's drawing, without literally following the plan. It includes the twin octagonal rooms (though they are not regular), and square chambers in the four corners (though there were no bed alcoves), stairways are tucked away similarly, and chimneys and fenestration conform in their placing (fig. 9.5). But the through hall is more diversified. It begins as a six-sided vestibule, narrows to a small square between the octagons, and becomes a straight passage leading to the back porch. A pair of closets or dressing rooms is included in the rear projection. On the whole the wood trim is rather plain, yet the mantels show a distinct personality (fig. 9.6). Pedestal-like flat uprights, tapering in and then expanding, and reeded at the top, support a course with an intertwined motif, above which is the frieze emblazoned with sunbursts, another narrow course—appropriately including octagon shapes, alternating with swirling swastikas—and then modillions bracing the serpentine shelf. Modifications to the plan and the un-Jeffersonian decor produce a more livable

Fig. 9.6 Parlor mantel, Farmington. Photo, 1964.

house than if the Virginia model had been followed verbatim.

Strangely enough, the exterior features of Farmington look less Jeffersonian than those of the brick pavilion at Chaumière: the roof sits too close to the top of the windows, which have smaller panes, and the delicate portico elements are unlike Jefferson's adherence to classic proportions (figs. 8.18, 9.7). Chaumière had no portico. That of Farmington has been compared to the one on nearby Ridgeway and, being earlier, probably served as its model (figs. 8.27, 9.7). The Farmington portico has a banister railing, which Jefferson seldom used, and the railings to the stairs are modern. Jefferson's door treatment was as simple as his fenestration, and he did not employ the Palladian motif, such as is incorporated in the Farmington frontispiece. The Palladian motif, attenuated columns, and entablature members of the portico, molded brick water table at first-floor level, and the nine-paned window sashes of Farmington are all Georgian features inconsistent with Jefferson's floor plan. They indicate the thin line of demarcation between Georgian survival and the classic phase in Kentucky Federal architecture.

The smaller of the interior stairways descends to what must have been John Speed's office at the south-

east corner of the basement, which also could be reached by entrances under the portico. The winter kitchen is at the northwest corner. The summer kitchen was a detached building in the yard. Other dependencies, of which something remains, are a smokehouse, carriage house, springhouse, and stone barn.

Farmington was taken over by the Historic Homes Foundation of Louisville in 1957. It was furnished and opened to the public as a house museum in 1959 and has been subsequently restored.

MOUNT AIRY. Col. Andrew Muldrow (1752-1829) acquired several thousand acres in the Grier's Creek area of Woodford County, near the DuPuy House (chapter 3) and about a mile from the Kentucky River, in 1804. He built a log house prior to the completion of the remarkable brick residence set atop a rounded hill to which Mrs. Muldrow gave the name Mount Airy. Materials were obtained near the site. Lumber was cut and seasoned four years, periodically turned over to prevent warping, and the house probably was completed between 1817 and 1820.[5] The recurring motif in the design was the half circle, used in the concentric stone steps to the portico, the arches spanning the slender Tuscan columns, and the fanlight over the front door and lunette (with an un-

Fig. 9.7 Farmington.
Photo, 1964.

Fig. 9.8 Mount Airy (ca. 1815-20), Woodford County. Photo, 1941.

usual muntin pattern within it) in the pediment, and it bridged the center light of Palladian windows right and left in the front walls and in the end gables (fig. 9.8). The extensive use of the semicircle might place Mount Airy in the geometric category were it not for the accompanying classic columns. Archivolts of the portico arches and frames of doors and windows were reeded. A dogtrot on the left side connected the kitchen, to which a servants' room was attached (fig. 9.9). On both porches were full round columns adjacent to the wall.

The plan of Mount Airy equaled the exterior in matters of simple refinements and ample proportions (fig. 9.10). Main-story ceilings were 14 feet high. The center hall was 12 feet wide and 48 feet long. The two front rooms measured 20 by 22 feet, and those behind 20 by 17 feet. Windows on the south side of the house were set symmetrically in the

wall, and rooms were accommodated to the openings. Stairways were Jeffersonian, rising as winders in square enclosures to either side of the hall in a projecting pavilion at the back, and continuing as straight flights to the second floor. One opened into the upstairs hall and the other into one of the three bedrooms. A storage room expanded into the space over the portico. Woodwork inside the house was elaborate and has been attributed to Matthew P. Lowery (fig. 9.11).

Mount Airy was much abused during the late nineteenth century. One side window was filled in and three others were cut, small panes were replaced by larger glass, the rear doorway was moved forward eight feet (presumably to let farmhands use the upstairs rooms without coming into the lower part of the house), banisters of the porch railings were removed, and the quarters were demolished. The

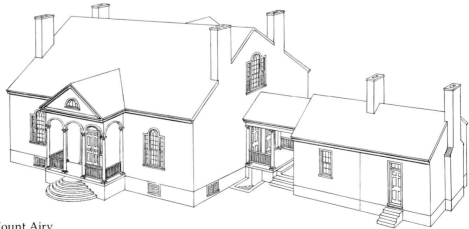

Fig. 9.9 Restored sketch of Mount Airy.

CLASSICISM 161

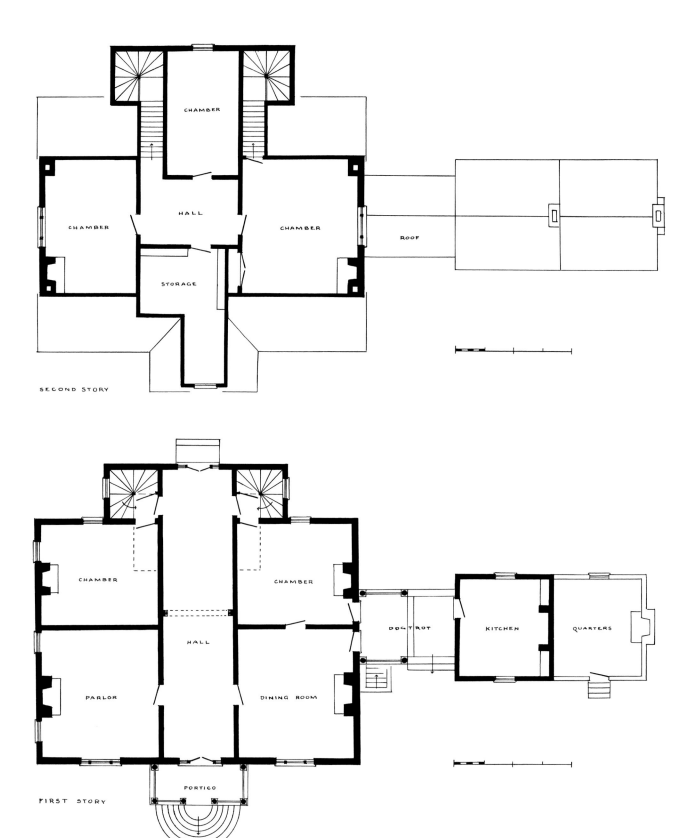

Fig. 9.10 Floor plans of Mount Airy.

Fig. 9.11 Detail of hall arch, Mount Airy. Photo, ca. 1939, by Lafayette Studio, Lexington.

house was undergoing restoration in 1945 when most of it was destroyed by fire. Northeast of the house site stands a two-room stone office with end chimneys, built in 1829, the year Andrew Muldrow died.

THE WARNER COTTAGE.   The arched portico was nowhere more prominently displayed than on the William A. Warner Cottage. It was unique in being the only known residence in Kentucky of the Federal period having a prostyle, or temple, form. This distinctive classic example was built on a narrow (37½ feet wide) lot on East Main Street in Lexington inherited by Warner in 1829.[6] The facade presented five elliptical (three-centered) arches, having fluted archivolts and square blocks for keystones, supported on Tuscan columns (fig. 9.12). The pediment contained a Palladian window, and steps up to the platform rose between pedestals in front of the center pair of col-

umns. Elements of the portico were of wood. The front wall contained a fanlighted entrance flanked by single rectangular windows. Chimneys rising above the outer walls indicate that the house was two rooms deep, and dormers show that use was made of the second story. The original front door would have had six or eight panels, in place of the two Greek Revival replacements that can be seen in figure 9.12. The Warner Cottage was razed soon after World War I, when the Esplanade was cut through the site.

The culmination of houses with arcaded porticoes was represented by two examples built of masonry in central Kentucky during the 1820s. They were called White Cottage and Pleasant Lawn.

WHITE COTTAGE.   This house was built on a ten-acre tract on the prominence above East Main Street opposite Rose Street conveyed in 1823 to Mary Ann Dewees by Henry Clay, executor of her uncle, James Morrison.[7] The owner was the wife of Farmer Dewees, a partner in the tobacco and oil manufacturing firm of Dewees and Grant. It has been said that the grounds were landscaped and gardened by the eccentric botanist Constantine Samuel Rafinesque, who concluded his seven-year sojourn in Lexington in 1826.[8] Quite aside from its fine natural or devised setting, the residence, called White Cottage, compelled notice (fig. 9.13). Its 35-foot-broad recessed portico featured a five-bayed arcade of geometric se-

Fig. 9.12 The William A. Warner Cottage (ca. 1830), Lexington. Photo, ca. early 1900s, courtesy of Charles R. Staples, Lexington.

Fig. 9.13 White Cottage (ca. 1824), Lexington. Photo, ca. late 1800s, courtesy of Mrs. John Johnstone, Lexington.

verity, with plain cylindrical posts, set each on a square pedestal and plinth, capped by a simple abacus, and holding up a square impost block, in response to which sections of the horizontal cornice stepped forward on axis. The rather steeply pitched pediment above was pierced by a Palladian window. Entrances with fanlights were at either end of the portico, and there were arched windows elsewhere in the facade. Those in the end pavilions were disguised as Palladians. Like the Morton House, White Cottage was of brick coated with stucco, and the corners were finished with dentated quoins (fig. 9.14).

An addition was constructed on the east flank, probably in the later 1820s or 1830s. The best lighted room evidently was the parlor, and the room in the center, with closets flanking the fireplace, must have been the dining room. Transverse passages were on either side of it, and the one to the east contained the

staircase to the second floor, with its four bedrooms. The only access to the great chamber on the main floor was from the portico, later modified by the addition of a narrow room behind, entered from the back hall (fig. 9.15). That the rear gallery was continued across to the new wing is conjectured for adequate circulation.[9]

The design of White Cottage was so unusual and its characteristics so unrelated to houses of earlier date in Kentucky that one is led to speculate on possible sources of inspiration. The treatment of the recessed portico is unlike those of the Gist or Singleton houses, Farmington, Ridgeway, or Elmwood. It compares favorably with the rear arcade of Clay Hill, Harrodsburg, built for Beriah Magoffin about eleven years before.[10] A suggested prototype is Thomas Jefferson's work. At the University of Virginia (1817-19) in Charlottesville, there is a brick arcade in the lower portico of Pavilion VII (the first erected and, it may be added, derived from Palladio), and there is overwhelming repetition of such arches in the outermost (student quarters) ranges, the last probably suggested by Robert Morris's designs.[11] The clear-cut quality of forms at White Cottage recalls the severity of the architecture of Claude-Nicolas Ledoux (1736-1806), whose architectural drawings were published in Paris in 1804.[12] Ledoux evidently was influenced by Mediterranean villas of lesser architectural pretensions. The type had been transplanted to America a century earlier, in French architecture of the lower Mississippi River region, which may have served as intermediary. New Orleans was a city abounding in arches when it came under the American flag in 1803, and the high elevation of White Cottage suggests what has been called

Fig. 9.14 Restored facade elevation of White Cottage.

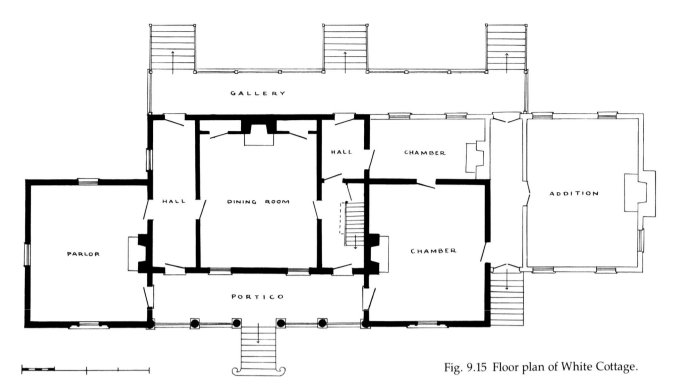

Fig. 9.15 Floor plan of White Cottage.

the "raised-cottage" type (prompted by soil saturation, if not floods) of the Deep South. The Lexington house could have been a local interpretation of Gulf Coast architecture. The name Dewees implies a French origin.

White Cottage was sold to Mathew F. Scott in 1840. During the early 1870s it became the residence of H. Howard Gratz, publisher of the *Kentucky Gazette*. After purchase in 1889, the Christ Church Women's Guild opened the Protestant Infirmary in the house, and ten years later it went under interdenominational Protestant management, with the name changed to the Good Samaritan Hospital. Adjoining buildings were erected and occupied until 1907, when the hospital moved to a new building on South Limestone Street. White Cottage deteriorated and was demolished in 1940.[13]

PLEASANT LAWN. A house having many points in common with White Cottage is Pleasant Lawn, built in 1829 for Daniel Jackson Williams in Woodford County between the Versailles-Frankfort and Lexington-Frankfort pikes, east of the Midway road. Daniel was a descendant of Roger Williams, founder of Rhode Island, and his parents had immigrated to Kentucky soon after the American Revolution. Unlike White Cottage, Pleasant Lawn was built without strict symmetry or architectural propriety. It may be described as being composed of two houses of equal

depth but facing in opposite directions. The outstanding motif of each is a pedimented arcade. That of the south front is at the western end of the original building. It consists of a recessed portico of nine bays, the centermost somewhat wider than the others, and with a Palladian window in the brick pediment (fig. 9.16). The principal doorway is aligned with the center bay, but the fenestration in this wall occurs without reference to the arched voids. The wing on the right side was added a decade or so later and serves to create a semblance of balance. The east portion is pierced by five windows in the lower story, equally spaced, with the last one set awkwardly close to the outer corner of the building. Unlike White Cottage, the main floor of Pleasant Lawn is close to the ground in front (fig. 9.17), but there is a respectable basement elevation at the back. Here is shown a more provincial combination of harsh forms, miscellaneous elements, and size discrepancies (fig. 9.18). The arcade of the east wing has slightly wider end bays, which two openings are furnished with steps, and there are closets or pantries beyond. A Palladian window is centered in the pediment, but it is aligned with neither the column nor the arch below. The supports of both porticoes repeat the plain cylindrical shafts set on thin plinths of White Cottage, yet they have a disk forming a transition to the abacus by way of a capital, and there are no advanced

Figs. 9.16, 9.17 Pleasant Lawn (1829), Woodford County with detail of front arcade. Photos, 1948.

imposts between the more rounded arches. The small protruding porch sheltering the rear entrance to the principal hall is without refinement. Pents over cellar stairs are on the two outer corners farthest from the porticoes.

The two parts of the house each have a hall and stairway; that in the west section has an open well, the other is enclosed (fig. 9.19). In the parlor were the murals by Alfred Cohen, considered earlier (figs. 6.12, 6.13). The three chambers over the west half and the two over the east half of the house were all rather poorly lighted and ventilated.

Daniel Jackson Williams died in the late 1850s. Pleasant Lawn stayed in the family for more than a century. It was sold in 1964, and toward the end of that year a fire broke out, destroying the murals and

inflicting considerable damage to the house itself. It was rebuilt and renovated, with dormers added, and copies of the Cohen murals, on canvas, were affixed to the parlor walls. Pleasant Lawn is now called Lane's End.[14]

So far, examples of the classic phase of Federal architecture have been buildings of one or one and one-half stories. They climaxed the early architecture of Kentucky, and with them design came to a high point and could go no further. The other aspect of Federal classicism consisted of larger, multistoried buildings. They, too, attained a higher degree of refinement but still became a channel for further architectural development. After the Gano House, discussed next, domestic buildings leveled off to a

Fig. 9.18 Restored sketch of rear of Pleasant Lawn.

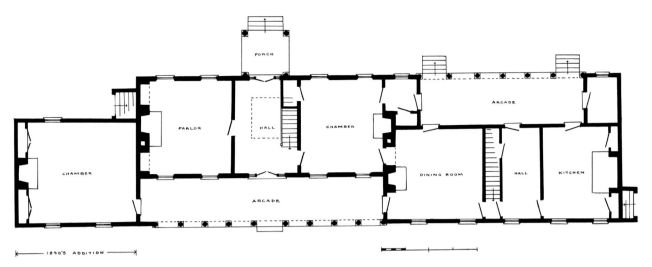

Fig. 9.19 First-floor plan of Pleasant Lawn.

standardized type; but this standardization in itself was indicative of the manner of building that was to follow.

THE GANO HOUSE. Perched on the promontory west of the confluence of the Ohio and Licking rivers, occupying land purchased in 1815 by Gen. John S. Gano, Richard M. Gano, and Thomas D. Carneal and by 1820 in the hands of Aaron Gano, the house now at the east end of Second Street has been claimed as Covington's oldest brick residence.[15] It was most likely designed about 1820 by Carneal, and like his own home, Elmwood Hall, it shows the influence of Palladio's architecture. The indebtedness is not in plan, however, like the Ludlow villa, but in elevation.

Fig. 9.20 The Gano House (ca. 1820), Covington. Photo, ca. 1960s, courtesy of the *Courier-Journal*, Louisville.

Recalling plates of the Villa Pisani at Montagnana or Villa Torre at Verona in Andrea Palladio's second book of architecture, the Covington house has an indented two-story portico centered on the facade (fig. 9.20). Following the accepted protocol (undoubtedly derived from the Colosseum), the sequence of orders is Corinthian over Ionic over Doric, omitting either the first or last where only two levels are involved. In the Gano House, Corinthian columns are on the second floor and Ionic on the first, and although the latter are Greek Revival replacements, one assumes that the originals were of the same order. Walls within the portico are stuccoed, and those elsewhere are of exposed brick, with a cut-stone belt course dividing the stories and stone-panel insets flanking the arches. Many early brick houses had stone belt courses, sills, and keystones, but this greater array of decorative elements borrowed from the sixteenth-century Venetian architect was not equaled elsewhere in Kentucky.[16]

There may have been an American intermediary between Palladio's work and the Gano House. The general impression of its facade favors the land side of Drayton Hall (1738) on the Ashley River in South Carolina.[17] But this remote building, five miles up-river from Charleston, built four-score years earlier, would not likely have been known to Thomas Carneal. A more probable candidate is the Michael Hancock residence (1808-1809) on North Fifth Street in Richmond, Virginia. It has two stories and its three-bayed portico spans two octagonal pavilions, with a continuous cornice running across the facade.[18] This adherence to a plane is unusual. Carneal employed it at both Elmwood Hall and the Gano House, and it leads one to speculate as to whether the poorly fitting pediment atop the latter house is not as much a later addition as is the row of post–Civil War brackets to the cornice. The Hancock House in Richmond does not have free-standing columns, but a Renaissance arch-and-pilaster combination, the arches relating to the windows in the Gano House. Here lower windows are enframed in stone moldings, and the upper openings are set in blind arches. The fenestration proper is slightly pointed and contains muntin tracery in the Georgian rococo-Gothic manner. A center pavilion projects five inches at the rear, corresponding to the portico in front, and is pierced by a window balancing a doorway in the first story, constituting the only departure from a strict bilateral symmetry on any elevation.

The house measures 30 by 60 feet, and it contains a straightforward and elegant plan (fig. 9.21). The front doorway has coupled colonnettes supporting a vigorous serpentine cornice beneath a fanlight both inside and out. The original mantel at the east end of this reception room had matching elements. Pointed doorways at either side had niches in their depth and opened into the drawing room occupying the right wing of the building. Sharing the corresponding space opposite are the dining room and stair hall. A blind window adjacent to the stairs contained louvered shutters outside (which existed nowhere else on the house) until a side door was cut in this

area. A cooking fireplace is in the basement, which is excavated only under the west half of the building. In all probability there was a summer kitchen in a detached pavilion nearby. Food from either kitchen would have been brought from outside through the rear door, accounting for its having been located nearer the west end of the hall. Inside frames around openings are rather heavy, corresponding to the almost baroque outline of the front-doorway cornice. Similar moldings exist at Elmwood Hall, and both sets belong to the second decade of the century.

A large wing later was extended back from the southwest corner of the house, connected to the embankment on the Licking River by a long, underground tunnel of stone. Curvilinear stone forms flanking the portico steps are contemporary with the Ionic columns, and a high retaining wall across the restricted front yard came into being when Second Street was cut through the property. The house now is a multiple-family dwelling.

THE KENNEDY HOUSE. Matthew Kennedy, Lexington's first classical resident architect, built his own home on the southeast corner of Mulberry (North Limestone) and Constitution (East Second) streets after the death of his former partner and joint owner of the lot, James W. Brand. Kennedy had been commissioned to design a new main building for Transylvania University in 1816, and elements of the classical-style scheme (fig. 9.31) that were rejected by the institution were included in his residence. The

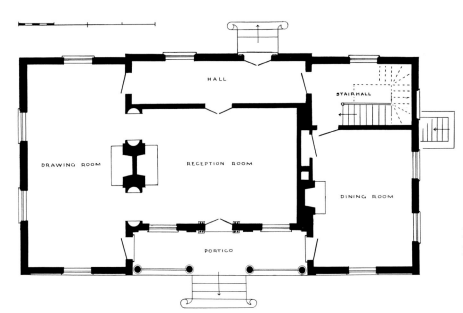

Fig. 9.21 Restored first-floor plan of the Gano House.

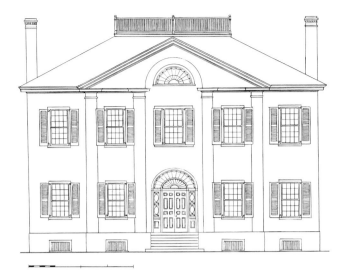

Fig. 9.22 Restored facade elevation of Matthew Kennedy House (ca. 1816), Lexington.

Kennedy House is characterized by a center pavilion incorporating giant pilasters tied together by a pediment (fig. 9.22). The horizontal cornice is broken in the middle bay, which is spanned by a blind arch, and a large lunette is centered in the pediment, reflecting the fanlight of the front doorway. A three-part window in the second story strengthens this axis. The unorthodox element is the direct connection of the pilaster shafts with the cornice. The uprights display a sort of necking, but advanced sections of the cornice itself answer for the capitals. The street facade of the Kennedy House recalls the garden front of the Matthias Hammond House (1773-74) in Annapolis, mentioned earlier in connection with Liberty Hall. The Maryland house, however, has a full entablature across the pilastrade but retains an archaism in a belt course at second-floor level, cutting uneasily across the pilaster shafts. The Lexington house has several blind windows included for balance on the north end, and it once was crowned by a balustrade at the crest of its truncated hipped roof. Its squared sills of windows and door forecast the Greek Revival.

Matthew Kennedy's plan is not unusual. A central transverse hall is divided by an arch, and the rear half, containing the staircase, is wider than the front (fig. 9.23). The closet under the first landing receives daylight from the north sidelight of the back door. The office adjacent to the stairs had a private entrance toward Second Street. The parlor and drawing room form a suite with the fore part of the hall across the front, and the dining room occupies the fourth corner of the main block. The service stairs and kitchen are in an attached wing, to which the storeroom section beyond is a later addition. Bedrooms on the second floor follow the same plan as below, with the exception of a small extra chamber over the front hall.

Most alterations were made a few years before the Civil War. Great sliding doors were placed between each pair of rooms on the first floor. The entrance was squared and sheltered by a portico of the composite order, the capitals derived from those of the Arch of Septimius Severus at Rome. The columns and hood molds added over the front windows are of cast iron, and blind windows on the north side have been filled with bricks. Single panes of glass in the window sashes were substituted probably nearer to the turn of the century. Recently the building has served as an antique shop, roominghouse, and rummage exchange, and now once again it is a private residence.[19]

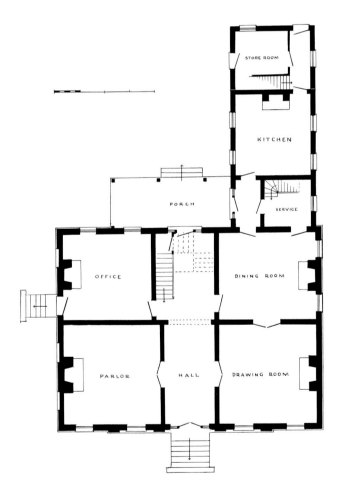

Fig. 9.23 First-floor plan of Kennedy House.

GRASSLAND. The home of Major Thomas Hart Shelby was built on a thousand acres of land given him by his father, Isaac Shelby, first governor of Kentucky. The estate lies in the southern part of Fayette County, between Walnut Hill and Jacks Creek roads, now connected by Shelby Lane, which the house faces. Major Shelby settled here in 1816, residing in a log structure until his fine brick residence, Grassland, was completed. The date 1823 is incised in the cornerstone at the northeast angle of the dwelling. The house strongly resembles the Kennedy residence, except it has a gabled roof, larger windowpanes, a gallery with round brick supports at the back, and is about six feet wider and deeper (fig. 9.24). The hall is not divided, and its staircase curves gracefully around a circular open well. Behind, a cross passage contains a secondary stairway, which encroaches upon the territory of the room in the southwest corner of the house (fig. 9.25). Twin parlors to the east of the main hall can be thrown together by means of a thirteen-foot-wide screen, composed of side doors that slide horizontally into wall pockets, and a double center section that lifts into the partition between upstairs bedrooms. The arch over the doors bridges a paneled tympanum (fig. 9.26). The sizeable room across the hall has a large closet and presses flanking the chimney. The mantel is a breakfront, with an elliptical panel in the center frieze block and paneled pilasters enframing

the stone facing of the fireplace. This large front room probably was used for dining on special occasions. The everyday dining room behind is considerably smaller, and, as in the Kennedy House, it opens into a rear entry with service stairs; the kitchen is beyond. In the cellar, a scooped-out log, nineteen feet long and a little over a yard in diameter, for salting meats, was undoubtedly deposited before the joists above were placed.

Grassland passed out of the Shelby family in 1895. Changes made through the years have been minor. A side porch off the dining room, gold-leaf bead molding on the hall ceiling, and a battlemented closet in a corner of an upstairs chamber have been added, and, of course, modern utilities.[20]

It is noteworthy that Grassland still presents a complete early-nineteenth-century country establishment. Included in the group of buildings are the washhouse (which, perhaps, also functioned as a summer kitchen), a two-story pavilion with the cook's room above; a square smokehouse and octagonal icehouse to the west; and a coach house with attached tack room and a double privy southeast of the residence (fig. 9.24).

THE WALLACE HOUSE. Of a number of other houses throughout central Kentucky that follow the pattern set by the Matthew Kennedy House, one of the closest in form is that of Samuel Wallace, built about 1825 in Woodford County not far from the

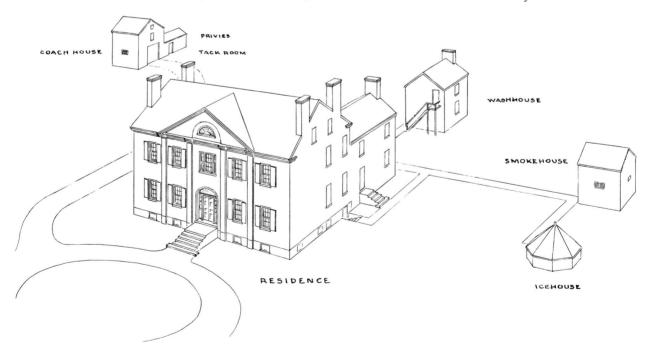

Fig. 9.24 Restored sketch of Grassland (1823), Fayette County, including residence and dependencies.

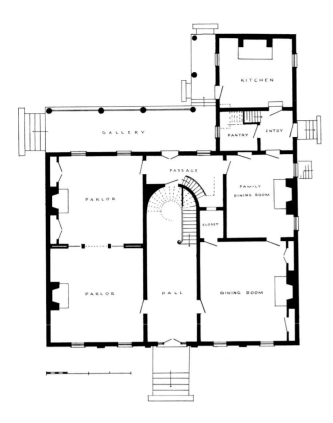

Fig. 9.25 First-floor plan of Grassland.

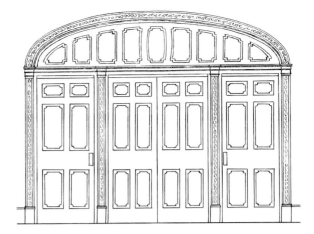

Fig. 9.26 Elevation of paneled screen between parlors in Grassland.

Fayette County line on the Lexington-Frankfort Pike (fig. 9.27). The outer differences are the larger window panes (like Grassland), and chimney shafts that break through the flank walls about the same depth as the front pilasters. The Greek Revival portico is a later appendage. The railing surmounting the hip roof was retained until the 1950s.

Details inside the house are rather provincial. Ap-

Fig. 9.27 The Samuel Wallace House (ca. 1825), Woodford County. Photo, 1941.

rons under the windows are embellished with three heavy sunbursts that look like flattened wheels with hubs, spokes, and oval rims. The parlor mantel has slim coupled banisterlike colonnettes supporting end blocks with vertical sunbursts resembling those under the windows, and a half sunburst in the center.[21] Delicate gold-leaf motifs in the frieze and cornice of this room are contemporary with the trim in the hall at Grassland. The staircase is a replacement.

A square brick smokehouse beyond the service ell had a turned wooden urn set on the apex of its pyramidal roof. This dependency was razed during the 1970s. The house proper was painted white at about the same time.

THE MEADOWS. Another house of the Kennedy type was built for Dr. Elisha Warfield during the early 1830s a mile east of Lexington, off present Loudoun Avenue. The breeder of Lexington, the most illustrious American race horse of his day, Dr. Warfield has been called the Father of the Kentucky Turf. Warfield's house, The Meadows, resembled Grassland, in more than name, though it had a hipped roof like the Kennedy and Wallace houses. The interior fittings were quite plain, the plan prosaic, but it was

Fig. 9.28 Restored floor plans of The Meadows (early 1830s), near Lexington.

quite large, especially in the length of the rear ell (fig. 9.28). The Meadows suffered extensively from fin-de-siècle modernization: the staircase and mantels were replaced, pressed tin ceilings installed, small windowpanes taken out, and an ugly eclectic porch was inflicted upon the entrance.[22] About 1950 a subdivision mushroomed along its driveway, and in the summer of 1960 the building was razed.

AUVERGNE AND BUCKNORE. Two later, related examples, Auvergne and Bucknore, are in Bourbon County. Auvergne is on the Paris-Winchester Pike, and Bucknore is in the Cane Ridge section, near Paris. Auvergne was built for Brutus Clay in 1837 and Bucknore for Walker Buckner several years later. It is

Fig. 9.29 Hall arch in Bucknore (1841), Bourbon County. Photo, 1941.

claimed Bucknore took seven years to build and the keystone over the arched front doorway bears the inscription "W. Buckner 1841." Both houses have gabled roofs, like Grassland, both have twenty-four-paned windows upstairs and twenty-eight-paned windows (sixteen over twelve) below, and both have wings.[23] The completion of Bucknore in the Greek Revival period explains the sliding doors flanked by Ionic columns between the parlors, and the arch in the stair hall supported on Greek Doric columns set on plinths (fig. 9.29). Chair railings common to a Federal house are omitted, and baseboards are increased to twice normal height for a Federal house.

KENNEDY DESIGN FOR TRANSYLVANIA UNIVERSITY. Even though the design was not executed, a rendering by Matthew Kennedy for the Main Building of Transylvania University, mentioned earlier, was among the more important of Kentucky Federal architecture, due to the influence it exerted on later buildings. It is one of two schemes in existence for the project making use of a colossal portico. The other consists solely of an elevation drawing in ink and watercolor, and the building it proposes flaunts a portico of four Roman Doric columns rising three stories (fig. 9.30). An oversized Palladian window in the center suggests the location of a two-story chapel between two entrance halls. An open bell tower accompanies irregularly spaced chimneys atop the long ridge of the roof. The drawing of the portico is not badly executed, but the disharmony between parts elsewhere indicates that the unknown delineator was not a professional.

The more significant proposal is signed and dated, "Matthew Kennedy 18 April 1816," and it includes both an elevation and plan. Like the preceding, it has pale red washes, indicating brickwork, but it differs in that in the best English tradition it leaves the doors and windows blank. The elevation is dominated by a wide pedimented pavilion, whose first story is given a basement treatment, and the second and third stories are united by two pilasters and four engaged columns, the latter set on advanced end sections containing arched doorways (fig. 9.31). As in the other scheme, the roof is an extended form with gables at the ends. The accompanying plan has been described as applying to the Georgian-type edifice that was built. On 29 April the trustees resolved that the design "be adopted with such alterations as the building committee shall think proper in regard to the internal accommodations of the house," which seems to have amounted mostly to the inclusion of a

Fig. 9.30 Ink-and-watercolor elevation rendering for a college building with a tall portico. Architect unknown. Courtesy of Transylvania University Library.

cellar, the windows of which are shown on the engraved sketch of the completed building (fig. 7.14). The characteristic elements of the classic design, although rejected by Transylvania, figured in Kennedy's own home and the various other domestic buildings resembling it, and ironically, some surfaced again in another building Matthew Kennedy designed, built by the university a decade later.

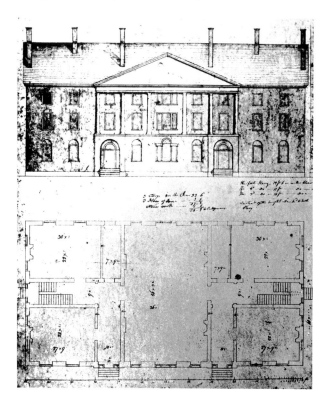

Fig. 9.31 Ink-and-water color elevation and first-floor plan for a Transylvania University building by Matthew Kennedy, 1816. Courtesy of Transylvania University Library.

THE TRANSYLVANIA UNIVERSITY MEDICAL HALL (1827). At the time of the consolidation of Transylvania Seminary and Kentucky Academy in 1799, Dr. Samuel Brown was named to the chair of chemistry and surgery. He taught in the old academy building, but by 1804, as the course of instruction grew and was divided among several professors, an effort had been started to produce a separate building for the medical department. Nothing happened until 1822, when the Kentucky General Assembly empowered a committee to raise by lottery a sum "not exceeding twenty-five thousand dollars, to be appropriated in the erection of a medical college . . . for the use and benefit of the Professors in the medical department of Transylvania University."[24] A design for the proposed building by Matthew Kennedy was adopted by the faculty on 23 January 1823, and Drs. Samuel Brown and B.W. Dudley were appointed to "confer with the citizens of the town for a suitable lot of ground to erect the building on."[25] The site selected was at the northwest corner of Market and Church streets in Lexington, extending toward Mill Street. The cornerstone was not laid until 16 April 1827.[26] The building was virtually completed when the school session opened on the first of November, although the anatomical amphitheater was not constructed until the following year (fig. 9.32). The facade of the main pavilion was a near-facsimile of the middle section of Kennedy's own home, three blocks away, and the flanks included pilasters, wide windows, lunettes, and blind arches. The second section, which looked like a row house, continued the form of the first, and the third was a small extension. At the end was the square anatomical amphitheater, with a cupola rising from the hipped roof. Accommodations of the group included a chemistry "lecture-room, forty five by fifty feet . . . a lobby, an anti-room, a chemical laboratory well supplied with all necessary apparatus, and a dormitory for a resident pupil who acts as librarian." The floor above contained "another spacious Lecture Room, fifty feet square; an extensive library room, fifty feet by twenty-five; janitor's apartment &c." A museum was installed later in a 75-by-20-foot gallery.[27]

After Transylvania acquired a new medical hall in 1839 (chapter 10), Kennedy's building housed a city hall (damaged by fire in 1854), a Methodist church, a public library, and a YMCA. It was razed in 1954.

LOUISVILLE MARINE HOSPITAL. This structure surpassed either of the Transylvania classic endeavors by having on one side two superimposed colossal

Fig. 9.32 The Transylvania University Medical Hall (1827), Lexington. Engraved view on a matriculation and library ticket. Courtesy of Transylvania University Library.

orders, each of two stories. The movement to build a hospital, "to take care of those engaged in navigating the Ohio and Mississippi Rivers who owing to fatigue and exposure incident to long voyages become sick and languish at the port of Louisville," was launched as a town project in 1817. The eleven incorporators were authorized to raise a sum not to exceed $50,000 for the hospital, which was to be supported by a 2 percent levy on auction sales in Jefferson County.[28] The building was begun on a five-acre lot between Walnut and Chestnut streets, west of Preston Street, which at that time was on the outskirts of the community. The project was delayed, and in 1822 the Kentucky legislature stepped in and offered assistance. A report made to the governing body at Frankfort on 8 November 1824 stated that the grounds were enclosed by a post-and-rail fence, the shell of the building was up, the windows glazed, but only four rooms in the basement were plastered and ready to have the doors hung, the remainder of the interior, including the staircase, being in need of considerable work. It was estimated that upward of $15,000 was needed to finish and furnish the Louisville hospital.[29]

The Marine Hospital was composed of a main block of three stories, with two-story wings on a high (two-story) basement at the back. The Chestnut Street facade was illustrated in *Ballou's Pictorial* in 1856. The Walnut Street front was depicted on a Staffordshire dinner plate of about 1825 (fig. 9.33).[30] The first shows a long flight of steps before an arched entrance with fanlight and sidelights, centered in the

five-bayed main pavilion, capped by an entablature and pediment. Attached wings contain recessed galleries supported by square piers rising from ground level, though the outermost, or fourth bays were enclosed. The Staffordshire view shows an applied arcade, embracing two stories, supporting an applied colonnade of equal height rising to an entablature with triglyphs, and with a pediment capping the main pavilion. Wings on this side are unadorned except for a cornice.

The Legislature Report of 1824 stated that the "Center Building" measured 61 feet across the front and was 50 feet deep. A foreign visitor to Louisville in 1826 related: "In the basement of the center building are the kitchen, the wash-house, the store-rooms, etc., and in the upper story the chamber for the meeting of the Directors, the apothecary's room, the steward's dwelling, and the state rooms for patients paying board and lodging. In the third story a theatre for surgical operations will be arranged." The wings accommodated "roomy and well aired apartments for the white patients, and in the basement, those for the negroes." In addition to having noted that the top floor of the main block was incomplete, he remarked: "There have been until now only one apartment habitable, in which twelve patients are lying. These have cleanly beds, but only wooden bedsteads." He estimated that when the hospital was properly outfitted,

Fig. 9.33 Louisville Marine Hospital (1817-24), depicted on a blue Staffordshire plate by Enoch Wood and Sons.

it could care for "at least one hundred and fifty persons with comfort."[31]

The Louisville Marine Hospital can be linked to a similar building in Philadelphia—the Pennsylvania Hospital, a three-unit composition designed in 1755 by Samuel Rhoads. The east wing, built on Pine above Eighth Street, was the earliest institution of its kind in this country. The center pavilion, redesigned in the classic Adam style by David Evans II and built between 1794 and 1805, may have been the model for the Louisville infirmary. It has five bays and three stories, the first of which is arcaded; the second and third levels are joined by Corinthian pilasters, and there is a pediment above, restricted to the three center bays.[32] The Kentucky edifice was enlarged in 1869 and was razed and replaced by the Louisville General Hospital in 1912-14.

THE SECOND STATEHOUSE. The first Kentucky statehouse of 1793-94 (chapter 3) burned in 1813, and its successor, which occupied the same location, was built from a plan by Matthew Kennedy in 1814-16.[33] It measured 100 by 62 (or 65) feet and contained two full stories and what was described as an attic. The first floor was divided by a wide hall and included court and committee rooms. Both houses of the General Assembly occupied the second floor. As later, in the Lexington courthouse, offices were relegated to dependencies, those of the treasurer and auditor in

Fig. 9.34 The second Kentucky State House (1814-16), Frankfort. After a sketch by Gideon Shryock in Richard H. Collins, *History of Kentucky* (Covington, 1874), facing p. 246.

the west, and those of the secretary of state and the land office in the east annex. The cost of the statehouse was $40,000, of which about half was contributed by individual subscriptions, the balance appropriated by the commonwealth.[34] The architectural innovation of the second capitol apparently was its colossal-order portico, whose columns rose two stories, the deep entablature either masking or precluding fenestration in the third story (fig. 9.34). Slightly less remarkable was the pilastered cupola with superimposed lantern or open pavilion rising from the roof. The illustration shown, however, contains an element of conjecture, having been engraved from a drawing made by Gideon Shryock some years after the building was destroyed.[35] Some elements look as though they belong more to the third than to the first quarter of the nineteenth century.

Although it was supposed to have been fireproof, the building was consumed by flames on 4 November 1824. The east dependency burned in 1865, and the west annex was demolished in 1912. Surviving from the main building are half sections of several stone column bases used as mounting blocks in front of residences at 401, 403, and 415 West Main Street in Frankfort.[36]

SAINT JOSEPH'S CATHEDRAL. Bardstown, known as Salem until incorporated in 1788, is one of the older towns in Kentucky and maintains much of its early identity. When the Roman Catholic church, whose early foothold among English-speaking people in the United States had been at Baltimore, created four new episcopal sees in 1808, Bardstown accompanied those at Philadelphia, New York, and Boston. The Rev. Benedict Joseph Flaget was named bishop, and he undertook to erect a suitable cathedral in his wilderness precinct. A small building, Saint Thomas, was built several miles out of town to serve the purpose temporarily (chapter 11), and the principal edifice in Bardstown rose simultaneously with the second phase of Benjamin Henry Latrobe's Baltimore cathedral that had been under way during 1808-12 and then abandoned for five years.[37] The cornerstone of the building at Bardstown was laid by Bishop Flaget on 16 July 1816, and Saint Joseph's Cathedral was dedicated on 8 August 1819. The only completed Roman Catholic cathedral in the United States at that time was Saint Louis Cathedral in New Orleans, dating from 1794. The Cathedral of the Assumption in Baltimore was not finished until 1821.

The architect John Rogers undoubtedly watched Latrobe's building in Baltimore progress until work was halted by the War of 1812. That edifice exerted some influence on the design of the Kentucky building, in its arches and low vaults inside (it had a cruciform plan with a dome at the crossing) and in its red-brick exterior, with stone panels above arched windows, a full entablature all around, and an impressive hexastyle portico in front. Of course not all these features had materialized before Rogers left Baltimore, but he may have observed their forms on the plans or seen them on subsequent visits. The simplified order of the Baltimore portico was that of the Tower of the Winds in Athens, dating from the first century B.C. Rogers's portico was to have Roman Ionic columns, but the order of the Tower of the Winds was used in the nave. It constituted the first notable appearance of a Greek architectural motif in Kentucky and previewed the Greek Revival style.

As initially completed, Saint Joseph's Cathedral bears affinities to Saint Thomas's Church in Nelson County, and by extension to the chapel of Saint Mary's Seminary in Baltimore (chap. 11). Saint Joseph's is twice the size of Saint Thomas's, and it has small flanking offices on the front plane like the chapel. The great difference is that Saint Joseph's is classical like Latrobe's cathedral rather than Gothic.

Its facade is pierced by round arched doorways, a single window above, and niches—here containing statuary. The building was a basilica plan with arches separating the barrel-vaulted nave from side aisles, and an apsidal end, like Saint Thomas's; but in addition it has a square entrance hall in back of the center front door, with twin stairways to the balcony over the western end of the church (fig. 9.35). The interior is wide and spacious (fig. 9.36).

The nine much publicized paintings in the church were given to Bishop Flaget by Louis Phillippe, duke of Orleans. Bills introduced in Congress during 1824 and 1832 applied for exemption from duties on "certain paintings and church furniture presented by the then Duke of Orleans, now King of the French, to the Bishop of Bardstown." The gifts stemmed from gratitude for care received by the exiled donor in Kentucky and for monetary assistance toward his return passage to France in 1800. The paintings were cut from their frames on 12 November 1952, but they were recovered in New York and Chicago by the Federal Bureau of Investigation. During the subsequent trial it was established that one of the pictures—the "Flaying of Saint Bartholomew," formerly attributed to Rubens—was a lost work by the seven-

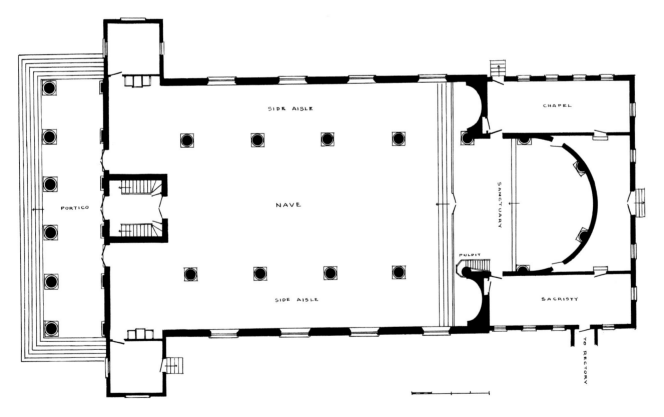

Fig. 9.35 Floor plan of Saint Joseph's Cathedral (1816-19), Bardstown.

Fig. 9.36 Interior of Saint Joseph's Cathedral. Photo, 1934, courtesy of the Library of Congress.

teenth-century Italian painter, Marria Preta, and the only one of worth.[38]

The tower of Saint Joseph's rises above the square stair hall at the front and is practically a duplicate of that atop the 1806 Fayette County Courthouse in Lexington. The colossal-order Ionic hexastyle portico was not on the cathedral at the time of its dedication. The cornerstone, marked only by a cross, was discovered in 1989 embedded in the basement masonry under the portico floor. Finished stonework indicates that the original steps spanned only the three doorways. The steps were eliminated by the portico, which was added at an early date. The portico also obscured a pediment flush with the facade (fig. 9.37). The present entablature is quite heavy, in this regard being more Greek Revival than Federal. Its inclusion was necessitated by the building of a second or upper roof incorporating the side parapets.

Saint Joseph's served as a cathedral through the 1830s, after which Bishop Flaget transferred the epis-

copal see to Louisville, first using the old church of Saint Louis and later building the Cathedral of the Assumption (chap. 11). The interior of Saint Joseph's was redecorated during the mid-1980s. The elaborate architectural designs on the vault were eliminated and the columns regrained with some gilding. The basic color throughout is a soft, warm gray, which with the blue stained glass in the windows creates a serene effect.

Within the sphere of Federal architecture are the most original, diversified, unique, tasteful, appealing, substantial, and beautifully detailed examples of Kentucky buildings. It was the period when refinement hit its stride—that happy moment between virile pioneering and secure sophistication, when the one still lingered and the other already had put in an appearance, and so both were present to complement and compliment one another. Aesthetic luxuries from longer-established communities to the eastward and south were brought in to enhance and serve as models for local production, and enterprising craftsmen found a ready market for their skills and trades. Inland Kentucky was eager to attain seaboard standards, and it did so in accordance with its own understanding and abilities. Exact copying would have been redundant, whereas those results stamped with the indigenous imprint are the more interesting, important, and worthy of our attention. The three types of Federal architecture—Georgian, geometric, and classic—each contributed notable examples to our heritage. Georgian-style Liberty Hall, for instance, built within only a few years of the natives' giving up their hold on Kentucky, could not have achieved the refinement it did without being influenced by the architectural development along the Atlantic seaboard. The Federal geometric phase fostered stylistic elegance in houses noteworthy for their unusual and fine arrangements (the Hunt House, Ridgeway, and Rose Hill), grandeur of conception (the Morton House, Ridgeway, and Elmwood Hall), and remarkable room shapes (the Pope House, Plancentia, and Woodlands; and the Georgian Ashland and classic Farmington). Striking facades are to be found mostly in the classic phase (Mount Airy, Warner Cottage, White Cottage, Pleasant Lawn, and the Gano House), extending to larger houses without freestanding porticoes (the Kennedy-House type). These buildings constitute the undisputed gems of Kentucky's domestic architecture. In addition to indicating the broad latitude of

Fig. 9.37 Saint Joseph's Cathedral. Photo, 1973.

family life through the rich legacy of residences, Federal architecture symbolized and provided for marked advancements in public life, in its notable government buildings, churches, colleges, and hospitals. Magnitude permitted these edifices a monumentality not possible in domestic works, and this ideal was seized upon and further explored and exploited during the ensuing period.

PART THREE

PARTICIPATION
IN THE POPULAR
REVIVAL STYLES

10 THE GREEK REVIVAL STYLE

THE GREEK REVIVAL style of architecture was classical insofar as it was based upon and furthered the most salient traits of the Federal style it supplanted. It was also romantic in that it burst upon the American scene in one specific building, rather than growing gradually out of its predecessor as the Federal had from the colonial Georgian. However, the Greek Revival style was in no measure as romantic as the contemporary Gothic Revival or the exotic styles that had practically nothing to do with what had gone before. Although Greek Revival architecture continued to use some Roman forms and a sprinkling of Egyptian elements, primarily it employed (as its name implied) Greek orders and Greek motifs. The mode adhered to the trabeated system, to the rectangular void in walls, although, upon occasion, as with the first Greek Revival building in the United States and the first in Kentucky, it resorted to round-headed openings and vaulted and domed interiors in public buildings. Otherwise, arched doorways and fan and Palladian windows became obsolete, along with the delicate carving that gave them grace and lightness. The Greek Revival was massive and heavy. It was masculine, as the Federal was feminine. The Greek Revival building acquired monumentality. The colossal-order portico came into its own on residences and public buildings alike. The entrance doorway often was recessed and glorified by columns of correct proportions, appropriate pilasters, and heavy entablatures. Windows became larger, often lowered to the floor or widened into three lights.

Greek Revival architecture took advantage of technical advances of the day. Its details were produced by steam-powered machinery rather than by hand carving, by iron casting rather than by hand forging, and by standardized molds rather than by hand modeling. Embellishments were designed by the architect and became more integral with the architectonic whole than when entrusted to the taste of the specialized carver, whitesmith, or plasterer. Inside doors frequently had wide enframements with "Greek ears" at the top of slightly battered sides. Mantels were in either columned-pilastered or eared forms, and often were of black, white, or mottled marble. Sometimes, deep entablatures encircled the rooms, connected to pilasters flanking windows and to great sliding doors between parlors, usually with columns set to either side in antis. Recessed in the ceiling was a round or rectangular centerpiece, from which hung the crystal or metal chandelier.

The architectural theme of the outer building infused itself through the interior. The objectives were bigness, spaciousness, graciousness, security, and consistency. Appropriate changes occurred in the furniture too, which became more bulky, and architectural orders were adapted for its elements. Although its inception was at the end of the eighteenth century, Greek Revival did not become the prevailing architectural fashion in the eastern United States until the 1830s, and a decade later in Kentucky. It struck a responsive chord in the New World inasmuch as the ancient Greeks maintained the freedom of independent city-states, and the modern Greeks rebelled (1821-27) against (Turkish) tyranny as had the American colonies half a century earlier. The Greek Revival was the national style until building operations were brought to a standstill by the outbreak of the Civil War.

The first monument in the Greek manner during

modern times was the garden temple built for Lord Lyttelton at Hagley, England, in 1758.[1] This was an ornamental or incidental building, not a serious piece of architecture, indicative of the British adherence to Palladian and Adam modes precluding much patronage of the Greek. The architect of the Hagley pavilion was James Stuart, who had conducted extensive archaeological investigation in the Aegean area during the middle of the eighteenth century. He and Nicholas Revett published four volumes of measured drawings, *The Antiquities of Athens*, between 1762 and 1818, with a supplement in 1830. These publications would provide authentic sources for architects on both sides of the Atlantic. Among the British influenced by the Greeks was Samuel Pepys Cockerell, under whom Benjamin Henry Latrobe (1764-1820) worked before opening his own office in London in 1791. That Latrobe was attuned to the dramatic power inherent in the Greek Revival is evident in two houses he designed within the next few years, Ashdown House and Hammerwood Lodge.[2] He was not long to practice in England, however. The building lag in the British Isles during the mid-1790s, the untimely death of his wife, his inheritance of his mother's lands in Pennsylvania, and the prospects of a promising career brought him to America in 1796.

After a sojourn in Norfolk, Latrobe proceeded to Philadelphia, where he conceived and built the first building of Greek Revival design in America, the Bank of Pennsylvania, begun in 1798 and completed during the summer of 1800. It was amphiprostyle, with a cubic center block, the walls pierced by a minimum of windows. The interior was dominated by a domed circular banking room lighted by a cupola.[3] The high basement with steps only at the ends was Roman, the columns styled after the order of the Ilissus were Greek. The blank pediments and friezes and the simplicity elsewhere were the taste of the architect. These features were to play an important role in the Greek Revival movement in America. Other Latrobe endeavors have been mentioned, and it is sufficient to recall that in his work on the nation's Capitol he created the corn order for the Senate vestibule, and the tobacco leaf order for the Senate rotunda.[4]

Latrobe's influence was spread by his own works and those of architects he employed and trained in his office. The most important were William Strickland (1787-1854), who came to Latrobe at fourteen and remained four years, and Robert Mills (1781-1855), who entered the office at twenty-one and

stayed seven years. Strickland was willful and lacking in responsibility, whereas Mills was steadfast; but Latrobe was fonder of Strickland and considered him the more brilliant.[5] His indirect contribution to Kentucky architecture will be discussed below.

The architects and designers whose works had a profound influence upon Greek Revival architecture in Kentucky were the compilers of builders' guides. Like earlier books of their kind they primarily furnished models for details. The first to offer the Greek orders was John Haviland's *The Builder's Assistant*, published at Philadelphia in three volumes from 1818 to 1821. Foliated rosettes (vol. 1, pl. 24) seem to have provided models for the plaster motifs (fig. 10.1) in the coffered ceiling of the senate chamber of the old statehouse (1827-30) at Frankfort. A design for a mantel (vol. 1, pl. 23) has pilasters with sunken panels in the shafts, enriched with anthemion reliefs at either extremity of the panels, which set the style for pilasters on a number of Kentucky doorways, such as that of the McCann House on Richmond Pike and Waveland on Higbee Mill Road in Fayette County (fig. 10.2). This feature reappeared in Asher Benjamin's *Practice of Architecture* (pl. 29) and Minard Lafever's *The Modern Builder's Guide* (pl. 87), both

Fig. 10.1 Detail of ceiling in the senate chamber, third Kentucky State House. Frankfort. Photo, 1940.

Fig. 10.2 Frontispiece of Waveland, Fayette County. Photo, 1941.

printed in New York in 1833. Meanwhile, the sixth enlarged edition of Asher Benjamin's second book of 1806, *The American Builder's Companion* (Boston, 1827), also presented examples of "Grecian architecture," although limited to the Doric of the Parthenon and Ionic of the Temple of the Ilissus, and a comparison of the Greek and Roman Doric. The principal sources of Greek designs published during the next two decades were in books by Benjamin and Lafever and those of Edward Shaw, William Brown, and Chester Hills.

A typical adaptation by a Kentucky builder of a printed design is that of plate 28 in Asher Benjamin's *Practical House Carpenter* (Boston, 1830) for the front doorway of Warwick, a residence constructed about 1850 in Danville (figs. 10.3, 10.4). The entablature and antas were virtually the same as Benjamin's version with the exception that the raised meander at the bottom of the anta panels had been omitted and the height of the plinth reduced. The parapet block and door paneling in Warwick had been simplified. Important elements in the Danville doorway not in the Benjamin design were Doric columns between the doors and sidelights.

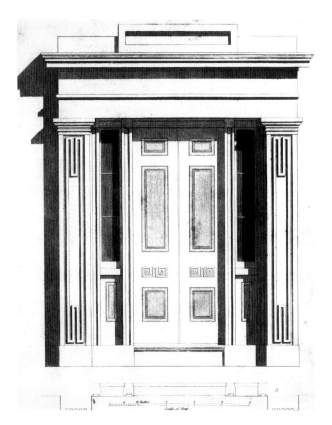

Fig. 10.3 "Design for Front Door Case." From Asher Benjamin, *Practical House Carpenter* (Boston, 1830), pl. 28.

Fig. 10.4 Front doorway of Warwick, Danville. Photo, 1941.

Edward Shaw's *Civil Architecture* (Boston, 1836), contributed further motifs to Kentucky architecture. Plate 37, for instance, delineating details of the Parthenon, served as source for the order of the Craig House on Cane Run Road near Georgetown (figs. 10.5, 10.6). Plate 78 is a design for a front entrance with Ionic columns in antis supporting a flat architrave stepping up in the center, with a sunken fillet whorled in angular key motifs at either end, directly above the columns (fig. 10.7). It was adapted for the frontispiece of The Elms, a large McMurtry-designed house that stood on the Harrodsburg Pike a mile south of Lexington (fig. 10.8). All the elements of the Shaw design were included, but they varied in proportions, and the recess was more shallow. Dual-leaf doors replaced Shaw's single door, sidelights continued up to lintel level, and the columns were more slender and without fluting. A copy of *Civil Architecture* was owned by the architect Thomas Lewinski, with whom McMurtry was associated on several projects.[6]

The books exerting the greatest influence upon Greek Revival architecture in America, and especially in Kentucky, were by Minard Lafever (1797-1854), whose five titles went into fourteen or

Fig. 10.6 Portico detail of the William G. Craig House, Scott County. Photo, 1946.

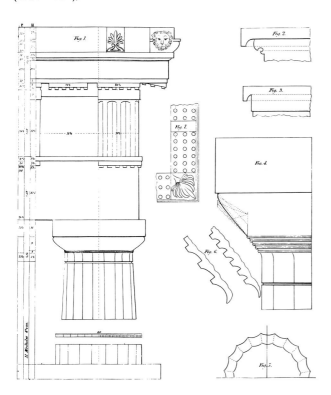

Fig. 10.5 The order of the Parthenon. From Edward Shaw, *Civil Architecture* (Boston, 1836), pl. 37.

more editions between the release of his first, *The Young Builder's General Instructor* (Newark, N.J., 1829), and the last, *The Architectural Instructor* (New York, 1856), published posthumously. Lafever, being "practically experienced in Architecture and House-Building business," understood and appreciated the problems and aspirations of his confreres, and to them he addressed his text and illustrations. *The Young Builder's General Instructor* has plates modeled after British guides of the eighteenth century, depicting alternate versions of each item. Plate 46 shows four mantel designs, one of which has the shelf supported on impost blocks set on Doric columns resting on cubic bases (fig. 10.9). A chimneypiece in the William Y. Davis House at Bloomfield appears to have been derived from the Lafever plate (fig. 10.10). The Davis mantel is simpler, omitting the panels on the frieze and substituting vertical moldings in the imposts, a treatment borrowed from the left-hand half of the plate. The column has a deeper echinus,

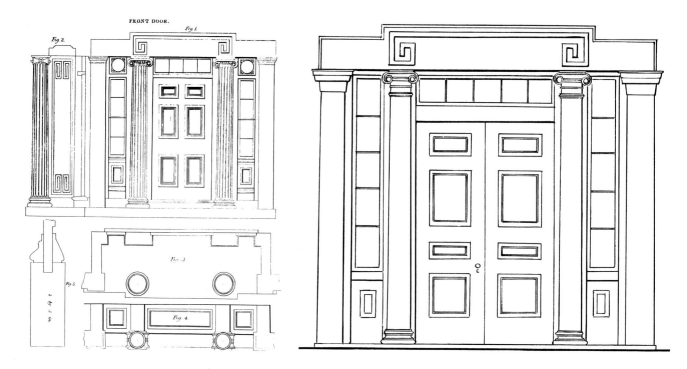

Figs. 10.7, 10.8 Design for a front doorway. From Edward Shaw, *Civil Architecture* (Boston, 1836), pl. 78. Diagram of frontispiece of The Elms, Fayette County.

fewer channels to the shaft, and the double plinth of the lefthand (Ionic) Lafever support. The cast-iron arch, diminishing the fireplace for the use of coal, is a subsequent alteration.

Lafever's second book, *The Modern Builder's Guide*, issued four years later, contains designs far superior to those of the first. Not all are by Lafever himself. A

front doorway, plate 63, is by James H. Dakin, the New York and New Orleans architect who designed the Bank of Louisville. The frieze pattern (fig. 10.11) is inspired by the north doorway of the Erechtheum and is separated from the plain architrave by a fillet, below which hangs a row of guttae. The entablature is supported by a pair of straight antas with simple

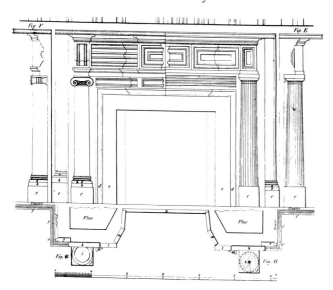

Fig. 10.9 Designs for mantels. From Minard Lafever, *The Young Builder's General Instructor* (Newark, N. J., 1829), pl. 46, figs. F-H.

Fig. 10.10 Parlor mantel in the William Y. Davis House, Bloomfield. Photo, 1941.

bases and egg-and-dart-enriched echini. This enframement, somewhat widened to accommodate dual-leaf doors, appears on the entrance to Rosehill in Richmond (fig. 10.12). The cornice cymatium is articulated after the manner of the anta capitals. Dakin's scrolled grille in the transom and Corinthian pilasters, however, have been ignored at Rosehill in favor of simpler treatment.[7] The recessed portico somewhat resembles plate 81, a doorway of corresponding members, although taller proportions. This plate also may have suggested the front door of the Hamilton Headley House, a late Greek example which stood on Tates Creek Road near Lexington (fig. 10.123). Plate 82 is the obvious model for interior doors at Glenwood, near Burgin in Mercer County (figs. 10.13, 10.14).

Lafever's third and most influential volume, *The Beauties of Modern Architecture* (New York, 1835) contains his own most highly evolved designs, including

one for a ceiling centerpiece which was the prototype for many in sophisticated Greek Revival houses in Kentucky. It is a radial device to support a chandelier composed of petals and tongues, egg forms, anthemions, and rosettes—an original and appropriate adaptation of traditional motifs to a new usage (fig. 10.15). The centerpiece was mass-produced in plaster castings and assembled with slight variations. Persian rosettes to the centerpiece in the stair hall of Rosehill somewhat resemble American sunflowers, (fig. 10.16). The outermost flowers are omitted from examples in the Ward and Craig houses near Georgetown, where the centerpieces are set in circular recessed panels (fig. 10.88).

A stunning doorway between parlors is delineated in plate 25 and detailed in plate 26 of *The Beauties of Modern Architecture* (fig. 10.17). Two recessed Ionic columns flank double doors that slide into the wall, and above them is a frieze of anthemion reliefs sim-

Figs. 10.11, 10.12 Design for a front doorway by James H. Dakin. From Minard Lafever, *The Modern Builder's Guide* (New York, 1833), pl. 63. Frontispiece of Rosehill, Richmond. Photo, 1941.

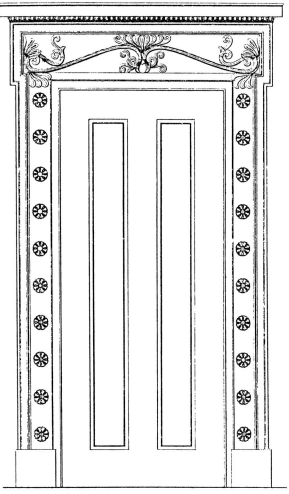

Figs. 10.13, 10.14 Design for a parlor door. From Minard Lafever, *The Modern Builder's Guide* (New York, 1833), pl. 82. Hall doorway to parlor, Glenwood, Mercer County. Photo, 1982.

Figs. 10.15, 10.16 Centerpiece design. From Minard Lafever, *The Beauties of Modern Architecture* (New York, 1835), pl. 21. Stair-hall ceiling in Rosehill. Photo, 1941.

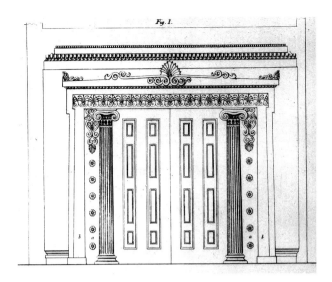

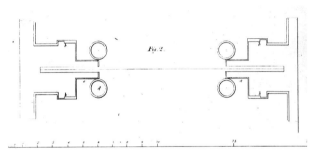

Fig. 10.17 "Sliding Door Design." From Minard Lafever, *The Beauties of Modern Architecture* (New York, 1835), pl. 25.

Fig. 10.18 Front doorway of Diamond Point, Harrodsburg. Photo, 1960.

ilar to that in plate 63 of the *Builder's Guide*. Plain jambs at either side have Greek ears at the top, and the enframement is crowned by an elongated whorled cresting with shell-like central motif, and antefixes at the outer corners. Lafever spoke of the design as "original in its features," and "classed with the richest compositions of the present style of finishing." It was adapted to the outside entrance of Diamond Point (after 1840) in Harrodsburg at the junction of Price Avenue and College Street (fig. 10.18). The columns have become Doric and are set closer together in response to the use of sidelights. Pendant reliefs, placed behind the columns in the Lafever scheme, are applied in abbreviated form to the enframement, and the anthemion frieze is somewhat adjusted. The egg-and-dart molding below the crowning member has been eliminated, and the points of the central shell are rounded. This cresting bears more affinities to the details given in Lafever's plate 26 than in the preceding plate.

Minard Lafever invented an eclectic Corinthian order shown in plate 11 of his *Beauties of Modern Architecture*. It is quite normal up to the capital, which is composed of a row of petals, a row of acanthus leaves studded with rosettes, and a campaniform top that curls outward and down, forming an edge of gadrooning, on which the abacus rests (fig. 10.19). It seems partly Egyptian lotus and partly the order of the Tower of the Winds at Athens, and not unlike a capital found at Delphi in the monastery of the Panaghia, included in James Stuart and Nicholas Revett's supplement to *The Antiquities of Athens*.[8] Columns of this form were used in the recessed entrance to the Philip Swigert House (1845) on Wapping Street in Frankfort, a large and gracious residence with an open gallery of two stories at the rear overlooking terraced gardens descending to the Kentucky River. Every detail of the capital was carried out except for the enrichment on the abacus (fig. 10.20). The entablature was derived from plate 12 in the Lafever book. It had an unusually tall cymatium, and a blocking course was added for good measure. The antas were similar to those of plate 63 in *The Modern Builder's Guide*, though without the echinus articulation (fig. 10.11). The house was razed in 1955.

Aside from the isolated use of Greek columns in the nave of the Bardstown cathedral (1816-19), repeated in miniature in the mantels of Wickland, and presumably in the Doric columns of Latrobe's Pope House portico, the responsibility for implanting the Greek mode in Kentucky rests with a young native,

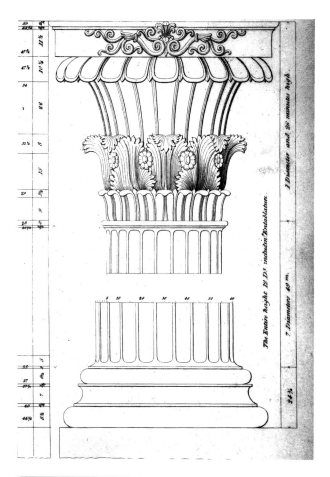

Figs. 10.19, 10.20 An original Corinthian order. From Minard Lafever, *The Beauties of Modern Architecture* (New York, 1835), pl. 11. Portal of the Philip Swigert House, Frankfort. Photo, 1940.

Gideon Shryock (1802-80). One of eleven children of builder Mathias Shryock, Gideon's early education was acquired at Mr. Aldridge's Lancastrian Academy for Boys in Lexington, after which he served as an apprentice to his father. At twenty-one he went to Philadelphia for a year to work and study architecture under William Strickland. On 21 October 1823, Shryock wrote home: "I have seen Mr. Strickland and he says he will do everything in his power to instruct me. I am to go with him tomorrow to look at some of the public buildings in the city and then he will let me know what I had better do."[9] Strickland already had to his credit an admirable list of edifices, including churches, institutions, government buildings, a theater, and banks.[10] The only one which had a marked bearing upon Shryock's later work was the Parthenon-like Second Bank of the United States. While in Philadelphia, Gideon obtained a copy of the American edition (1775) of Swan's *British Architect* and inscribed it. It is now in the Special Collections of the University of Kentucky Library. Early in 1824, he wrote his parents that he hoped to visit Baltimore and Washington on his return to Kentucky, but whether he got to see these seaboard centers and examine their architecture is not known. His first work in Kentucky, however, is well known.

THE THIRD STATE HOUSE. As Shryock was establishing his practice in Lexington, the second statehouse at Frankfort burned on 4 November 1824. Despite the urgency for replacement, the bill for a new capitol was not passed until 20 December 1826.[11] A design competition was advertised with a premium of $150 to the winner and the selection date was set for 20 February 1827. The specifications stated that the building should be "100 by 62 feet, (the dimensions of the old building) or disregarding that boundary, not exceeding 120 by 70 feet. The building to contain a Senate and Representatives' Chamber, with Lobbies and Galleries attached to each; two Court Rooms, one of which with Jury Rooms attached thereto; and two or more Committee Rooms." It was to be as "nearly *fire-proof* as practicable," and cost estimates and working drawings were expected to accompany plans submitted.[12] Despite his youth and inexperience, Shryock won.

Upon receiving the commission, Shryock moved to Frankfort and there in 1829 he married Elizabeth P. Bacon. Of their ten children, only one, Charles, followed his father's calling.

Dr. Theodore Bell, Shryock's intimate friend from childhood, would later remark "even competitors yielded the pre-eminent palm to . . . [his] plans." Dr. Bell, however, lamented that unfortunately Shryock "was saddled with that great incubus on such work—a building committee. But for that Kentucky would have one of the most tasteful and beautiful State Houses in the West."[13] One wonders what the limitations were that Dr. Bell had in mind. The cupola is a simple cylinder pierced by windows in plan, less attractive than the column-encircled version realized. The building reflects the strength, simplicity, and fine proportions indicated on Shryock's elevation rendering preserved at the Kentucky Historical Society. It has a remarkable clarity of layout.

Shryock's plans took advantage of the greater dimensions allowed by the specifications, exclusive of the portico. The two-story building is of prostyle form, the columns silhouetted against a plain wall with a single entrance such as is proper to Greek temples (fig. 10.21). Shortly after the building was opened, a description appeared in *Atkinson's Casket*, "furnished by Mr. Gideon Shryock, the accomplished architect, who planned the building and superintended its construction."[14] We are informed that the hexastyle portico was "taken from the temple of Minerva [Athena] Polias, at Priene in Ionia." Shryock's account continued:

The exterior walls present a smooth surface of polished marble of a light grey colour, obtained from inexhaustible quarries on the banks of the Kentucky River, near Frankfort. The Portico is built of a darker grey marble. The columns are four feet in diameter and thirty-three in height, supporting a marble pediment and entablature which is continued entirely around the building. The whole of the roof is covered with copper; from the middle of it rises the cupola, the basement of which is formed by a square pedestal of twenty-five feet on each side; which rises two feet above the apex of the roof; and on which is placed a lantern, twenty-two feet in diameter and twenty feet high, surmounted by a hemispherical dome. The flanks of the building have side doors to enter a passage leading across the house; and the rooms appropriate for the Federal Court and Court of Appeals.

He described the interior upon entering from the portico (fig. 10.22):

The door opens into a vestibule twenty feet broad and thirty-three feet long; having a committee room of the same size on either side, and a lobby in front leading to the stairway, which is of marble and enclosed by a circular wall, having an entrance in front and on either side, and is lighted from the Cupola above by twelve large windows. The ascent is by a straight flight of steps to a large plat-form

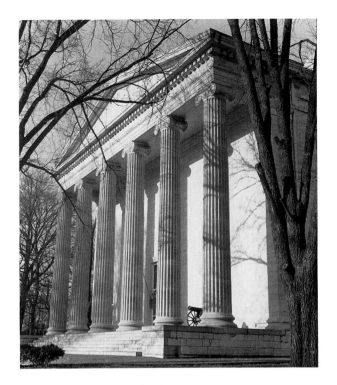

Fig. 10.21 The Kentucky State House (1827-30), Frankfort. Photo, 1940.

about five feet high; from each end of which there is a circular flight, which traverses the circular wall and meets in a platform at the top. The stairway leads to a lobby (on the second floor) thirty-five feet square, having the well-hole of the stairs (which is enclosed by an iron railing) in the centre. From this lobby there are doors communicating with the several apartments of the second story. This part of the building is arched with a spandrel dome, the angular spaces are filled with pendentives, terminating in a circular ring, on which a cylindrical wall is built, supporting the Cupola. The interior of the Dome is finished with raised pannels and ornamented with stucco, superbly executed; and produces that pleasing magic effect usual with a vast concave in such a situation.

The Senate Chamber is on the second floor in the front part of the house; being thirty-three feet broad by sixty-two feet long; having a spacious lobby with elevated seats at one end, separated from the Chamber by two Ionic columns and proper antia [antas]; supporting a full entablature; the frieze and cornice continuing entirely around the room; the ceiling richly ornamented with square sunk pannels. The floor is covered with a rich and durable carpet, made in the Penitentiary; and is occupied by the mahogany chairs and tables of the Senators.

The Representatives' Hall is in the opposite end of the second story, being forty-eight feet broad and sixty-two feet long, and having a lobby and gallery on the south side of the room. The ceiling of this room is also elegantly finished with square sunk pannels and other ornaments in

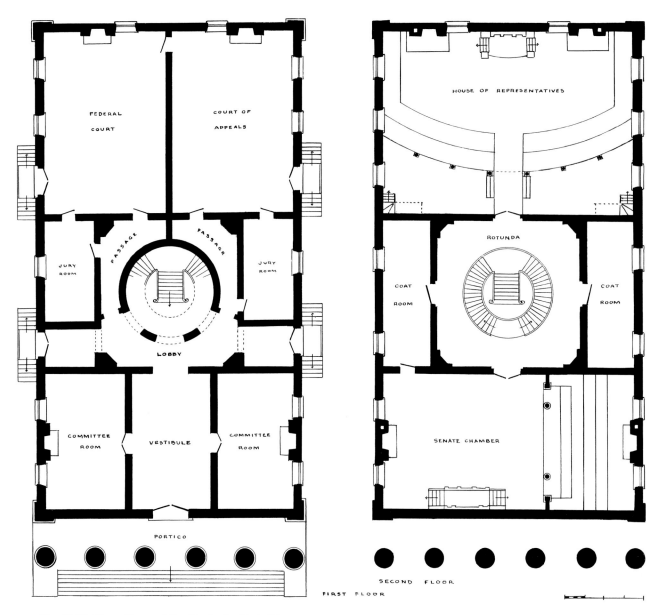

Fig. 10.22 Floor Plans of the Kentucky State House.

stucco. Behind the Speaker's chair hangs an elegant full length portrait of Lafayette, executed by Jewett [Matthew H. Jouett], at the order of the State.

The building was commenced in the spring of 1827, and finished in the fall of 1830; and cost ninety-five thousand dollars.

The old Kentucky State House has points in common with the Virginia capitol, which Jefferson had collaborated with Charles-Louis Clérisseau to design forty years earlier. The similarities include the hexastyle Ionic portico with plain pediment, antepodia enframing the front steps, the cella behind having seven-bayed flanks including side entrances, the en-

circling full entablature, and rooms distributed around a square, domed rotunda. The chief differences are that the Richmond building has a Roman portico two-bays deep, its front wall is pierced by two ranges of windows, and there are pilasters along the flanks, unlike the archetypal model sent from Paris that had pilasters only at the front corners.

The masterwork in the Kentucky State House is the stairway, which is graceful and beautiful, and a remarkable engineering feat. Gideon Shryock later visited the structure with his son Charles, then an apprentice in his father's office, and he told his son "he had worked out all the lines for the templates of each stone step when he made the original drawings of the building," and that

the lines used in working out this stairway are the same as those in the vousoirs [voussoirs] for an arch in a circular wall, the top joint at the angle of tread and riser, running below to the proper center; ten straight steps run to a platform on the rear wall of a circular rotunda, forming the springing of the arch; the circular steps run right and left around the wall of the rotunda to a landing . . . [at the front of the rotunda on the] second floor, forming the key-stone. A straight development of one flight would give one-half side of an elliptical arch.

Charles related that his father also called attention "to the third or fourth step on the right hand flight on the outer string. He said it was cracked by an accident before the false work was removed."[15] The architect reportedly commented that if the keystone shifted one-sixteenth of an inch, the entire structure would fall. It still stands, and the only perceptible flaw is the crack mentioned. The round well and the square rotunda are related by the enveloping dome (fig. 10.23). Plaster relief decorations consist of rosettes in two rows of panels beneath the cupola oculus and a stylized horn-and-acanthus motif in the triangular pendentives.

The stairway-rotunda relationship bears an affinity to New York's city hall (1803-12), by Joseph François Mangin and John McComb II, where a ring of Corinthian columns is at the brink of the stairwell supporting the dome, and a circular gallery is outside; the steps are cantilevered rather than self-supporting. The effect misses the lightness of the stairway in the Kentucky capitol. The model for the New York example was the stair hall in Wardour Castle (1768-76), Wiltshire, designed by James Paine. The rotunda in the Frankfort statehouse has the feeling of the old Dividend Office in the Bank of England (1795-1827) by Sir John Soane.[16]

Charles Shryock also furnished information about the execution of work on the Kentucky capitol. Prisoners in the state penitentiary not only made the carpeting in the senate chamber but did the quarrying and dressing of the stonework. He recalled: "A convict, an expert blacksmith, did the iron forging, the most important of which was the iron band around the spring stones of the brick arch of the dome. Other convicts worked on the building, mostly as laborers or at some ordinary mechanical work." He provided the names of several employed artisans: the stonecutters David Nevin, John

Fig. 10.23 Detail of rotunda dome over stairway, Kentucky State House. Photo, 1964.

Holburn, and Joseph Smith; and a carpentry framer, John Card.[17] Both Nevin and Holburn would work with Gideon Shryock in Louisville on the Jefferson County Courthouse.

The old State House was supplemented by the construction adjacent to it of the State Offices Building in 1869-71. Their function was taken over by the present capitol in 1910. The Shryock building became headquarters of the Kentucky Historical Society. It was named a National Historical Landmark in 1972, and in 1975 underwent extensive restoration.

Gideon Shryock was asked in 1833 to design a statehouse to be built at Little Rock, where John Pope was territorial governor of Arkansas. His drawings were delivered by George Weigart, Shryock's superintendent and pupil. In the summer of 1837, notice appeared in the *Kentucky Gazette* soliciting bricklayers, carpenters, plasterers, and other mechanics to work in Arkansas.[18] Although this building is outside the commonwealth, it is worthy of some consideration as its designer and at least some of its builders were Kentuckians. As completed in 1842 on West Markham Street, the Arkansas statehouse was modified from the Shryock scheme. The main building is a two-story prostyle form with four Doric columns. Its plan consists of a T-shaped hall separating two rooms at the front, a narrow crosswise section beyond with curved ends in which twin staircases rise in opposition, and an inversion of the T-shaped hall arrangement at the back. Two separate two-story flanking pavilions are in balance. The complex was remodeled in 1885 and was abandoned for the new statehouse in 1911.[19] The old structure became the War Memorial Building in 1921.

MORRISON COLLEGE. Transylvania University received a bequest from the estate of Col. James Morrison in 1827 to erect "an Edifice in the Town of Lexington to be called the Morrison College," and the sum was estimated "at not less than Thirty Thousand Dollars, and may reach Fifty Thousand."[20] When Transylvania University's Main Building burned on 9 May 1829, the Morrison legacy offered the means of replacing it. Soon after the fire President Woods obtained a drawing for a new building inscribed by "a Mr. Lawkins."[21] It is a tight and abbreviated line elevation for a two-story building of

seven bays with a tetrastyle Tuscan portico in the center and a domed rotunda rising above the parapet masking the roof. The elements are ill-proportioned. Windows are blank and oversized, columns are squat and weighted down by a plain entablature and steeply pitched pediment, and the drum of the dome is narrower than the portico. It was not accepted.

The commission was given to Gideon Shryock. This became his second important work in Kentucky as a result of a fire loss. His proposal of 17 February 1830 recommended alterations to a plan already submitted. The structure was to be built on or near the site of the old academy, with a porticoed center pavilion and wings whose walls were to be "rough cast or finished with plastering in imitation of stone," and it was to cost $20,000.[22] In May the site was changed to a recently acquired and larger lot above Third Street, and in June Shryock was authorized to proceed with an enlarged plan. The excavation and construction work already accomplished were to be filled in and removed.

Fig. 10.24 Morrison College (1830-34) of Transylvania University, Lexington. Photo, 1966.

The Morrison College building, planted on the summit of a low hill commanding a fine vista of Lexington, has a basement, a ground floor, an elevated first floor, and a second floor. The center pavilion is 68-feet across and features a pedimented hexastyle Doric portico with a broad flight of stone steps in front of the three middle bays, and great cubic antepodia on either side (fig. 10.24). The last were a startling innovation, appearing just after Strickland had used similar forms on the octastyle Ionic portico of the United States Naval Home, built in Philadelphia between 1827 and 1833. The channeled columns are of brick, stuccoed over like the walls. The frieze of the wooden entablature is enriched with triglyphs.[23] The main block extends back 115 feet, including the portico and steps. It contains a wide entrance foyer on the main floor, flanked by stair halls, and it originally had a chapel at the rear with balconies across the east and west sides on a level with the second story. Balanced wings, each 32 feet across and 45 feet deep, accommodating the library and classrooms of the academic and law departments, are capped by parapets masking the roof. It was a bold composition and set a precedent for simplicity in the Greek Revival movement that it inaugurated in the Bluegrass. Gideon received about $5,000 for his work on the building.[24]

Although not yet finished, Morrison College's dedication ceremony was held on 4 November 1833. That was the year of Lexington's terrible cholera epidemic, during which Gideon's father, Mathias, succumbed. A contract was let to John McMurtry and Charles A. Keiser in 1834 to complete the carpentry and painting.[25]

Toward the end of the nineteenth century, pilasters were added to the front walls of the wings, together with a new frieze and cornice all around and a new roof with gables at the ends surmounted by articulated, "Queen Anne"-style chimneys, and the windows were enlarged. In 1961 the building was restored except for retention of the enlarged windows. It burned in 1969 and again was renovated externally to its 1961 form.

THE FRANKLIN COUNTY COURTHOUSE. After his work on Morrison College, Shryock returned to Frankfort and built the Franklin County Courthouse on St. Clair Street. The plan had been adopted in June of 1832, and the building was completed in 1835.[26] Set on a terrace, it is a plain brick structure with a Doric tetrastyle portico reached by a monumental stairway (fig. 10.25). The portico has the se-

Fig. 10.25 The Franklin County Courthouse (1835), Frankfort. Photo, 1940.

verity of a Mills design. The column shafts are round and tapering, the architrave is divided into two fascia, and the frieze and pediment are without ornaments. On the truncated pyramidal roof is set a rusticated square base supporting an octagonal cupola or belfry, each face of which is pierced by a louvered opening, and at the corners eight Tuscan colonnettes sustain a circular entablature. Two sections are superimposed. Extensive remodeling of the building occurred in 1909. The back end was torn out and the building was made thirty feet deeper. The new work, in concrete, provided fireproof rooms for the county and circuit clerks' offices. The top was taken off and provisions were made for extra rooms on the second floor to house the courtroom, justices' office and sheriff's office, which were originally on the first floor. The upper windows are almost half above the level of the entablature of the portico, and small panes were replaced by a single pane to each sash. Subsequently the superstructure was modified; deeper cornices give it a pagoda look.

The Franklin County Courthouse established a pattern for this species of building erected in smaller Kentucky towns during the next two decades. Included are the Owen County Courthouse (1857-58) in Owenton, the Madison County Courthouse in Richmond (1848-50), and the Harrison County Courthouse in Cynthiana (1851-53).[27] The Maysville City Hall, later used as the courthouse for Mason County also bears some resemblance (fig. 10.38).

THE JEFFERSON COUNTY COURTHOUSE. Increased river traffic resulting from the canal opening in 1830 created a boom for Louisville, and the need arose for a good-sized building to house city offices and the courts. Consequently a joint city hall and county courthouse was proposed and a design competition ensued in 1835. Gideon Shryock's concept was selected by the city council, and he was also retained as the first city architect.[28] His plans were for an impressive building of stone, two stories on a high basement and over 200 feet long, eleven bays wide and five deep, the walls pilastered, and having four-columned porticoes on the ends and a hexastyle portico dominating the facade (fig. 10.26). The order was based on the Doric of the Temple of Poseidon on the promontory at Sunium, the remains of which had been measured by Nicholas Revett in 1765. Shryock conceived an original and dramatic approach to the main entrance. The cascade of frontal steps was broken by antepodia projecting forward from the first, second, fifth, and sixth columns, and there were two similar blocks set at right angles on the lower terrace. Steps to the side porticoes ascended laterally under those shelters. As at Morrison College, the columns were channeled and the frieze elaborated with triglyphs but without sculptured reliefs. A low parapet surmounted the cornice. On a square block rose the cylindrical cupola, with four clocks on axis in the lower drum, and the lantern similar to that of Shryock's statehouse in Frankfort.

Adversity dogged the project. The site originally proposed on Prather Square facing Walnut was finally changed to a part of the public square on Jefferson between Fifth and Sixth streets. The plans had to be modified to provide more space for city needs. Before the building reached the height of the entablature, the argilaceous limestone of which it was constructed began to decompose, and Shryock tried to seek some means for preserving it. Oiling proved unsuccessful, and later the stone was scored and stuccoed. A durable stone, however, was found on the Salt River for the entablature and portico. Problems over expenditures and the use of the building also caused prolonged delays. Shryock resigned in 1842, before the building had been completed, al-

Fig. 10.26 Shryock's original scheme for the Jefferson County Courthouse (1835), Louisville. From Lewis Collins, *Historical Sketches of Kentucky* (Cincinnati, 1847), p. [361].

though the structure was in use. In 1858 the city engaged Albert Fink and Charles Stancliff as architect and superintendent to finish the building, which they did in 1860.[29]

The building realized was a curtailment of the noble external form, yet it retained the original capacity. The superstructure and side porticoes were eliminated, and the front portico was reduced from six to four columns (fig. 10.27). On the lower floors long crosswise halls led from the rotunda to stone staircases at the extremities, rising as twin flights against the outside walls to a landing and continuing to the next level by a center flight (fig. 10.28). There were also stone stairs located in the area north of the rotunda, which later were removed and replaced by a monstrous cast-iron staircase. The ground floor is covered by vaults, and rooms more than one bay wide are divided by squat, Doric column supports. Circular walls carry the load of the rotunda and colonnade above. The rotunda portion of the first floor originally was open. Spatially, this unified the core of the building and brought daylight down into the middle of the basement. Then Albert Fink designed a metal floor closing the well, and the great round hall was finished in the prevailing Renaissance Revival

Fig. 10.27 The Jefferson County Courthouse (1835-60). From *Williamson's Annual Directory* . . . (Louisville, 1865), frontispiece.

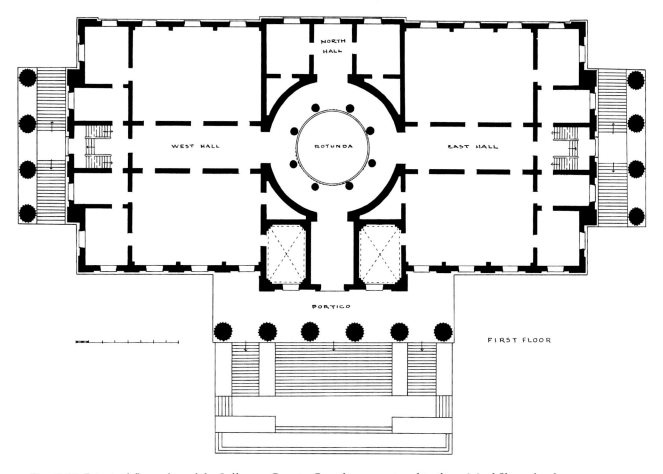

Fig. 10.28 Principal floor plan of the Jefferson County Courthouse restored to the original Shryock scheme.

manner. Its columns are Roman Ionic, with capital volutes on the diagonal rather than parallel front and back, the overhanging cornice in the upper well is supported by heavy consoles, and the second-story railing is a balustrade.

Rooms served various uses over the years. The top story, before completion, was a drill hall and arsenal for voluntary military companies. The library of the Law Department of the University of Louisville once was housed there, following its sojourn in the basement. When Gen. Kirby Smith's Confederate army occupied Frankfort in 1862, the legislators met in the west hall on the second level. But mostly, the building accommodated the mayor, city courts and councils, officers and their staffs, and county records.[30] Relief from crowding was provided in 1873 when a separate city hall opened across Sixth Street. In 1901 an annex was constructed on Court Place, and the courts were transferred to new quarters. A fiscal court building went up in the late 1930s, yet by the mid-1940s a huge office building was proposed to replace the courthouse; the project was thwarted by Prof. Justus Bier of the University of Louisville, art editor for the *Courier-Journal*, and the allies he assembled.[31] The building was completely renovated between 1977 and 1980.

THE LOUISVILLE MEDICAL INSTITUTE. As city architect, Gideon Shryock undertook to build the Louisville Medical Institute. The cornerstone was laid on 22 February 1838, and the building was ready for use in November, though not completed for several months. Facing Chestnut Street at Eighth, the center motif consisted of a steep flight of steps between antepodia rising to a projecting-recessed portico with two Ionic columns in antis, and an entablature and parapet carried around the building (fig. 10.29). The steps and columns were of stone from Madison, Indiana, and the brick exterior walls were painted stone color.[32] Above the portico rose a square pent on which was set a circular cupola, crowned by a dome. A contemporary account described the building as containing "three lecture-rooms capable of seating between four and five hundred persons each."[33] The largest, which occupied most of the east wing, was the chemical lecture hall, with seats arranged in tiers rising from the basement to the third level. The medical lecture hall was on the main floor in the west wing, and the center area was occupied by a vestibule and library (fig. 10.30). The third of the "lecture rooms" was the anatomical theater over the vestibule and library, lighted by the cupola. The top floor of the west wing, including the area of the stair corridors, was entirely devoted to a museum. The basement contained a chemical laboratory and four dissecting rooms. The Louisville Medical Institute was illuminated by gas, and every facility could be carried on by night as well as by day. All rooms were well ventilated. The cost of the building was given variously as from $30,000 to $53,000, the larger amount perhaps including equipment.[34]

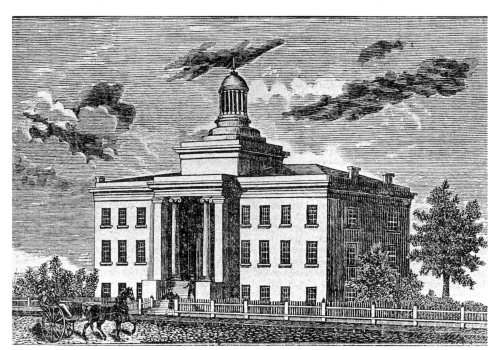

Fig. 10.29 The Louisville Medical Institute (1838). From *Family Magazine*, 1841, p. 358.

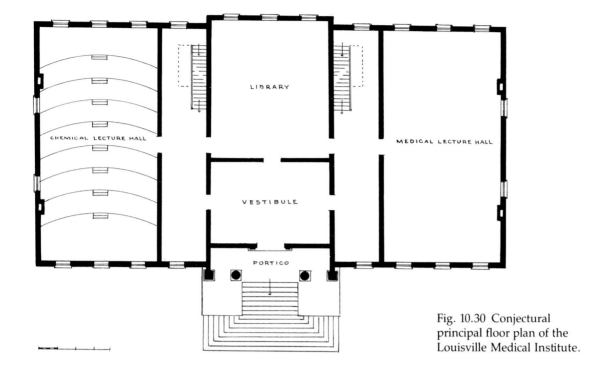

Fig. 10.30 Conjectural principal floor plan of the Louisville Medical Institute.

The medical institute burned in 1856, and another was built on the foundations the following year by Henry Whitestone. The new building also made use of parts of the portico, although now pedimented and with sloping antepodia (as on the completed Jefferson County Courthouse). It had three full stories above the basement, the wings were three-bayed instead of four, and it was without a superstructure. The Whitestone building later served the Louisville Board of Education and the Louisville Free Public Library. It was destroyed in 1972.

THE BANK OF LOUISVILLE. The names of three notable architects are associated with the Bank of Louisville, located on the south side of Main Street between Third and Fourth streets. John Rogers, followed by Gideon Shryock, superintended construction, and the designer was James Harrison Dakin (1806-52), a native of Hudson, New York.[35] We have seen Dakin's design for a front doorway in Lafever's second book used as model for the frontispiece of Rosehill (figs. 10.11, 10.12). His architectural career was begun as an apprentice draftsman in the newly formed partnership of Town and Davis in 1829, and three years later he became a full-fledged member of the New York firm. Dakin was practicing independently in 1834 when commissioned to design the Bank of Louisville. The form is based upon that of a Delphic treasury, an appropriate ancient

archetype featuring a distyle portico in antis. Dakin furnished a number of facade variations, one employing square Doric piers (without cresting elaboration), another with Corinthian columns, the others having Ionic supports, like that executed (fig. 10.31). One is struck by the sloping wall sections as outer supports,

Fig. 10.31 Elevation rendering for the Bank of Louisville (1834) by James Dakin. Courtesy of James H. Dakin Collection, Louisiana Divison, New Orleans Public Library.

in place of antas, the battered wall being an Egyptian device for funerary chambers (mastabas) and temple gateways (pylons). It is crowned by an architrave and broken cornice, the middle portion consisting of an elaborate palmetto on whorled taenia terminating in antefixes. Below, alternate courses of stone were in two colors, as in the walls of Near Eastern Moslem and medieval Venetian buildings. The design seems to have been carried out faithfully, assuming the flanking screen walls were meant to be fanciful. The palmetto cresting was cast in iron. It resembles that of the parlor doorway shown in plates 25-26 in Lafever's *Beauties of Modern Architecture* (fig. 10.17). The motif was used on several buildings attributed to Lafever, which, like the book, postdate the Dakin design.[36] Their former professional association may account for the borrowing.

The Bank of Louisville contains a public room measuring approximately 35 by 60 feet, with two pairs of columns forming screens at the ends of the six-bayed interior and carrying an elliptical coffered dome over the four center bays (fig. 10.32). The free-standing columns are patterned after those of the fourth-century (B.C.) Choragic Monument of Lysicrates, which order constitutes plate 43 of Lafever's *Beauties of Modern Architecture*. The profile of the entablature follows that depicted on plate 44 in the same book, and the three doorways in the south wall reflect elements in plates 1, 6, and 14, especially the paterae on the overdoor frieze of the last. The doorways led to a stair hall flanked by an office and vault across the rear of the building.

Dakin reportedly stopped in Louisville in 1835 en route to New Orleans, where he launched a practice with his younger brother, Charles, and James Gallier, both also former associates of Town and Davis. Soon after, Dakin was called upon to furnish a skylight for the oculus of the banking-room dome. It was made and shipped in December of 1836. The remarkable aspect of this dome is its elliptical shape (fig. 10.33). The breaking away of the curved frieze from the rectangular architrave, however, creates awkward leftover spaces in the corners, and the dome falls short of the good effect of Shryock's on pendentives in the statehouse (fig. 10.23).

The Dakin building later served as headquarters for the National Bank of Kentucky, the Louisville Credit Men's Association, and in 1973 it became the foyer to the Actors Theatre of Louisville.[37]

THE LOUISVILLE HOTEL.   The Greek Revival had been anticipated in Louisville before Shryock and

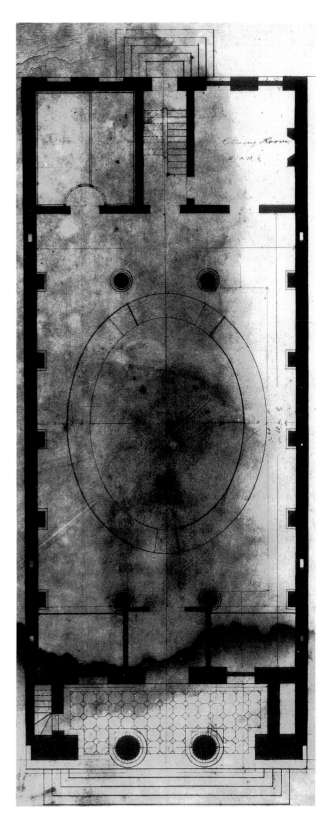

Fig. 10.32 Dakin's plan for the Bank of Louisville (1835-37). Courtesy of James H. Dakin Collection, Louisiana Divison, New Orleans Public Library.

Dakin appeared. The Unitarian Church, the U.S. Branch Bank, and the Second Presbyterian Church (perhaps by Thomas U. Walter) all date to 1832. Of the same year was the Louisville Hotel, which was an English Regency version of the Greek Revival style, resembling John Nash's projects on Regent Street and Regent's Park in London. Designed by a relative newcomer to the city, Hugh Roland, the hotel was built on Main Street west of Sixth. Roland was born in Ohio about 1795 and was in Nashville before 1818, when he planned and built the Masonic Hall on Spring Street.[38] He designed the Episcopal Christ Church in Gothic Revival style about 1829 before moving to Louisville, where his first work (1830) was the Catholic Saint Louis Church, also Gothic.

The Louisville Hotel had a high basement with three additional stories, and the 124-foot-wide front wall was stuccoed and grained to resemble marble (fig. 10.34). The main doorway was reached by a flight of steps that interrupted the projecting basement accommodating a bar and various shops, with arched service entrances at each end. The basement front served as a podium for ten Ionic columns rising two stories. The entablature formed a balustraded terrace for the top floor, and windows at that level were recessed individually in panels. A parapet, rising to a low peak in the middle of the facade, highlighted the long entablature. The 1832 city directory claimed that the Louisville Hotel "will surpass in elegance and arrangement any in the western country and in extent will exceed most in the United

Fig. 10.33 Interior of the Bank of Louisville. Photo, 1973, by David S. Talbott. Courtesy of the Actors Theatre of Louisville.

Fig. 10.34 The Louisville Hotel (1832). Lithograph dated 1 January 1849 by William Endicott, New York City. Courtesy of the Louisville Free Public Library.

States, covering a surface of 16,000 square feet, being 3,000 feet greater than that of the Tremont House in Boston." The Tremont House, built by Isaiah Rogers three years earlier, is considered to have been the first modern hotel in America. Like the Boston hostelry, the Louisville Hotel had a circular rotunda directly in back of the entrance. It was 22 feet in diameter. Passages led crosswise to the public and private rooms, and there were staircases at the extremities. The dining hall, in the west wing, was as wide (30 feet) as that in the Tremont House and 20 feet longer (90 feet). Similarly placed at the back were "Bathing Houses and every other convenience," which were accessible from porches surrounding the area. The parallels between the two hotels testify to Roland's familiarity with Rogers's achievement. Ironically, Isaiah Rogers and Henry Whitestone were the architects of the second Louisville Hotel, which replaced Roland's building in 1855.

GIRON'S CONFECTIONERY.   M. Mathurin Giron came to Lexington about 1810 and introduced French pastries and candies to the Bluegrass. In 1837 he erected Giron's Confectionery on the west side of Mill Street, between Main and Short streets.[39] The two-story building, seven bays across, bore a strong resemblance to such establishments in New Orleans, whence Giron had come. The first story had an entablature carried on a range of half-round Tuscan columns of wood engaged to square brick piers, and it was divided into two shops by a wide central doorway opening into a stair hall leading to the floor above (fig. 10.35). The broad overhanging cornice provided a balcony for the second floor that was enhanced by a pretty wrought-iron railing with a few cast parts. The upper story had brick pilasters dividing alternating doorways and windows, the doors dual-leafed with square panels, and the windows with twelve-paned sashes. The upper level accommodated ballrooms with their "great paneled folding doors of polished cherry, opening to the high frescoed ceiling," and each contained columned mantels. Here suppers prepared by Giron's famous Swiss chef, Dominique Ritter, were served. Later, Gus Jaubert ran a saloon in the first story of the south half, which has been demolished. A newsstand and restaurant have occupied the north half, and remodeling has obliterated most of the original features.

FRANKLIN SPRINGS.   The rural counterpart of the urban hotel, the watering place took on a new look and an increased affluence during the Greek Revival

Fig. 10.35 Giron's Confectionery (1837), Lexington. Photo, late 1800s, courtesy of Lafayette Studio, Lexington.

period. Franklin Springs had been established in Franklin County, six miles southeast of Frankfort on Lawrenceburg Pike, toward the close of the eighteenth century. In 1838 a structure was added that mirrors Shryock's statehouse, only in a smaller denominator. The portico is hexastyle but Tuscan, walls are of brick, and the cupola (added later) is octagonal rather than circular (fig. 10.36). The shafts of the columns are stuccoed brick, with only the bases and capitals of stone, and the entablature and pediment are wood. First-story windows on the portico begin at floor level. The recessed doorway is unadorned and leads into a central hallway bisecting the main pavilion, which is two rooms deep. A doorway at the back opens onto a gallery, and an adjacent door on the north side gives access to an enclosed stairway. The four adjoining rooms were parlors and dining hall. A long wing extends back from the south suite, the rooms reached from the L-shaped gallery, with an open-air stairway at the far end. The building was sold in 1845 to Col. R.T.P. Allen for the establishment of the Kentucky Military Institute.[40] The cupola and Victorian Gothic interior features postdate this era, as do additions at the end of the ell and on the right flank, where the short arm of the gallery was lengthened and another stairway added. Supplemented by later buildings on the five-hundred-acre estate, it serves the Stewart Home School, an institute for the mentally retarded opened in 1893.

GRAHAM SPRINGS. Dr. Christopher Columbus Graham, graduate of Transylvania Medical School, purchased Greenville Springs in 1827 and his father-in-law's Harrodsburg Springs a year later, combining them under the title of Graham Springs. In 1834 the establishment was described by a Cincinnati visitor as being composed of a number of buildings. The main hotel, he reported, has "a piazza extending the whole front which forms an admirable promenade. It contains a dining-room, in which one hundred and fifty persons may be comfortably seated, an excellent ball-room, parlors, chambers, &c., and two rows of very comfortable cabins."[41] A new and greater edifice was built in 1842-43, costing upward of $30,000, "full four stories high . . . [with] massy colonnade, rich capitals and lofty entablature."[42] The alignment of eight Ionic columns, embracing three stories, had two bays of windows in the interspaces (like several Greek Revival houses still standing in Harrodsburg), and the entablature was exceptionally deep (fig. 10.37). The ballroom measured 50 by 150 feet, and the building contained a bowling alley and "saloon for the accommodation of patients who may wish for other kinds of physical exercise." Facilities could provide for a thousand visitors.[43] Graham sold the property in 1853 and it became the Western Military Asylum; the buildings burned down in 1856. Although a revival of the springs was undertaken from 1911 to 1934, it proved unsuccessful, and the Mercer County Hospital took over the grounds.[44]

MAYSVILLE CITY HALL. On the intersection of Court and Third streets in Maysville stand two noteworthy buildings, the old Greek Revival city hall (1844) and the Gothic Revival Presbyterian church (1850), the two in near balance and both now painted white. The city hall was built by Stanislaus and Ignatius Mitchell, Christopher Russell, and L. Pernell. It has a high basement with a double staircase rising to a pedimented portico of four plain Doric columns, resembling the market hall in Charleston, South Carolina, completed in 1841 by Edward B. White.[45] The Maysville building has pilastrades on the flanks em-

Fig. 10.36 Franklin Springs (ca. 1838), Franklin County. Photo, 1941.

bracing the main and second stories and supporting a full entablature. A tower, rising in back of the front plane of the building proper, is composed of a cubic clock section and octagonal belfry crowned by a dome topped by a spar with ball and weathervane (fig. 10.38). The clock with four faces is said to have been made by a Flemingsburg blacksmith, although

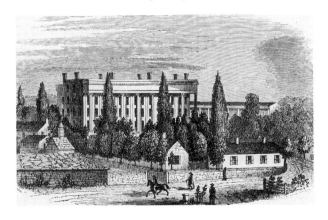

Fig. 10.37 Graham Springs (1842-43), Harrodsburg. From Lewis Collins, *Historical Sketches of Kentucky* (Cincinnati, 1847), facing p. 449.

Fig. 10.38 Maysville City Hall (1844). From Lewis Collins, *Historical Sketches of Kentucky* (Cincinnati, 1847), p. 431.

most of its parts are of wood. The building became the county courthouse in 1848, when the seat of Mason County was moved from Washington to Maysville. A detached one-story clerk's office in complying style was built on the west side in 1860.

THE TRANSYLVANIA UNIVERSITY MEDICAL HALL. The Medical Department of Transylvania University had outgrown its building by Matthew Kennedy when a committee of three was named on 21 March 1839 to procure plans for a new edifice and dormitory. John McMurtry, whom we first encountered as the builder of the Lexington and Ohio Railroad Station, was approached, and twenty-four days later he submitted plans for both buildings.

McMurtry (1812-90), whose parents—like the Shryocks—had come from Maryland, was born on his father's farm in Fayette County northwest of Iron Works and Russell Cave roads. He moved to Lexington in 1833 to become a builder and lodged as an apprentice with Gideon Shryock in the old Robert S. Todd House on West Short Street. It has been noted that in the following year Shryock sublet a contract for finishing the Morrison College building to McMurtry and Charles Keiser. McMurtry had a carpentry shop on West Main Street in the basement of Matthew Kennedy's Masonic Hall when it burned on

29 August 1836, and his later shop was on Short Street near the site of the Todd House.

John McMurtry and Michael Gaugh contracted for the carpentry work on the dormitory, erected northeast of Morrison College. The Medical Hall was delayed several months because of insufficient funds, until $5,000 was amassed by the professors to achieve the total cost of $24,600.[46] The teaching facility was on the northwest corner of Second Street facing Broadway. It was prostyle in form; its facade was taken practically verbatim from the center section of Morrison College, and it was about 10 feet wider (fig. 10.39). Above five of the ten pilasters on each flank rose chimneys; and as on Shryock's capitol, a circular lantern was set on the roof ridge. Its cornerstone was laid in 1839 on the Fourth of July, and it was dedicated on 2 November 1840. Dr. Robert Peter later described the accommodations, which were similar to those of the Louisville Medical Institute.[47]

It contained three great lecture rooms, with ample provision for light and ventilation. The amphitheatre was immediately below the cupola, being by this means lighted from above. There were three other large apartments—for the library, the anatomical museum, and for other medical teaching. Smaller rooms accommodated the laboratory, Faculty room, janitor's room, etc. Besides which were long halls or galleries utilized for natural history collections, museums of zoology, ornithology, geology, etc., as also for apparatus of diverse sorts. The costly and complete chemical apparatus was well displayed and conveniently arranged in the immense lecture room for that department.

Fig. 10.39 The Medical Hall (1839) of Transylvania University, Lexington. From *Catalogue of the Students of the Medical Department of Transylvania University . . .* (Lexington, 1856), frontispiece.

In the great hall at the front of the building, students and townspeople heard not only learned discourses by "incumbent professors" but were "charmed with concerts by Ole Bull, Stakosch, Adelina Patti—who sang there on her first tour in this country—and other celebrities of the period." When it was nearing completion a Lexington newspaper declared the building "ornamental to the City . . . a proud monument of the munificence of the authorities of our town, and of their patriotic devotion to the cause of Education. It is a noble edifice, and better adapted, perhaps, than any similar building in the United States, for the purposes of its design."[48] During the early days of the Civil War, the loss of students in the medical department led to its partial use by the literary and classical faculties of the university. It was serving as a Union hospital when destroyed by fire on 22 May 1863.[49]

GIDDINGS HALL OF GEORGETOWN COLLEGE. Georgetown College, a Baptist affiliated school, was founded in 1829. Dr. Rockwell Giddings became president in 1838 and lived to preside over the college only one year, but he is said to have designed the stately hall bearing his name. Another account, how-

ever, attributes the design to J.E. Farnam, professor of physical science. Giddings Hall was built in 1839 of bricks made on the campus, and much of the labor was furnished by students.[50] It is prostyle with a portico of six Ionic columns, the shafts being of brick (presumably always exposed) and the bases and capitals of stone (fig. 10.40). The wooden entablature and pediment are deep and heavy. Front steps span only the three center bays of the portico. The doorway is plain with Greek ears at the top. Windows, divided into two lights, are of a later period; those on the flanks retain Victorian hoods. The building has a center transverse stair hall with rooms on either side. Changes were made during the early 1970s to accommodate administrative functions.

THE CAPITAL HOTEL. Just as architectural taste in ancient Greece changed from an almost exclusive use of the simple Doric order to an acceptance of the foreign Ionic by the end of the sixth century B.C., leveling off for two centuries until the ornamental Corinthian came into prominence during the Hellenistic and Roman periods, so in America the more accelerated Greek Revival underwent a notable

Fig. 10.40 Giddings Hall (1839) of Georgetown College. Photo, 1968.

Fig. 10.41 The Capital Hotel (1853, 1855), Frankfort. From J. Soule Smith, *Art Work of the Blue Grass Region of Kentucky* (Oshkosh, 1899), n.p.

change from the use of the Ionic and Doric modes of the 1830s and 1840s to a preference for Corinthian during the 1850s. Corinthian columns were prominent in the Capital Hotel in Frankfort, designed in 1852 by Isaiah Rogers (1800-69), who was renowned for such buildings.

After making a name for himself building the Tremont House in Boston, Rogers constructed the similar Bangor House (1832) in Maine and then surpassed both in the Astor House, or Park Hotel (1834-36), in New York City. At mid-century he turned southward and designed great hostelries in New Orleans, Louisville, Cincinnati, and Nashville. It was after building the second St. Charles Hotel (1851) in New Orleans that Rogers undertook the Capital Hotel in Frankfort, where he was assisted by Henry Whitestone. The hotel was constructed on Main Street between Olive and Ann streets, the principal part dating from 1853, with a large wing added in 1855. Unlike earlier hotels, limited to an almost flat facade adjacent to the street, the Capital Hotel front stepped in and out 15 to 20 feet (fig. 10.41). In this regard it reflected the forecourt arrangement of Rogers's earlier Burnet House (1850) in Cincinnati, with a monumental stairway leading up to the domed central pavilion.[51] The main block of the Frankfort hotel had a colossal-order portico of six Corinthian columns, reminiscent of the middle section of the St. Charles but with broad steps up to the portico in place of a basement entrance. Rogers similarly incorporated such a portico in his Commercial Bank of Kentucky (1855) at Paducah. The Capital Hotel walls were not of large, uniform blocks of dressed marble as in the statehouse but of roughly squared blocks of limestone of varying sizes fitted together as in early Kentucky stone houses. Windows were exceptionally large. In back of the first range of rooms the center pavilion rose to three stories and was surmounted by a sixteen-sided cupola. The outer pavilions were connected by wings forming inner courts. The hostelry was commissioned by the city of Frankfort at a cost of $70,000.[52] It burned in 1917 and was replaced by a Colonial Revival building.

LEXINGTON CEMETERY RECEIVING VAULT. The Lexington Cemetery was incorporated in 1848 and located beyond the city limits at the west end of Main Street. A Gothic Revival gateway was erected by John McMurtry soon after (chap. 11), and around the drive in a hillside to the left an Egyptian-style receiving vault was constructed in 1857. Bodies awaiting interment were placed in it, especially during the winter months when the ground was too frozen for graves

Fig. 10.42 Lexington Cemetery receiving vault (1857). Photo, 1942.

to be dug. The style of ancient Egypt in its association with the royal cult of the dead was considered appropriate for funerary use. Mount Auburn Cemetery at Cambridge, Massachusetts, established in 1831, has a five-part Egyptian gateway by Jacob Bigelow completed in 1842. Other examples of the decade include Isaiah Rogers's small Egyptian gate to the Old Granary Burying Ground in Boston, his duplicate in the Touro Memorial Gateway at Newport, Rhode Island, and Henry Austin's larger Grove Street Cemetery gateway in New Haven, Connecticut.[53] The facade of the receiving vault in Lexington bore a resemblance to the Cambridge gateway in that it was a complex composition of symmetrical parts and decorated with torus and gorge moldings (fig. 10.42). The portal, with the date 1857 in Roman numerals carved over the bronze doors, was flanked by plain walls, each interrupted by a tall, buttresslike shaft capped by a cavetto, the ends dropping steeply to low terminal posts resembling pedestals. A wide masonry vault formed the interior. Cast-metal coffins of the period simulated Egyptian mummies, the body coverings treated less as wrappings than drapery folds gathered around the arms crossed over the chest.[54] The receiving vault was demolished in the 1950s.

The Greek Revival broke precedent with earlier styles in Kentucky—appearing initially in public buildings and afterward in residences. For the most part, the time lag was considerable. Few residences in the Greek Revival style predate 1840, in Kentucky. This has prompted in this chapter a reversal in the sequence of discussion of residences and public buildings. It has been pointed out that the first example of Greek Revival in the United States was a public building and that the prostyle form was more suitable to great edifices. The colonnade spanning one face or encircling the building was adapted during the Federal period to domestic uses, especially in the Deep South, and it became more prevalent during the Greek Revival. But the peristyle is not to be found in Kentucky, and only rarely did the portico embrace the entire facade. It figured primarily as an impressive entrance shelter and secondarily in porches as open-air living spaces.

THE ORLANDO BROWN HOUSE. The only residence known to have been designed by Gideon Shryock, who fostered the Greek Revival during his early period, is the Orlando Brown House in Frankfort. It shares the Wilkinson Street block with Liberty Hall and was commissioned by John Brown for his

Fig. 10.43 The Orlando Brown House (1835), Frankfort. Photo, 1940.

younger son. On 23 April 1835 he contracted with the builder Harrison Blanton for a dwelling "agreeable to a plan drawn by Mr Shryock."[55] John Brown's Liberty Hall shows a marked conservatism, and apparently the same disposition exerted itself over the plans made almost forty years later. The Orlando Brown House is transitional in style from Federal to Greek Revival. Early features include the half columns against the front wall of the portico (as at Ridgeway), the banister railing above (as on the entry to Woodlands), a small-paneled front door with reeded frames having corner blocks (as in the Hunt House), the pilastered triple window in the second story (of the Kennedy type and not unlike the upper window at Liberty Hall, although lacking the arch), and a lunette in the pediment (also in the manner of Matthew Kennedy houses) (fig. 10.43). The pediment of the facade could be either Federal or Greek Revival, whereas the definitely later characteristics

Fig. 10.44 Parlor mantel viewed through hall door, the Orlando Brown House. Photo, 1940.

are the narrow window frames and the portico with Grecian Ionic columns. Inside, the earlier tradition dominates. There is a central transverse hall divided by an arch; the staircase in the back half with a railing is similar to that in Liberty Hall. Mantels have colonnettes supporting entablature imposts, central frieze panels, and a broken cornice shelf. Doors have three horizontal panels over a pair of vertical panels, and they are enframed in moldings of early-nineteenth-century pattern, with the addition of a square panel above the plinth at the base (fig. 10.44). Typical of the Greek Revival style, however, chair railing has been eliminated in favor of a higher baseboard. The house was opened as a museum in 1957 by the Colonial Dames.

THE KEATS HOUSE. George Keats, brother of the English poet John Keats, came to America to seek his fortune, and after a failed business venture with John James Audubon in Henderson, he settled in Louisville.[56] He prospered and in 1835 constructed a house on the south side of Walnut Street, west of Third.[57] Although an exact contemporary of the Orlando Brown House, which remained largely Federal in style, the Keats residence was wholly Greek Revival.

Keats had left England at the advent of the greatest flurry of the Greek Revival there. Sir Robert Smirke began the British Museum in 1823, and Decimus Burton erected the Triple Arches in Hyde Park Corner about two years later. Both made use of the Ionic order. This appeared in the Keats house, as did the high English basement of the London Regency townhouse rows by John Nash (fig. 10.45). There were three openings at the front of the podium, the center one arched. A flight of steps curved up from the street at the east end to the main level of the portico. Stairs, portico platform, and the premises were protected by wrought-iron railings or fences. The floor plan must have resembled that of Ward Hall near Georgetown, although the rear rooms apparently were not full-sized and had corner fireplaces (fig. 10.87).

George Keats died in 1841. The property was sold to James Trabue for $8,000. During and after the Civil War it was the home of Hampton College for Young Ladies. In 1900, it was converted into the headquarters of the Elks Club and was disfigured by a rusticated fore structure with balustraded stairs to either side. The building was demolished in 1924 and an extension to Stewart's Department Store was later built on the site.[58]

THE HIGGINS MANSION. The Greek semblance of monumentality was exerted in Bluegrass residential architecture first through an addition to the late-eighteenth-century home of Elijah Smith, a two-story brick, center-stair-hall house on the ridge overlooking Town Fork of Elkhorn Creek in Lexington. It was acquired by and extensively remodeled for Joel Higgins during the mid-1830s. The grandiose new facade consisted of a great portico of six rectangular brick piers supporting a heavy wood entablature and pediment, with an upper balcony enhanced by a delicate wrought-iron railing. Attached at the sides were low wings, whose pilasters, frieze, and cornice reflected members of the portico (fig. 10.46). The featured frontality of the Greek Revival style is manifested in the total concept. The full entablature of the pediment continues on the sides of the main pavilion only to the depth of the portico, beyond which the roof drops to a lower level (as on Morrison College), and the pilaster bases and capitals alone bend around the corners of the wings. The front door was changed to the tall-paneled Greek type, and window sashes of the original house were altered from twelve small to

Fig. 10.45 The George Keats House (1835), Louisville. Photo, ca. late 1800s, courtesy of the Filson Club.

six large panes. Bearing testimony to the success of the effect, MacCabe's Lexington city directory for 1838-39 listed the house as "Higgins Mansion," the only building designated as a mansion. Later in the century, Lexington Avenue was cut between High and Maxwell streets and beyond and came to within a few feet of the west side of the house. Upon conversion of the building into apartments, a new two-storied front pavilion enveloped the west wing.

THE GIBSON HOUSE.   More worthy of being called

a mansion was the already sizable house on Lexington's West Second Street, between Broadway and Jefferson Street. Built for Thomas January early in the 1800s, it was acquired by the Bank of the United States in 1820 and in 1834 became the home of the Episcopal Theological Seminary.[59] At that time the building consisted of a two-story center mass three bays wide, with a low porch on the front and wings of one story at the sides. The facade corresponded to that of Jefferson's Brandon and Battersea, lacking the

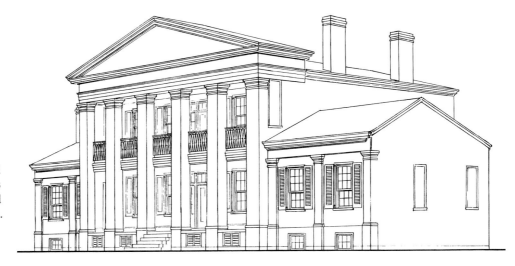

Fig. 10.46 Restored sketch of Higgins Mansion (remodeled mid-1830s), Lexington.

Fig. 10.47 The Thomas January House (early 1800s) and dependencies when serving as the Episcopal Theological Seminary, Lexington. View during early 1840s, P. Desobry's Lithography, New York.

end pavilions, but the form was two rooms deep with lateral extensions embracing a rear court (fig. 10.47).[60] The property was purchased in 1846 by Tobias Gibson of Louisiana, and Thomas Lewinski was commissioned to make "proposed alterations and improvements."[61] Major Lewinski contributed the giant tetrastyle Ionic portico set in front of the two-story pavilion, and very likely he combined the front room and passage into a large reception hall. Two years later John McMurtry made further changes, demolishing the west rear (former chapel) wing, building up the flanking wings and service ell on the east to two full stories, and adding a gallery of two levels along two sides of the new court.[62] Front openings were enframed by cast-iron moldings with Greek ears, and clusters of octagonal chimneys rose above the parapets masking the roof (fig. 10.48).

The principal internal improvement on the first floor was the removal of the partition between the two rooms in the right wing, making a double parlor divided by "an Entablature supported by handsome

Fig. 10.49 Detail of screen between parlors in the Gibson House. Photo, 1940.

Ionic Columns fluted also Pilasters against the wall." McMurtry also was "to run around said Parlor Ceilings A Handsome & appropriate cornice in Plaster and Put up in each ceiling an appropriate Center Piece in Plaster finished in Good style and Taste" (fig. 10.49). The centerpieces were modeled on the Lafever design (fig. 10.14). Matching marble mantels were brought from Louisiana by the owner. Access to the gallery was provided through the tall rear windows. Provisions on the first floor were also made for a library in back of the reception hall, a pair of rooms for dining opposite the parlors, and an entry, pantry, kitchen, and scullery in the ell (fig. 10.50). The layout of the upper level corresponded roughly to the rooms below, except that the stair hall continued through to the front of the building, a narrow passage extended off to the southwest bedroom, and a dressing room was inserted between the chambers

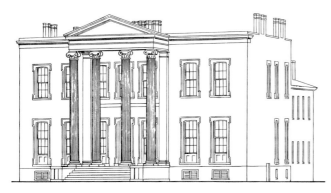

Fig. 10.48 Restored sketch of the Tobias Gibson House (remodeled 1848), Lexington.

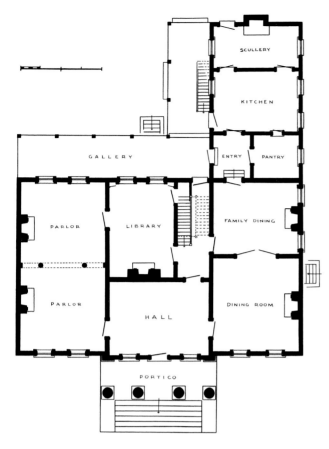

Fig. 10.50 First-floor plan of Gibson House.

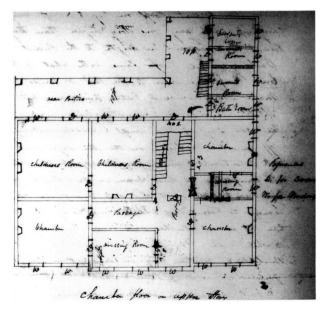

Fig. 10.51 "Chamber floor or upper story" of the Gibson House. Sketch indicating proposed remodeling by John McMurtry in letter to Tobias Gibson of 11 July 1848. Courtesy of Mrs. Sarah Buckner, Lexington.

over the dining rooms (fig. 10.51). A bathroom was over the pantry.

Later changes included acquiring single-paned sashes and elaborate hood molds over the front openings and concrete disks in the place of the original column bases. Early in the present century the house became the Campbell-Hagerman College for Girls, then it served the Lexington Conservatory of Music, and finally it was divided into apartments.

THE ALBERTI HOUSE. In 1821 Dr. John C.M. Alberti purchased thirty acres nine miles east of Lexington on the Winchester Pike for $900.[63] A log house was standing on the farm, and Dr. Alberti added a frame section to it. In 1853 his son John Leer Bledsoe Alberti enlarged the landholding and probably the house as well.[64] With a new brick section at the rear keyed in with extensive remodeling, the Greek Revival mode was used to unify and give a sense of formality to a rambling country house that had come into existence haphazardly (fig. 10.52). The log structure was made the entrance pavilion by the addition of a front portico, in which tall square piers supported interpenetrating roofs, with a pediment over the wide center bay and smaller pediments at the ends. There were benches and false windows between the outer pilasters. A projecting balcony above spanned the width of the portico on a level with the paneled parapet over the east gallery. Porches practically encircled the house, except for the outer flank of the brick pavilion and a short segment on the other side at the rear. Square piers, smaller than those of the portico, formed the east range; one was at the front west corner, while elsewhere the supports were rustic posts (at least in modern times), and there were no parapets above (fig. 10.53).

The assortment of rooms was connected by a labyrinth of passages and the outer galleries and by inside and outside stairs (fig. 10.54). Most of the interiors were somber because of the scarcity of windows and the depth of the galleries. The kitchen was the exception, being amply supplied with openings. Its floor was continuous with the brick paving of the back gallery. A serving window opened into the shallow closet alongside the dining-room mantel. As in many southern plantation homes, the room used for dining was the largest and most centrally located. The only cellar was under the bedroom part of the brick section, and there is a lack of basement elevation proper to a Greek Revival design. The house might have been mistaken for a country inn. All but the brick wing was razed about 1960.

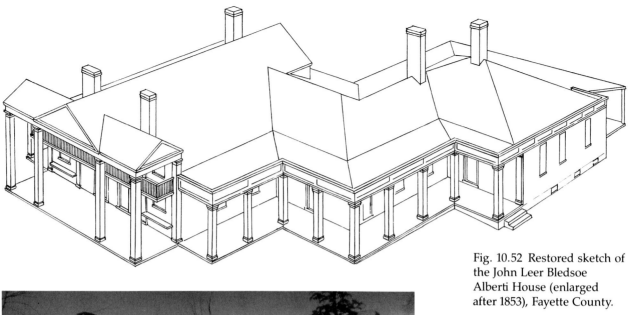

Fig. 10.52 Restored sketch of the John Leer Bledsoe Alberti House (enlarged after 1853), Fayette County.

Fig. 10.53 Rear view of the Alberti House. Photo, 1943.

Fig. 10.54 First-floor plan of the Alberti House.

EDGEMOOR. A building showing enough similarity to the Alberti House to have been a model for its enlargement is Edgemoor, built for James M. Barclay about 1851 at the eastern limits of Versailles.[65] In its low, spreading forms, covered with hip roofs, the house also resembles the group of Federal houses from Lewis Manor to Ridgeway—in seeming contradiction to the ideals of the Greek Revival style. In the regional manner, pavilions expand asymmetrically at the rear, rather than being placed laterally in perfect balance (fig. 10.55). The Alberti House featured a box-like entablature that carried over both closed and open forms, and square piers on portico and gallery. Edgemoor, however, is a house of some pretensions, and refinements include such architectural details as dentils beneath the cornice, a row of guttae on the molding separating architrave and frieze, and a

Fig. 10.55 Edgemoor (ca. 1851), Versailles. Photo, dated 1851, courtesy of James H. Barker, Nantucket, Mass., and Palm Beach, Fla.

Greek-key motif at the necking of the piers (fig. 10.56).

The interior is a blend of elegance and stark simplicity, but it should not be overlooked that rich fittings, such as heavy draperies and carved and upholstered furniture, would have contributed considerably to the atmosphere. The long transverse hall, with a single door in each side opening to the parlors, leads to a cross passage containing the enclosed stairs (fig. 10.57). The dining room opposite with chambers distributed around it is the hub of the house. The stairway to the garret presents a puzzle because three bottom steps are missing and there is a doorway where they would have abutted the wall. Dual-leaf doors here are hinged together and open back against the winders in the corner. Depressions on the back side of the doors indicate decades of banging against the nosing of the fourth riser. One surmises that a moveable unit, like library steps, was fitted at the base when needed. It would resemble the stairway in the dressing room at Elmwood Hall (chap. 8). The other quandary at Edgemoor is the one-room cottage opposite the porch door, which seems to predate the house proper. One wonders whether it was used as a chamber or kitchen. If the latter, then cooking would have been performed on a stove rather than in the small fireplace now existing. About ten feet beyond the cottage stands a two-story brick dependency of four rooms, with the long axis running east and west. Tradition labels it the servants' quarters. Beneath it is presumably a root cellar—a windowless, brick-vaulted basement, with outside entrance at the far end. Back of it was a large, circular icehouse (demolished), and down the hill built into the bank is the milkhouse.

Fig. 10.56 Portico detail of Edgemoor. Photo, 1927, by Tebbs and Knell, courtesy of the Library of Congress.

For many years Edgemoor has served the local school system, formerly as residence for the principal of the adjoining high school and now as offices for the board of education. Dentils have been removed from the entablature, and a small wing was added to the old quarters.

THE HUNT HOUSE. The best developed of spreading Greek Revival houses belonged to Francis Key Hunt and was on the north side of Barr Street in Lexington. Hunt was a man of means and connec-

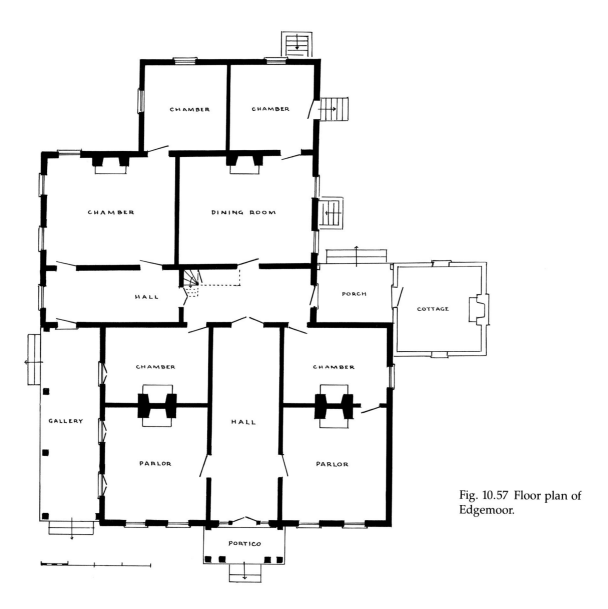

Fig. 10.57 Floor plan of Edgemoor.

tions, his father being John Wesley Hunt and his father-in-law, Dr. Elisha Warfield of The Meadows. His wife, Julia G. Hunt, received the 90-by-290-foot lot as a present in 1843 from her mother, Maria Warfield.[66] Their house was set back 40 feet from the sidewalk, and the front yard was suitably terraced. On the facade of the main block, pilasters rose from ground level, supporting a full entablature, and a substantial flight of steps ascended to a pretty columned doorway set in a deep recess (fig. 10.58). Unprecedented for such an early date in Kentucky was the use of unbonded (all-stretcher) brickwork in the facade. Narrow wings had flounder roofs masked by parapets in front, and a brick wall screened the service court on the east side (fig. 10.59). The court was paved with brick, and a narrow walk ran in back

to the outbuildings, including a smokehouse, quarters and privies, an icehouse and stable, a carriage house, and a cow shed. Sharing the north extremity on the alley with the cow lot was a vegetable garden, and the middle area was a greensward bordered by flowers. The relationship of house to court and garden was comparable to that at the John Wesley Hunt home.

The living area of the Barr Street house was divided from the sleeping rooms by a transverse hall (fig. 10.60). Only the two chambers adjoining the hall and that at the front of the wing were original; the later ell contained three others. The corner fireplace in the small outer chamber was unusual for the Greek Revival period. Being well supplied with closets was innovative and became characteristic of Greek Re-

Fig. 10.58 Doorway of the Francis Key Hunt House (ca. 1843), Lexington. Photo, 1940.

Fig. 10.60 Floor plan of Hunt House.

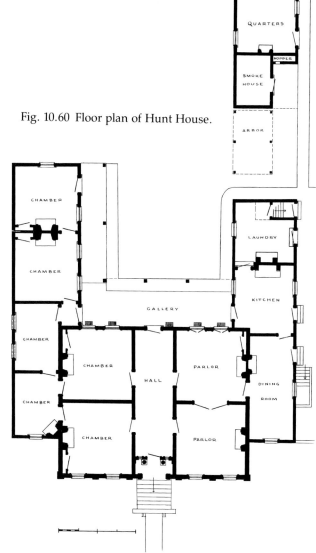

Fig. 10.59 Perspective sketch of the Hunt House and dependencies, restored with advice from Mrs. Eleanor Parker Hopkins, Lexington.

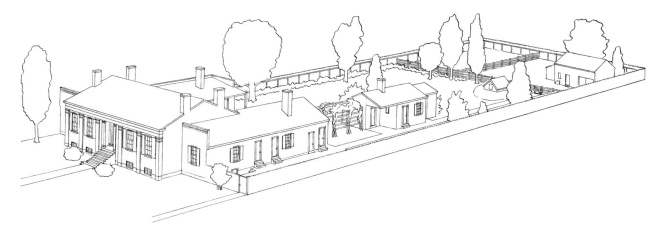

vival residences. The rear parlor windows had hinged panels beneath the sashes for egress to the open gallery, and iron grilles in the porch floor were a safeguard over basement airshafts. The dining room was long and narrow (26 by 11 feet), had an off-center fireplace, and opened to the courtyard and kitchen. A laundry with servants' room above completed the east wing. The decor was as plain as that of Edgemoor but more delicate. Mantels in the main rooms were of marble, white in the parlors and mottled in the chambers. They were pilastered but otherwise reduced to a minimum of elements, recalling the design of plate 73 in Edward Shaw's *Civil Architecture* (revised and enlarged in 1834). Door and window trim had running moldings and corner blocks not unlike that in the earlier Hunt House on Mill Street and certainly archaic for the forties. Baseboards were a bit higher than in the father's house, and there was no chair railing. Doors throughout were of the two-panel variety, like the front door. An elliptical plaster centerpiece was affixed to the transverse hall ceiling.

Francis Hunt sold the property in 1851, when he built Loudoun (chap. 11). The dependencies disappeared many years before the residence, which served as a parish house for Saint Peter's Church and School from 1911 until its demolition in 1953.[67]

MANSFIELD. Built by Henry Clay for his son, Thomas Hart Clay, Mansfield is located beyond Ashland on the south side of the Lexington-Richmond Pike. It was designed in 1845 by the architect Thomas Lewinski, Henry Clay's friend and his children's French teacher.[68] Mansfield has a high basement story. Its facade sports a shallow tetrastyle Ionic portico with frontal steps, the antepodia apparently added later (fig. 10.61). Coupled pilasters unify the walls of the nearly square house, sustaining a deep entablature on all sides. Pilastered triple windows are in the wide center bays front and back, and single blind windows are set in the interspaces on the sides; curved-headed windows are recessed in applied arches in the pediments above. Chimneys are prominent and have a heavy capping.

Mansfield's plan is simple, consisting of four equisized rooms flanking a divided hall, with staircase in the rear half (fig. 10.62). Window frames protrude into the rooms for shutter recesses. Wide double doors connect parlor and dining room. In addition to those on the first floor, two bedrooms are on the second. Kitchen and service rooms occupy the basement, as in most Greek Revival houses without wings.

Additions of 1927 by Robert McMeekin made Mansfield into a five-part composition resembling Ridgeway, a Federal, outmoded form for Greek Revival styling. The connectors cut awkwardly through pilasters of the old end walls.

The Greek Revival came into its own domain in the two-story house, on which its most salient feature could be applied—the colossal portico. Lewinski's improvement to the Tobias Gibson House (before McMurtry's enlargement) produced a result which

Fig. 10.61 Mansfield (1845-46), near Lexington. Photo, ca. 1926, by Robert McMeekin.

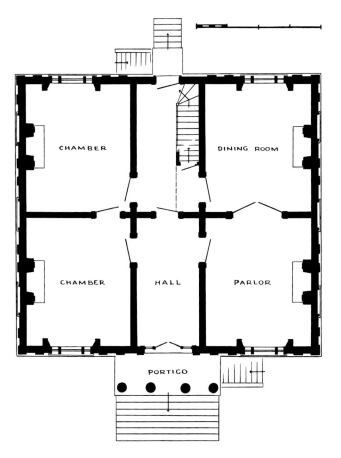

Fig. 10.62 Restored first-floor plan of Mansfield.

resembled the only pre-Revolutionary residence in this country endowed with a great portico. It was Whitehall, Gov. Horatio Sharpe's retreat, built during the 1760s in Anne Arundel County, Maryland.[69] The house shape, composed of a high, porticoed center mass with low, balanced flankers, perhaps served as the model for a group in Kentucky, the first of which was the Weir House.

THE WEIR HOUSE. The residence on the northeast corner of Limestone and Third streets in Lexington was commissioned by James Weir just prior to his death in 1832. Construction was resumed during the regime of a nephew of the same name a decade or more later; and the house attained final form in the early 1850s, owned then either by James H. Woolfolk (1851-52) or Chief Justice Thomas Mitchell (after 1852).[70] The house exhibits the heavy, cubic quality of nearby Morrison College, for which reason it has been attributed to Gideon Shryock. Its portico has broad steps between antepodia, and the Doric columns had bases (now missing) and have plain shafts (fig. 10.63). The entablature is boxlike, the unadorned frieze and architrave of three fascias are in reverse position, separated by a row of guttae, and a course of dentils is between the misplaced architrave and stumpy cornice. Such lack of protocol relieves

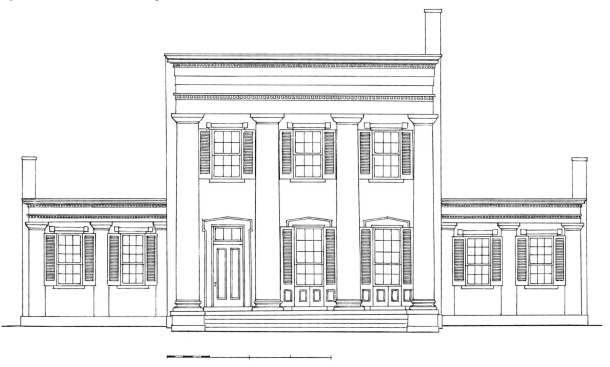

Fig. 10.63 Restored front elevation of the James Weir House (1832-early 1850s), Lexington.

Fig. 10.64 Parlor detail of the Weir House. Photo, 1942.

the Strickland-trained Shryock from design responsibility. The three parts of the facade are articulated by pilasters, and the doorway is in the north bay of the two-story pavilion, which contains a long stair hall and two parlors on the first floor. The parlors are divided by a screen of Corinthian columns supporting an entablature with a modillioned cornice, the latter encircling both rooms (fig. 10.64). The chimney breasts have matching marble mantels in whose spandrels are carved figures of Nike and putti in low relief, with a female bust in high relief on the cartouche keystone over the arched fireplace. This eclectic Renaissance decoration dates from the middle of the century.

The service ell was destroyed about 1910 and a new wing of two stories was built in its stead, joining the south flanker. Both flankers acquired a second story. Blank sashes replace the original nine-over-six-paned windows in the first story and six-over-six in the second. The building now serves as the Whitehall Funeral Chapel.

THE COCHRAN HOUSE. The most refined of the Weir House type stood on Hill (now East High) Street in Lexington west of the present Harrison Avenue viaduct. It was built for James W. Cochran probably soon after he purchased the lot in 1840.[71] The portico was pedimented and had four Ionic columns inspired by those of the north porch of the Erechtheum, here set on pedestals with steps in between (fig. 10.65). The entire facade was pilastered, as on the Weir House, but on the wings the shafts rose from ground level. The entablature continued along the sides of the lower forms, whereas on the main pavilion it cleared only the portico. The wings were embellished with frieze grilles aligned to the front windows, scrolled ornaments atop the cornice abutting the portico piers, and antefixes at the corners. Such crestings were unusual on Kentucky domiciles. The doorway was enframed with a simple, wide molding having Greek ears and cornice hood at the top.

Upon demolition of the Cochran House about 1905, its columns were incorporated in a new portico on the McConathy House next door. The McConathy House became part of the Kentuckian Hotel before it was razed in the mid-1960s.

THE BRYAN HOUSE. A comtemporary but less sophisticated, more rural version of the Weir House type is the George Byrd Bryan House on the Lexington-Harrodsburg Pike near Wilmore. The Ionic portico has pilasters only at the corners. The doorway, in the reverse position, is recessed and enframed with Ionic colonnettes, pilasters, and an

Fig. 10.65 The James W. Cochran House (early 1840s), Lexington. Photo, ca. early 1900s, courtesy of Dr. W.O. Bullock, Lexington.

Fig. 10.66 The George Byrd Bryan House (1840s), Jessamine County. Photo, 1941.

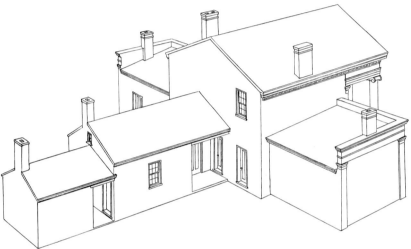

Fig. 10.67 Restored sketch of the rear of the Bryan House.

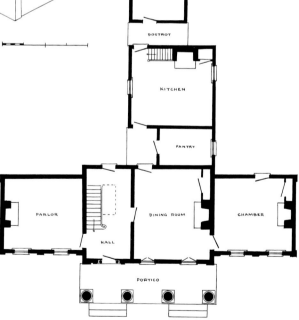

Fig. 10.68 First-floor plan of the Bryan House.

entablature (fig. 10.66). The front mass is only one room deep, and with a dummy chimney over the stair hall and entablature parapets masking shed roofs on the wings, it presents the sham effect of a two-dimensional stage set (fig. 10.67). The front range contains three rooms downstairs and a bedroom over the dining room (fig. 10.68). The low ell at the back has an open entry off the dining room connecting to the pantry and kitchen. A stairway alongside the chimney ascends to a garret room over the kitchen. A servants' room is across the dogtrot beyond. Convenience of circulation seems to have been little considered in the planning of this house.

LEMON HILL.   More commodious and complex in arrangement but less well-proportioned is the country house Lemon Hill. It was built in the 1840s for Abraham Lunsford Ferguson on property he inherited from his father on the east side of Cleveland

Road, two miles north of the Winchester Pike in Fayette County.[72] Its portico is similar to that of the Bryan House, except its columns are more slender, its architrave is more shallow, its pediment has rustication in the tympanum, an elliptical centerpiece is in the ceiling, and railings connect the supports of the end bays. Bases of the columns and railings are of iron. The doorway may have been derived from plate 50 in Minard Lafever's *Young Builder's General Instructor* of 1829; it is centered and has a window of three lights above it (fig. 10.69). The wings have pilasters only at the outer corners, and their roofs, instead of being masked by the entablature, rise above it almost to the cornice of the principal pavilion, providing

rooms in the upper space (fig. 10.70). The effect reflects that of Redwood Library (1748-50) in Newport, Rhode Island, or an early version of Jefferson's Monticello, adapted from Robert Morris.[73] A recessed doorway on the right flank has simplified Doric pillars and an entablature similar to that of the front door. For the sake of symmetry, a blind window is inserted on this side of the house nearest the front corner, and there is another on the left flank.

A thirty-foot drawing room occupies the fore part of the principal mass, and behind it are the dining room and stair hall (fig. 10.71). A false door in the great room balances the real one to the hall. The drawing-room centerpiece has an inner motif identi-

Fig. 10.69 Lemon Hill (early 1840s), Fayette County. Photo, 1940.

Fig. 10.70 Restored sketch of the rear of Lemon Hill.

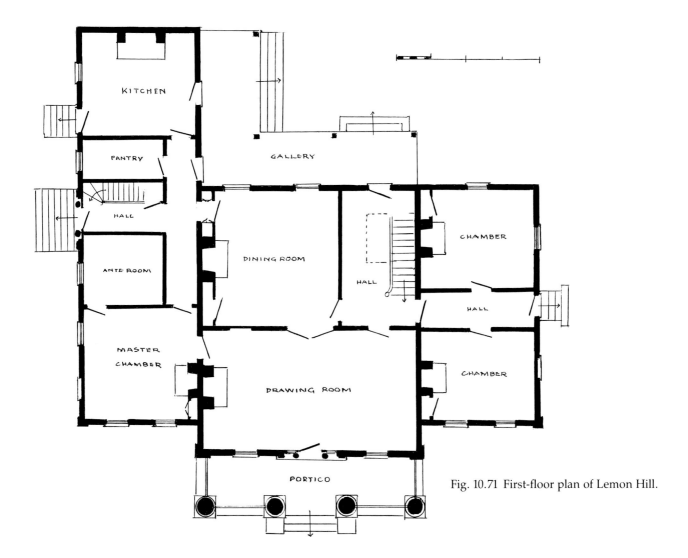

KITCHEN

PANTRY

GALLERY

HALL

ANTE ROOM

DINING ROOM

HALL

CHAMBER

HALL

MASTER CHAMBER

DRAWING ROOM

CHAMBER

PORTICO

Fig. 10.71 First-floor plan of Lemon Hill.

cal to that in the Gothic Revival Elley Villa in Lexington (chap. 11), whereas the outer border contains a whorled vine with flowers, and both have heavier molded frames (fig. 10.72). Rooms in the wings are considerably smaller, with lower ceilings. Steps from the second floor of the main part of the house lead down to the upper rooms in the wings, which have sloping ceilings and windows almost at floor level. The only basement is under the north wing, with a fireplace under the kitchen. The casual treatment of the rear of Lemon Hill contrasts remarkably with the formality of the front.

THE DILLARD HOUSE. The Kentucky house which most completely reflects indebtedness to a specific builder's guide design is that of Robert Dillard in Hopkinsville. It was built in the mid-1850s, and the planter Dillard moved to it in order that his daughter might acquire the graces and advantages of

Fig. 10.72 Centerpiece in drawing room, Lemon Hill. Photo, 1952.

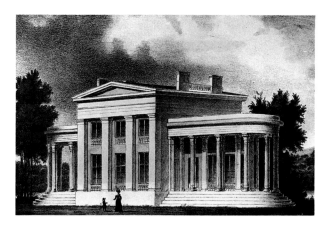

Fig. 10.73 "Perspective View of a Design for a Country Residence." From Minard Lafever, *The Modern Practice of Staircase and Hand-Rail Construction* (New York, 1838), pl. 3.

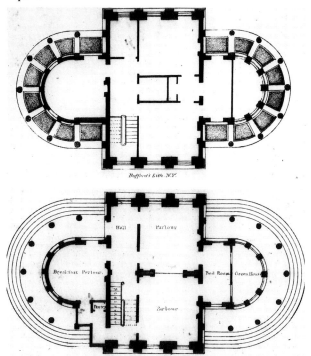

Fig. 10.74 Floor plans of the design from Minard Lafever, *The Modern Practice of Staircase and Hand-Rail Construction* (New York, 1838), pl. 4.

urban life. The prototype came from Minard Lafever's *The Modern Practice of Staircase and Hand-rail Construction*, a little book of only forty-seven pages, issued probably in a small quantity in New York in 1838.[74] Besides showing staircases with strong resemblances to those in Peter Nicholson's books, there are colored perspective views and plans for two original villas.[75] The more distinguished of the two

Fig. 10.75 The Robert Dillard House (ca. 1847), Hopkinsville. Photo, 1940.

has perfectly balanced columned galleries encircling the curved end of lower wings right and left of a pilastered rectangular mass (fig. 10.73). It is labeled "a design for a country residence which presents elegance and conveniences suitable for a gentleman of respectable circumstances." Fretwork panels appear beneath windows and between the chimneys of the main block of the house. Colonnades at the sides make use of Lafever's own Corinthian order delineated on plate 11 of his *Beauties of Modern Architecture* (fig. 10.19). The first-floor plan consists of a stair hall and twin parlors separated by sliding doors, a "breakfast parlour" (dining room) in the annex adjacent to the hall, pantries between this room and the rear of the hall, and a bedroom and conservatory opposite (fig. 10.74). The second story contains five chambers.

The Dillard House in Hopkinsville is simpler than the Lafever design. It sits close to the ground. The colonnades are Doric and the architrave and frieze are differentiated only by a fillet (fig. 10.75). Parapets above the wing cornices mask the roof, which slopes downward toward a valley in the center. The walls are wood, and the surfaces between pilasters are given a rusticated treatment. Windows in the wings appear only in the flat surfaces front and back. The house reverses the hall-parlor arrangement, the dining room could be reached only from the porch, and the opposite wing contains a single chamber (fig. 10.76). Two large bedrooms and a small hall room occupy the second floor. Lafever had suggested that this house "may be built with all necessary conveniences, on the rear of the plan"; and his advice was taken in the Dillard House, where a pantry and kitchen of two stories opened off a dogtrot. The room

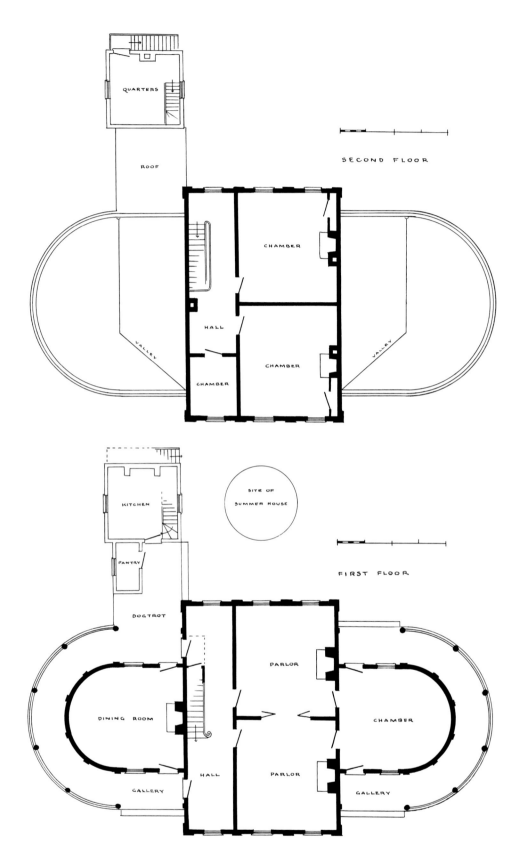

Fig. 10.76 Restored floor plans of the Dillard House.

over the kitchen was reached by inside and outside stairs. A round summerhouse stood nearby.

Pedestals have replaced the lower part of the wing columns, a door has been cut through the wall at the foot of the staircase to the dining room, the kitchen has been razed and parts of it incorporated into a one-story wing adjoining the house, and a bath has been installed in the upper hall. The house now serves as an antique shop.

The most characteristic Greek Revival houses have two full stories and an equally tall entrance portico. The prototype for this species may have been Horn Quarter, a transitional Federal–Greek Revival house in King William County, Virginia, built for George Taylor in 1829-30.[76] The portico has three interspaces, and the windows have three lights; by far the widest of each is in the center. Thoroughly in the Greek idiom is Sachem's Wood in New Haven, Connecticut, the Greek Revival house of 1828 by which New York architect Alexander J. Davis launched his career.[77] The main differences are that Sachem's Wood lacks triple windows, and the outer supports of its portico are square.

THE CRAIG HOUSE.   The first Kentucky house of this type to be considered is on Cane Run Road near the Georgetown-Frankfort Pike in Scott County, built for William G. Craig during the 1840s (fig. 10.77). Its Doric columns are slightly attenuated, their channeled shafts of stuccoed brick rest on stone plinths, and the capitals, entablature, and pediment are of wood. The full entablature continues across the front and around the sides of the building, carried on pilasters, having triglyphs in the frieze, and mutules with guttae and anthemions on the soffit of the cornice. Except for the channels penetrating the necking, the model for the order is that of the Parthenon, probably taken from plate 37 of Edward Shaw's *Civil Architecture* (figs. 10.6, 10.7). The pilastered doorway is restrained, the door itself unusual in its single panel. Triple windows above and at each side repeat the motif of the front door with sidelights. Walls are of unbonded brickwork. The forms of the chimneys are especially handsome. Side porches had square wooden piers, and railings ran around the upper decks. The appeal of the building resides in its good proportions and attention to details. From oral tradition, the stonework was executed by convict labor, presumably while Capt. Newton Craig was a keeper at the Kentucky penitentiary from 1844 to 1849.[78]

On 9 May 1845 Thomas Lewinski noted in his diary that he "Ordered of Mr. N. Craig two cap stones for the pedestals of the Honbl. H. Clay Steps." This connection and Lewinski's ownership of Shaw's

Fig. 10.77 The William G. Craig House (1840s), Scott County. Photo, 1955.

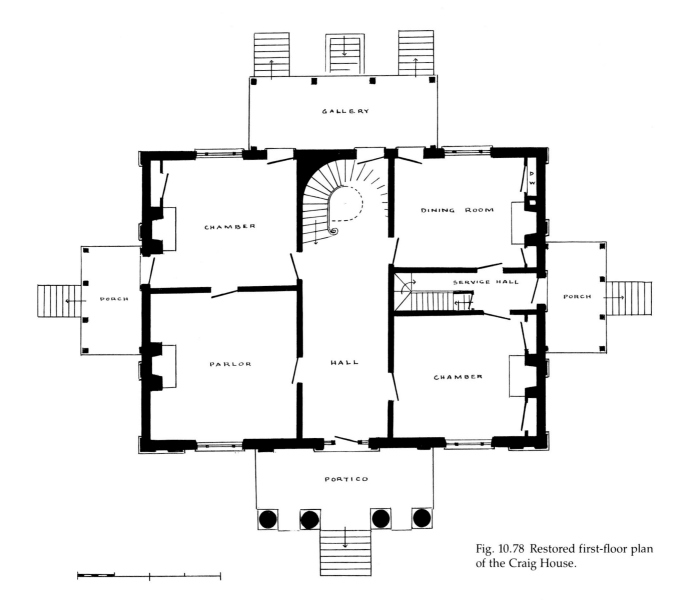

Fig. 10.78 Restored first-floor plan of the Craig House.

Civil Architecture might lead one to suspect that he designed the house, but the project is not mentioned in his diary, which covers the period from 24 March 1845 to 5 July 1847, nor is there any known documentary evidence to support such a supposition. Room variations and irregular placing of doors seem unlike Lewinski's work (fig. 10.78). In the parlor ceiling is the circular Lafever centerpiece; the centerpiece in the hall is rectangular with a center motif like that in the Lemon Hill drawing room. An open newel staircase winds around the curved back of the hall. The kitchen is in the basement, and a dumbwaiter brought food up to the dining room.

The Craig House and 462 acres of land were sold in 1857 to George C. Branham, whose daughter, Sallie Branham Johnson Bradley, inherited the property eight years later.[79] The residence and about a third of the acreage were acquired in 1891 by H.C. Allen, whose great-grandson, Allen Porter, is the present occupant.[80]

Kentucky contains many simplified versions of the Craig House, lacking its refinements but pleasing and substantial buildings nevertheless. The Noah Spears House (1854), on Pleasant Street in Paris, has square piers for outer supports to the portico, like Town's Sachem's Wood, and between them are piers with polygonal shafts, giving the impression of fluting.[81] Some of the houses with four identical columns are compact and two rooms deep, like Colonial Home at Bethel on the county line between Fayette

Fig. 10.79 Buenna Hill (late 1840s), Fayette County. Photo, 1943.

tispiece is attractive, with smaller Ionic columns supporting an entablature whose frieze is emblazoned by anthemions resembling those in the north portal of the Erechtheum, probably derived from a plate in Lafever's *Modern Builder's Guide* (fig. 10.11). Stone portico stairs extend to the outer sides of the inner columns, the lowest step being characteristically wider than the others. Brick paving, averaging six feet across, encircles the house. Aligned to the left flank is the long ell, altogether consisting of eight bays, the middle four having recessed galleries. The entablature is full, and the roof is hipped, except for a gable at the end of the ell and of course the portico pediment.

Rooms are square and similar in size; each has a projecting chimney breast and windows in two walls (fig. 10.81). The drawing room and parlor adjoin the front stair hall. The informal family room and the dining room behind are flanked by open galleries, and the kitchen at the end has an extension in back of the pantry serving as a rear entry. The first and last rooms in the ell have stairways in one corner.

Brick dependencies close to the main house in-

and Scott. Most have a shallow front and a rear ell of two stories, like Buenna Hill, built for Robert Innes by John McMurtry during the late 1840s nine miles north of Lexington on old Cynthiana (Russell Cave) Pike (fig. 10.79).[82]

WAVELAND. Perhaps the most typical Kentucky house of the group is Waveland on Higbee Mill Road near the Nicholasville Pike, five miles below Lexington. It was constructed in 1847 for Joseph Bryan by the builder Washington Allen.[83] The portico has closely paired Ionic columns, and all the front windows have three lights (figs. 10.2, 10.80). The fron-

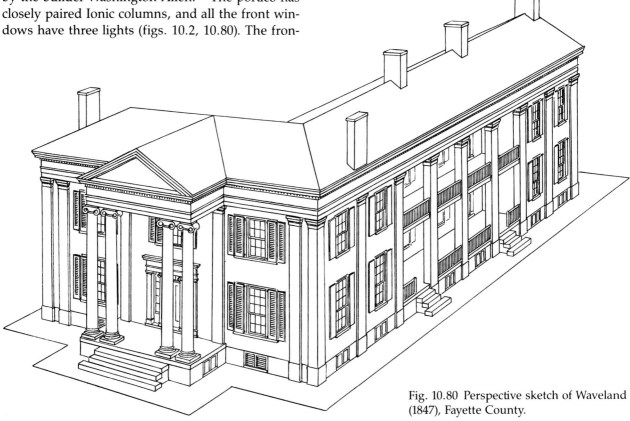

Fig. 10.80 Perspective sketch of Waveland (1847), Fayette County.

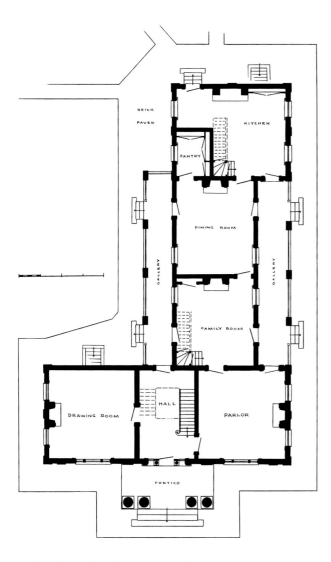

Fig. 10.81 First-floor plan of Waveland.

signed by John McMurtry and completed by him in September of 1854.[85] It is larger and more elaborate and employs a T instead of an L plan. Of special note is the fine modeling of the cast-iron column capitals of the Corinthian order that give title to the house (fig. 10.83). They were inspired by those of the best preserved temple of the Romans, the Maison Carrée at Nîmes, France. Limestone steps extend across the entire portico. The lower front windows are unusually tall, rising from floor level and expressing the ceiling height. Great sliding doors between the hall and parlors permit the front suite to be thrown into a single interior fifty-eight feet long. The main stair hall is behind, and the dining room lies between it and a secondary stair hall and two open galleries on the flanks (fig. 10.84). The kitchen is in the basement, accessible from the rear stairs. The two chambers at the back were perhaps meant to accommodate business associates. There are five bedrooms on the second floor. The newel post at the base of the main staircase is a console mounted on a plinth, the end of the handrail forming a volute at the top (fig. 10.85). Wood trim is narrow and out of scale with the massiveness of the house. Plaster flower centerpieces on the parlor ceilings are trivial. These inferior details

clude two-story servants' quarters, smokehouse, and icehouse, all connected by brick walks to the terrace (fig. 10.82). The property passed out of the Bryan family in 1894, and the Commonwealth of Kentucky became its owner in 1956. Waveland is now a museum.

A facade practically identical to Waveland's is on the Benjamin McCann House, six miles from Lexington on the Richmond Pike, built in 1847 and attributed to John McMurtry.[84] It differs in that the main part is two rooms deep and the extension at the rear, which includes a kitchen connected to the serving room by an open dogtrot, is much smaller.

CORINTHIA.   Resembling Robert Innes's Buenna Hill in form and built across Russell Cave Road for his brother, Charles Webb Innes, Corinthia was de-

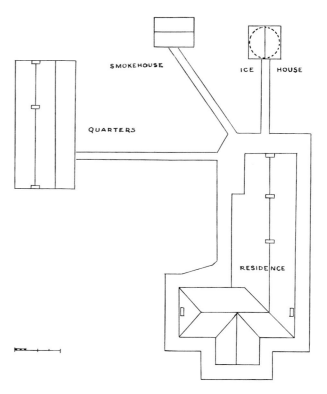

Fig. 10.82 Restored plan of roofs and walks of main house and dependencies at Waveland.

Fig. 10.83 Corinthia (1854), Fayette County. Photo, 1941.

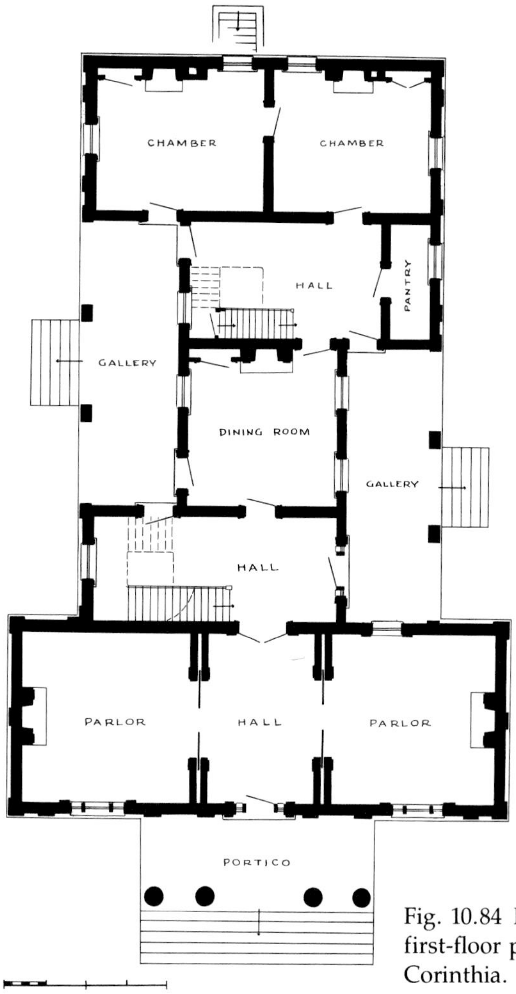

show the beginning of the stylistic breakdown of the Greek Revival.

Two contemporary houses similar to Corinthia were Fairlawn and the Pettit House. Fairlawn was built for Thomas Hughes on the Paris Pike six miles from Lexington, and it was renamed Greentree after its purchase by Payne Whitney in 1926. The William B. Pettit House stood on the Nicholasville Pike just north of Stone Road. From 1887 to 1900 it was operated as a boys' school called Alleghan Academy.[86] The building was razed in 1966.

Fig. 10.84 Restored first-floor plan of Corinthia.

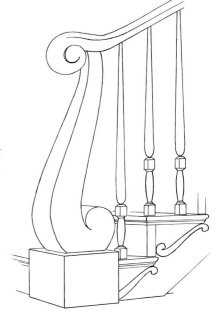

Fig. 10.85 Sketch of newel post at base of main staircase, Corinthia.

WARD HALL.   The most imposing Greek rural residence in Kentucky is that built for Junius Richard Ward on the Georgetown-Frankfort Pike in Scott County, not far from the Craig House. It is said that upon completion of the building in 1859, the contracted amount of $50,000 was paid in gold to the builder, with a $500 lagniappe in appreciation for the excellence of the work.[87] The Ward mansion has an exceedingly high basement. The portico order is the same as at Corinthia, only here the column shafts are fluted, and the pilasters have acanthus capitals, rather than plain Doric ones. Antepodia flank the portico steps, and a platform spans the entire facade (fig. 10.86). Stone paving at ground level extends out from the building eight feet in front and six feet

elsewhere, except at the portico and stoops, where subsidiary strips link the interrupted walk. An attic treatment, with pedestal forms aligned to the coupled pilasters at the ends and a stepped parapet in the center, is at front and back, and chimneys rise over the pilasters on the flanks. The terminal bays on the sides contain blind windows.

It has been suggested that Thomas Lewinski designed Ward Hall based on the similarity of its architectural dress to Woodside, Henry Bell's house in Lexington, known to have been conceived by Lewinski during the mid-1840s.[88] As with the nearby Craig House, however, no documentary evidence yet found supports this contention.

The large scale, clarity of plan, and richness of

Fig. 10.86 Ward Hall (late 1850s), Scott County. Photo, 1964.

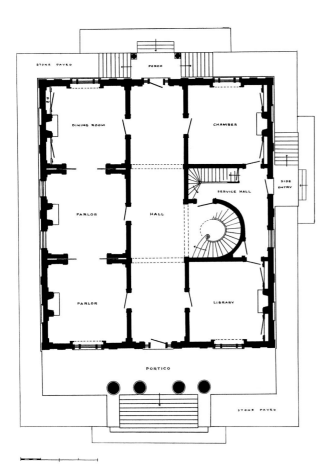

Fig. 10.87 Restored first-floor plan of Ward Hall.

Fig. 10.88 Ceiling detail and chandelier in front parlor of Ward Hall. Photo, 1964.

detail also produce a magnificent interior. The space is divided into nine almost equal parts, the three down the center constituting a sixty-five-foot hall; an elliptical staircase on the west side of the middle bay spirals up to the third floor (fig. 10.87). Above the natural walnut doorways, which have battered sides and Greek ears at the top, a cornice is adorned with exquisitely carved acroteria in the Lafever style. Pilasters farming the sliding doors and in the corners of the rooms of the east suite, as well as those dividing the hall, support a full entablature, which is ornamented with egg-and-dart and acanthus bands. Plaster centerpieces in the principal rooms are recessed in circular panels, and they retain their original colors of pink, yellow, pale green, and blue (fig. 10.88). From them hang silver-and-crystal chandeliers whose globes are etched with classic figures. Door hardware is of Sheffield plate, and white marble mantels are carved with grapes and foliage.

The kitchen was in the southeast corner of the basement, and food was sent up on a dumbwaiter alongside the dining-room chimney breast. In the second-floor bedroom opposite the stairway was a rare survivor of Greek Revival decoration. Baseboards were marbleized, and the walls and ceiling were divided by strips of paper, stamped with Pompeiian designs, into large panels and borders, which were painted in flat colors. This decor was obliterated during the 1940s. Doorways on the third floor are enframed by a design from Lafever's *Young Builder's General Instructor* (fig. 10.89, 10.90). The stair to the roof pent has a neat railing and square-shaped newel post. A copper cistern in the garret provided running water. The sheet copper that covered the roof was removed and sold during the Civil War. Financial reverses forced Junius Ward to sacrifice the mansion. It was purchased by Allie DeLong, and the Wards went to live on their Mississippi plantation. The subsequent owner, Col. Milton Hamilton, offered the house to the commonwealth for $50,000 when the Frankfort capitol was in bad repair. It was an absurd proposal if only because Ward Hall is but half the size of the Shryock building.

HARTLAND AND HIGHLAND HALL. Many two-story Kentucky houses have square piers instead of columns, to their porticoes. Typical is Hartland, built for John Hart during the 1840s on Armstrong Mill Road, five miles below Lexington. It is an L-shaped building, with facade neatly laid in Flemish-bond brickwork. The piers are closely coupled, and the only pilasters and full entablature are limited to this

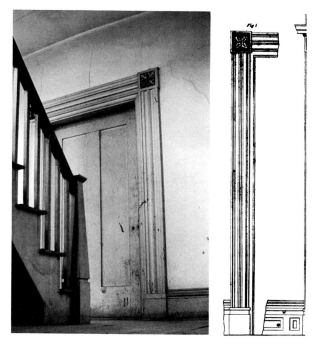

Figs. 10.89, 90 Third-story doorway, Ward Hall. Photo, 1940. Design for a door frame. From Minard Lafever, *The Young Builder's General Instructor* (Newark, N.J., 1829), pl. 29, fig. 1.

portico (fig. 10.91). The chaste doorway includes channeled Doric columns in antis and a transom enframed in small panes. All front windows have three lights. The roof is hipped, except for the pediment of the portico, whose tympanum has a later trefoil vent hole. A subdivision now overspreads the site.

Highland Hall is a few miles away on the Richmond Pike. It dates from the eve of the Civil War and represents the last phase of the style. The outer piers of the portico are spaced farther apart and the roof pitch is lower than in other examples discussed. The doorway is narrower, lacking column supports between the antas. Windows are of two equal lights. This feature solves the shutter problem adequately but does little for the appearance of the house. A photograph of Highland Hall was exhibited at the Philadelphia Centennial of 1876 as representing a typical Kentucky house (fig. 10.92). It cost $20,000 to construct.

Highland Hall has the widest portico in relation to the breadth of the front wall of any house discussed so far. In the next group of houses to be considered, the porticoes span three bays of the five-bay facades. We have already considered the earliest of this type—by fifteen to twenty years—the Keats House of 1835 in Louisville. It is possible, of course, that the portico of the Keats residence was added by a subsequent owner, James Trabue, about the time the others in the group were built. Photographs do not suggest this, but without examination one cannot be sure. One difference between it and the others is that the spacing of the columns in the Keats House was more nearly the same, whereas in the rest the center two supports are proportionally wider apart. In the two latest, The Elms and Cedar Hall in Fayette County, the middle bay of the portico in one is almost twice as wide as the outer bays and the other is more than twice as wide. No other of the group has quite such a

Fig. 10.91 Hartland (1840s), Fayette County. Photo, 1942.

Fig. 10.92 Highland Hall (ca. 1860), Fayette County. Photo, ca. 1874, courtesy of Alfred Andrews, Newtown, Conn.

high basement story as the Keats House, nor was any other urban residence built as close to the street.

THE McCAULEY HOUSE. A subclass of the Keats House type features the Doric order and has no pediment to the portico. The first example discussed has almost a full third story, though hardly apparent from the front. John McCauley's house was built by John McMurtry on the five-acre tract on Maxwell Street in Lexington acquired in 1850.[89] The portico columns are of wood with channeled shafts, and the entablature across the front surmounts short third-story windows (at floor level), with iron grilles of anthemion pattern (fig. 10.93). As the entablature turns the corners of the facade only for the depth of the pilasters, there is full fenestration in the upper ends of the house, and parapets masking the roofline connect the chimneys. The front doorway is deeply indented in the center bay, its Ionic columns having unusually thick shafts. Identical supports coupled with antas flank both sides of the sliding doors between the double parlors (fig. 10.94). Other openings are enframed by pilasters and the entablature encircling these rooms, the doors having awkward leftover spaces above them. Ceiling centerpieces are of the Lafever design. Marble chimney pieces are geometrically severe, with a suggestion of pilasters. A long staircase occupying the rear of the hall has a heavy newel post with volutes at top and bottom, somewhat like that at Corinthia. The service ell is an earlier, two-story dwelling converted to this purpose. Appurtenances once included a stable, a smokehouse, and a two-story servants' house.[90] The grounds have dwindled to a fraction of their original extent, with a church encroaching on the front yard. The house now is accessible from Lexington Avenue. Besides a residence, it has served as an Episcopal seminary, Prof. A.I. Totten's School for Boys, a so-

Figs. 10.93, 10.94 The John McCauley House (early 1850s), Lexington. Photo of front, late 1800s, courtesy of the University of Kentucky Libraries. Detail of enframement of sliding doors between parlors. Photo, 1940.

rority house, a university dormitory, and apartments.

Similar to the McCauley house is the main block of Walnut Hall, on the Newtown Pike north of Lexington, built for Victor Flournoy in 1842 and now considerably enlarged.[91] A second example is Scotland, outside Frankfort near the junction of Georgetown and Versailles pikes, unique in having a brick entablature, even to the portico.[92]

ROSEHILL. Col. William Holloway acquired a thirty-two-acre tract on East Main Street at the edge of Richmond in 1849.[93] A two-story brick house already on the site was retained, as in the McCauley House, and became the rear ell to a new Greek Revival front. The house, called Rosehill, has a pedimented tetrastyle Ionic portico, like the Keats House, but the main mass is shallow and without a basement (fig. 10.95). Unusual features include steps at the sides as well as in front of the portico, columns with stone bases, anthemion reliefs on the neckings of columns and pilasters, and two rows of dentils in the entablature, the unorthodox set separating architrave and frieze (fig. 10.96). The handsome doorway has been pictured and discussed earlier as derived from Lafever (figs. 10.11, 10.12). The mid-century addition with its 22-foot-square rooms outscales the old part, which contained the dining room as well as the kitchen and was accessible only across porches (fig.

10.97). The elliptical staircase in the main hall is a thing of beauty, its railing carried on finely shaped banisters of Egyptian inspiration, its consoles carved into a bird-leaf pattern, a great lion's paw forming the base of the stairway string, and the first few steps curving out gracefully (fig. 10.98). The circular plaster centerpiece is especially suitable here (fig. 10.16).

A one-story wing was attached to the left flank of the house after its purchase by Maj. Jonathan T. Estill in 1860. The rear ell was demolished shortly after World War II, and recently the Holloway pavilion has served as the Telford Community Center.

A house with a similar facade is Cumberland View, southeast of Richmond, built for Alec Tribble in 1855. In Cumberland View, however, antepodia break the continuity of front and side steps, and the pilasters as well as the columns have bases. The McHatton-Showalter House at Georgetown and Aspen Hall at Harrodsburg are among other members of this group.[94] The last and the two to follow are or were without fluted columns.

THE ELMS AND CEDAR HALL. Two houses resembling the Holloway House, only with the entablature limited to the portico, were The Elms and Cedar Hall. As has been noted, the spacing between their center columns was exceptionally wide, and their architraves came below lintel level of the upstairs windows.

Fig. 10.95 Rosehill (ca. 1850), Richmond. Photo, 1941.

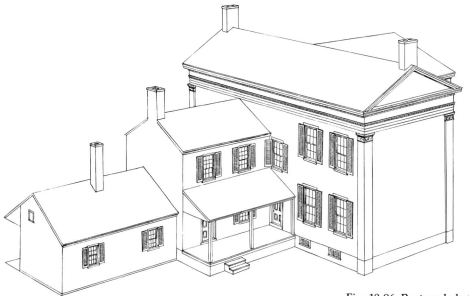

Fig. 10.96 Restored sketch of the rear of Rosehill.

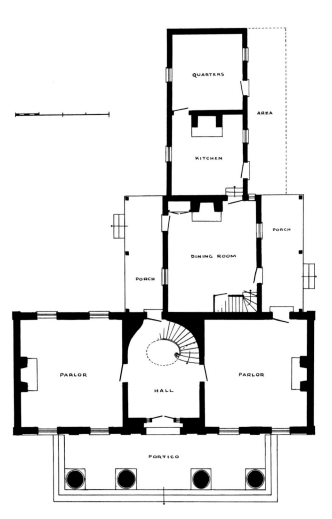

Fig. 10.97 Restored first-floor plan of Rosehill.

Fig. 10.98 Base of staircase in Rosehill. Photo, 1941.

Fig. 10.99 The Elms (before 1854), Fayette County. Photo, ca. 1900, courtesy of Mrs. P.G. Savage.

The Elms was built by John McMurtry for William Leavy before 1854, the year the architect became the owner.[95] The house presided over an estate of more than 350 acres, a mile from Lexington on the east side of the Harrodsburg Pike. Steps spanned the front of the portico, and the columns had stuccoed brick shafts on limestone bases (fig. 10.99). The doorway has been shown as an adaptation from a design by Edward Shaw (figs. 10.7, 10.8). Windows were fifteen-paned in the first story and twelve above. The house was large and consisted of reduplication of similar rooms 20 feet square, arranged on either side of an ample stair hall or off an open gallery on axis 62 feet long (fig. 10.100). The staircase rose gracefully up to the third floor, and there were projecting forms in the lower hall containing niches for life-size sculptures. Dependencies included a brick servants' quarters, a large carriage house, stables, barn, and a gristmill, according to a newspaper description when the property was auctioned in 1856.[96] McMurtry had run into financial difficulties building the School for the Deaf in Danville (chap. 12), and he had to sacrifice The Elms. During the present century the house has been an orphanage and then part of Lafayette High School. It burned in 1940, and the remains were pulled down for a new building.

Cedar Hall is about seven miles out from Lexington on Bowman's Mill Road, near the Harrodsburg Pike. George H. Bowman, the owner, offered it for sale in 1858, declaring it to be "newly built."[97] The front steps are only the width of the middle bay of the portico, the doorway is quite conventional, and windows are fifteen-paned on both levels (fig. 10.101). In the hall the staircase ascends in straight flights. The element surpassing that of its sister house is refinement of interior trim. Enframements in the main rooms reflect the design of plate 49 in Lafever's *Modern Builder's Guide*. The columned

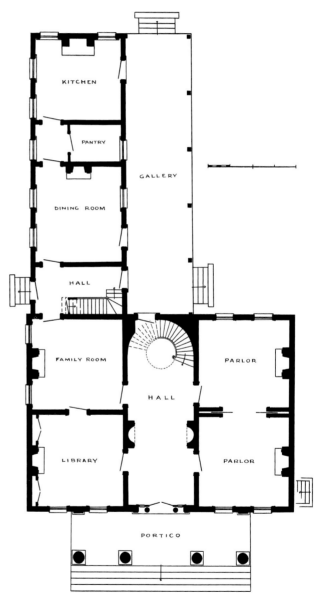

Fig. 10.100 Restored first-floor plan of The Elms.

THE GREEK REVIVAL STYLE 235

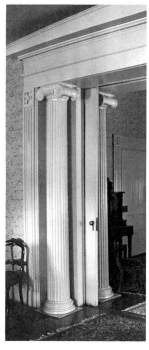

Figs. 10.101, 10.102 Cedar Hall (1850s), Fayette County. Front, detail of doorway between parlors. Photos, 1941.

Fig. 10.103 The Daniel Stagg House (after 1835), Harrodsburg. Photo, 1964.

doorway between parlors is lighter, and its entablature does not encompass the room as in the McCauley House (fig. 10.102).

The trend toward widening the portico, which reached three-fifths of the facade width in the Keats House, attained three-fourths in Cedar Hall, due to the greater breadth between the middle two columns. The outer bays of the portico had only to equal the middle, and the building would be prostyle. Doricham, the mid-nineteenth century house of Daniel Stagg at 409 North College Street in Harrodsburg exemplifies this type (fig. 10.103). As at Graham Springs, portico bays each span two windows, and there is no pediment. The windows have external frames like interior woodwork, and the front doorway bears a resemblance to that of nearby Diamond Point at the corner of Price Avenue (fig. 10.18). It has a portico across its three-bayed facade,

with two round Doric columns between square piers at the corners, the entire structure being covered by a hip roof. A third example whose form was related to the two in Harrodsburg was on the Lexington-Nicholasville Pike near the county line. It is said to have been built for the Bryan family in 1856. Although the facade was as broad as that of the house on College Street and it had a tetrastyle portico, the front wall had only a single window on either side of the doorway.

THE BURGESS HOUSE.   One of the oddest houses ever to have a porticoed front is outside of Mayslick in Mason County, built during the mid-1850s for Michael R. Burgess, a founder of the Maysville Savings Institute.[98] The first floor is nearly at ground level, and the portico abuts the house without pilasters a little short of the wall width (fig. 10.104). The two center supports are fluted Ionic columns, and

Fig. 10.104 The Michael R. Burgess House (mid-1850s), Mayslick. Photo, 1940.

Fig. 10.105 The Staircase in the Burgess House. Photo, 1940.

the outer are smooth square posts with angular voluted capitals that are unique in the annals of classic architecture. A row of small dentils divides architrave and frieze, and another of larger dentils separates frieze and cornice. The ceiling of the portico is level with the soffit of the architrave, and this boxiness carries around the building in the plain parapet, the depth of the portico entablature. Originally a heavy balustrade crowned the parapet, with chimney pots conducting smoke to the top of the railing. Chimneys are partly inside and partly outside the wall planes. The front door is a shuttered opening not unlike the parlor windows. Two blind windows are in the north wall, adjoining the stair hall. The staircase is at the back of this hall, the handrail curling over an urn set on a plinth, forming the newel post (fig. 10.105). Parlor and dining room open to the south, and a kitchen and pantry are in the ell, a stairway from the dining room ascending to the back room upstairs (fig. 10.106). The mantel and centerpiece in the parlor belong to a later period.

WARWICK. A notable house with porticoed front was Warwick, built by Robert Russell, Jr., for Dr. Joseph Weisiger on a South Second Street lot in Danville purchased in 1843.[99] Like Higgins Mansion in Lexington, Warwick had a pedimented hexastyle portico flanked by wings of two bays; but the wings were two storied, and the portico contained round Ionic columns in antis (fig. 10.107). Though simplified, all elements were architecturally proper, unlike those of the Burgess House. The well-proportioned Doric doorway has been compared to a design from Asher Benjamin's *Practical House Carpenter* (figs. 10.3, 10.4). The stair hall was across the front of the main block of the house, lighted by windows opening on the portico. On entering, the staircase was to the left, as in the Thomas Bodley House in Lexington (chap. 8). Warwick became part of the School for the Deaf in 1885, and it was razed in 1957. Its form is reflected in the Yeiser-Kinnaird-Chestnut House on East Lexington Street in Danville, the result of a number of additions and changes. Its upstairs windows are three-quarters above the line of the architrave.[100] As in Warwick, the wings of the house come forward to the antas and thus the portico is more recessed than projecting.

THE BARBEE-McCLURE HOUSE. A house with an unqualified recessed portico is that also built by Robert Russell, Jr., about 1850, for Samuel Porter Barbee at 304 South Fourth Street in Danville (fig. 10.108).[101] It sits low to the ground, like the Burgess

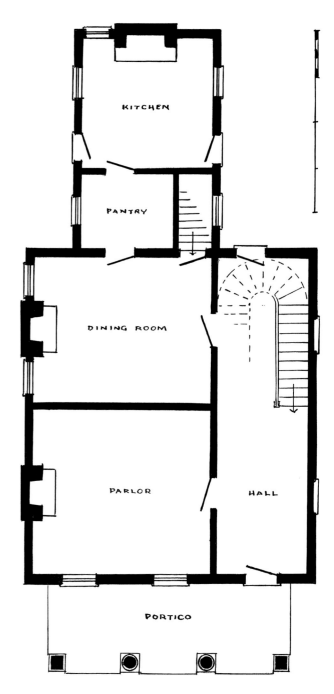

Fig. 10.106 First-floor plan of the Burgess House.

House. The three equal units of the facade are crowned by a full entablature. The plan is T-shaped, with square rooms grouped around the junction, which area is divided equally into porch and stair hall (fig. 10.109). An open side porch with louvered screens extends back from the chamber along the left flank of the dining room and kitchen. Three bedrooms are upstairs. In 1908 the house was acquired

Fig. 10.107 Warwick (after 1843), Danville. Photo, 1940.

by Professor George M. McClure, by whose name it is generally identified.

An attractive variation on the recessed-portico theme is the John B. Clark House (1843) on State Street in Bowling Green, which has superimposed Doric columns in two levels of polygonal porches.[102] Walls are of exceptionally fine Flemish-bond brickwork.

The indented portico proved a great convenience in providing an entrance shelter to buildings erected adjacent to the street, as in the William Y. Davis House in Bloomfield, from which a mantel has been illustrated (fig. 10.10). The lower doorway has no more prominence than the portal to the Francis Key Hunt House, attaining portico status only through superposition. The upper entablature is ornamented

Fig. 10.108 The Samuel Porter Barbee House (ca. 1850), Danville. Photo, 1964.

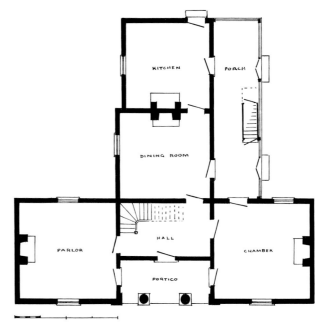

Fig. 10.109 Restored first-floor plan of the Barbee House.

Fig. 10.110 Portal of the William Y. Davis House, Bloomfield. Photo, 1941.

Fig. 10.111 Restored sketch of the Bayles-Oldham House (1846), Lexington.

with triglyphs, and mutules with guttae are suspended from the cornice (fig. 10.110).

The colossal-order portico may have been the Greek Revival's most distinguished feature, but it was by no means essential. During ancient times the porticoed facade was used in public buildings including palaces, but not in private dwellings. It could be humanized by being reduced in scale; and in becoming less imposing, it became more inviting. This will be seen in the next few examples.

THE BAYLES-OLDHAM HOUSE. The house that stood on Hill (now East High) Street facing present Stone Avenue in Lexington was built by Jesse Bayles in 1846 and acquired by Edward Oldham the following year.[103] In form it resembled the Matthew Kennedy House, a quarter of a century older, having the center three bays of the facade gabled, and giant pilasters connected directly with the cornice (figs. 9.22, 10.111). The Bayles-Oldham House included only two pilasters, and they had beautifully modeled brick bases between the cellar windows at ground level. Arched openings had been eliminated, and the

plainness of fenestration served to focus attention on the portico. It had a high platform with small, coupled Ionic columns set on antepodia with paneled fronts. Steps rose half under the entablature, which had advanced end blocks over the paired columns, and there were aligned pedestal-like posts above, connected by balustrades. Paired pilasters against the wall responded to the outer supports, and matching columns stood in antis at the entrance to the deeply receding doorway (fig. 10.112). The floor plan was a normal center-hall type, and there was an open gallery at the back of the house overlooking Town Fork of Elkhorn.

Hood molds were added over all the front windows, panels with cutout patterns inserted in the

Fig. 10.112 Portal detail of the Bayles-Oldham House. Photo, 1942.

angles of the gable cornices, and dormers set on the roof before the present century; much later the walls were painted white. An iron fire escape was affixed to the facade when the building was converted into a business school. A twin to the Bayles-Oldham House was that of Dr. David Bell built during 1845-46 on the west side of Broadway south of High Street. Both residences were razed early in the 1970s.

LEAFLAND. Six houses dating from about 1850-55 east of Lexington on or just off the Winchester Pike may be considered together, having in common a heavy two-storied form crowned by a low-pitched hip roof, the facade pierced by three triple openings in each level, and the center doorway prefaced by a small portico. All but the one nearest town (the Darnaby House, on the South side between Chilesburg and Cleveland roads) have broad pilasters incorporated in the walls, supporting a deep entablature, the exception substituting a sunken-panel effect in brickwork. The second house out from Lexington is Leafland, the Jacob Hughes residence, on the north side of the road a short distance past the Alberti place. Its pilasters are unusually thick and its voids constricted; the entablatures of both house and portico,

and the square wooden piers of the latter, are simplified to essentials (fig. 10.113). Wings, not in equal balance, flank the main pavilion. Four rooms on each floor are accessible from the central transverse stair hall. Ceilings of the first story are 14 feet high, and those of the chamber level are 15, taking advantage of the space over the windows afforded by the entablature. Other members of the group differ slightly. Edgewood, across from Leafland and beyond Combs Ferry Road, has two-story wings on both sides. Dunreath (Scottish for Wooded Hill), on the same side of the pike as Leafland and near the county line, lacks the low west wing.[104] The names of all six have tree connotations.

THE BUTLER HOUSE. In 1846 John McMurtry built the residence of James C. Butler north of his own home (chap. 11) and two doors south of the Dr. David Bell House on Main Cross Street (Broadway) in Lexington.[105] The main block resembled a row house, except for having an ell attached to the southwest corner (fig. 10.114). The severity of these forms was relieved by iron anthemion grilles in the garret windows or in sunken parapet panels, and a small distyle Ionic portico placed before the columned

Fig. 10.113 Leafland (1850s), Fayette County. Photo, 1941.

Fig. 10.114 Restored sketch of the James C. Butler House (1846), Lexington.

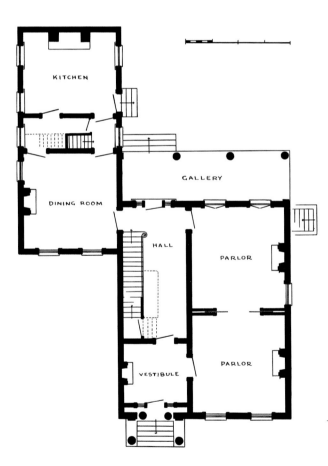

Fig. 10.115 First-floor plan of the Butler House.

entrance. The projecting ends of the entablature and indented stairs were elements seen in the portico of the Bayles-Oldham House. The front door opened into a square vestibule with a fireplace (fig. 10.115). In the hall behind, the staircase faced the back door, and the windows of the rear parlor had hinged panels beneath the sashes for access to the gallery, orienting the principal block toward the garden. The wing was set far back and the dining room faced the front. Both parts of the house had a full second story, and there was a third floor over the living section. Interior fittings were plain, including a matching pair of clean-cut black marble mantels with Greek ears in the parlors. The Butler House was demolished in 1974.

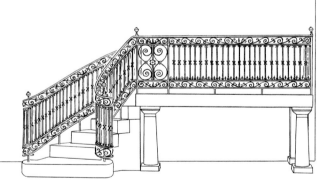

Fig. 10.116 Restored sketch of the stoop of the Dr. James Fishback House (1838-42), Lexington.

Fig. 10.117 Restored facade elevation and details of Honeysuckle Hill (early 1840s), Harrodsburg.

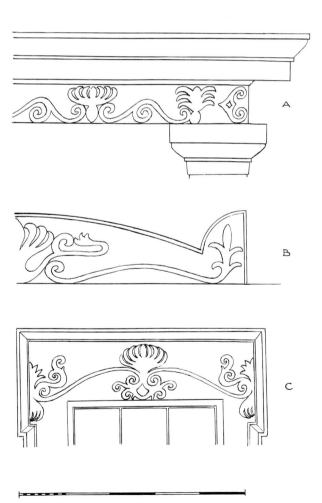

The portico was eliminated from many contemporary townhouses though the recessed portal remained. High basements called for stoops, usually having stone steps and iron railings. One of the handsomest belongs to the house at 176 North Broadway in Lexington, built by McMurtry and sold to Dr. James Fishback in 1838. The stoop consists of five winders ascending to a slab supported on a pair of tiny Doric columns set on plinths (fig. 10.116). The wrought-iron railings have whorled borders at top and bottom, joined by uprights decorated with small cast pieces. A horizontal spiral over the first step and a panel with balanced volutes over the column relieve the regularity of the design, and brass-ball finials accent the corners and ends of the railing. Later alterations to the building and the sidewalk detract from the effect.

HONEYSUCKLE HILL. The unique suburban house of substantial size at 712 Beaumont Avenue, Harrodsburg, was built for Dr. Guilford Runyan. He had been the physician in the Shaker village at nearby Pleasant Hill, but "returned to the world" in 1839 and purchased the thirty-five-acre tract for his home. He intended to marry a lady from the lower Mississippi region, but she died before the wedding. The residence in which Dr. Runyan lived with his two

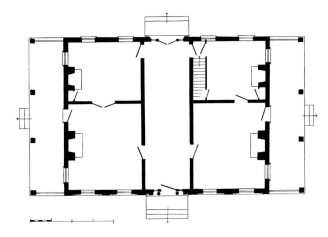

Fig. 10.118 First-floor plan of Honeysuckle Hill.

sisters has a seven-bayed flat facade divided by pilasters and with square piers at the extremities; there are two-storied galleries across the ends. These are screened from the front by louvered panels at the first level and shaped wood floral (honeysuckle) motifs above, the latter suggesting New Orleans ironwork patterns (fig. 10.117). The frieze beneath the front cornice, that over the recessed and colonnetted frontispiece, and the eared frames over the windows are embellished with cutout motifs in the Lafever manner, resembling those at Diamond Point and the Stagg House shown earlier (figs. 10.18, 103). The floor plan was straightforward, having a central hall with two rooms on either side and enclosed stairs between the back of the hall and the southwest room (fig. 10.118).

After Dr. Runyan's death, his sisters sold the house and returned to the Shakers.[106] In 1881, the new owners built a service ell at the rear, incorporating the detached kitchen. Subsequently the name Honeysuckle Hill was changed to Fair Oaks, and in 1905 a colossal-order Doric portico was added across the three center bays of the facade. In 1949 a stairway around an open well was installed in the transverse hall. The attached kitchen, front portico, and hall staircase lessened the singularity of the original scheme.

The breakdown of the Greek Revival style set in a few years after the mid-point of the nineteenth century, when robust proportions began to give way to distortions and attenuation of members, and features of romantic architecture were absorbed among its elements. We have seen a suggestion of this at Corinthia. The most lethal of adopted romantic motifs was

the bracket, which could support a deeper overhanging cornice but defaced the entablature it was intended to ornament. The bracket figures prominently, if inharmoniously, on the examples that follow.

MAUVILLA. During the mid-1850s, Jack Taylor built a home for his bride, Eliza, daughter of James Robertson, once governor of Tennessee. The house overlooked the broad Ohio River a mile above Westport in Oldham County and was called Mauvilla after a Cherokee chief.[107] It is said to have duplicated Robertson's residence, but considering its late characteristics, Mauvilla could have followed little more than its plan. Like the first Greek order employed in Kentucky at the Bardstown Cathedral, the columns of the portico were Tower of the Winds Corinthian (fig. 10.119). Coupled brackets set in a deep frieze supported a wide cornice. A square belvedere crowned the roof, and polygonal bay windows projected from the flanks of the house. Windows in the main story extended to the floor and had a segmental arch head with hood molds springing from small consoles. The recessed entrance was surmounted by an upper doorway with balcony whose railing was a Gothic tracery pattern. The railing, consoles to the doorways, column capitals, and egg-and-dart and bead-and-reel moldings outlining sunken panels in the ceiling and the inner plane of the entablature were of cast iron (fig. 10.120). The main staircase in the transverse hall had a broad and flat rail supported by shaped and tapering newel post and banisters characteristic of the mid-Victorian period (fig. 10.121). Small, pointed niches were set in the curved

Fig. 10.119 Mauvilla (mid-1850s), near Westport. Photo, 1941.

walls. Door and window frames were tall, and those of the first story were flanked by pilasters, which connected with consoled cornices encircling the hall and rooms. Plaster centerpieces were circular and embellished with acanthus leaves. Arched windows in the belvedere provided superb vistas of the river and valley. The house was demolished during the mid-1950s.

THE HEADLEY HOUSE.   One of the last Greek Revival residences to be constructed in Kentucky was in the 1860s for Hamilton A. Headley three miles southeast of Lexington on the Tates Creek Road.[108] It belonged to the Waveland type in form and style yet showed more affinity for vertical proportions (fig. 10.122). The tall columns had fluted shafts, and their bases and capitals were of marble; the pediment was more steeply pitched, and brackets were evenly spaced under the deep cornices. The design of the front door may be compared to plate 81 in Lafever's

Fig. 10.121 Second-story hall looking toward staircase, Mauvilla. Photo, 1941.

Fig. 10.120 Portico ceiling detail from second-floor balcony, Mauvilla. Photo, 1941.

Modern Builder's Guide, a seventh printing of which had come out in 1855. The Kentucky doorway displayed more fastidiousness of detail, having lacelike scallops edging the narrow door panels, fluting recessed in the pilasters, more elaborate consoles, and transom and sidelights divided by muntins and filled with colored glass, anticipating the Eastlake style (fig. 10.123). Carved rinceaux on the frieze were somewhat rococo. The plan of the Headley house resembled that of Waveland, except that the ell had been doubled back, forming the owner's initial (fig. 10.124). The service stair hall at the back almost duplicated the front hall.

The property was acquired by Joseph Clark in 1878, and four years later it passed to Archival Logan Hamilton, who gave it the name of Kirklevington, after a breed of cattle. The nearby black settlement, originally called Frog Town, adopted the title, but by 1900 the inhabitants were pronouncing it "Kirk-

Fig. 10.122 The Hamilton A. Headley House (1860s), Fayette County. Photo, 1966, by J. Winston Coleman, Jr.

Fig. 10.123 Elevation of front doorway of the Headley House.

Fig. 10.124 First-floor plan of the Headley House.

livingston." The Headley House was destroyed in 1970.

Other houses in Kentucky reflect the curious bracketed phase of the late Greek Revival. The pilastered John Clark Miller House at Millersburg has a tall, narrow tetrastyle Corinthian portico, with coupled brackets over each of the columns and pilasters. There are cut-out pendants hanging from the cornice over the front windows, with matching bargeboards to the raking cornice of the portico.[109] The five-bayed Hezekiah C. Ellis House at 209 West Main Street in Mount Sterling is Greek Revival only in the plain symmetry of the facade and columned recessed doorway.[110] The entablature of both doorway and house bristle with evenly spaced brackets.

The Greek Revival appeared in the United States at the beginning of the nineteenth century, fostered by its nationalistic association with the independent city-states of ancient Greece. Its big and bold form and the flexibility in producing ornament were wholly acceptable to the ideals and technical advances of the American people. Its formality, architectonic overlay, and sense of depth and spaciousness gave new life to Federal-style buildings. Manifestly suitable to large buildings, the Greek Revival first determined the design of public buildings and then accrued converts in the residential field. It filtered down to rambling cottages. From the 1830s through the 1850s the bulk of American building was in the Greek vein. In Kentucky, there can be little question about the most notable building in the style being its first, Gideon Shryock's statehouse at Frankfort. One of its most impressive would have been the same architect's city hall and courthouse in Louisville, if it had been built as designed. And one of its most exquisite essays is James Dakin's Bank of Louisville, built by John Rogers and Shryock. Translyvania's Morrison College and the Medical Hall were impressive pacemakers in the Bluegrass. Hugh Roland's Louisville Hotel must have been among the most attractive hostels of its period in America. Domestic examples ranged from such charming spreading houses as Edgemoor in Versailles and the Francis Hunt cottage in Lexington to such elegant residences as the Keats House in Louisville and Ward Hall in Scott County. The Greek Revival became diluted by romanticism shortly after mid-century, its elements mixed with other styles in what has been called synthetic eclecticism, which altered its proportions and principles—and its virility—leading to a loss of identity. The Greek Revival submerged into the realm of the romantic dream styles; diluted, it entered a channel that swept it away into oblivion.

11 THE GOTHIC REVIVAL STYLE

ALTHOUGH AS A STYLE the Gothic Revival enjoyed duration and distribution in America equal to the Greek Revival, it fell far short in patronage. Its use got off to a slow start at the beginning of the nineteenth century, but by the middle of the century building activities in Gothic matched those in Greek. As with the Greek Revival, the archetypes for Gothic Revival architecture were predominantly religious buildings, but instead of being ancient temples of the Mediterranean, they were medieval cathedrals and lesser parish churches of western Europe and especially England. As the religion itself was transplanted and these forms were suitable for later worship needs, the style was to figure prominently in churches in the United States. The Gothic Revival also sought inspiration from late medieval domestic dwellings—castles, manors, and cottages. Here adaptation was considerably modified, as over the intervening centuries life had become quite different. Distinctions between dwellings and public buildings are more apparent in the Gothic Revival than in the Greek, where a portico made all kinds of buildings into temples. The Gothic used monumental portals on ecclesiastical buildings along with towers and buttresses, and great tracery windows. Residences are clearly discernible by their low, wide porches, consciously scaled to human occupants, and by the prominence of chimneys, that concomitant of the domestic hearth. The steeply pitched Gothic roof, devised for heavy snowfall in northern countries, made it better adapted to the upper part of the United States than elsewhere. But the Gothic Revival was no more restricted to New England and the upper Midwest than the Aegean style, with its low-pitched roof and portico, was to the South. One wonders why the Gothic Revival, having been derived partially from domestic antecedents, did not accrue more residential patronage. Evidently, overhanging eaves, deep verandas, narrow windows (often including colored glass), slender towers, and parapets were too somber and confining, and appealed only to a romantic minority conditioned to appreciate them.

Gothic Revival stood foremost among romantic architectural styles in America and it was the only noteworthy one prior to the Civil War. Its antecedents are English, but Englishmen's relation to Gothic architecture was quite different from their relation to Roman or Greek. Although the late-medieval style had been made obsolete by the Renaissance, its monuments were still in existence, and some continued to be used. Thus, unlike Roman examples, which were scarce, or Greek, of which there were none at all in Britain, Gothic models were readily available. The medieval manner persevered in unregenerated, rural districts as a folk style and traditional way of building; and sophisticated architects working in the classic tradition, such as Sir Christopher Wren, Sir John Vanbrugh, Nicholas Hawksmoor, and Robert Adam condescended when occasion required to build in Gothic. Still, it made no appreciable impression upon their principal projects or the steady evolution of English Renaissance-baroque and Classic Revival architecture. The upper classes had come to consider the medieval mode backward and uncivilized, as indicted by its very name, "Gothic," referring to the Goths, barbarians, those who had destroyed the Roman Empire and its culture. This reproach was eased somewhat by recognizing that Gothic could not be accused of being pagan; and in large measure its association with Christianity was responsible for the revival of interest in it. In the early nineteenth century the Gothic Revival served a very practical resolution for the English problem of lawlessness and relaxation of morals. The success of the Church Building Society, organized in 1818, shamed the government into enacting analogous legislation. It originally set aside a million pounds for erecting churches. The sum was increased sixfold within the next fifteen years. The appropriations fostered the building of 214 houses of worship, of which 174 were in a style described as Gothic.[1]

An interesting sidelight, pertaining to Gothic Revival architecture as a whole, is that the preference for the style stemmed largely from economy. Churches could be built with plain brick walls, unadorned pointed windows, simple portals without porticoes, gables without pediments, and relieved inside by a few plaster details at a cost less than that required for the elaborations of the classic styles.

Sentiment among the numerous literati, antiquarians, and semileisurely churchmen in England played an important role in launching and advancing the Gothic Revival. To them, architectural forms were imbued with emotion-provoking references to the legendary Middle Ages. Turrets were retreats for fair damsels, battlements shielded brave archers defending the citadel, cloisters and chapels were the abode of kindly priests bestowing spiritual counsel, and great halls were the scene of yeomen paying homage to the mighty lord and of traditional holiday reveleries. During the industrialized nineteenth century, the persistence of the Gothic dream relied on a continuing literature whose roots go back to the beginning of the Renaissance. The Gothic mood was explored poetically in Edmund Spenser's *The Faerie Queen* of the sixteenth century and John Milton's "Il Penseroso" of the seventeenth. In 1717, Alexander Pope's "Eloisa to Abelard" was published, replete with mention of mossy walls and crumbling ruins, shadowy halls and dismal woods, decay, death, and places of burial. Such melancholia prompted a group known as the Graveyard Poets. The best-known member was Thomas Gray, author of "Elegy Written in a Country Churchyard," who was both a scholar and an archaeologist. It is said that he could discern with precision when each part of a cathedral had been executed, which was no small feat at a time when pointed arches were assumed to be Saxon.[2] Thomas Gray advised on the remodeling and enlarg-

ing of Horace Walpole's Strawberry Hill in the Gothic style. This introduces us to the prose writers, Walpole having conceived the pace-setting romance *The Castle of Otranto* (1764), initially issued as a translation from a work by an Italian, Onufrio Muralto, a shallow disguise of his own name. Strawberry Hill was a small farm on the Thames not far from London inherited by Walpole in the middle of the eighteenth century. He undertook to convert its modest dwelling into an extensive castle. *Otranto* and Strawberry Hill are literary-architectural equivalents of romantic sham, the latter sporting cardboard crenelations outside and groin vaults stamped on ceiling wallpaper inside.[3] The house set the pattern for later compositions of its kind no less than had *Otranto*.

Two other novelists and builders of castellated homes must be mentioned. The first was William Beckford II, who inherited great wealth and indulged his tastes by writing an oriental extravaganza called *Vathek*, and by sponsoring Fonthill Abbey, a dramatic palace in the Christian style. It was designed by James Wyatt and constructed in Wiltshire at the end of the eighteenth century.[4] Its principal tower was 276 feet tall and its impressive architectural character reduced Strawberry Hill to a decorator's showcase. Compared with either, Sir Walter Scott's castle is without much character. Abbotsford was constructed by William Atkinson on the Tweed River thirty miles from Edinburgh in 1812.[5] Scott's writings far outstripped those of his predecessors in quantity and popularity, his *Lady of the Lake* and *Ivanhoe* having secure places among the world's literary classics. Their historic setting provided architectural acceptance for the Gothic Revival.

Published designs supplied tangible motifs and models for buildings. They came in several categories. Batty Langley's early book with the high-sounding title *Gothic Architecture Improved by Rules and Proportions in Many Grand Designs* was issued in 1742. The Vitruvian approach is sheer bravado: the plates depict incidental parts of structures. The work was condemned by Thomas Gray as "a book of bad designs."[6] The *"Batty-Langley-Manner"* (Gray's term) is used interchangeably with "rococo-Gothic," referring to a shallow Georgian interpretation of Gothic, as in Chippendale "Gothic" furniture.

Supplementing the bizarre phase of the Gothic Revival was a deep-seated conservatism favoring archaeological correctness. Among the chief exponents were the Augustus Pugins, father and son. Augustus Charles Comte de Pugin fled France during the Revolution and took a position in the office of John Nash when the demand for castellated manors was at its height. He was charged with collecting authentic designs to be used on commissions, and these were published in 1825 as two volumes of engraved plates entitled *Specimens of Gothic Architecture*. A second collection was *Specimens of the Architectural Antiquities of Normandy*, to which the younger Pugin also contributed. Augustus Welby Northmore Pugin became totally immersed in the Middle Ages, to the extent of converting to Catholicism. That the era was far more beautiful than his own time became the theme of his three books, *Contrasts* (1836), *True Principles of Pointed or Christian Architecture* (1841), and *An Apology for the Revival of Christian Architecture in England* (1843). *Contrasts* presented a series of engraved views showing contemporary towns, with their factories, warehouses, iron bridges, and jail, and equivalent visas as they might have looked four centuries earlier, with picturesque walls, gateways, masonry bridges, and soaring church spires. Pugin *fils* built over sixty-five churches in the United Kingdom and many other types of buildings there and in the colonies. His most significant commission was in collaboration with Sir Charles Barry to replace the old Palace at Westminster, which burned in 1834, with the Houses of Parliament, for which he devised all the elaborate fittings in the Tudor style.[7] That the most important edifice of the mid-nineteenth century in England adhered to the Gothic Revival gave tremendous impetus to the movement.

Even though Englishmen seemed to worship their medieval buildings as much as (or even more than) they worshiped in them, Americans paid them only the slightest attention, even on the literary level. Buildings in Edgar Allan Poe's Gothic tales of the 1830s and 1840s are not like any in the United States. Washington Irving's creation of Sunnyside during the late 1830s, with quaint corbie gables, purporting to be a restoration of Wolfert's Roost, was pure fantasy.[8] The setting for Nathaniel Hawthorne's *The House of the Seven Gables* (1851), though based on an existing dwelling in Salem, is inaccurately described. No attempt was made to study, delineate, and publish plates of early buildings.

Of course none of the Gothic edifices in this country could compare with the great medieval monuments of the British Isles, but the New World had a few interesting examples. Two in Virginia are of brick. The Arthur Allen House (ca. 1655), better known as Bacon's Castle, in Surrey County, is a two-

story, cross-plan building with impressive Jacobean curvilinear gable parapets and clustered chimney stacks. The Newport Parish Church (1682)—Saint Luke's—at Smithfield, has a square tower, quoins, buttresses, an arched doorway, and traceried windows. Equivalents in the Massachusetts colony are of frame construction. The Rev. Joseph Capen House (1683) at Topsfield has a second-floor overhang in front, gable overhangs on the flanks, and a pilastered chimney. The Old Ship Meetinghouse (1681) at Hingham originally measured 45 by 55 feet and was covered by a double-pitched roof supported by three trusses. In typical medieval fashion, these buildings had exposed structural members inside, leaded casement windows, batten doors, and handwrought hardware.[9] Medieval features were not limited to the seventeenth century in America. We have noted some in Kentucky dating to the late 1790s and early 1800s, some showing rococo-Gothic affinities (chap. 4).

The advent of the Gothic Revival proper in the United States occurred in 1799 at Philadelphia, in the building of William Crammond's country seat, Sedgeley. Its architect, Benjamin Henry Latrobe, also had the first Greek Revival design in America to his credit. Sedgeley was a symmetrical mass crowned by a hip roof, with a projecting rounded entrance pavilion preceded by a porch, square open flankers at the corners connected by galleries across the flanks, pointed arches, hood molds, and scalloped bargeboards on the main eaves (fig. 11.1). The house is no longer in existence, but judging from the heaviness of details on a dependency still standing in Fairmount Park, the builder actualized something of a caricature of Latrobe's drawings. The tendency to grossness characterized a fair percentage of buildings that were to follow.

Latrobe also did a set of plans for the Roman Catholic Cathedral in Baltimore (1805) that was Gothic, but it was not executed. His Philadelphia Bank (1807-1808), at Fourth and Chestnut streets, had a plain facade pierced by a tall recessed Tudor portal, a superstructure with rose window between buttresses capped by obelisks, and narrow lancet windows to either side. It was demolished about 1832.[10] A larger building of similar character was William Strickland's Masonic Hall (1809-11), at Eighth and Chestnut streets. Its square tower of two stories and polygonal spire surmounted by a weathervane presented the appearance of a church.[11] Presumably the first American townhouse in the Gothic manner

Fig. 11.1 Sedgeley (1799-1801), near Philadelphia.
Courtesy of the Historical Society of Philadelphia.

was that designed and built in Philadelphia by John Dorsey in 1810. The three-story building on Chestnut Street had a 60-foot facade divided into three pavilions, the center one recessed, the outer framed by buttresses topped by pinnacles. Ornaments included recessed pointed panels, quatrefoil tracery, hood molds over the fenestration, and an obtuse gable over the great triangular window centered in the top story. It was razed in 1851.[12] Besides these Philadelphia manifestations, Saint Patrick's Cathedral (1809), at the corner of Mott and Prince streets in New York City, might be mentioned. Designed by Joseph François Mangin, it had square towers (their summits never completed) flanking the facade, a steep center gable crowned by an aedicula, and pointed windows. It burned and was rebuilt in 1866-68.[13]

These early examples testify to their creators' insecurity in the style. It was only during the 1830s that the Gothic Revival in America gained grace and showed signs of taking its place as a rival to the Greek Revival. Among its chief exponents was Richard Upjohn (1802-78), an Englishman who came to this country in 1829. A few years later he conceived the Tudor house of cut stone for Governor R. H. Gardiner at Gardiner, Maine, as well as Saint John's Church at Bangor, rebuilt at the turn of the century. Upjohn's masterpiece was the third Trinity Church in New York, built on the site of a rococo-Gothic building from plans begun in 1839. He was responsible for many other Gothic Revival churches and a few houses in New York City and Brooklyn and in New Jersey, Maine, Rhode Island, Massachusetts, Con-

necticut, Maryland, North Carolina, and Texas. He was requested to submit designs for stained-glass windows for Christ Church in Lexington, Kentucky, in 1849, but nothing seems to have come of it.[14]

The architect of Kentucky's finest Gothic Revival residence, Loudoun, was Alexander Jackson Davis (1803-29), America's most prolific designer of Romantic villas. Born in New York City, he showed a remarkable penchant for drawing and at twenty made renderings for A.T. Goodrich's guide books, as well as plans and perspectives for the architect Josiah Brady. As a practicing architect, his first accomplishment was Sachem's Wood (1828) at New Haven, the house suggested as prototype for the Craig House group in Kentucky. In 1829 Davis became the partner of the established architect and engineer Ithiel Town (1784-1844), whose work had been mostly in the Classic and Greek Revival styles, and whose engineering included bridge building. The association produced an upsurge of Gothic designs. Among them were the building for New York University (1832-36, razed 1894); Glen Ellen (1832-34), the Robert Gilmore residence near Baltimore; and Lyndhurst, the Gen. William Paulding castle in Tarrytown, New York, which Davis enlarged for George Merritt in 1865. After the Town-Davis partnership dissolved in 1835, Davis conceived many other Gothic residences in the Hudson River Valley, New York City, and Brooklyn, and in New Jersey, Connecticut, Massachusetts, Pennsylvania, Virginia, Michigan, and Kentucky.[15] He was the originator of most of the designs of cottages, farmhouses, villas, and village churches in the series entitled *Rural Residences,* published in New York in 1837.[16]

Gothic Revival domestic architecture got its greatest boost in America from A.J. Downing, whose publications and lectures on country living promoted houses as appropriate coordinates to landscaping and horticulture. Andrew Jackson Downing (1815-52) was born in Newburgh, New York, the son of a nurseryman, whose business he and his brother Charles inherited. Early in life he became interested in the mineralogical and botanical features of the neighborhood from which his preoccupation with landscape gardening and planting developed. He also was influenced by the Englishman John Claudius Loudon, whose writings included books on botany, gardening, horticulture, the laying out of gardens and grounds, and the placement and construction of farm buildings and residences. Downing's reputation was established by his publication *A*

Treatise on the Theory and Practice of Landscape Gardening (1841), in which a long chapter was devoted to "Landscape or Rural Architecture." The book was followed in 1842 by *Cottage Residences,* containing ample text and designs for ten houses, increased to fifteen in a later (1847) edition. Downing's definitive work, published in 1850, was *The Architecture of Country Houses,* a tome of 484 pages, 36 plates, and 318 figures. Many of the designs were by A.J. Davis, some from suggestions by Downing, and a few were the work of Richard Upjohn. Downing was antagonistic to the Greek Revival, believing the ancient Mediterranean temple was an unsuitable model for the American home. He favored those styles having domestic prototypes, such as the late medieval manors and cottages of England, and the earlier Romanesque or Norman, the Italian villas of the Renaissance, and Swiss chalets. *Country Houses* included an original style, labeled "bracketed," derived from the Italian Swiss types. It also featured the species of house called "villa," a term alike in "Latin, Italian, Spanish, and English" meaning "a country house," and related to the word "village," which is "a small collection of houses in the country."[17] No matter in what style, all rural houses greater than cottages were designated villas, though the word seemingly applied best to those in the Italian manner.

In the first section of *The Architecture of Country Houses,* Downing follows a discussion of "The Useful in Architecture" with "The Beautiful in Architecture," stating that as the first satisfies the physical wants of man, the second ennobles him with its divinelike grace. The Beautiful in Architecture strives to attain the ideal in proportion, symmetry, variety, harmony, and unity, as in fine classic buildings. Counterbalancing the "Beautiful," he says, is the "Picturesque," wherein beauty is "manifested with something of rudeness, violence or difficulty. The effect of the whole is spirited and pleasing, but parts are rude." The Picturesque applies to the romantic styles, to the Gothic Revival—especially the castellated—and to the Irregular Villa (chap. 12). According to the comparison, the Beautiful has to do with the relatively simple, compact, and regular Greek Revival domicile, whereas the Picturesque applies to the complex, loosely formed, asymmetrical Gothic Revival residence, characterized by advancing and receding pavilions, pierced by pointed doors and windows, with projecting oriels, deep verandas with slender colonnettes, steep roofs with tracery bargeboards, and prickly outlines achieved by parapets, pinnacles, towers, turrets, and clustered chimney stacks. Such elements have a pictorial sufficiency. Inasmuch as he designated that which is virtually formless "Picturesque," he would have done well to have called the well-formed "Sculpturesque" instead of "Beautiful," thus relating the two architectural types more meaningfully to their sister arts.

Villas in either category called for a special kind of landscape setting. The Beautiful (or the Sculpturesque) was to be surrounded by level or gently rolling meadows, and to have straight drives, and round, deciduous trees. The Picturesque was set in rough terrain, crossed by twisting drives through jagged, pointed evergreens. In the Bluegrass, the stately old white pines, not native to the region, owe their existence to Downing. He was thought of highly in Lexington: the Maxwell Springs Fair Association's board of directors made him an honorary member on 5 October 1850.[18]

The first few Kentucky examples of Gothic Revival to be discussed contain incidental features, and belong mainly to a previous period. The first Catholic church in Louisville, built in 1811 by Father Stephen Theodore Badin for ministering to a group of French families at Shippingport, was a brick building supposedly in the Gothic manner, but a sketch of it showing semicircular arches on the door and windows hardly substantiates the report.[19] In the following year Father Badin went to Lexington, where a "gothic chapel of brick" was constructed in the "Catholic graveyard, on Winchester [East Third] street," to replace a log church.[20] The primitive character of both buildings would classify them as survival Gothic at most. The following example shows more architectural pretensions.

SAINT THOMAS CHURCH. In 1810 Thomas Howard willed his farm of 340 acres, four miles south of Bardstown, to Bishop Benedict Joseph Flaget, head of the first Catholic diocese in the west. Flaget occupied the log house on the property and set about to establish a seminary there, naming it after the saint for whom the land donor was namesake. On 23 August 1813 he laid the cornerstone for a church whose design reportedly had been furnished by the Baltimore architect Maximilian Godefroy.[21] Apparently work on the building did not progress to Flaget's satisfaction, and in 1814 he called John Rogers from Baltimore to complete it. It is a small church in the rococo-Gothic manner, its Flemish-bond brick facade having a fanlighted doorway re-

Fig. 11.2 Saint Thomas Church (1816), near Bardstown. Photo, 1960s, by J. Winston Coleman, Jr.

cessed in a pointed arch, with pointed niches on either side and five small Gothic recesses flanking a center circular plaque in the parapet above (fig. 11.2). The scheme is a simplified version of the chapel Godefroy designed for Saint Mary's Seminary in Baltimore. This prototype, built in 1807-1808, is more complex. It is elevated on a high basement, and colonnettes and archivolts enframe the pointed doorway and niches; other features are given more elaborate architectural treatment, and small pavilions flank the facade (fig. 11.3). A slender axial tower and pinnacles at the corners failed to materialize. The Kentucky version has a brick block atop the parapet supporting the stepped base of a cross. Both buildings have rather plain lancet windows in the sides. They are a contrived Gothic—a step removed from legitimate Gothic Revival. Saint Thomas Church, dedicated on 13 August 1816, served as Flaget's cathedral until Saint Joseph's in Bardstown was completed three years later (chap. 9).

Although John Rogers's source of inspiration for Saint Joseph's Cathedral seems to have been Latrobe's classic cathedral in Baltimore, he was somewhat influenced by the form of Saint Thomas Church. They follow a similar plan, and that the Bardstown cathedral is exactly twice the size of the seminary church perhaps recalls that Solomon's tem-

ple was twice the size of Moses' tabernacle. Both cathedral and church are of basilica shape, ending in a curved sanctuary (figs. 9.35, 11.4). They have round columns supporting arches (pointed in Saint Thomas) dividing nave from side aisles, with other round supports—rather than pilasters—at the corners where nave and sanctuary meet. The two build-

Fig. 11.3 The chapel of Saint Mary's Seminary (1807), Baltimore. Photo, 1960s, by Wayne Andrews.

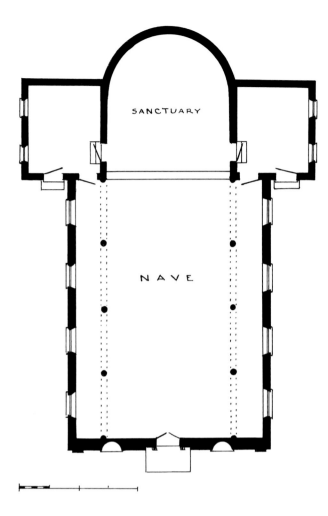

Fig. 11.4 Floor plan of Saint Thomas Church.

ings were innovative in introducing a new architectural style to Kentucky, Greek columns modeled on those of the Tower of the Winds in the cathedral, and modified Gothic elements in Saint Thomas Church.

A number of stone country churches in Kentucky, of the period of Saint Thomas Church, have pointed windows, but they seem to be later changes, as in Old Providence Church (ca. 1793) midway between Winchester and Boonesboro, and Pisgah Church (1812, remodeled 1868) on Pisgah–Mount Vernon Road five miles from Versailles. Saint Francis, a Catholic church of brick, on the Frankfort-Georgetown Pike, seems to have had pointed windows from the beginning, but it was built in 1820, several years after the Bardstown vicinity church.[22] Its interior is similar to that of Saint Thomas, having arches at the side and a rounded end. Also of brick, David's Fork Church, on Cleveland Road, east of Lexington, is a mid-nine-

teenth-century pilastered and pedimented building, Greek Revival except for the pointed windows.

HOLY TRINITY CHURCH.   The little brick Episcopal church on Main Street in Danville was commenced by the builder Robert Russell, Jr. (1792-1873) in 1830 and dedicated by the Rt. Rev. William Meade, assistant bishop of Virginia, on 17 April 1831. It has a square tower, containing the entrance vestibule, set before the gabled rectangular auditorium. Doorway and fenestration are Gothic arched (fig. 11.5). Dr. J.R. Cowan recorded:

The windows were just as they are now, except for two small ones in the south wall, closed in the reconstruction of 1860 [after the building was damaged by fire], and were furnished with plain glass and Venetian blinds. The ceiling was supported by a double row of Doric pillars. There was no recess, and the chancel floor and railing projected out from the rear wall centrally, encircled by a cushioned kneeling step, the floor inside the railing being one step higher. A large reading desk and in the rear a larger pulpit built against the south wall, and reached by a stair on either side. . . . roomy, high, straight-backed pews, painted glistening white on the exterior and capped with a cherry red railing . . . locked alms-chest below the organ gallery seems to have completed the furniture.[23]

Fig. 11.5 Holy Trinity Church (1830-31), Danville. Photo, 1988.

A spire was added to the tower in 1842, "built according to plans drawn by Bishop [Benjamin Bosworth] Smith who was an excellent architect and who designed St. Phillips Church, Harrodsburg."[24] The church became more Gothic following the 1860 fire, the "Doric pillars" being replaced by an open-timber roof, and a separate chancel enlarging the north end.

THE CHURCH OF SAINT PETER. John McMurtry included pointed openings in his second known commission, following that of the Lexington and Ohio Railroad Station (chap. 4). The building was a combination of Greek and Gothic features. The Catholic Church of Saint Peter stood on the east side of North Limestone below Third Street in Lexington, and it was completed and dedicated on 3 December 1837 (fig. 11.6).[25] The description of it in MacCabe's city directory the following year enumerated parts. The dimensions were given as 90 by 50 feet, plus a polygonal sanctuary on the end. Eight pointed windows lighted the auditorium, which had a vaulted ceiling, 28 feet high to the crown. The facade featured "a splendid gothic door, having on either side a handsome doric pillar and two corresponding pilasters, all capped by a well proportioned entablature, upon which rises a parapet . . . that forms the butment of the steeple." The steeple was of wood and consisted of five sections. The first was 18 feet square and housed the bell. Superimposed were an octagonal and two circular sections, the last "finished somewhat like a pedestal, with points resembling the Irish crown, out of the top of which rises a conic roof, terminating against a spire pole, capped with a gilt ball of three feet in diameter, and crowned with the emblematic cross, which is seen glittering over the city at a considerable distance."[26] The church was razed in 1930.

SAINT PAUL'S EPISCOPAL CHURCH AND THE FIRST PRESBYTERIAN CHURCH. Two Louisville churches completed in 1839 make an interesting comparison. Both were on Sixth Street, Saint Paul's Episcopal near Walnut and the First Presbyterian at the southeast corner of Green (Liberty), which it faced. Both were designed by John Stirewalt whose background included training in Town and Davis's office.[27] There were thirteen churches in Louisville when they were built. Promoters of Saint Paul's were proud of introducing a new style of architecture (Gothic) to the town. Its forms were square and contained by buttresses at the corners, which ended in crenelated turrets (fig. 11.7). The four-storied entrance tower

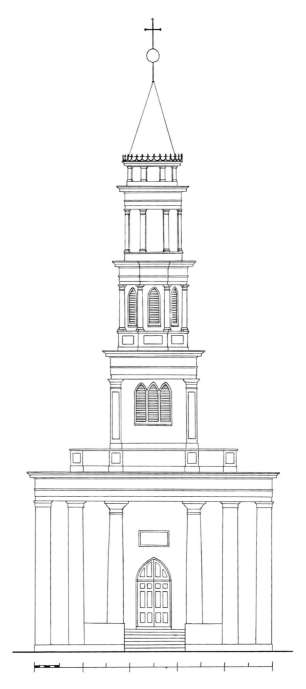

Fig. 11.6 Reconstructed facade elevation of the Church of Saint Peter (1837), Lexington.

had a Tudor-arched doorway that looked stunted because of the exceedingly tall window above. Over the window was an escutcheon bearing the name of the church, and twin louvered openings were in each side of the belfry. The tower was surmounted by an octagonal spire. On a plane with the front of the tower and three-fourths as tall were narrow wings containing secondary entrances, and attached to

Fig. 11.7 Saint Paul's Episcopal Church (1837-39,
Louisville. From Lewis Collins, *Historical Sketches of
Kentucky* (Cincinnati, 1847), p. [357].

their outer walls were lesser forms, set back, altogether creating a screen facade. The interior was
composed of a nave "with pilastered walls and a
groined ceiling." The auditorium was practically
square. The cost of the lot and construction was
$50,000.

In 1872 an addition at the west (chancel) end took
the form of transepts wider than the length of the
original building, making it into an "Egyptian cross"
(ankh) plan, and a chapel-like Sunday-school pavilion was built in the yard on the north side.[28] The
congregation deserted the building in 1891, after
which it served a black Methodist organization up
through the middle of the present century. A parking
lot currently occupies the site.

Stirwalt's design for the First Presbyterian Church,
more so than that for Saint Paul's, testifies to his

being an architect well versed in the medieval ver-
nacular.[29] The square tower was recessed half into
the building proper, its portal, superimposed window in the perpendicular manner, and openings in
the bell section all were in proper scale (fig. 11.8).
Buttresses had proper setbacks and were capped by
crocketed octagonal pinnacles. Slender piers applied
to the top of the tower met in pointed arches and
were surmounted by crenelations. Crenelations also
appear on each side of the tower along the sloping
parapet masking the auditorium roof. Pinnacle-cap-
ped buttresses aligned the flanks of the main body of
the church. The awkward forms and strained proportions of nearby Saint Paul's threw into sharper relief
the agreeable disposition of parts and refined treatment of details in the First Presbyterian Church. This
building and its setting cost $66,516, or almost a third
more than the Episcopal project.[30] The land was
more extensive, but the finer architectural effect also
must have accounted for some of the difference.

The First Presbyterian Church also later acquired a
Sunday-school building at the rear. In 1889 the property was sold to the Louisville Gas Company for
$40,000. The Jefferson County jail was built there in
1902-05.

CHRIST CHURCH. An entry in Maj. Thomas
Lewinski's account book testifies to his beginning
drawings for the "Episcopal Church" on 18 December 1845. It is Christ Church, at the northeast

Fig. 11.8 The First Presbyterian Church (1846-47),
Louisville. From Lewis Collins, *Historical Sketches of
Kentucky* (Cincinnati, 1847), p. [357].

Fig. 11.9 Christ Episcopal Church (1846-48), Lexington. Photo, ca 1900, courtesy of the *Courier-Journal*, Louisville.

corner of Market and Church streets in Lexington. Many references by Lewinski follow, and on 2 September 1846 is the notation: "Final arrangement with Episcopal Church Committee for design & specification." The plans were displayed in the office of the building committee chairman Francis Key Hunt for the purpose of receiving bids on the construction work, which was to start on 12 October.[31] John McMurtry was the successful bidder. Three previous places of worship for the congregation had been on this site, the immediate predecessor being Mathias Shryock's brick church built in 1814. Christ Church was completed in May of 1848 and consecrated 2 June 1849.

The western facade is dominated by a square tower with the principal portal at its base, a large window above, and narrow twin louvered openings in the belfry section (fig. 11.9). Lesser doors were in the front of the auditorium at either side of the tower, with blind arcades in the sloping parapet above (cut down to roof level in fig. 11.9), and stepped buttresses were set diagonally at the corners and crowned by cast-iron crocketed pinnacles five to

eight feet tall.[32] The six bays on the flanks were separated by buttresses capped by iron plates. The external walls were coated with a mixture of lime and sand to resemble stone.

The original auditorium was rectangular and spanned by level-crown intersecting vaults thirty feet high, with modeled bosses at the junction of the ribs. An extension was proposed in 1858, but lack of funds and the outbreak of the war held it up until 1862. By 1864 the building had acquired transepts and a polygonal chancel beyond, bounded by narrow side aisles three bays deep. Vaulting similar to Lewinski's was repeated, apparently executed by McMurtry. In 1897, as Christ Church Cathedral, the building became the center of the new Episcopal Diocese of Lexington. In 1912-13 the parish house was added on Church Street. About this time new fittings were installed in the chancel, and a full set of bells was hung in the tower.[33] The pinnacles were taken down a few years later, following the removal of the front parapet. In 1949 a small chapel was built off the garden on the north side of the church; in 1955 a new stained-glass window was installed over the main doorway, and the wall behind opened up to the auditorium. In 1962 the Margaret Helm Building was constructed beyond the garden.[34]

THE MCCHORD PRESBYTERIAN CHURCH. Before Major Lewinski had completed the drawings for Christ Church, he was already designing a Presbyterian Church a few doors north of it on Market Street. It was to be named for the Rev. James Mc-Chord, founder of the Presbyterian congregation in Lexington. On 21 March 1846 Lewinski noted in his account book that he "commenced estimate for the McChord Church from . . . [his] own design"; and on the twenty-third he "handed in a tender for the same." The selection was made from an open competition, and the number of hours Lewinski spent on his design did not ensure that it won. The church appears to have been the work of John McMurtry. A floor plan and perspective, both executed in delicate pen lines and shaded in watercolor (fig. 11.10) turned up in the church archives in 1950. Comparison with old photographs of the constructed building leaves little doubt about these being the archetypal design. Under the perspective view, to the right of the title, is the signature: "J. McMurtry, Acht." Although an erasure to the left of the name arouses suspicion, the document probably would not have been preserved as it was if the inscribed authorship were not valid.

Fig. 11.10 The McChord Presbyterian Church (1846-47), Lexington. Architect's wash rendering, courtesy of the Second Presbyterian Church, Lexington.

The square tower and rectangular auditorium repeated the forms of Christ Church, crenelations abounded, and pinnacles ornamented the corner piers and the tops of the buttresses on the sides. Unlike Christ Church, a portal and traceried window filled the shorter square tower, which was surmounted by a spire attaining a height of 160 feet. The McChord Presbyterian Church was dedicated on 31 October 1847, shortly after which a newspaper reported: "The basement contains a large and commodious Sabbath School room, with library and session rooms, together with a furnace for heating the whole building with warm air. The upper room, calculated to seat 700 persons with ease and comfort, is at once striking in its *tout ensemble,* elegant and commodious. The windows filled with stained glass imported direct from Germany, are the first of that kind which have been used to any extent in this place."[35] The cost of the building was about $18,000. The steeple was removed before 1900. A fire, which also threatened Christ Church, consumed the McChord Presbyterian Church on 21 May 1917.

THE CHURCH OF SAINT MARTIN OF TOURS. The Church of Saint Martin of Tours for German Evangelical Catholics was built in Louisville on Shelby Street facing Gray Street in two stages. The nave was constructed in 1853-54, and the transepts and chancel, and presumably the tower, were added during the early 1860s.[36] On either side of the church stood a Franciscan convent and the School of Saint Martin, which although different in style were similar in shape. The front wall of the church was given a soaring prismatic tower (fig. 11.11). The low-pitched roofline of the three building forms gave dramatic emphasis to the upward thrust of the tower. Its first stage rose three times its diameter; the corners were braced by buttresses that diminished at equal intervals and were capped by attenuated pinnacles rising to include the clock level. Each face of this stage is crowned by a gable. The slender spire sheathed in copper, and once interrupted by tiny dormers half-

Fig. 11.11 The Church of Saint Martin of Tours (1851-54, 1860s), Louisville. R.G. Potter Collection, courtesy of the University of Louisville.

way up, ends in a finial and cross. Twin doorways in the splayed sides at the base of the tower opened into an octagon with steps leading directly up to nave level. Stairs at the top branched right and left and ascended around the sides of the polygon to the balcony over the west end of the auditorium. This stair arrangement resembles that in the old statehouse at Frankfort. The nave is broad and the transepts are of equal width and form short projections. The chancel at the east end is narrow and made up of five sides of an octagon, reflecting the shape of the tower opposite. Originally there was a rather flat coved ceiling articulated by liernes and containing circular paintings of saints. The present plaster vaults springing from bosses on the walls are later. The windows, made in Munich, marble altars, and communion rail date from the mid-1890s. In 1903 a shallow stone front with squat, cumbersome flankers was added, destroying the pristine effect. The older buildings on either side are gone.

THE CATHEDRAL OF THE ASSUMPTION.   The Chapel of Saint Louis, planned by Hugh Roland and under construction in 1830-32 on the east side of Fifth Street near Walnut in Louisville, was a stuccoed brick structure. Bishop Flaget moved from Bardstown and took up residence nearby in 1841 and made the church Saint Louis Cathedral. By 1845, planning for a new cathedral had begun and funds were being collected. Though appropriate to the city of Louisville, the name of Saint Louis was changed to the Cathedral of the Assumption. It avoided confusion with the diocese church in New Orleans but identified with that of Latrobe's cathedral in Baltimore. In 1849 construction began around the old church, which was later razed. William Keely (1805?-76) was the architect. The building like its predecesor had stuccoed walls. It cost upward of $70,000, and was dedicated on 3 October 1852. The soaring octagonal spire designed by Rogers and Whitestone was completed in 1858.[37]

The tower is centered on the western facade (fig. 11.12). Octagonal buttresses are set at the corners and become pinnacles above the square form of the bell section of the tower. The eight-sided clock section and the slender steeple rise to the impressive height of about 285 feet. The principal doorway is at the base of the tower, with secondary entrances right and left. Inside, wide steps lead up to church level. Octagonal piers separate the nave and side aisles, and they support pointed arches below the clerestory, which space is covered by a level-crown vault

(fig. 11.13). A balcony over the western end is reached by narrow stairs off the entrance in the tower; it is said that one side was for children and the other for slaves. The sanctuary at the far end is the width of the nave and depth of a single bay, but it is covered by more elaborate vaulting. A high pointed window is in the east wall. Originally two small vestry rooms opened off the sanctuary, but now a large structure has been built on the south side and rear, and the north aedicula has been removed.

Extensive remodeling of the building was carried out in 1910. The flooring was replaced, and smaller

Fig. 11.12 The Cathedral of the Assumption (1849-52), Louisville. *Art Work of Louisville* (Chicago, 1897), part 7, n.p.

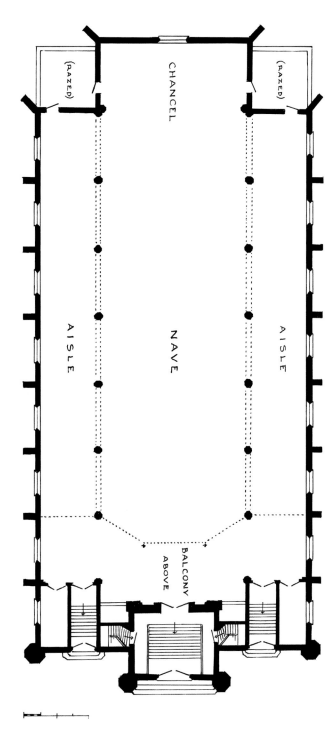

Fig. 11.13 Restored floor plan of the Cathedral of the Assumption.

doors as well as a new marble main altar and communion rails were installed. In 1912 the present stained-glass windows replaced the originals of plain glass, except those in the chancel. The old iron fence in front went to the scrap-metal drive during World War II. An extensive and stark refurbishing was undertaken in 1969, which included the opening of a side door in the south aisle reached by a ramp, installation of platforms in the east part of the church, new pews, and carpeting. It was followed by a study to determine how to restore to the cathedral some of the character removed twenty years previously.

NAZARETH ACADEMY. Another of the institutional seeds that bore fruit at Saint Thomas Seminary was a community of women, the Sisters of Charity of Nazareth. Six nuns were under the instruction of Father (later Bishop) John Baptist David by 1813. The following year they were joined by Sister Catherine Spalding, who became the first superior. In 1822 the sisters moved to the permanent location a few miles north of Bardstown. Here their school flourished as Nazareth Academy, comparing favorably with the high standards of neighboring Saint Joseph's College.[38] William Keely came to Nazareth from Louisville, and in 1853-54 he built the Saint Vincent de Paul Church, designed in the Gothic manner for Catherine Spalding in 1850. In 1855 the main part of the present academy building was completed, and Keely's name appears on the original plans (fig. 11.14).

The academy is of brick, stuccoed and scored to resemble stonework. Its three-story long center section ends in advanced pavilions crowned by low pediments, with wings of two stories beyond. Two cupolas are set on the roof ridge. Except for openings of three lights over the main doorway, windows are coupled, their casements traceried at the top, and originally they were capped with hood molds. Each bay is set in a Tudor arch, which creates a pleasing rhythm across the facade. The entrance hall, with reception rooms at either side, leads to a long cross corridor, beyond which is the great refectory. Stair halls adjoin the refectory, and in the pavilion on the right end is an amphitheater and an examination hall. The second story contains class and study rooms and an infirmary; and in the third story are dormitories and lavatories. An unusual and distinctive device inside the building is a semicircular, horizontal iron hoop protruding near the top of each window. The double casements are hinged on the center post and open inward; the outer edges of the casements follow

Fig. 11.14 Nazareth Academy (1855), Bardstown. Photo, 1973.

the circumference of the hoops and may be fastened by a series of notches at any desired angle.

The academy building subsequently was greatly enlarged, the auditorium part being built in 1870-71. Although Nazareth Academy no longer functions as such, it provides a pleasant setting for retreats.

THE ABBEY OF OUR LADY OF GETHSEMANI. Trappists and Dominicans both established their presence in Kentucky in 1805. The Trappists built a crude log monastery about fifteen miles southeast of Bardstown. It burned in 1808, and after a short sojourn in the Mississippi Valley, the monks returned to France.[39] The Dominican friars also built a monastery, then a college, and they remained near Springfield. In 1811 the Rev. Benedict Joseph Flaget came to Kentucky to establish the Catholic Diocese. He must have regretted the Trappists' departure from the Bardstown area, for thirty-five years later he sent an invitation to the abbot of Melleray in France to establish an order here. Conditions at Melleray were crowded, and Father Eutropius Proust was placed at the head of a band of forty bound for America. At New Orleans they reembarked for Louisville and then proceeded to the farm that had been purchased for them from the Sisters of Loretto in Nelson County, near New Haven. They set about constructing

Fig. 11.15 The Abbey of Our Lady of Gethsemani (1852-55), Nelson County. Isometric sketch from Rexford Newcomb, *Old Kentucky Architecture* (New York, 1940), pl. 128.

wooden buildings, and on 21 July 1850 Pope Pius IX rewarded their efforts by calling the settlement the proto-abbey of the New World. Dom Eutropius Proust was made first abbot.[40] At this time Trappists determined to replace their wooden buildings with a brick complex. William Keely was hired on 13 October 1852 to prepare the plans and superintend construction, which he did for more than three years. The abbey the Trappists erected over the next sixteen years was medieval in concept and style. It consisted of a broad, walled-garden forecourt and a church with three-storied wings enclosing a cloister 100 feet square (fig. 11.15). Off the cloister were the rooms of the hierarchy, the refectory, chapter house, and a meeting place for lay brothers. Dormitories were above, and an infirmary and service buildings behind, with the cemetery encircling the apse of the church. The church was long and narrow, lacking side aisles. The nave was covered by eleven level-crown vaults, and about half of it was devoted to the choir (fig. 11.16). The tower rose over the crossing. Square transepts were on either side, and the church broadened at the back, with five low radial lady chapels off an ambulatory around the chevet.

The abbey later was faced with concrete blocks but retained its Gothic character. Subsequently the

Fig. 11.17 The State Arsenal (1850), Frankfort. Photo, 1942.

church was stripped of all architectural dress, the windows were squared and filled with brown, amber, and translucent white glass, and the interior was finished in the geometric International style of the 1930s. The cloister was remodeled to look like a Bauhaus factory surrounding a Noguchi garden. Air-conditioned buildings in modern style were added. The monks' garb was changed to overalls.

THE STATE ARSENAL. The old "gun house" in Frankfort was pulled down in 1834 and replaced by one at the northeast corner of the public square that cost $2,000. It served until mid-century, when Ambrose W. Dudley, E.H. Taylor, and Philip Swigert were appointed commissioners to select a site "not less than ½ mile from the capitol," and obtain plans for a new arsenal. Constructed at a cost of $8,000 in 1850 on the lower part of Town Hill, above the junction of East Main and Capitol Avenue, it is of brick on limestone foundations, with two tiers of openings, three-bayed on the ends and five on the flanks. The State Arsenal was designed by Nathan C. Cook in the castellated style, having square towers or turrets dividing each bay and stationed at the corners, with crenelations at the top of the walls and capping the towers and turrets (fig. 11.17). Hood molds cover doors and windows. A contemporary companion structure since destroyed was the small (19 by 20 feet) stone magazine built at the northeast corner of the Frankfort Cemetery. On 30 June 1933 an explosion in the arsenal destroyed weapons valued at $150,000,

Fig. 11.16 Interior of the church at Gethsemani, view of the nave from the choir. From Rexford Newcome, *Old Kentucky Architecture* (New York, 1940), pl. 30.

Fig. 11.18 Paris Cemetery gateway (after 1847). Photo, 1940.

and repairs to the building amounted to $30,000 or almost four times the original cost.[41] The Louisville and Nashville Railroad tunnel penetrates Town Hill below Main Street and passes directly beneath the arsenal, which presently houses exhibits of the Kentucky Historical Society.

PARIS AND LEXINGTON CEMETERY GATEWAYS. The pastoral cemetery that became popular in the 1840s and 1850s differed greatly from the old church graveyard. Known variously as the garden, or rural, cemetery, it derived from the English park, which has been characterized in connection with the grounds around Chaumière near Lexington, and it related to picturesque villa landscaping. The vogue was inaugurated in the early 1830s in the United States with the opening of Mount Auburn Cemetery in Cambridge, Massachusetts, whose monumental gateway was in the Egyptian style. Soon after, Richard Mitchell Upjohn designed an ornate Gothic style gateway for the new Greenwood Cemetery in Brooklyn, New York.[42] John McMurtry designed two gateways in Gothic Revival style for such cemeteries in Kentucky, using motifs that had appeared on the churches he had built lately on Market Street in Lexington. Both McMurtry structures were simpler and more compact than the eastern examples.

The Paris Cemetery Company was incorporated on 30 January 1847, and ground was set aside for burials at the southwest edge of the Bourbon County seat. The gateway is composed of a wide Tudor arch for carriages between narrower pedestrian entrances of similar shape; buttresses surmounted by iron pin-

nacles stand on each side of the openings, with keepers' lodges at either end (fig. 11.18). Windows originally would have been of the casement type capped by hood molds. A horizontal cornice on brick brackets spans the entire structure, and battlements break the skyline. The sides of the center arch have been cut back to the buttresses for the passage of automobiles.

Proposals for a gateway to the Lexington Cemetery, at the northwest limits of the city, were considered in 1849, and McMurtry's design was chosen.[43] The form resembled that of the Paris entrance, except for octagonal piers, and the triple windows in the pavilions (fig. 11.19). Piers were two deep and provided shelter over the pedestrian entrances. Crenelations dropped to a lower level over the two lodges, and the hood molds were identical to those over the

Fig. 11.19 Lexington Cemetery gateway (ca. 1850). Photo, before 1890, courtesy of Lafayette Studio, Lexington.

windows of McMurtry's own home in Lexington (fig. 11.26). Dedication ceremonies took place on 25 June 1850, and the structure lasted four decades. Ironically it was razed the year McMurtry died and replaced by a stone Romanesque building.

MAXWELL SPRINGS AMPHITHEATER. The Maxwell Springs Company and the Kentucky Agricultural and Mechanical Association were organized and united by mutual agreement in the early 1850s.[44] They developed a fifty-two-acre tract for the fairgrounds southwest of Rose and present Euclid Avenue in Lexington, now the oldest part of the University of Kentucky campus. Buildings erected on the grounds included "a large and handsome amphitheatre, 810 feet in circumference, with a shingle roof over the seats and offices, a beautiful gothic cottage for the accommodation of the ladies, one hundred and fifty stables belonging to the Association, besides many others which have been built by individuals, and also several houses for the accommodating of grooms."[45] By his own testimony John McMurtry was responsible for the amphitheater and presumably most of the other buildings.[46] The amphitheater was circular, bearing some resemblance to an Elizabethan theater, consisting of two tiers of Tudor arches, the upper level reached by external stairways (fig. 11.20). Stadiumlike rings of spectators' seats sloped downward for viewing horse shows and other county fair contests. The Maxwell Springs fairgrounds were used as a camp and drill field by Union troops during the Civil War, and the amphitheater

Fig. 11.20 Maxwell Springs Amphitheater (early 1850s), Lexington. Detail from J.T. Palmatary, *View of the City of Lexington, Ky.* (Cincinnati, ca. 1857).

was burned on the night of 18 December 1861 "through the carelessness of some recruits of Colonels Crisby and Anderson's command."[47] After the war the Maxwell Springs Company was awarded damages for the loss by the federal government.

In form, size, and period the Maxwell Springs Amphitheater related to that of the Southwestern Agricultural and Mechanical Association at Crescent Hill, Louisville.[48] The structure at Crescent Hill, however, was without Gothic or any other architectural stylistic reference. It survived until the mid-1870s, when the land was sold off into building lots.

THE CRAIG, ELLIOTT AND COMPANY BUILDING. Lexington's first commercial cast-iron facade had Gothic detailing. The Craig, Elliott and Company Building at 216 West Main Street was erected between the purchase of the property in 1854 and publication of a cut depicting the store in a local newspaper in 1857 (fig. 11.21).[49] The iron-front tradition in the United States had been inaugurated in John Haviland's classic design for the Miners' Bank at Pottsville, Pennsylvania, built in 1830; and it reached its full stride in James Bogardus's Edgar Laing Stores at Washington and Murry Streets in New York City, of 1848. John McMurtry built the Lexington example, three-storied and four-bayed, with slender colonnettes supporting Tudor arches in the first story that allowed for ample display windows and entrances. Narrow piers rose above the colonnettes, interrupted by molded courses at each floor level and capped by pinnacles. These vertical members accentuated the height of the facade, with a screen parapet and crenelations at the top masking the summit of the flounder roof, which drained at the back. Windows became more pointed in each ascending story, and they were hooded with drip molds. The casements had some tracery at their tops.

At the time of construction, McMurtry owned the foundry established (1816) by Joseph Bruen, located in a relatively new building on the north side of Water Street, west of Spring Street, where the cast-iron pieces for the store facade would have been manufactured. Some of them had been obliterated before the Craig, Elliott and Company Building was razed by Urban Renewal in 1971.

THE PROPOSED HENRY CLAY MEMORIAL. On 12 April 1855 committee members of the Clay Monument Association met in Lexington to select a design for a mausoleum and memorial to Henry Clay to be erected in the Lexington Cemetery. From more than

Fig. 11.21 The Craig, Elliott and Company Building (mid-1850s), Lexington. From the *Lexington Observer and Reporter*, 13 June 1857, p. 1.

one hundred designs submitted from across the nation, first place, accompanied by a premium of $500, was awarded to the Cincinnati architect J.R. Hamilton. His entry was for a polygonal Gothic pavilion set on a stepped terrace, with open lobed arches in the first story, the form diminishing gracefully above by means of curved flying buttresses; a clerestory crowned by a series of gables encircled an ogee dome ending in a point, on which stood a winged angel (fig. 11.22). A sarcophagus containing the remains of Henry Clay was to be in a crypt at the base of the monument, on which a heroic-size statue of the great statesman was to be centered and at a level to be seen through the ring of arches. The upper story was to house a collection of memorabilia belonging to the deceased. The building was to be thirteen-sided, symbolizing the number of original states, with a carved American eagle perched on the cresting over each arch. At the summit of the clerestory buttresses, protruding like gargoyles, were "angels with trumpets surrounding the base of the dome, like a glory."[50] *Ballou's Drawing-Room Companion* lavished praise on the design, comparing it to the memorial of Sir Walter Scott in Edinburgh and stating:

From what we saw of it, we have no hesitation in saying that, although excelled by others in size and costliness, if we consider its adaptation to the purpose intended, its elegant outline and proportions, and exquisite richness of detail, this design for a mausoleum is beyond all question the most beautiful thing of the kind with which we are acquainted in the new or old world. . . . We have been so long accustomed to look upon nothing but obelisks and columns in our burial places, our artists seem so paralyzed by hackneyed devices in all architectural efforts for obituary purposes, that it is truly refreshing to meet with something bold, practical and original. . . . [We] congratulate our Kentucky friends upon their selection in this important undertaking, and if they execute this model in its integrity, they will add another to the very few monuments in this country worthy of the great objects to which they are dedicated.

At a meeting of contributors, the president of the Clay Monument Association, Henry T. Duncan, announced that only $50,000 had been raised, and Hamilton's design would require $90,000 to build.

Fig. 11.22 Design for the Henry Clay Memorial and Mausoleum (1855). From *Ballou's Pictorial Drawing-Room Companion*, 25 August 1855.

The architect responded that the scheme could be reduced to cost only $60,000 or $65,000 without compromising it much, but an alternate proposal costing $55,000 was erected. It is a gigantic Corinthian column mounted on an Egyptian base, with a statue of the statesman on top. The resident engineer was Thomas Lewinski, and the contractor was John Haly.[51]

THE LEXINGTON OPERA HOUSE. The Lexington Odd Fellows Hall Association incorporated the opera house in its building of 1856-57 on the southeast corner of Main and Broadway. The architect, Cincinnatus Shryock (1816-88), son of Mathias Shryock and younger brother of Gideon, had been working as a builder in Lexington since the early 1840s.[52] The opera house and Odd Fellows Hall was built in the perpendicular style, of brick, except for the first-story facade, which was of stone (fig. 11.23). Above rose polygonal buttresses, which framed tall, pointed windows lighting the main or second story, and which continued upward embracing coupled blind arches at attic level, creating a broken skyline with crenelations between on the Main Street front. On the side, a flat, panel effect replaced the buttresses. Wirt and Wilgus were the contractors, and construction cost $40,000. Stores occupied the street level, and the Independent Order of Odd Fellows held lodge meetings on the top floor. The main floor housed the opera house, or concert hall, which had a seating capacity of over a thousand persons; dressing rooms were in back of the stage. Opening night was

Fig. 11.24 The Episcopal Burying Ground Chapel (1867), Lexington. Photo, late 1800s, courtesy of E.I. Thompson, Lexington.

20 May 1857 with a performance of Sheridan's *The Rivals*. The building was destroyed by fire on 15 January 1886, after which Lexington acquired the tiered-theater-type opera house on the west side of Broadway above Short Street.[53]

THE EPISCOPAL BURYING GROUND CHAPEL. The site of the Episcopal cemetery on East Third Street in Lexington was purchased in 1832 and extensively used for interments during the cholera epidemic of the following year. Burial plots were laid out in groups of ten on each side of a 17-foot central axis; and a 10-foot alley separated the blocks, with the exception of the main cross axis, which was 16 feet wide.[54] At the junction of the two principal axes a small T-shaped building was erected in 1867. The projecting stem and crossbar have the full dimensions that their intersection allowed. G.D. Wilgus contracted for the simple structure with low brick walls, hood molds over the openings, steeply pitched roofs, and carpenter Gothic details on the overhanging eaves (fig. 11.24).[55] Its eaves' elaboration, with half-round moldings and turned pendants, differ from bargeboards of antebellum Gothic cottages, which were carved from a single plank. The pattern on the side eaves is plain and without relief. Although referred to as a "cottage" in the contract, the dual-leaf doors of the entrance, open ceilings in all three rooms, and built-in furnishings indicate its purpose as a chapel, with vestry and record rooms (fig. 11.25). Each room has a fireplace. The two small-

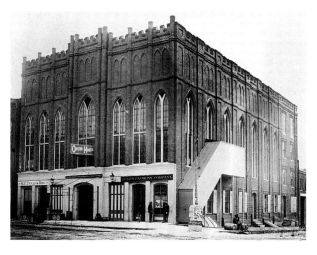

Fig. 11.23 The Lexington Opera House (1856-58). Photo, before 1886, from the Lafayette Studio Collection, Lexington.

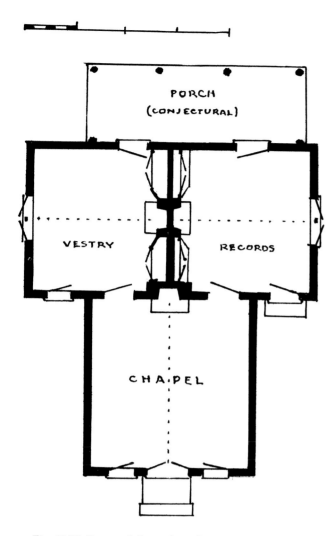

Fig. 11.25 Restored floor plan of Episcopal Burying Ground Chapel.

er rooms share a square chimney. The large room uses only the center flue of a triple-stacked chimney, the outer shafts being decorative. The fireplaces have arched panels, and half-boss corbels support the mantel shelves. Wardrobes in the vestry room have octagonal piers at the corners and crenelations at the top, continuing across the chimney breast separating them. Cabinets with shelves in the adjoining room are of similar character. Originally there may have been a porch or lean-to at the back. The building and the grounds were restored by a committee from Christ Church in 1947. The Episcopal cemetery "cottage" long has been used as a dwelling.

THE McMURTRY HOUSE. Perhaps the first Kentucky example in what Downing called the "pointed" or "rural" Gothic manner was the home of architect-builder John McMurtry, located on the west side of South Broadway, between High and Maxwell streets, in Lexington. During the 1840s McMurtry bought and sold a number of lots in the block, and he built his own house on one acquired in 1845.[56] To the north was the house he built for James C. Butler. The architect's residence was a three-part composition. Its slightly advanced central pavilion and ends were gabled and had overhanging eaves adorned with bracketed bargeboards, which continued in this instance along the connecting horizontal lengths (fig. 11.26). The fenestration throughout consisted of small-paned casements of three lights, except for the projecting bay windows in the first story at each end; the square-headed windows and doorway had drip molds over them. Chimneys were exceedingly tall and articulated into triple stacks. Octagonal piers to the veranda were joined by traceried railings and supported wide Tudor arches with pierced trefoil spandrels. The low arch with hollow spandrels became something of a McMurtry signature, appearing not only on his Gothic Revival houses but on the classic exterior of Botherum and the Italianate villa Lyndhurst. According to the Middleton, Wallace and Company 1857 bird's-eye view of Lexington, the McMurtry House had a long two-story ell at the back with superimposed galleries, and there was a small separate dependency to the rear on a line with the south flank.

Fig. 11.26 John McMurtry House (late 1840s), Lexington. Stereoscopic slide, ca. 1870-80s, courtesy of Lexington Public Library.

A transverse hall in the main pavilion accommodated a long straight flight of steps, which confronted the visitor upon entering. A coved cornice and molded ribs framed and diagonally crisscrossed the flat ceiling of the parlor on the south side. The mantel had colonnettes and trefoil spandrels beneath the shelf. Pilasters flanked a similarly arched mirror on the chimney breast and matched others spaced around the room.

By World War I the McMurtry home had lost its bay windows and most of its bargeboards; the casement windows had been changed to sash, the veranda railings altered or removed, chimneys truncated, and dormers added on the roof. Much rebuilding had occurred at the back. The structure served as a roominghouse known as The Britling for many years prior to its demolition in 1961.

THE BAYLES-BECK HOUSE. John McMurtry built a house in Lexington on East High Street facing Lexington Avenue for Jessee Bayles in or after 1845. It was then probably remodeled for James Burnie Beck, who acquired it in 1848.[57] There is a clear separation between Greek and Gothic elements, the bulk of the design being the former, and the latter reserved for the crenelated crowning. The building is cubic, with unbroken side walls (where grapes were grown on trellises), and openings limited to front and back. The facade is divided into five shallow planes, the outermost almost as narrow as piers, and the centermost, containing the frontispiece, being slightly advanced.

Fig. 11.27 The Bayles-Beck House (late 1840s), Lexington. Photo, late 1800s, courtesy of Mrs. J.T. Shannon, Lexington.

The doorway, enframed by sidelights and transom, was sheltered by a plain portico supported by coupled Roman Doric columns on antepodia, between which rose the front steps (fig. 11.27). A single window above had shutters in side recesses, resembling an opening of three lights; and the intervening wall spaces had single shuttered windows on each of three levels, including the basement. In contrast to the severity below, the parapet is quite elaborate. The first two levels correspond to architrave and frieze. The brick "triglyphs" were capped by round-headed merlons (now leveled on top), making a lacy skyline. The interior arrangement is simple, with four square rooms flanking a transverse stair hall. A rectangular centerpiece ornaments the hall ceiling. Fireplace openings are rounded and have a cartouche keystone between paneled spandrels; the shelves have a wavy outline.

In 1911 the portico was replaced by a long front porch with angled volute, Ionic columns, and balustrade. It was reduced nearer to the original size in the mid-1980s; the 1911 column shafts were reused with Doric capitals.

BOTHERUM. Another McMurtry-built residence in Lexington is as distinctly divided between classic and romantic as the Bayles-Beck House, only the two styles here are employed about equally, one notably on the outside and the other on the inside of the building. The stone cottage on West High Street (now reached from Madison Place) facing Town Fork of Elkhorn is called Botherum. The unusual architectural character of the house probably stemmed largely from its eccentric owner, the lawyer Madison Conyers Johnson. He received highest honors when he graduated from Transylvania University in 1823 at fifteen and he was the model for the main character in James Lane Allen's *Two Gentlemen of Kentucky*. The land for Botherum was purchased in 1844, and its construction date, 1851, was chiseled in the stone over the basement door.[58] The building was U-shaped, with an open court formerly at the back. It had three Corinthian porticoes at the main entrance, that with a distyle projection roofed over with a small vault (fig. 11.28). The placing of columns on brick paving at ground level instead of on a substantial podium belies the external classicism. This hugging the ground, and the use of bay windows, lozenge-paned French doors containing stained glass, an octagonal turret at the crossing of the roofs, and a Tudor arch over the west entrance are Gothic Revival elements in accord with the interior.

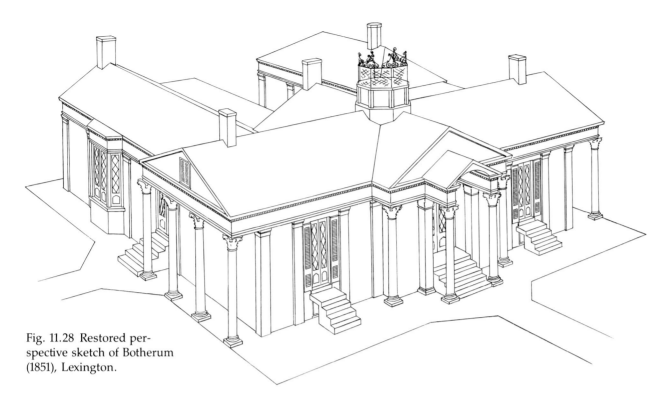

Fig. 11.28 Restored per-
spective sketch of Botherum
(1851), Lexington.

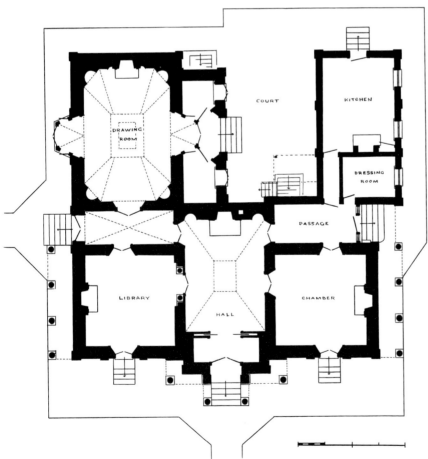

Fig. 11.29 Floor plan
of Botherum.

The elegance of the interior arrangement outstrips its magnitude (fig. 11.29). The focal point is a cloister-vaulted hall lighted by a skylight. It is flanked by a library and chamber and connects with passages behind leading to the drawing room and kitchen in the rear ells. The front rooms were dark, each having only a single opening, whose casements have colored glass. The east passage and drawing room are vaulted, the latter octagonally, with niches in four corners and a rectangular centerpiece in the ceiling bordered by gamopetalous flowers molded in plaster. This motif is repeated around the Tudor-arched mirror over the marble mantel (fig. 11.30). Light is provided in the drawing room by bay windows, the one on the court side opening into small anterooms. In the court an iron stairway ascended to the lookout atop the turret. The west wing contained the kitchen and dressing room. There being no dining room, it is probable that Major Johnson either ate alone in the west passage or banqueted in the hall. An exception to the inner Gothic uniformity is the Ionic doorway set in the thick wall of the library adjoining the door to the hall. McMurtry was not too concerned with the inconsistency in combining two historic styles, one ancient and the other medieval. He was more conscious of construction than the period of architectural dress. He once wrote: "All styles may be divided into two classes. One derived from the post and lintel and the other from the arch; the Grecian being the type of the first and the Roman or Gothic of the second."[59] The fact that the Corinthian order was much more

widely used by the Romans than by the Greeks would reconcile the envelope having the medieval enclosure; and we need not press the matter of the single interior, Greek doorway detail. The various parts of the house add up to a thoroughly charming whole, making it one of the outstanding examples of romantic architecture in America.

The grounds around Botherum were ample, extending out to the Versailles turnpike. The entrance had an iron gateway that opened and shut automatically by a mechanism triggered by the wheels of a carriage passing over it.[60] A servants' house is behind the kitchen wing, beyond the present diminished property line. The court has been filled by a dining room, the stairway to the lookout obliterated. Windows in the east bay of the drawing room have been given large-paned sashes over a seat, and narrow windows have been cut in the side walls to the north of fireplaces in the library and chamber. The east flank of the house faces Madison Place, and the portico here has been extended one bay to shelter the side hall door, making it the main entrance. The land was divided into building lots for the Woodward Heights subdivision in the 1880s, but recently the lot to the north has been added to the Botherum property, and with it a gingko tree given to Madison Johnson by Henry Clay.

LOUDOUN. The first and foremost castellated villa in Kentucky is Loudoun. Its construction was financed by the sizable patrimony received in 1849 by Francis Key Hunt, then living on Barr Street. The fifty-six-acre tract on the northern outskirts of Lexington was given by and adjoined that of his wife's parents.[61] Francis Hunt engaged the outstanding architect A.J. Davis of New York, who at the time was working almost exclusively in the romantic styles. First studies of the house were begun on 3 April 1850, and the final drawings were sent in July 1851. Hunt was in New York that December and made the final payment amounting to a little over $300. Several schemes were submitted, the one labeled "Plan No. 2" bears a close resemblance to the house as built (fig. 11.31). The porch end of the house is similar; the remainder is more monotonous because of the sameness of window treatment and wall height. The stairway is restricted to the tower section, which Hunt found unacceptable. As executed, the service ell is drawn out with more grace and variety, and the stairs are in a central position. One notes that the roofs are mostly low-pitched (befitting a southern house), though the overall effect is steepness (proper to a

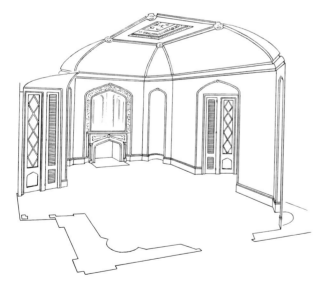

Fig. 11.30 Restored perspective sketch of drawing room in Botherum.

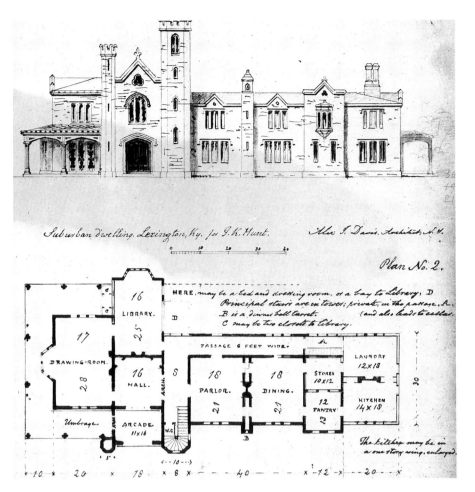

Suburban dwelling, Lexington, Ky., for J.K. Hunt. Alex J. Davis, Architect, N.Y.

Plan No. 2.

HERE may be a bed and dressing room, or a bay to Library. D
Principal stairs are in tower; private, in the passage. A.
B is a dining hall turret. (and also leads to cellar.)
C may be two closets to library.

The kitchen may be in a one story wing, enlarged.

Fig. 11.31 "Suburban Dwelling, Lexington, Ky., for F.K. Hunt." Plan no. 2 (1850) by A.J. Davis. Courtesy of the Print Department, Metropolitan Museum of Art, New York.

Fig. 11.32 Loudoun (1850-51), Lexington. Photo, late 1800s, courtesy the Lexington Public Library.

THE GOTHIC REVIVAL STYLE 271

Gothic building) because of gable parapets and the roof slope of the left end pavilion (fig. 11.32). The walls may have been the first use of hollow-wall brick construction in Kentucky, the system having been introduced to America by Ithiel Town in New Haven, Connecticut, villas.[62] The brick pattern repeats four stretchers and one header in each tier. The walls of Loudoun were coated with sand and paint to simulate stonework. Details are cut limestone. Windows are lozenge-paned, some enframed by narrow rectangular glass in stained vine patterns. The bay window on the second story was after a design used by Davis at the Virginia Military Institute (fig. 11.33). A half-tunnel encircles the main foundations to eliminate moisture from the footings of the walls and give added stability. The builder was John McMurtry, who reported that construction cost $30,000.[63] The castle was named after one of Mrs. Hunt's favorite songs, "The Bells of Loudoun."

One enters through what Davis called the "arcade," a porch covered by a level-crown vault, open-

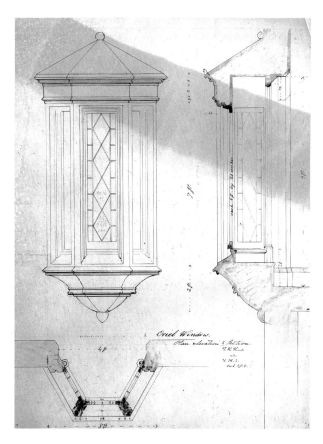

Fig. 11.33 Plan, elevation, and section of an oriel window for Loudoun, by A.J. Davis. Courtesy of the Print Department, Metropolitan Museum of Art, New York.

ing on one side to the umbrage, both paved with a tessellation of gray and white marble. The massive staircase in the main hall has a cut-out apron pendant from the outer edge of the soffit. The ceiling is crisscrossed with ribs, and the beam spanning the stairwell springs from grotesque protomas modeled in plaster. The drawing room is 20 by 30 feet, and is lighted by a great curved oriel as well as twin windows at front and back, in which casements and louvered shutters slide back into wall pockets (fig. 11.34). Shutters elsewhere fold into special recesses. Walls of the drawing room were stenciled al fresco in a large fourteenth-century Italian floral pattern, and squares between the ceiling beams were stenciled in geometric designs. A gilded lambrequin fitted over the arch to the oriel, and a pair of gold mirrors in perpendicular style sat at each side. These and the marble mantel originally in this room are in the residence where Mrs. Hunt went to live after the death of her husband, on Mill Street adjoining the John Wesley Hunt House.

The library is in back of the staircase, lighted by a bay window, and opposite are full-length bookcases on either side of a red-brown polished stone chimneypiece. The ceiling is divided by ribs connected to attenuated colonnettes along the walls. The parlor has an interesting shape by expanding into the base of the tower. Its mantel is a white marble specimen simpler than that in the drawing room. The ceiling centerpiece is a foliage-flower design modeled in plaster. Cupboards flank the fireplace in the long dining room. A water closet at the foot of the service stairs on the first floor corresponds to another directly above it. Ceiling heights downstairs are 14 feet, except for the drawing room, which is 2 feet higher. The service-room ceilings are considerably lower. Dressing rooms adjoin the principal bedrooms, and a bath is over one of the pantries. Servants' rooms are above the kitchen and laundry.

Loudoun has become Castlewood Park. The porches have been removed, minor curtailments made about the parapets, and a gymnasium was added at the back. A few of the big trees survive, giving the place an atmosphere of lingering grandeur. The villa is now used by the Lexington Art League.

INGELSIDE. A castellated villa similar to Loudoun, the home of Henry Boone Ingels, was built at the west limits of Lexington. The date, 1852, was incised on a stone escutcheon in the principal tower. The house was designed and built by John McMurtry, who borrowed motifs from Loudoun and Christ

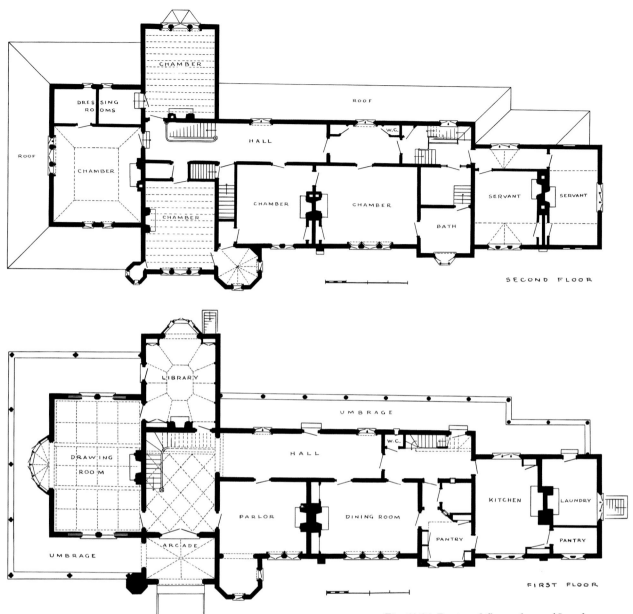

Fig. 11.34 Restored floor plans of Loudoun.

Church, executing many in cast iron at the Bruen foundry, which had been under the supervision of Ingels since 1848.[64] Ingelside was situated on three hundred acres, purchased in 1843 by Ingels's father-in-law, Joseph Bruen.[65] The gate house on the Harrodsburg Pike was a severe stuccoed brick block with an arched carriageway through the center, having a half upper story beneath a flounder roof masked by a crenelated parapet (fig. 11.35). Merlons at the angles were chimneys for corner fireplaces.

The facade of the castle was symmetrical, its form reminiscent of Blithewood, the house for Robert Donaldson of Fishkill, New York, designed by A.J.

Davis and included among designs in *Rural Residences*, 1837, but never realized.[66] The traceried porch of Ingelside, however, was in the Downingesque cottage style (fig. 11.36). Like Blithewood, the main tower was on the right flank, and the ell extended back on that side. Ingelside was the more interesting composition, the rear of Blithewood resembling a child's toy fort. Although nearly as large as Loudoun, the Ingels villa had a more homelike atmosphere due to its more compact shape, its intimate entrance shelter, and its veranda being limited to the rear (fig. 11.37).

Ingelside had an entrance hall with a crisscrossed

THE GOTHIC REVIVAL STYLE 273

Fig. 11.35 The gatehouse at Ingelside, Lexington, with a sketch of the rear. Photo, early 1900s, by Harvey Watkins.

Fig. 11.36 Ingelside (1852), Lexington. Photo, early 1900s, courtesy of Mrs. Dunster Duncan Foster Pettit, Lexington.

ceiling like Loudoun's, off which opened the large drawing room and smaller parlor, the latter expanding into a recess at the base of the tower. The library, dining room, and services were farther away (fig. 11.38). The staircase was in a separate hall at the inside angle of the building, eliminating the need for a long hallway downstairs and creating an attractive L-shaped hall upstairs. A small stairway to the garret and tower ascended over the main flight. Dressing rooms were provided on the chamber floor, and three octagonal turrets made corner closets. Interior fittings were similar to those of Loudoun, although plainer, the doors having less detail and the windows having stained glass in solid colors. In the center of the higher ceiling of the drawing room was a large circular centerpiece modeled after a medieval geometric rose window (fig. 11.39). The white marble mantel had a half-round arched fireplace, with low-relief foliage in the spandrels and a keystone more organic than architectural in character. The chimneypiece in the library was of polished gray stone. In other rooms were marbelized iron mantels of the kind sold at Henry Ingels's store.[67] The centerpiece in the dining-room ceiling came from the same die as that in the Loudoun parlor.

Fig. 11.37 Rear perspective sketch of Ingelside.

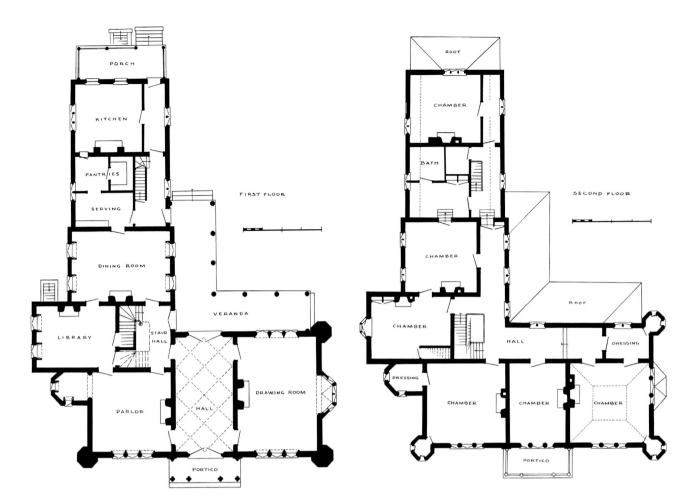

Fig. 11.38 Restored floor plans of Ingelside.

Fig. 11.39 Centerpiece on drawing-room ceiling, Ingelside. Photo, 1941.

Behind the kitchen wing at Ingelside stood an octagonal hip-roofed brick smokehouse, demolished in 1938. Farther back was a servants' cottage of six rooms in the pointed manner. When the property was portioned off into building lots, the gatehouse was enlarged into an apartment house, and recently it has been converted into a shop. The villa and shrunken setting became a trailer camp in the 1940s, and twenty years later the residence was demolished.

THE ELLEY VILLA.   The best and the most characteristic of Kentucky villas in the pointed manner was the home of William R. Elley, built in Lexington on an eight-acre tract south of Maxwell Street and east of Rose Street in 1851.[68] As constructed by John McMurtry, it is an adaptation of design 25 in Andrew Downing's *The Architecture of Country Houses* (fig. 11.40). Downing contended (pp. 304-305) that the scheme was "no copy of any foreign cottage," but its elements had been "suggested by the country life of those who live in residences of this size in the Middle

Fig. 11.40 "A Country House in the Pointed Style."
From Andrew Jackson Downing. *The Architecture of
Country Houses* (New York, 1850), design 25.

United States." Although the view and plans illustrated in the book were delineated by A.J. Davis, this design was by Downing himself. He enclosed it in sketch form in a letter to Davis on 27 January 1848, when the book was in preparation.[69] The main difference between Downing's plan and McMurtry's execution is wall height, the latter having a full second story, with small gables affording tall windows at the front of the wings (fig. 11.41). In a house of this style, Downing would have specified casement rather than sash windows. The bargeboards of the principal gables are based on details supplied by the Downing book, copied from an Augustus Pugin rendering of a sixteenth-century example (figs. 11.42, 11.43). It, however, has a solid background, whereas Downing's version and McMurtry's example are pierced. Pugin points out that the "pinnacle is modern and of a mean style unsuitable to the sides." It was given slightly more shape but less height in *Country Houses*. The veranda has plain octagonal piers rather than columns with bases and capitals, and the chimney stacks are square rather than eight-sided. The published design of the interior arrangements and those of the actualized house are similar. Downing described the main axis of the first story: "The entrance hall . . . unoccupied by stairs . . . [makes] a fine apartment, and being connected with a library of equal size, by large sliding doors, the effect of this suite of 44 feet, when thrown into one, will be very agreeable on entering the house. This will be heightened by the position of the large bay-window at the end of the library."[70] In Elley Villa tall folding doors substitute for large sliding doors. The staircase is in a cross hall behind the dining room. The conspicuous difference in plan is that in place of a bedroom in back of the parlor there is a second parlor, and the two rooms are connected by wide openings flanking the chimney (fig. 11.44). The conservatory at

Fig. 11.41 The William R. Elley Villa (1850-51), Lexington. Photo, ca. 1910, by Louis Edward Nollau, courtesy of the University of Kentucky Libraries.

Fig. 11.42 "Verge-Board." From Andrew Jackson Downing, *The Architecture of Country Houses* (New York, 1850), fig. 137, p. 310.

Fig. 11.43 "Wooden Gable." From Augustus Pugin, *A Series of Ornamental and Timber Gables from Existing Examples in England and France of the Sixteenth Century* (London, 1839), pl. 18.

this end of the Elley Villa did not project as much as illustrated in the book but was finished by a bay window on the south. There are also slight variations in the service rooms and conveniences. Although Downing's plan shows a door to the second-story bathroom from the landing, the difference in level made it an impossiblity. Servants' rooms are restricted to the garret in both.

Colored glass enhances the bay window in the Elley Villa library, and frosted glass with intaglio flower patterns embellishes the transom and sidelights of the front doorway. Matching rectangular centerpieces ornament the ceiling in the hall and library, with a high-relief gamopetalous vine bordering an anthemion in a sunken panel, identical to those in the Botherum drawing room and Bayles-Beck House stair hall. The white-marble mantels in the parlors are of the Ingelside type. That in the dining room makes use of several thin slabs of stone in juxtaposition, with beveled edges following curved outlines, and a single console of contrasting depth supporting the projecting mantel shelf (fig. 11.45).

William R. Elley sold the property to John L. Barclay in 1856. Twenty years later it was leased from a subsequent owner, Judge W.C. Goodloe, by the Sisters of Charity of Nazareth and made into a hospital. A few years later it became the home of W.T. Withers. When purchased by Oliver Perry Alford in 1885, it was given the name of Aylesford, and for the next decade was one of the showplaces of the Bluegrass. In 1925 it became a fraternity house and was painted—inappropriately for its style—white. Since 1944 the villa, facing Linden Walk on a diminished lot, has been a private dwelling.[71]

Mound Cottage and Warrenwood. Gothic Revival villas of the mid-1850s around Danville have been attributed to McMurtry, as he was there constructing the main building of the School for the Deaf (chap. 12). The most attractive of these houses is Mound Cottage on Maple Avenue, built in 1856 for J.T. Boyle, who would rise to the rank of brigadier general in the Union army (fig. 11.46).[72] Mound Cottage is a center-hall, two-chimney house, and it has three front gables and triple-light windows in the upper facade, like the Elley villa. Unlike the Lexington house there are lozenge-shaped panes in all sashes, and a tracery railing carries around the upper level of the front porch and bay windows at each end. The house and chimney forms are more bulky than those of the Elley Villa. There is only a slight projection of the center pavilion, and the porch does not

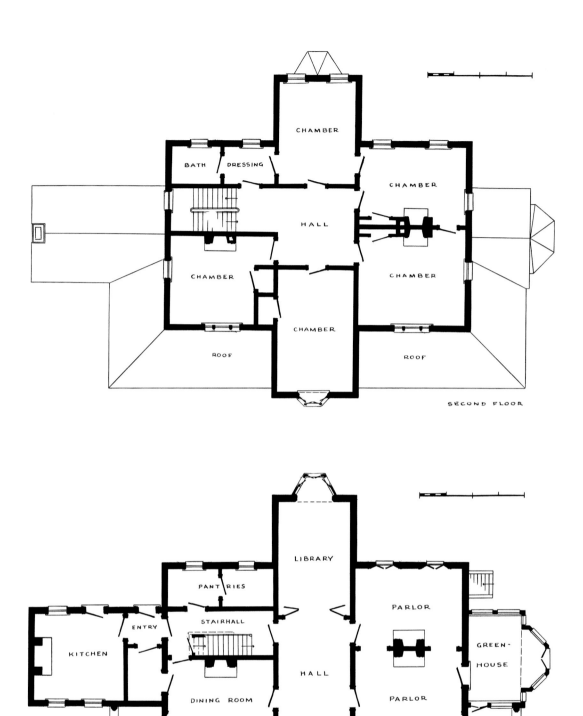

Fig. 11.44 Floor plans of the Elley Villa.

Fig. 11.45 Dining-room mantel of the Elley Villa. Photo, 1941.

Fig. 11.46 Mound Cottage (1856), Danville. Photo, 1940.

turn the corners to meet one-story wings at the sides. Bargeboards are more lacelike. Rooms are repetitious in shape, and the interior lacks the interest of the Lexington house. A modern porte cochere has been added on the right flank, prompting removal of a bay window.

Warrenwood, on the Danville-Hustonville Pike, was built by John Fouche Warren in 1856.[73] Like Mound Cottage it has twin chimneys, three front gables, and a veranda spanning the facade, but the porch has brackets on a flat lintel, and there are coupled windows except over the entrance. Variations of this type abound throughout Kentucky.

WALNUT GROVE. The farmhouse of John McClintock, called Walnut Grove, in Bourbon County just north of Millersburg, is a good example of carpenter Gothic, or the vertical-board type of construction set forth in Upjohn's *Rural Architecture* (New York, 1852).[74] The story-and-three-quarters building features six gables with restrained wavy-edged bargeboards both on overhanging horizontal eaves and gables, and there are flat cut-out pinnacles at the summits (fig. 11.47). Sash windows are given a wide upright muntin in the middle to resemble casements, and they are shuttered; the upper fenestration is surmounted by triangular louvered panels giving the appearance of corbel-arched openings. A pointed-arch Palladian doorway over the main entrance opens onto the upper deck of the bracketed-style veranda. Walls are composed of boards over a foot wide, stripped by five-inch vertical planks that are capped by half-round arch forms beneath the eaves, and windows and doors are carefully regulated by

Fig. 11.47 Walnut Grove (late 1850s), near Millersburg. Photo, 1976, by Patrick Snadon.

these members, with lintels slightly peaked and having corbeled ends. The regard for symmetry and a set module is indicated further by the use of five blind windows, two on the east flank of the front pavilion, one on the west, another farther back on that side of the wing, and one at the back. Double windows on two sides of the parlor preclude the need for additional light in this room, and the other three blind windows occur opposite closets or the kitchen stairway.

Walnut Grove is an L-shaped dwelling, with an open-newel staircase in the main hall between square rooms, a narrow hall with partly enclosed stairs at the junction of the ell, and the dining room and kitchen behind (fig. 11.48). Both halls and the rear rooms open onto a wide porch running along the east side of the ell. Interior fittings are plain, the

Fig. 11.49 Dependency at Walnut Grove. Photo, 1976, by Patrick Snadon.

fireplaces being framed by pilastered Greek Revival mantels.

Several dependencies at Walnut Grove reflect the features of the residence (fig. 11.49). A carriage house is square and has bargeboarded gables meeting at each corner. A servants' cottage is elongated, with twin gables in front separated by a space containing the doorway.

THORN HILL. The early-nineteenth-century house that stood on the southeast corner of Limestone and Fifth streets in Lexington was the birthplace of John Cabell Breckinridge (statesman and vice-president of the United States), the home of Joseph Cabell Breckinridge (secretary of state under Gov. John Adair) and Charlton Hunt (first mayor of Lexington). Called Thorn Hill, the house may have resembled that of the Rev. James McChord, several doors south on Limestone, a one-story building with gabled center pavilion. In 1857, Thorn Hill was extensively remodeled in the pointed manner for Nancy Warfield.[75] It was made two full stories at the front and enlarged at the back. In the main part of the house, fireplaces were brought to the inside wall, and windows were cut through the outermost walls (that on the north end made a bay window). A traceried porch with paired octagonal piers was set before the entrance. Pointed windows were placed in the second story. The wide gables probably once had bargeboards. The design was climaxed by tall dia-

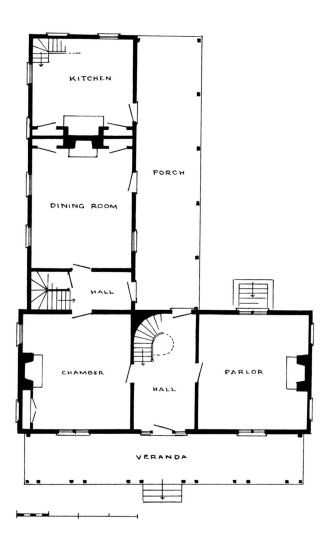

Fig. 11.48 Restored first-floor plan of Walnut Grove.

Fig. 11.50 Thorn Hill (re-modeled 1857), Lexington. Photo, 1955.

mond-stacked chimneys (fig. 11.50). Detracting from the effect were inappropriate hood molds added over the lower windows and single panes of glass per sash. Even though Thorn Hill always was a "rule-of-thumb" house—casual in its symmetry and inconstant in its measurements—in its heyday it achieved some degree of good external appearance.

Its room arrangement also had some merit (fig. 11.51). The hall was a bit odd with a short vestibule at the front and staircase behind. But the isolation of the north room, the stair hall opening to the gallery and dining room, the south room also communicating with the dining room, and the complexity of the services and kitchen were well handled. The early kitchen pavilion and detached quarters had been but slightly altered. The entire complex was demolished in 1963.

BUFFALO TRACE.   On an eminence overlooking the Ohio River above Maysville, Buffalo Trace was built for William Henry Wadsworth in the Gothic cottage style about 1862, which is the date incised in a stone set in the gable over the front doorway of a small brick dependency behind the house. Like the Elley Villa group, Buffalo Trace has a projecting entrance pavilion and symmetrical wings, but it differs

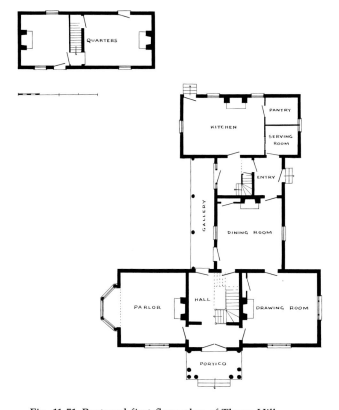

Fig. 11.51 Restored first-floor plan of Thorn Hill.

Fig. 11.52 Buffalo Trace
(1862), near Maysville.
Photo, 1967.

in having parapets rising above gable walls (rather
than bargeboarded overhangs) and in the absence of
porches (perhaps because the house was not completed; fig. 11.52). The form relates to a scheme by
Davis published as design 30 in Downing's *Country
Houses* (fig. 11.53), but the narrow doorway flanked
by small separate windows in place of an open arch,
higher walls on the sides with heavier battlements,
and the lack of a veranda make a less graceful composition. Plan similarities between Buffalo Trace and
design 30 begin and end with the front suite: a hall
flanked by parlors with oriels at each end (fig. 11.54).
The published plan has smaller rooms behind. The
Maysville house is somewhat U-shaped, the dining
room and kitchen-service wings extending back from
the parlors, and the stair hall filling most of the cusp.
The layout resembles the first story of another Davis
house, a story-and-a-half residence built in New Bedford, Massachusetts, and included as design 23 in
Country Houses. One need only substitute the dining
room for the library and invert its position with the

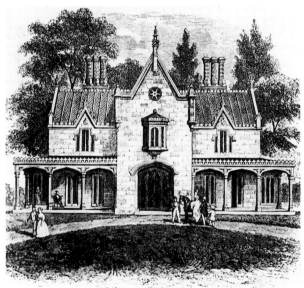

Fig. 11.53 "Villa in the Pointed Style." From Andrew
Jackson Downing, *The Architecture of Country Houses*
(New York, 1850), design 30, fig. 160.

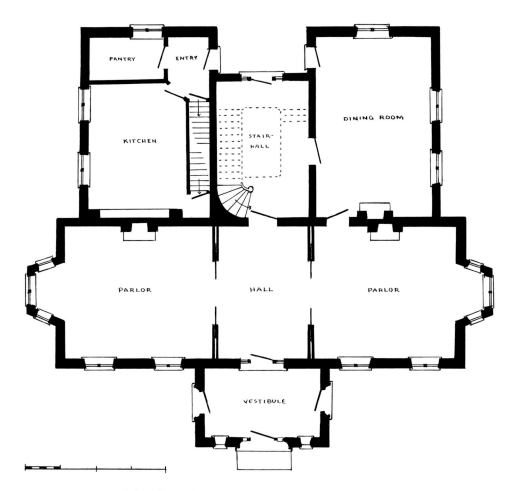

Fig. 11.54 Restored first-floor plan of Buffalo Trace.

kitchen. Unique to Buffalo Trace was the interior isolation of the kitchen from the dining room until it was connected later by a sizable back porch. Interiors are plain, perhaps because the construction took place during the war. The most elaborate fittings are mottled marble mantels with semicircular openings in the parlors, resembling those in the dining room and library at Ingelside. Staircase newel and banisters are heavy, polygonal uprights supporting a broad handrail, characteristic of the Reconstruction period. The house was occupied by William Henry Wadsworth's decendents until recently.

The Gothic Revival was the romantic style par excellence. It had a double heritage. It was imported mature from England but developed somewhat in its own way in America because of sophisticated enthusiasts like Downing and Davis, well versed in its principles and archaeological background, and provincials like McMurtry, who interpreted it according to their own tastes. In Kentucky, as throughout the United States, the way was paved for this fully developed Gothic Revival by certain amorphous predecessors in the rococo-Gothic manner. These were manifested in the Saint Thomas church near Bardstown and as pointed or "Christian"arches in otherwise styleless churches. Similar openings carried over into the Greek Revival. Churches by John Stirewalt in Louisville became completely Gothic Revival during the late 1830s, and the style later spread throughout the commonwealth. Other types of buildings adhering to this appearance were mausoleums and cemetery gateways, a monastery, arsenal, fairgrounds amphitheater and other structures, an opera house, and a store. In residences there is a clear-cut division between the lordly castellated and plebeian pointed or cottage varieties. The best examples of both were built in the Bluegrass, most of them by John McMurtry. The pointed style first appeared in McMurtry's own home in Lexington, and shortly thereafter he built the outstanding castle Loudoun after a Davis design. It unquestionably provided the details for Ingelside, many of which were cast in iron. Imitation of materials played an important part in the romantic style, iron overspreading the facade of the Craig, Elliott and Company building, and stucco or sanded paint for a stone effect being used on both public and private buildings. The vertical-board house and church, popularized without historic precedent, was employed in Kentucky no less than elsewhere in the United States. Buffalo Trace demonstrates that the Gothic Revival persisted up to the eve of the Civil War, and the Episcopal Cemetery Chapel in Lexington that it survived the war. The pure Gothic Revival then fell into disuse, though an eclectic High Victorian Gothic continued to determine the design of some churches, public buildings, and large houses through the balance of the nineteenth century. The style was to be supplanted by an archaeologically correct rural Gothic during the first third of the twentieth century.

12 THE ITALIANATE STYLE

MOST KENTUCKY BUILDINGS predating the Civil War belong to stylistic categories already discussed in the preceding chapters. The residue are designated rather loosely under a heading having a geographic import, which pertains to the peninsula of Italy. As Gothic Revival examples may be divided into the castellated and the pointed or the cottage varieties, so the Italianate may be parceled into those that are indebted to the sophisticated architecture of the Renaissance and those that derive from less pretentious, mostly residential, buildings in rural areas. The former type of Italianate architecture actually has a two-fold ancestry, the more remote being the marble edifices of ancient Rome, as understood through the ruins of forums, temples, basilicas, baths, theaters and amphitheaters, triumphal arches, memorial columns, and so on, and the more recent being the palaces and churches of the fifteenth and sixteenth centuries by such famous architects as Brunelleschi, Alberti, Michelozzo, Bramante, Sangallo, Peruzzi, Raphael, Michelangelo, and Palladio. The second category of the Italianate was inspired by buildings belonging to the most enduring architectural tradition in the Western Hemisphere, with roots going back to the Etruscans, and late manifestations postdating the Renaissance. It may be considered a sort of folk architecture; its builders were anonymous. In accordance with those phases in American building influenced by the monuments of Greece or of the Gothic period, the first within the Italianate is known as the Renaissance Revival style. The second is not as conscious of style as of form, and it is subdivided into two types of buildings. One is compact and perfectly balanced right and left, and it is designated by locale, the Tuscan Revival. The other is of complex masses, asymmetrically disposed, and it is referred to simply as the irregular Italian villa. Unlike all other types heretofore considered, including even the pointed style of the Gothic Revival, this last as its name implies was used exclusively for dwellings, mostly of moderate size.

In an inland region like Kentucky, the Renaissance Revival played a lesser role in the early Italianate movement than the more casual phase, and its background is more clearly defined and can be traced in a few sentences. The Renaissance Revival was a nineteenth-century resurgence of the rebirth of ancient Roman culture and needs only to be placed in its chronological context. The original Renaissance (rebirth), of course, was the cultural ferment that started in Italy by the fourteenth century and spread north and westward during the next few hundred years, outmoding the Gothic. In the seventeenth century it took an emotional turn, known as the baroque, which in architecture is distinguished by twisted and reduplicated members, dynamic and complicated forms. The Renaissance and baroque styles had amalgamated in England before any influence was felt in America. One of the first examples here was the Col. John Foster House (ca. 1688) built on North Square in Boston. It had a pedimented doorway, giant pilasters applied to the walls, and a balustrade topping the cornice.[1] Such features had become widespread, if not prevalent, throughout the colonies by the middle of the eighteenth century. The Hammond House (1773-74) in Annapolis, designed by William Buckland and mentioned in connection with Liberty Hall and the Kennedy House (chap. 7), serves to illustrate the type. A new international movement came into being about the time of the American Revolution, advocating a return to purer forms. This included the Louis XVI, Directoire, and Empire periods in France, the Adam and Regency in England, the Biedermeier in Germany, the Empire and neoclassic in Italy, and the Federal in the United States. Thomas Jefferson's prostyle capitol (1785) at

Richmond shows the rigid imitation of the style. Federal classicism had run its course and had been replaced by the Greek Revival when again the need was felt for a return to that enduring fount of authority in Western architecture, prompting the Renaissance Revival to come into being.

It will be recalled that the Greek Revival supplanted the Federal style gradually, giving rise to a number of transitional buildings, in which Roman and Greek elements were blended. Roman domes and arches appear in Shryock's statehouse (1827-30) in Frankfort. Pilastrades were more Roman than Greek, yet characterize McMurtry's Medical Hall (1839) at Transylvania University and many Greek Revival Kentucky residences. By the early 1850s classic buildings had taken on such motifs as cornice hood molds and pediments over doors and windows, console supports to cornices and balconies, fully developed quoins and rustication, and true balusters and balustrades. They were Roman classic or Renaissance, and in no way Greek. They differed from the earlier, delicately hand-carved Federal ornaments in more closely approximating archaeological archetypes, not only in shape and form but in scale and architectonic effect. Like the elements of contemporary Greek and Gothic Revival buildings, they were fabricated by methods technologically advanced. When assessing the Louisville Water Company pumphouse complex or the School for the Blind, we may justifiably ask whether these are Greek Revival designs with extraneous elements inserted (like the dome in the statehouse) or a different breed of architecture. By way of differentiating them from the pure Greek, they are considered in this chapter as specimens of the Renaissance Revival.

The Renaissance Revival's initial American monument was Richard Upjohn's remodeling of the Stephen Van Rensselaer House in Albany, New York, during 1840-44. The form of the old two-story colonial building was retained, its facade consisting of a three-bayed center pavilion and identical two-bayed wings. The new dress given it by Upjohn was mostly in stone and included a rusticated basement story, quoins at the extremities of the three divisions, cornice hoods over the first-story windows and pediments above the second, a main cornice on consoles, a balustraded porch with columns on pedestals, and temple fronts to windows preceded by balconies in the low annexes with balustraded flat roofs.[2] The new sophisticated elements consummated the original intent of the design.

Renaissance Revival buildings constructed from the ground up soon followed. The Atheneum on Washington Square in Philadelphia, the work of John Notman, was built in 1845-47. With its three-story walls of stone, its palazzo affinities are unmistakable. Three-bayed in front and nine-bayed on the sides, with center doorway in each facade, the first-story walls are rusticated, and quoins at the ends continue up to the entablature. The main story has a balcony supported on consoles across the narrow front, and windows here are capped by consoled hoods, those on the side at this level being plainer. Upper windows are square and set in the frieze. A row of modillions is tucked under the deep cornice. An engraving of the building is in Louisa Caroline Tuthill's *History of Architecture* (Philadelphia, 1848). Also reproduced is an image of the two-story Bank of the North America in the same city, having a three-bayed facade with pedimented center doorway, eared windows flanking it, and arched, hooded windows above, the front framed by rusticated pilasters and an entablature with an overhanging cornice on consoles. The palazzo mode was immediately adopted in the brownstone townhouse, beginning with the Herman Thorne residence (1846-48) on West 16th Street in New York City.[3]

A French building put up soon after this had the effect of popularizing the Renaissance style all over the world. It was the Nouveau Louvre, in Paris, constituting sections of the palace built around the Place Louis Napoleon by Louis Visconti and Hector Lefuel during 1852-57. The new work was no further removed in style from the original sixteenth-century pavilions by Pierre Lescot than the seventeenth-century additions by Jacques Lemercier. The Renaissance Revival absorbed this baroque tendency to overelaborate, which made it easy prey to eclectic infiltration from other styles, especially in America during the Reconstruction period. The Renaissance Revival showed commendable propriety, however, in limiting colossal-order porticoes to public buildings.

The less dressy phase of the Italian mode—the Italianate proper—was better suited to the agrarian civilization of Kentucky. The source of inspiration was the indigenous Mediterranean farmhouse or small villa, which displayed very little ornament and was about as straightforward as a building can be. It was not lacking in picturesqueness, however, appearing as an integral part of its setting, which often was the result of changes and additions made over many centuries. Like preceding styles, even those of exotic origins, the Italianate came to America from England. An early milestone in London was the Church of Saint Paul, Covent Garden, dating from 1631-38. It was conceived by Inigo Jones, whose patron, the earl of Bedford, ordered a building "as simple and inexpensive as a barn." Jones modeled it after an Etruscan temple. The portico had a pair of 30-foot-tall Tuscan columns between square antas, with arches on the sides connecting the piers to the cella. A plain architrave encircled the rectangular building, with thin, deep cornices cantilevered on beams, and an unadorned pediment in front. One consideration in the design was that it accord with the arches of Covent Garden Market opposite.[4] Two factors about Saint Paul's remained true for other Italianate buildings. The first was that, because of its simplicity, it was not costly; and the second was that it had wide eaves, upheld by projecting beams or brackets. The bracket became the hallmark of the Italianate.

A minor vogue for Italianism was witnessed in England during the middle of the eighteenth century. It will be recalled that Italy was the setting of Horace Walpole's *The Castle of Otranto*, which was published at this time. The four books of Andrea Palladio were brought out in an English edition in 1742, and notwithstanding the large size and wasted space of Palladian designs, many were of restrained ornamentation. All concepts could be reduced in scale, as was done in the plan for Elmwood Hall, in Ludlow. Indicative of the trend is plate 32 (no. 10, p. 27) in William and John Halfpenny's book, *The Modern Builder's Assistant* (London, ca. 1757), which shows a design for "a low Building, supposed to be situated in a Country Villa." The form of the building is no clearer than the wording of the caption.

Italianate architecture came into its inheritance in England during the early nineteenth century. William Beckford built and moved into an Italian villa when he sold Fonthill Abbey. This was some years after John Nash created Cronkhill (1802) for Lord Berwick's agent, at Attingham, near Shrewsbury. Cronkhill was an informal, compact residence of square and round masses of various heights, crowned by low-pitched roofs with deep bracketed eaves, and with arched fenestration and an arcaded loggia (fig. 12.1). This design, reputedly the first of its kind, soon was followed by a host of published plans of the same ilk. One champion of the style was Joseph Gandy (b. 1771), who at the age of twenty-three went to Italy for several years, afterward earn-

Fig. 12.1 Cronkhill (1802), Attingham, England. From John Summerson, *John Nash, Architect to King George IV* (London, 1955), pl. 3.

ing his living by making architectural renderings for Sir John Soane. Gandy conceived two books, *Designs for Cottages, Cottage Farms, and other Rural Buildings* (1805), and *The Rural Architect* (1806).[5] Obviously his concepts for unadorned structures composed of long, low forms with wide roofs and occasionally an elevated loggia or tower were modeled on what he had seen around the Mediterranean. Of the same period were Robert Lugar's *The Country Gentleman's Architect* (1807) and *Architectural Sketches for Cottages* (1815). The earlier work included an Italianate "Farm House" with a three-story tower at the right, a projecting pavilion in the middle, and a low service wing ending in an octagonal beerhouse with cupola at the left (pls. 6 and 14). The later presented an asymmetrical house labeled "Italian Villa" (pls. 27-28).

The 1820s produced two interesting publications. The first was T.F. Hunt's *Architettura Campestre: Displayed in Lodges, Gardeners' Houses, and other Buildings . . . in the Modern or Italian Style . . .* (1827). Linkage of the words "Modern" and "Italian" is noteworthy. The other was G.L. Meason's *On the Landscape Architecture of the Great Painters of Italy* (1828), illustrated with facsimiles of canvases by Raphael, Titian, Giotto, Poussin, Veronese, Claude, Giorgione, and others. The preponderance show imaginary buildings with round towers, turrets, pediments, crenellations, and other such features; most of the buildings reside in rugged scenery, it being Meason's opinion that a building appears "most agreeable when backed by wood or rising ground."[6] The important point this opus brought out is that the Italianate house belongs to the category of picturesque and romantic architecture.

From Paris, in 1804 and 1846-47, came the two-volume portfolio of *L'Architecture considérée sous le rapport do l'art, des moeurs et de la législation*, by Claude-Nicolas Ledoux, the French designer (1736-1806) whose use of simplified architectural forms was mentioned in connection with White Cottage. The Dewees residence (mid-1820s) in Lexington had, and Pleasant Lawn in Woodford County (1829) retains, some features that are not Roman—and therefore not properly Federal—but virtually Italianate. Included are the geometric masses, severe arches, unrelieved Palladian windows, and stuccoed walls with quoins in the case of the Lexington house. All the wood fittings—doors, trim, mantels, and staircases—were in the Federal style, however, and determined the classification of them here.

The Latrobe design for the John Pope House (1811) was somewhat Italianate, especially the treatment of its entrance porch. A link between certain aspects of Federal and Italianate is not to be denied; rather, it may be confirmed by pointing out that the later style revived features from the early period, such as round arches, belt courses, quoins, and polygonal rooms, though the last figured in the Gothic Revival too.

American publications spread the Italianate as they had other nineteenth-century styles. Apparently the first illustrating the mode was of "a small villa suitable for the summer residence of a genteel family," in John Haviland's three-volume *The Builder's Assistant* of 1818-21, cited earlier as the first issued in the United States to present the Greek orders. Plate 60, in volume 2, shows the front elevation of a symmetrical, two-story composition of three parts, with a small cubic office attached to each end. Projecting beam ends support the overhanging eaves, and the gabled center pavilion has an indented portico of two stories. The design had been actualized in the John Cridland House in the outskirts of Philadelphia. A similar scheme appeared in volume 3 (pls. 109-110), which, decked out in Greek garb, was somewhat plagiarized by Minard Lafever in 1829 in *The Young Builder's General Instructor* (pl. 44). Plans for three villas appeared in A.J. Downing's *Cottage Residences* of 1842, as designs 6, 8, 9. But it was Downing's magnum opus, *The Architecture of Country Houses* (1850), which popularized the term *villa*, and as expected, included several Italianate specimens. They range from a small "Suburban Cottage" (design 7) to a large "Southern Villa" (design 32), the latter identified as in the Romanesque style, but an Italianate house nevertheless. Design 27 is of Edward King's

villa in Newport, Rhode Island, built by Richard Upjohn in 1845. William H. Ranlett's *The Architect* (New York, 1847-49) and Charles Wyllys Elliott's *Cottage and Cottage Life* (Cincinnati, 1848) also contributed a few examples, and Samuel Sloan's *The Model Architect* (Philadelphia, 1852) quite a few more. Sloan designed many houses, among them the well-known octagonal oriental villa Longwood (1861) for Dr. Haller Nutt at Natchez, Mississippi.

It will be seen from this list that the Italianate predated the Renaissance Revival style in the United States, Haviland's villa for John Cridland having preceded the Atheneum also in Philadelphia by a quarter of a century. The Cridland House was symmetrical; and by way of completing the story it should be noted that the first picturesque, or asymmetrical, villa in America was conceived by the architect of the Atheneum, John Notman. This was the residence of Bishop George Doane at Burlington, New Jersey, built in 1837.[7] By having designed in both phases of the style, Notman accrued a double distinction; and inasmuch as he resided and worked in the same city as Haviland, Philadelphia may be said to have been the hotbed of Italianate architecture (as also of Greek and Gothic Revival) in America.

The foremost exponent of the Italianate in Central Kentucky was Maj. Thomas Lewinski (ca. 1800-82), architect of Christ Church in Lexington (chap. 11), designer of the portico added to the Gibson mansion, and creator of Mansfield, near Lexington. Born in London of a Polish father and an English mother, Lewinski was educated for the Catholic priesthood. Finding army life more to his liking, he joined the British regiments and fought in Spain. He continued his soldiering in South America, where he lost one eye. Lewinski first appeared in Kentucky as an instructor at the University of Louisville. He also trained the Kosciusko Cadets, gave French lessons at O.L. Leonard's seminary, and married Hannah Carey. He came to Lexington in 1843 and was associated with Cassius Marcellus Clay, whose views as publisher of the antislavery paper *The True American* Lewinski defended. He taught French (mostly to young ladies) and drilled the Lexington Rifles. His first wife died in 1845, and the following year he married Mary Watkins, a niece of Henry Clay and sister of Thomas Watkins, who had married a daughter of John McMurtry. At this time Lewinski was actively practicing architecture. His professional diary has been preserved covering the period from 24 March 1845 through 5 July 1847. He continued to practice until he became secretary to the Lexington Gas Company in the mid-1850s, and after that he occasionally engaged in remodeling. He functioned mainly as an architectural designer, making drawings and specifications for buildings and checking the work of his builders; but he assumed the role of construction engineer on the Henry Clay Monument, built in the Lexington Cemetery during the late 1850s. John McMurtry was the builder of the church on Market Street in Lexington designed by Lewinski, and as we shall see, they worked together on Cassius Clay's White Hall. Lewinski assembled an architectural library, including Samuel Sloan's *The Model Architect*, from which his liking for the Italianate style may have been derived.[8]

The principal advocate in Kentucky of the Italianate, with leanings toward the Renaissance Revival, was Henry Whitestone (1819-93). Born in Innis, Ireland, of English descent, he practiced architecture there, designing the County Clare Courthouse (ca. 1840-50), a Greek Revival building with a hexastyle Ionic portico. He came to Kentucky with Isaiah Rogers, with whom he worked on the old Capital Hotel in Frankfort in 1853. Afterward, Rogers opened an office in Cincinnati, and Whitestone an associated office in Louisville. It is thought that they worked together building the Burnet House (1850) in Cincinnati, and on remodeling the old Galt House in Louisville in 1853. Whitestone built the second Galt House a block east of the first in 1869. In 1853 Rogers and Whitestone constructed the enlarged Louisville Hotel—a five-storied, fifteen-bayed building. Whitestone was responsible for many fine residences in and around Louisville, the architect's favorite being the Silas Miller House (1872) on the south side of Broadway between Second and Third streets, no longer in existence.[9]

Another advocate of the Renaissance Revival style was Francis Costigan (ca. 1810-65). He was born in Washington, D.C., and first worked as a carpenter in Baltimore, moving westward and settling permanently in Indiana about 1836. He was in Madison until 1851 and spent the last fourteen years of his life in Indianapolis. In Madison, Costigan completed Saint Michael's Catholic Church, begun before his arrival, the first Gothic Revival building in the state; and he designed and built the Madison Hotel, as well as the James F.D. Lanier Mansion and the Capt. Charles Shrewsbury House, during the 1840s. At the Indiana capital in the 1850s, Costigan supervised the construction of the Institute for the Blind, the Hospi-

tal for the Deaf and Dumb, and the Hospital for the Insane. He designed and built the Odd Fellows' Building and several residences there, and to this period belongs his Kentucky School for the Blind in Louisville.[10]

As in the two preceding chapters, public buildings will be taken up before residences. During this period from the mid-1840s to the mid-1860s, buildings in both categories of the Italianate were fairly simple at the beginning and became progressively more complex and elaborate.

The United States Marine Hospital. The first building discussed here in the Italianate style is Italianate by default, as its prototype was Greek Revival, and various conditions altered its characteristics. Also, it introduces into this study a building that was not designed for Kentucky or built by a Kentuckian. It derived from a national model conceived for the treasury department in Washington. Its out-of-state origin provided a precedent for later buildings in the commonwealth and forecast a practice that would become common in modern times. In erecting marine hospitals the early federal government followed the lead of colonial legislators. The new element was building them not only on the east coast but also on inland waterways. The Louisville Marine Hospital proposed in 1817 was a local undertaking, although the building was completed by state financial assistance from 1822 to 1824. The United States Marine Hospital begun at Portland in 1845 was sponsored by and built on land purchased by the United States Treasury Department.

Prototypes for marine hospitals were designed by Robert Mills, who was appointed federal architect in 1836. Mills designed two types, a smaller one to accommodate fifty patients, and a larger for one hundred. They were Greek Revival in style. But in 1845 they were modified for economic reasons by Secretary of the Treasury R.J. Walker. The one in Kentucky was further simplified by Stephen Harriman Long, who was "on loan from the Corps of Topographical Engineers to the Treasury Department with orders to build a marine hospital at Louisville, Kentucky." The Portland building was simplified even more by Long's assistant, Charles A. Fuller, and by their Cincinnati associate architect, Joseph O. Sawyer. As late as 1849 Sawyer changed Mills' classic columns to Italianate-style square piers.[11]

The United States Marine Hospital is of the one-hundred-bed variety. It has three stories, with advanced square pavilions at the corners (fig. 12.2).

Fig. 12.2 The United States Marine Hospital (1845-52), Portland. From *Louisville Illustrated* (Chicago, 1889), part 12, n.p.

Recessed open galleries are on the longer north and south sides, and an octagonal cupola on the low-pitched roof admits light to the center of the building. A wide transverse hall is flanked by four wards, each subdivided by sliding doors into two units. The corner pavilions contain smaller wards, service rooms, and staircases. Side passages lead to the wings. The hospital was completed and occupied in 1852. Stephen Harriman Long built similar buildings at Paducah, Natchez, and Napoleon, Arkansas, but not one of them has survived. The Portland building has become part of the Louisville Memorial Hospital for the aged and infirm.

THE UNITED STATES POST OFFICE AND CUSTOM HOUSE. Two lots, with a frontage of 150 feet on the west side of Third Street and 135 feet on the south side of Green (Liberty), were purchased in 1851 for the new U.S. post office and customhouse at Louisville. Elias E. Williams (1794-1880) was named architect, and contracts were let to Michael Gillion for stone, Henry Vanseggern for wood, and Henry J. Mead for iron.[12] The design would have been quite an innovation in Louisville had the building been completed in 1851; but with problems of funding, scaling down the plans, acquisition of stone, and labor disputes, work dragged, and it was not ready for occupancy until August of 1858. By that time the palazzo form had become somewhat commonplace. Construction cost $246,641. The customhouse had two similar facades, with a rusticated first story and smooth walls above, and it was crowned by a bracketed cornice and parapet, all of limestone from

Bedford, Indiana (fig. 12.3). Doorways at street level and windows above were arched, the windows elaborated with drip molds and most of them composed of two lights with a circular motif in the tympanum. Each facade was divided into five pavilions, the second and fourth recessed, the broader front on Third Street having a three-bayed center mass. Compared to contemporary custom houses elsewhere by Ammi B. Young, Mills's successor, Williams's building looks rather blocky, its Italianate forms being not thoroughly digested, which might explain why the designer described the style as "Anglo-Norman."[13] It provided space for the surveyor of customs, the postmaster, officers of the U.S. Circuit and District

Fig. 12.3 The United States Post Office and Custom House (1851-58), Louisville. From *Williamson's Annual Directory of the City of Louisville . . .* (Louisville, 1865), facing p. 326.

courts, and the inspector of steamboats. The post office was on the ground floor. The courts did not move into the building until 1860. Less than a quarter of a century later all the tenants moved to the new post office and customhouse at the northeast corner of Fourth and Chestnut streets. The old building was changed principally to house the *Courier-Journal* and the *Louisville Times.* Many of the lower arches were enlarged to rectangular openings, and the second story was divided into two levels. Practically nothing of the original interior is apparent, except for the piers of the first story, where the post office was located. At present it is an office complex called the Morrissey Building.

THE MASONIC TEMPLE. A second major undertaking in Louisville by Elias E. Williams was the Masonic Temple on the southwest corner of Fourth and Jefferson streets. The building had three stories and had seven bays on the north and south ends and nineteen on the long front. The street level was devoted to commercial enterprises, and the accommodations above climaxed with the Grand Concert Hall. Built between 1851 and 1857, it was an early example of the Renaissance Revival style and displayed a certain immaturity. It somewhat resembled John B. Snook's Odd Fellows' Hall, built of brownstone on Centre Street in New York City during the late 1840s.[14] The first story of Williams's edifice consisted of rusticated piers modulating shop entrances and display windows and supporting an entablature, above which rose colossal pilasters of modified Corinthian style. They were spaced at each bay across the north and south flanks, and they organized the Fourth Street facade into a hexastyle center pavilion and tetrastyle terminal pavilions, with plain connectors between them (fig. 12.4). A full entablature with bracketed cornice and parapet above crowned the pile. Squeezed in the narrow spaces between columns were tall rectangular windows with hood molds on consoles, and hooded round-headed windows above. A horizontal molding at third-floor level cut awkwardly across the connectors and threaded between the pilasters on the north and east fronts. In its place on the south end were elliptical windows, which may have been utilitarian but were no asset to the design. Williams was no better as a structural engineer than as an architectural composer. His claim against the Masonic fraternity for unpaid fees was answered by a counterclaim for $4,655 to cover expenses for erecting oak trusses in the Grand Con-

Fig. 12.4 The Masonic Temple (1851-57), Louisville. Photo, late 1800s, from the R.G. Potter Collection, Photographic Archives, courtesy of the University of Louisville.

cert Hall to sustain its ten girders, which were said to have settled from 5 to 9 inches and to be in a precarious condition.[15] The Masonic Temple was torn down in 1903.

THE KENTUCKY ASYLUM FOR THE DEAF. The full name of this institution (prior to 1882) was the Kentucky Asylum for the Tuition of the Deaf and Dumb. Its four-story Italianate brick building, designed by Thomas Lewinski and built by John McMurtry during 1855-57, is in the south end of Danville.[16] The compact mass has a basement treatment to the first story, and the three upper stories are unified by vertical shafts joined at the top by half-round arches. Coupled brackets support exceedingly deep eaves on the low-pitched roof, which is crowned by an octagonal belvedere (fig. 12.5). The facade is divided into three pavilions, each three-bayed, the center one stepped forward and surmounted by a wide, almost flat gable. Preceding this section is a heavy one-story piered portico, identical at the front and back of the building except for the additional advanced bay at the main entrance with channeled Doric columns in antis. In its fore structure and arched wall treatment the design recalls Lewinski's James B. Clay Villa, built a decade earlier in Lexington (fig. 12.11). The doorway of the Kentucky Asylum for the Deaf is framed

Fig. 12.5 The Kentucky Asylum for the Deaf (1855-57), Danville. Photo, 1988.

with transom and sidelights and opens into one arm of a cruciform hall. The square crossing is divided by wide arches, and an octagonal well, encircled by a banister railing in each of the upper floors, admits daylight from the cupola. Major staircases are in the west and north halls, and service stairs are in a narrow space off the south hall.

John McMurtry grossly underbid a number of projects in the mid-1850s, notably the asylum in Danville. In the summer of 1855 he attempted to check the impending catastrophe by selling property in Lexington, amounting to a dozen houses (including his former residence on North Broadway) and fifteen lots. Before the year was out, he had lost or mortgaged his carpenter shop and plank yard in Lexington and several farms in Fayette County, the principal one being The Elms, where he was living. In June of 1856 he was declared insolvent.[17] To his credit, he managed to complete the Danville asylum the following year.

THE KENTUCKY SCHOOL FOR THE BLIND. A building that was mostly Greek Revival in style but had a few Renaissance Revival features, warranting its inclusion here, was the Kentucky School for the Blind on Frankfort Avenue in the Clifton section of Louisville. It was designed and built in 1855 by Francis Costigan, whose Institute for the Blind at Indianapolis was reflected in the Kentucky building, notably in the three-pavilion disposition of forms. Renaissance elements included rustication, consoles on doorway and main-story window hoods in front, modillions on the cornice of the entablature, arches under the main stairs and arched windows in back, a large dome on an octagonal drum capping the main block, and smaller domes on the three octastyle temple superstructures.

Above the high basement of rusticated stonework in front were four stories of stuccoed brickwork in

Fig. 12.6 The Kentucky School for the Blind (1855), Louisville. Photo, 1934, courtesy of the Library of Congress.

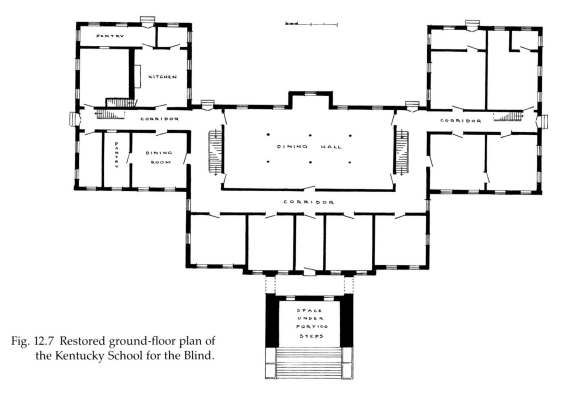

Fig. 12.7 Restored ground-floor plan of
the Kentucky School for the Blind.

the main part and three in the wings. A two-story tetrastyle Ionic portico was centered on the facade, with a wide stairway between stepped antepodia (fig. 12.6). Carved in the face of the two upper setbacks were dogwood blossoms, reminiscent of frieze and mantel motifs at the Morton House in Lexington. The great dome atop the main pavilion, as well as the two wings, had identical small circular octastyle temples serving as crowning devices. Their columns had Corinthian-type capitals with gadrooning at the top, as on the Lafever design in plate 11 of *The Beauties of Modern Architecture* (1835). The height of the windows in each tier diminished slightly as they ascended above the basement. The entablature displayed dentils, as well as modillions, and two sets of bead-and-reel moldings between.

A crosswise corridor cut through each of the three parts of the building on all floors, with the main staircase in connecting halls at right angles, and lesser stairs to the lower levels in the wing corridors. Classrooms and reception rooms were on the ground and main floors, with dormitories and bedrooms above. A 30-by-65-foot dining hall filled the space between the stair halls at the back at grade level, and a private dining room and kitchen occupied the west wing (fig. 12.7). An assembly room had the central position on the principal floor. A gymnasium with arched windows took up the area over the dining hall in the second and third stories.

The building later acquired two additions, four-storied pavilions behind at the outer corners of the wings. They matched the old structure in details, but the walls were left exposed brick. The entire building was razed in 1967.[18]

THE LOUISVILLE WATER COMPANY PUMPHOUSE COMPLEX. The precedent for masking starkly utilitarian buildings with elegant classic veneer was set in this country by Benjamin Henry Latrobe in the Philadelphia waterworks, particularly in the Centre Square Pumping Station (1800). It was a square stone building with a recessed portico, above which rose a tall, circular drum providing clerestory lighting. Smoke from the steam-powered machinery was emitted through the apex of the crowning dome as through the oculus of the Temple of Vesta, Roman goddess of the hearth.[19] When the Louisville Water Company was established over a half century later, the classic was still the proper clothing for such a structure. Like the Kentucky School for the Blind, the water company group was predominantly Greek Revival in style, but Renaissance in that there were arches, pedimented hoods over doors and windows, pedimented pilastered pavilions, consoles in the entablature, imposts over columns, pedestals, and balustrade. Begun in 1858 and finished after 1860, at River Road and Zorn Avenue on the outskirts of Louisville, the entire system was designed by Theodore R. Scowden (1815-81), "civil and mechanical

Fig. 12.8 Pumphouse and standpipe of the Louisville Water Company (1856-60), near Louisville. Photo, 1969.

capitals are of terra cotta. Small pedimented blocks accentuate wings at either side. Originally a tall smokestack soared upward beyond each end pavilion, and coal houses were outside and somewhat in advance of them, making a more attractive composition than at present, the vertical forms of the smokestack relieving the strong focus of the standpipe.[21] Cast-iron figures of gods, goddesses, and other subjects are perched atop the balustrade pedestals of the peristyle around the colossal column, which had to be rebuilt after the 1890 tornado.

A larger pumphouse was subsequently built nearby. The old plant was named a National Historic Landmark in 1971 and was renovated in 1978-80 for the Water Tower Art Association.[22]

THE FALLS' CITY TERRA-COTTA WORKS. Patrick Bannon, a native of County Down, Ireland, came to Louisville in the early 1850s and began a plastering business. In 1858 he started manufacturing ornamental terra cotta for "the exterior and interior decoration of Buildings, embellishment of Gardens, &c." His establishment, the Falls' City Terra-cotta Works, located on Fifth Street opposite the Catholic Cathe-

engineer and architect" for the Louisville Water Company; Scowden was responsible for such waterworks in Cleveland and Cincinnati.

The Louisville complex consisted of "an engine and boiler room, a stand-pipe tower, two offices and two coal houses. The engine and boiler room is a structure one hundred and fifty-eight feet in length, fifty-five feet in breadth and twenty-one in height. . . . [The tower] attains an elevation of one hundred and sixty-nine feet above its base, and is . . . surrounded by a cupola lookout."[20] The symmetrical group is dominated by the iron-plated water tower, like a commemorative Doric column, encircled by a peristyle of the Corinthian order at the base and a balustrade atop the entablature (fig. 12.8). A belvedere set on the abacus and the tower's bulbous dome give it the appearance of a minaret. The placing of the standpipe is unfortunate in being set directly in front of the main pavilion, which is a two-story temple-type building having a four-columned Corinthian portico with steps across the front. Windowsills and column and pilaster bases are of cast iron, and the

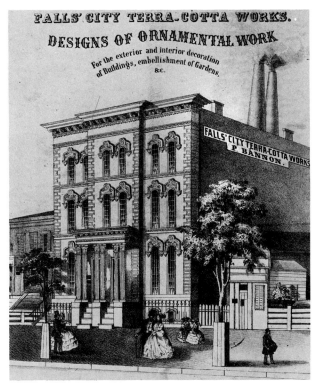

Fig. 12.9 The Falls City Terra-Cotta Works (1858), Louisville. Lithograph, ca. 1859, by Hart and Mapother, Louisville, courtesy of the Library of Congress.

dral, resembled a duplex townhouse in the eclectic Renaissance manner (fig. 12.9). It had three full stories and a basement. The facade was divided into three two-bayed pavilions, the centermost stepped forward and the corners enriched with quoins. The levels were separated by belt courses continuous with windowsills, and the building was crowned by a deep overhanging cornice supported on intricately detailed consoles. Windows were capped by heavy and complex hood molds, and the twin entrances were sheltered by a portico featuring three coupled piers of the Corinthian order set on antepodia between which steps ascended. A number of articulated moldings were included in the portico entablature, its cornice on consoles a smaller version of that at the top of the facade. Probably all these elements were of terra cotta. One can only speculate as to how much Bannon products were incorporated in buildings being constructed in Kentucky at mid-century, and how much they were used to modernize and spoil old ones, as on the Gibson, Peck, and Butler houses in Lexington. Evidently, however, the decorative architectural output did not prove as lucrative as more utilitarian items. In 1868 Bannon erected a plant at 431 West Jefferson Street and began manufacturing a new product, which was memorialized in the subsequent title of his concern, the Louisville Sewer Pipe works.[23]

THE CLAY VILLA. During the time Thomas Lewinski was involved with Mansfield for Thomas Hart Clay, he was working on the Clay Villa for another of Henry Clay's sons, James B. Clay, also in Lexington. The Clay Villa fronted on East Main Street but now is accessible from Forest Avenue. The first entry about it in Lewinski's diary is dated 11 June 1845, and his statement that he "surveyed Building and took dimensions for steps to Portico," indicates the house was already under construction. Subsequent remarks noted his inspecting progress and making additional drawings for such details as door, mantels, gates, lamps, icehouse, "Cabinet d'aissance," and furniture. Lewinski referred to it simply as a villa; A.J. Davis would have classified its style as Tuscan.

The two-story residence was symmetrical and heavy looking, its walls enriched by applied segmental arches on wide engaged piers with sunken panels; the porch that enclosed the lower portion was composed of brick corner pavilions connected by galleries having thick coupled square wooden posts supporting a deep entablature (fig. 12.10). Some of its

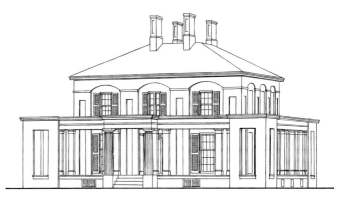

Fig. 12.10 Restored sketch of the James B. Clay Villa (1845-46), Lexington.

features were to be reflected on the Kentucky Asylum for the Deaf in Danville. The form of the Clay Villa may be compared to that of Latrobe's Sedgeley (1799) near Philadelphia (fig. 11.1). Similarities include the hipped roof with chimneys rising above interior walls, and flankers connected by colonnades; but the Kentucky design is more ponderous, with the porch continuing across the front, and maintaining a single cornice level. The Clay Villa also should be compared to Hayfield, the house at the end of Tyler Lane in Louisville, built for Col. George Hancock about the time Lewinski arrived there. The main block is squarish and has four chimneys rising from a truncated hip roof. Pilasters support a deep entablature, and a heavy piered gallery spans the facade, with steps between antepodia. The Lexington house seems a further development of the Hayfield design. As its gallery encircled the building, its windows had to be of maximum size (fig. 12.11). The unusual half-panes at the sides, the pattern of octagonal and rectangular glass in the doorway, and the Doric columns flanking the front steps came from plate 77 in Edward Shaw's *Civil Architecture* (1836), a copy of which Lewinski owned (fig. 12.12).

The floor plan relates to that of Mansfield, consisting of four equisized and similarly arranged rooms, though one of them is relieved by niches in three corners (fig. 12.13). The hall is not divided and the stairs turn around an open well. The services were housed at the back, in what the Hart and Mapother map of the mid-1850s shows to be a shallow projecting form between the rear flankers, perhaps a sort of lean-to. Marble mantels in the double parlors have round arched fireplaces, like those at Ingelside, and the one in the library is pilastered. The chamber level had the same arrangement except for two dressing

Fig. 12.11 The Clay Villa, detail of entrance before removal of porch. Photo, 1940.

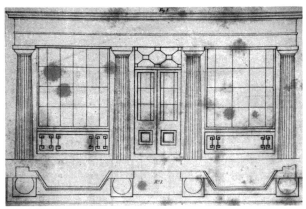

Fig. 12.12 Design for shop front. From Edward Shaw, *Civil Architecture* (Boston, 1836), pl. 77, fig. 1.

Fig. 12.13 First-floor plan of the Clay Villa.

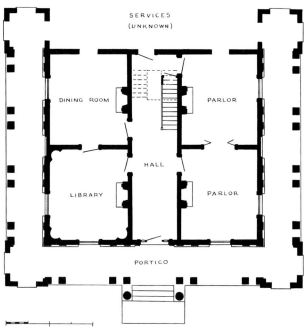

rooms at the front of the hall. The lowness of the windows in the second story reduces their efficiency in providing light and ventilation. The center bay of each flank at both levels originally contained a blind window.

Bracketed gables and wide eaves were added after the Civil War, and the staircase was continued to the garret. The partition between parlors was removed, and folding doors were installed in the hall wall. About 1945 the porch was razed and the building was converted into apartments; since then it has served various uses.[24]

OCTAGON HOUSES. The mid-nineteenth-century cult of octagonalism in the United States was promulgated by Orson Squire Fowler, lecturer, author, publisher, phrenologist, and advocate of hydropathy, vegetarianism, and abstinence from alcohol and tobacco, who himself lived in an eight-sided residence. Through his book *The Octagon Mode*, first published in 1848, Fowler set forth the rationale for this form of dwelling. It afforded the utmost inside volume for external covering. It required no stylistic trim. With the stairway in the center, accessible to all rooms, no space was wasted in passages. Its many-sidedness offered more exposures to light and ventilation, and its encircling porches provided more sheltered places for exercising and relaxing. Fowler advocated central heating, a cupola to light the core of the house, and (after his 1853 copyright) poured concrete for construction of walls with obtuse angles. These recommendations were followed in his own home at Fishkill, New York, but they were not, of course, in every octagonal house.

Kentucky's principal example took little advantage of being octagonal, and its simplicity in architectural dress justifies its inclusion under Italianism.[25] The Andrew Jackson Caldwell House was built probably in the early 1850s six miles north of Franklin on the Bowling Green Pike in Warren County.[26] Great care was lavished on the construction of the Flemish-bond brick walls, even including the basement from grade up, all sides being equal in width and each having a centered window or doorway (fig. 12.14). A cupola once surmounted the roof. The plan has little to do with what Orson Squire Fowler advised, fireplaces with prominent chimney breasts substituting for central heating, and a vestibule in front and stair hall at the back in place of a staircase in the middle (fig. 12.15). The arrangement is as though meant for a square or rectangular house that happened to have its four corners cut back to form an eight-sided building. The windows occur at odd places in the rooms.

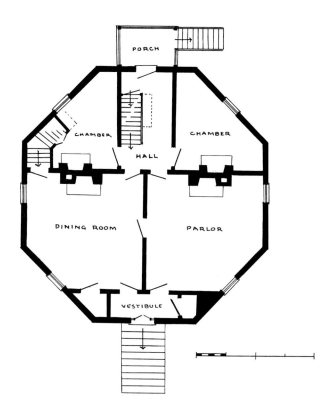

Fig. 12.15 First-floor plan of the Caldwell House.

It seems that the house was not finished by the builder. A grandson sold the property to Dr. Miles Williams, of Nashville, Tennessee, in 1916, and about a dozen years later he set about to complete and remodel the house.[27] The doorway and the treatment of the windows above it date from this era.

It should be noted that a one-story frame octagon cottage was built about 1850 in Barren County; and in adjacent Allen County, the brick courthouse of 1819 was in the same configuration.

CANE RUN. One of the most attractive medium-sized, irregular Italianate villas in America was Cane Run, named for the property's watercourse, three miles north of Lexington on the Newtown Pike. It was built in 1853-54 for Alexander H. Brand by George Batcheller after a design by Thomas Lewinski. The tight plan and bilateral symmetry of Lewinski's houses of the 1840s have given way to a variegated arrangement of rooms and interesting informal massing in Cane Run. Pavilions of diverse widths, covered by low-pitched roofs with deep overhanging eaves supported on graceful brackets, a pedimented tower, projecting bays, an arcaded porch, and arched windows over tall, wide windows (like those of the Clay Villa) were combined in harmo-

Fig. 12.14 Andrew Jackson Caldwell House (1850s), Franklin-Bowling Green Pike. Photo, 1977, by Hughes Photographers, Bowling Green. Courtesy of the Hobson House Association, Bowling Green.

Fig. 12.16 Cane Run (1853-54), Fayette County. Photo, 1941.

Fig. 12.17 Floor plans of Cane Run.

nious composition as focus to an idyllic setting (fig. 12.16). The pilaster-panel effect, used with regularity on the Clay Villa, occurred spasmodically here, and details were more restrained. The plan was made up of rooms of square, rectangular, and octagonal shape, with axes running in various directions, and arranged in suites (fig. 12.17). Especially noteworthy was the way the narrow transverse hall was cut by a visual axis in front of the arch separating the staircase part. The doors on either side were aligned with the center line of the drawing room and its bay window at one end, and an off-center window in the parlor at the other. Wide sliding doors joined the parlor and dining room. The drawing room had twin marble mantels matching the one in the corresponding room at Ingelside. Its ceiling was higher than in other rooms, and featured an octagonal recess. The eight-sided anteroom at the base of the tower had niches in alternate sides, as in the corners of the library of Clay Villa. From the second floor a staircase wound up inside the square tower to a lookout. Several brick dependencies of chaste design stood a short distance behind the villa.

After the death of Alex Brand, Jr. in 1881, the property was sold to Joseph C. Anderson, who rechristened it Glengarry. The house burned down in 1970.[28]

THE PROPOSED PETER VILLA. The University of Kentucky library is the repository of an interesting set of wash drawings by Thomas Lewinski, the design of a villa for Dr. Robert Peter that was not built. There are eight sheets, drawn to a scale of ⅒ inch to the foot, including three floor plans, a transverse cross section, and four elevations (fig. 12.18). In the English manner, the windows are shown without sashs, those open are indicated by a tone, the blind ones without. The architectural style bears a strong affinity to that of Cane Run, with arcaded porch, arched windows above, brackets under the horizontal eaves but not under the raking eaves (as at Cane Run) and a panel effect on the wall at the side. That the dominant pavilion is symmetrical, and a two-storied mass expands from one side only, gives a sense not of informal balance but of unfinish. The building was to be placed on a site that sloped down at the back, so the kitchen, washhouse, and bath in the basement would be at ground level. On the main floor, one would enter a crosswise "Corridor" with transverse stair hall behind at one end. The arrangement is reminiscent of what Lewinski had achieved in the Gibson House many years earlier through

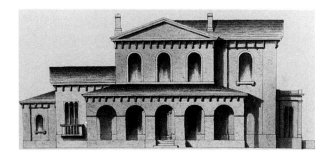

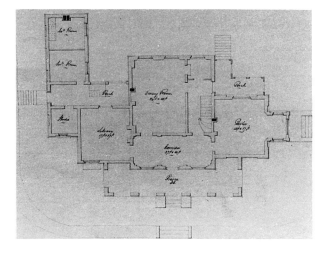

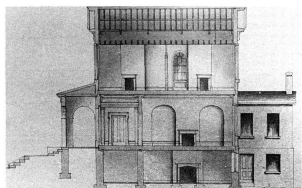

Fig. 12.18 Elevation, plan, and section of a proposed villa for Dr. Robert Peter. Drawings by Thomas Lewinski, scaled ⅒ inch to the foot. In Special Collections, courtesy of the University of Kentucky Libraries.

remodeling. Servants' rooms are in a side wing off an open porch with a stairway to the lower level. There are blind windows on the outer side. The Peter Villa design does not measure up to that of Cane Run, which points up the dire loss occasioned by the destruction of the latter.

THE SECOND ASHLAND. After the death of Henry Clay in 1852, his home was purchased from the estate by his son, James B. Clay. For some years the walls of

Fig. 12.19 The second
Ashland (1856), Lexington.
Photo, 1944.

the Lexington house had been settling, a process
thought to have been initiated by the series of earthquakes of 1811-12. The structure finally had to be
rebuilt, and to do the job, Clay chose Thomas
Lewinski, who had constructed a plain gardener's
cottage at Ashland in 1846.[29] The new Ashland was
resurrected on its own site, following the same plan,
probably using parts of the old foundations, as well

as bricks and ash wood salvaged from the old structure. The residence was completed in 1856. Although
Ashland's original form, its colonnetted doorway
with half-round fanlight, and Palladian window
above with banister railing around the projecting
entrance bay were repeated, the style of the building
is mid-nineteenth century (fig. 12.19; *compare* fig.
7.10). Quoins were added, cornices were made heav-

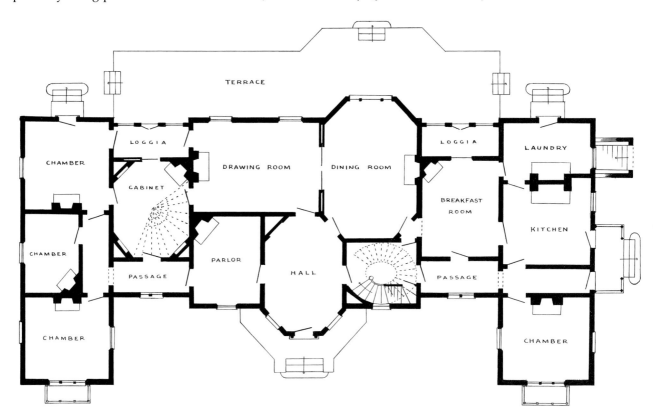

Fig. 12.20 Restored first-floor plan of the second Ashland.

ier, chimneys elaborated, window headings arched, cast-iron hoods were applied on the principal block, sashes were given large panes of glass, a platform was placed in front of the entrance bay and a broad terrace at the back, and cast-iron balconies were affixed to the front windows of the end pavilions. An iron porch was set before the service passage and kitchen doors at the south end of the house. Alongside, leading to the basement, was a brick pent with a curved roof. Downspout bases all around were of cast-iron dolphins.

The plan consists of rooms of interesting shapes, including three octagons and a domed elliptical stair hall (fig. 12.20). Interiors were in the taste of the period of the rebuilding, with wide wood moldings around doors and windows, arched marble mantels, and elaborate plaster centerpieces and cornices. One of the few subsequent alterations was replacement during the 1880s of the elliptical staircase by a massive oak structure of straight flights. The domed ceiling of the hall was mostly obliterated in the change. Ashland was opened as a museum in 1950 under the auspices of the Henry Clay Memorial Foundation.[30]

THE WOOLLEY HOUSE. The cottage of John Norton, built about 1826 on Hill (now East High) Street near Limestone in Lexington, was acquired by Judge George Woolley and enlarged and renovated into a bracketed house about 1859.[31] Thomas Lewinski may have been responsible for the work, having been engaged on Judge Woolley's former home, according to entries in the architect's diary during 1846. The cottage consisted of a squarish main block, with two small flankers projecting at the front, and a semi-detached one-and-a-half-story service wing at the back, connected by an open gallery. The principal part was increased from one to three stories, and the flankers were incorporated in a long, low porch across the front (fig. 12.21). Square chamfered posts reflected the old ones on the rear gallery, and brackets and cast-iron railings, crestings, hood molds over windows, and grilles in the garret openings brought the design up to date. A one-story wing of three rooms, two of which were polygonal, extended back from the east flanker. The rear porch continued over to the new wing. The original rooms remained unchanged in function with two exceptions. A new staircase was installed in the small square back hall, which entailed permanently closing one of the doors to the front hall, against which the first flight of steps ascended, and the adjoining room, formerly a chamber, was opened to the big drawing room by means of double doors (fig. 12.22). The addition of the second and third stories, which included about ten rooms, greatly increased the size of the house. An especially pretty feature in the modernized interior was the cast-iron mantel in the east flanker, which had Geor-

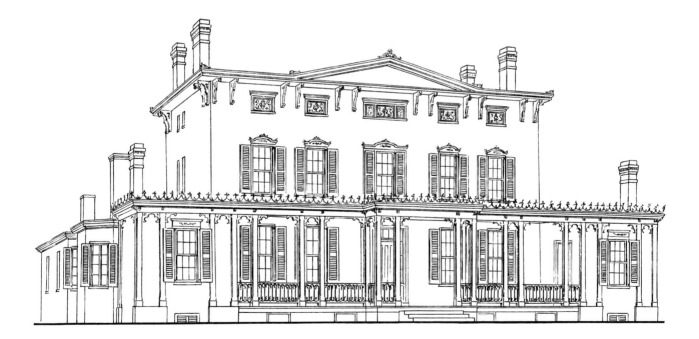

Fig. 12.21 Restored sketch of the George Woolley House (1859), Lexington.

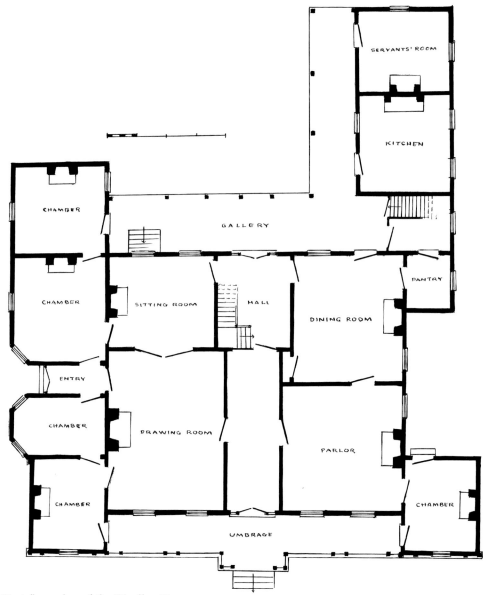

Fig. 12.22 First-floor plan of the Woolley House.

gian console-type outlines and parrots among tropical vegetation painted under glass in the spandrels of the fireplace arch. The house was razed in 1946.

THE FORD MANSION. James Coleman Ford, a native of Bourbon County, Kentucky, and owner of plantations in Louisiana, Mississippi, and Arkansas, bought a 150-by-250-foot lot on the southwest corner of Prather (now Broadway) and Second streets in Louisville, and he commissioned Henry Whitestone to design his house.[32] Mrs. Ford wanted it to be in the Italian villa style, and Ford himself insisted on central heating. Whitestone drew several versions, and the selected design was built in 1858-59. The two-story facade of dressed stone from Bedford, Indiana,

had a rusticated treatment below and plain walls framed by quoins and a full entablature above. Lower windows were rectangular and the upper arched, and the entrance was enhanced by a tetrastyle Ionic portico preceded by wide steps and surmounted by a balustrade. Another balustrade crowned the truncated hipped roof (fig. 12.23). The portico columns are said to have been made in Italy. Curved side pavilions maintained the perfect balance seen from the street; the convex glass in their windows was imported from France.[33]

The first floor of the main part of the Ford Mansion was similar to Elmwood Hall in plan. One entered a vestibule with free-standing columns in the corners,

Fig. 12.23 The James Coleman Ford Mansion (1858-59), Louisville. Photo, ca. early 1900s, courtesy of the Filson Club.

and there were square rooms on either side. The principal suite was behind, but instead of being adjoined and with recessed porticoes outside, here the twin rooms were separated by a hall and extended into curved projections (fig. 12.24). A fine rosewood staircase occupied the center division at the back, and a breakfast parlor was to the west. A screen of Corinthian columns separated the drawing room from the anteroom in the northeast corner, and French windows on either side of the drawing-room fireplace opened to the loggia, here called a conservatory, where arches sprang from column capitals decorated with tobacco leaves and flowers, similar to the order devised by Latrobe for the Senate rotunda of the nation's capitol. The hall floor was of blue-and-white tile; other floors were oak parquetry. Carved marble mantels and a goodly amount of plaster work contributed to the richness of the interior. At the southwest corner an attached second structure, more than half as large as the first, contained the services; in addition to the kitchen and laundry rooms and two stair halls were a porch and a room off the side entrance used as an office or dressing room.[34] At the back of the lot a two-story stable, upward of seventy-three feet long, had an icehouse attached at one end. A "fowl house" stood nearby.

The Civil War disabled southern plantation owners like Ford, and with the mansion heavily mortgaged soon after its completion, the owners lived in less style than they had anticipated. They died in the early 1880s, and the house was sold to Dr. Norvin Green, president of the Western Union Tele-

graph Company, in 1883. After 1914 it was occupied by the YWCA for almost a half-century, and in 1964 it was razed.

LYNDHURST. In 1860 William R. Fleming purchased an eleven-acre tract adjoining Rose Street, between High and Maxwell, where he proposed building the finest villa in Lexington.[35] The site was between the John Pope House on the east and the Higgins Mansion on the west. John McMurtry was engaged as architect, and the derivation of his design was "An Ornamental Villa" in *The Model Architect*, published in 1852 by Samuel Sloan of Philadelphia, whence Fleming came. The building Sloan depicted had exceedingly deep eaves on numerous brackets,

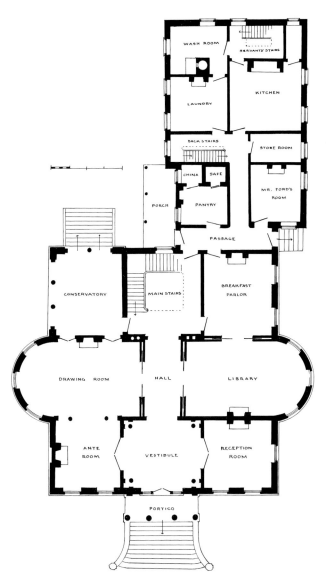

Fig. 12.24 First-floor plan of the Ford Mansion.

Fig. 12.25 "An Ornamental Villa." From Samuel Sloan, *The Model Architect* (Philadelphia, 1852), vol. 1, design 9, pl. 30.

an abundance of balconies, and an octagonal cupola on the roof (fig. 12.25). His text admitted that the "ornamental appendages are expensive. But it is to be hoped that the time is or is coming, when such near-sighted utilitarianism will give way to more liberal views of life, and that he who builds for himself a home, will aim beyond mere physical comfort."[36] The rooms were arranged around an eight-sided hall with a circular opening in the ceiling, admitting light from above (fig. 12.26). Also influenced by Sloan was the use of hard-burned bricks in place of stone for the foundations. They figured at Longwood, the oriental mansion of Dr. Haller Nutt at Natchez, designed by Sloan and illustrated as the initial design in his second book, *Homestead Architecture* (1861). The Fleming project, like Longwood, was interrupted by the Civil War, during which it remained in an unfinished state. McMurtry estimated that the house cost $25,000 to build.[37] In 1867 the property was sold for $35,000 to Joel Walker of Richmond, Kentucky, who had it completed for a favorite niece and her husband, Robert R. Stone, who had been living in Canada. They purchased furnishings and sculpture for the niches in New York and called the house Lyndhurst after a Hampshire town in England.[38]

McMurtry's version was larger than the *Model Architect* scheme, having greater depth, with projecting pavilions on all four sides, a third floor, and a belvedere as a superstructure on the entire rotunda (fig. 12.27). Appendages were more restrained, with fewer and smaller brackets, and porches flanking the entrance projections front and back instead of so many balconies. A rounded conservatory was on the

east side. The Lexington architect's familiar "signature" was affixed in the Tudor arch with open spandrels over the front steps.

As in the Sloan plan, the octagonal rotunda was the core of the house, only it was more fully developed at Lyndhurst, formed by round arches in four sides separated by walls with niches on both first and second floors, and here it was twice the height (12.28). The original intent was to have marble flooring and balustrades, but wood was substituted, and a

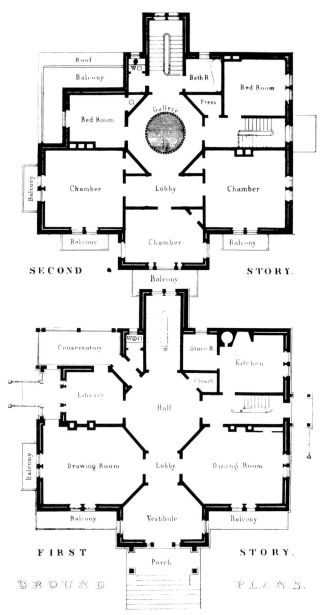

Fig. 12.26 Floor plans of "An Ornamental Villa." From Samuel Sloan, *The Model Architect*, (Philadelphia, 1852), vol. 1, design 9, pl. 36.

Fig. 12.27 Lyndhurst
(1861-67), Lexington.
Photo, 1941.

Fig. 12.28 First floor of rotunda, Lyndhurst. Photo,
1962, by Philip Poynter, courtesy of the *Sunday Herald-Leader*, Lexington.

proposed fountain in the rotunda (like Longwood) was replaced by a gas chandelier with clusters of glowing bulbs at each story, suspended from the ceiling of the cupola. The drawing and dining rooms of the Ornamental Villa became twin parlors at Lyndhurst, their white marble mantels having carved figs, grapes, plums, and pomegranates in the spandrels; equally lush plaster cornices and center-pieces combined intricate acanthus leaves, beads, shells, and tiny faces (fig. 12.29). Despite the strict bilateral symmetry outside, the interior showed re-markable differences in room size, shape, and ar-rangement (fig. 12.30). The largest was the dining room. The main bedroom above was only slightly smaller because of a door in an angle wall in the northeast corner, opening to the dressing room. One of the two adjoining bathrooms was entered through a door in the fireplace wall, and beyond the service stairs in the back hall on the second floor were stor-age closets with windows. Ample closets as well as dressing rooms were provided throughout. Both the handsome curved main stairs and a simpler service stairway continued to the third floor for access to the billiard room in front, and servants' quarters or stor-age spaces elsewhere. Narrow stairs inside the rotun-da ascended to the belvedere. The property was

Fig. 12.29 Fireplace in west parlor, Lyndhurst. Photo, 1940.

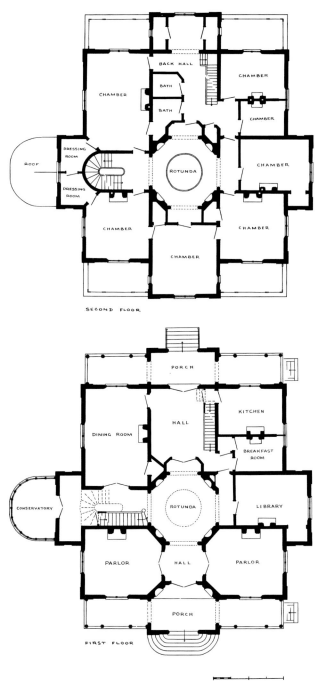

Fig. 12.30 Floor plans of Lyndhurst.

subdivided in 1919 and the villa was demolished in 1964.

RIVERVIEW. The Col. Atwood Gaines Hobson House, at the west edge of Bowling Green, is a miniature mansion, about the size of the service wing of the J.C. Ford residence in Louisville. Called Riverview, from its site commanding a superb vista of the Barren River and valley, the building reflects the form and plan of Hobson's earlier home (1852) on College Street, a cube crowned by a low-pitched hipped roof and cupola, with projecting entrance bay, in front of which stood a one-story portico.[39] Riverview was begun before the Civil War and was temporarily

roofed over for a munitions magazine by the Confederates when they occupied Bowling Green. Soon after the war the house was completed, and Colonel Hobson moved his family into it. The two-story brick structure on a high stone basement is in the bracketed style, the restraining effect of the war showing in the plainness of the arched windows and the absence of intended balconies over the entrances

Fig. 12.31 Riverview (1861-66), near Bowling Green. Photo, 1977, by Hughes Photographers, Bowling Green. Courtesy of the Hobson House Association, Bowling Green.

(fig. 12.31). The front stoop with curved stairs on either side is a graceful structure of stone. A terrace planned for the rear was not realized during the builder's lifetime, and the wooden porch constructed by his son in its stead was later removed.[40]

The formality of the interior is satisfying, with a balance of rooms not unlike in Ward Hall, discussed earlier, though on a smaller scale. Two parlors are on the north side of a transverse hall, and stairs lie between the rooms on the south (fig. 12.32). Fritz Lieber was brought from New York to paint flower and Eastlake designs on the parlor ceilings. The black and golden-wood trim is wide and gives an especially appealing unity to the corners of the rooms with adjoining windows. Marbelized mantels are small, enframing coal-burning fireplaces. The ceiling of the second-story hall is of wood, and a circular opening in the center transmits light from the cupola. A unique and engaging motif is the circular stairway that winds around the light shaft up to the cupola (fig. 12.33). Pipes from a wooden reservoir under the roof immediately in front ran to the bathroom opposite the stairs. This water supply was never used, however. A cistern, above ground level, was installed alongside the side stoop to furnish water to the basement kitchen under the dining room.

Riverview was acquired by the Hobson House As-

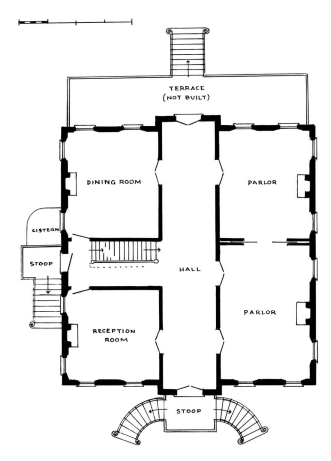

Fig. 12.32 First-floor plan of Riverview.

Fig. 12.33 Oculus in second-story ceiling, showing spiral staircase to the belvedere of Riverview. Photo, 1973.

sociation, organized in 1966. It has been carefully restored, appropriately furnished, and is open to the public as a museum.

VINEWOOD.   Ben B. Groom has his name and the year 1861 incised in the semispherical copper button he set on the newel post of the balustraded staircase

in Vinewood, his villa near the east side of Clark County on the Winchester–Mount Sterling Pike. The house was reportedly copied from a manor house in England.[41] Its plan is unlike any other in Kentucky, as is its staircase. The closest analogue to the latter although Gothic Revival in style, is in Loudoun. The main facade of Vinewood resembles a medium-sized symmetrical Tuscan Revival house, with a deep bracketed veranda in front, but a large square tower is attached to one side (fig. 12.34). The narrow advanced entrance bay is pedimented, and behind it rises a group of chimneys, each divided into several square stacks; another chimney projects above the rear of the tower. Windows and the front door are rectangular, except for the coupled arched windows fitted into round-headed openings in the third story of the tall pavilion. A multipiered porte cochere with arches front and back is attached to the left side of the house. A polygonal single-story bay window projects from the opposite flank, and an indented porch occupies the rear corner on this side. Stone belt courses at the second-floor and windowsill levels connect with the railings of the back porch and indicate that corresponding railings were once around the top of the front veranda.

The entrance hall is narrow, its end framed in an arch on Corinthian pilasters opening into the 16-by-24 foot stair hall forming the nucleus of the house. The staircase rises in two flights to the balustraded

Fig. 12.34 Vinewood (1861), Clark County. Photo, 1971, by John C. Wyatt, courtesy of the *Sunday Herald-Leader*, Lexington.

Fig. 12.35 Staircase in Vinewood. Photo, 1971, by John C. Wyatt, courtesy of the *Sunday Herald-Leader,* Lexington.

balcony that encircles most of the well, which is lighted by a skylight (fig. 12.35). The suite of rooms to the west consists of unequal double parlors connected by sliding doors, with open porches at each end (fig. 12.36). A pair of Corinthian columns stands in the bay-window recess opposite the mantel in the front parlor. Two smaller square rooms are adjacent to one another across the hall. A long dining room behind the stair hall connects with the kitchen through pantries. A narrow breakfast room off the porte cochere has an outside door facing the service stairs, and two other outer doors open into the kitchen and stairs that are the only access to the "Texas," or vagrant's, room over the kitchen. At the head of the main staircase on the second floor, a door opens to steps leading to the garret; another flight ascends to the tower and yet another to the roof of the tower. The tower room is unique in being separated from the stair compartments and having its own fireplace.

WHITE HALL. Cassius Marcellus Clay may have been inspired to remodel his father's house, Clermont, in Madison County by his cousin's rebuilding of Ashland. He employed the same architect, Maj. Thomas Lewinski, but the motive behind the work was different. James B. Clay had to rebuild Ashland because it was structurally unsound. Cassius Clay wanted to enlarge and remodel White Hall (he had

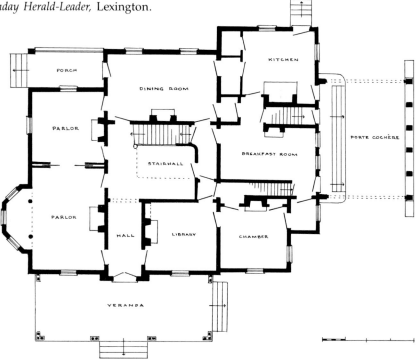

Fig. 12.36 First-floor plan of Vinewood.

Fig. 12.37 White Hall (enlarged 1862), Madison County, detail of south flank. Photo, 1957.

Clay was to look after and approve the work. There is some question whether Cassius was aware that his father's house was being drastically altered.

Lewinski's renovation called for an entirely new east front to be added on the old house's left side. The old part became most of the right flank and rear ell. The drawing-room half of Clermont grew to three stories, and a new side porch with stone columns replaced the former front portico (fig. 12.37). Windows in the south wall of the late-eighteenth-century pavilion were given two-paned sashes, and the cornice was extended and acquired coupled brackets. The alterations enabled the old to be tied to the new. The newer east facade is dominated by a tall, narrow center pavilion, with pilasterlike accents at the corners, and the wider wings on either side are divided into bays by applied upright shafts (fig. 12.38). Windows are thin and attenuated in the constricted divisions, and they maintain the same proportions by being coupled over the doorway. Low-pitched gables, on brick dentils and wood corbels, surmount the center pavilion and middle divisions of each wing. The deck of the square-piered porch and balcony have cast-iron railings. The exterior character seems as much McMurtry's as it is Lewinski's, indicating the builder assumed some of the design function.

changed the name from Clermont in the 1840s) to make it a more impressive and fashionable residence. In 1862, when in Russia serving as ambassador at the court of the czar, he wrote his brother, Brutus Junius Clay, to let contracts for the project. John McMurtry was the builder, and Mrs. Cassius

Fig. 12.38 White Hall, later east facade. Photo, 1967.

The front addition strives for a palatial effect, albeit distinctly provincial. Upon entering the high-ceilinged hall, one is to be impressed with the great sweep of the staircase to the left and with the thirty-two-foot-square ballroom to the right, divided by a screen of Corinthian columns supporting an entablature with an elaborate modillioned cornice encircling both parts of the room (fig. 12.39). The outer part has niches in the corners and a projecting bay window. The fireplace opposite is insignificant and mostly decorative, as a hot-air furnace in the basement below supplied heat. The only part of the old house connected by the main hall is the big drawing room. Its two old north windows were closed yet retained as recesses. The stairways in the west rooms were removed, but that in the dining room was replaced by a closet, which makes an odd projection in a room already small in comparison with those surrounding it (fig. 12.40). Service stairs were provided in the adjoining rear projection. The ell remained unchanged except for new wood columns and a brick arch at the end of the porch.

Two sizable bedrooms, each with double dressing rooms, occupy the space over the ballroom, and the balance of the area in the upper floors is a maze of rooms and passages on various levels. The second story of the addition is between the second and third levels of the old house. Especially awkward are the three little dark cubicles at the back of the chamber over the drawing room; two steps up from it is the room over the little reception room. A bathroom off the service hall contains a zinc-lined tub provided with water by a storage tank overhead. Stairs opposite ascend to the third floor over the east section, most of which is restricted in height.

Although Cassius Marcellus Clay lived at White Hall forty years, the house was never finished. The ballroom walls remained unpainted, and its fireplace was unadorned by a mantel. The house was purchased by the commonwealth in 1968, and it was decorated, furnished, and opened to the public as a museum in 1971.[42] Mid-nineteenth-century marble mantels taken from the Hunt-Morgan House in Lexington were installed in the ballroom and reception room.

THE FRAZER VILLA. Just north of the Greek Revival Weir House on North Limestone Street in Lexington stood a similar building, presumably also erected by James Weir. It was altered and enlarged into an Italian villa by Dr. Warren Frazer, who bought the property in 1863.[43] In its Greek Revival stage, it

Fig. 12.39 Detail of entablature and ceiling in ballroom, White Hall. Photo, 1964.

was a compact, two-story cubic block with portico and symmetrical one-story wings. Heightened to two and one-half stories, it was covered by a low-pitched roof with deep overhangs supported on brackets and surrounded by a porch having square posts and a flat roof (fig. 12.41). The original sashes remained in the second-story windows, and those in the wings were moved above, whereas all the tall lower windows were given two sashes each of four large panes. The door enframement was simplified. Cast-iron hood molds were set over the windows of the chamber story, cast-iron grilles were inserted in the garret openings, and a railing was added to the porch deck. To mask the prominent and out-of-character Greek podium, an earth terrace was heaped around the structure.

The old transverse stair hall and rooms in the center pavilion were retained, though the stair railing was modernized, and sliding doors and marble mantels were installed in the parlor and dining room. On the north side of the hall was a huge drawing room with two fireplaces and a projecting bay window which terminated the umbrage on that side (fig. 12.42). A door opened on the recessed veranda of two stories at the rear. A narrow service ell

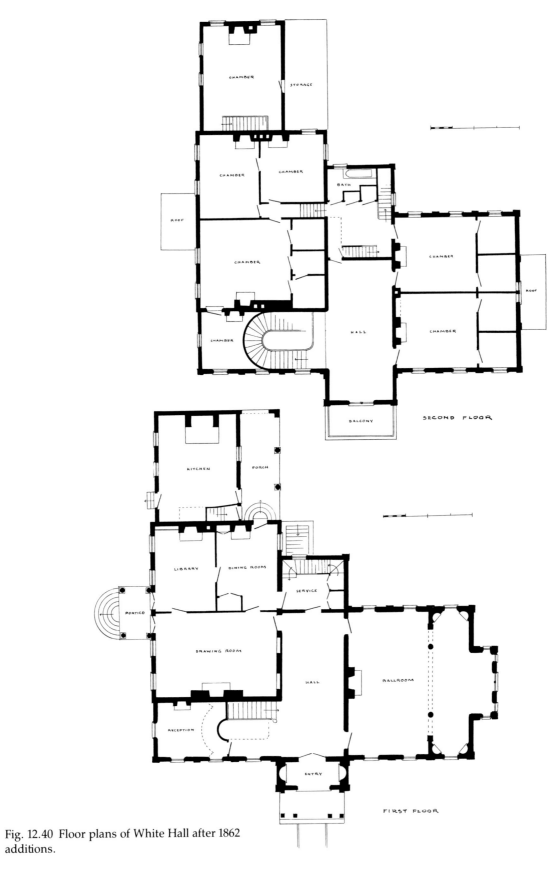

Fig. 12.40 Floor plans of White Hall after 1862
additions.

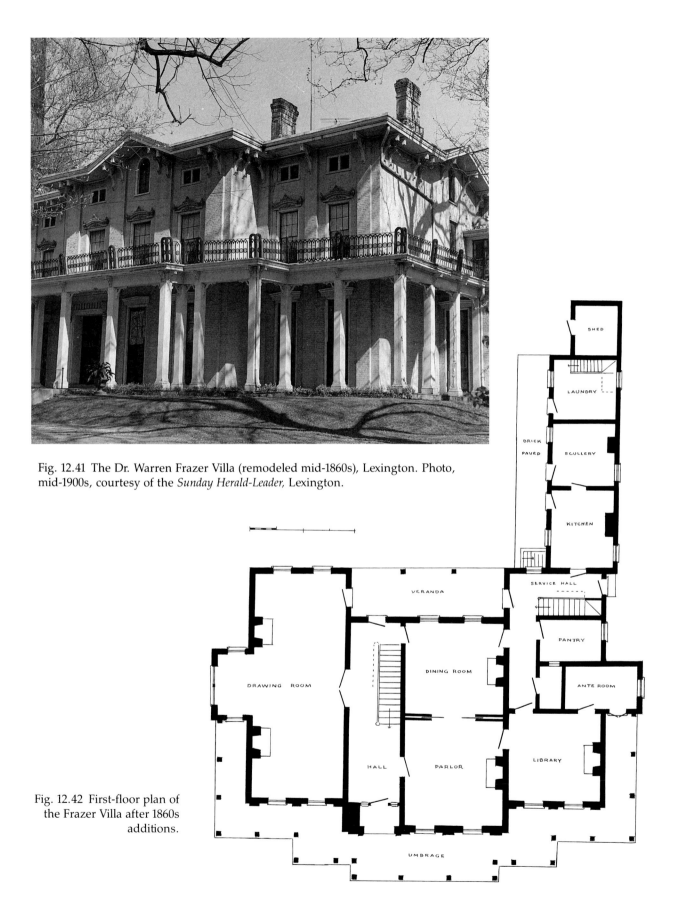

Fig. 12.41 The Dr. Warren Frazer Villa (remodeled mid-1860s), Lexington. Photo, mid-1900s, courtesy of the *Sunday Herald-Leader*, Lexington.

Fig. 12.42 First-floor plan of the Frazer Villa after 1860s additions.

extended back from the southeast corner of the main part of the villa. The building was razed in 1965.

The culture of the Italian peninsula, which for centuries had prompted drastic Renaissance changes upon the art of western and northern Europe, England, and America, was manifested anew, especially in architecture, under the aegis of romanticism during the nineteenth century. This resurgence sought inspiration in anonymous villas, characterized more by form than style (unless it is the bracketed), which had enjoyed an unbroken continuity since time immemorial. The Gothic Revival paved the way with asymmetrical massing for the most characteristic type of nineteenth-century Italianate house. Informal composition, with towers, bay windows, octagonal blocks, and especially porches appeared in Italian guise. Some of the most delightful dwellings of mid-century Kentucky were villas like Cane Run and Vinewood. The more blocky version, or Tuscan phase, produced an unusual and charming example in the Clay Villa at Lexington, and the Marine Hospital at Portland. The customhouse at Louisville, the Asylun for the Deaf in Danville, Lyndhurst and the remodeled Frazer Villa in Lexington, are particularly noteworthy.

The counterpart of the villa movement was the more staid Renaissance Revival, which was rigid in plan and usually well endowed with architectural dress. But, when handled with restraint, the results could be most attractive, as in the Ford mansion in Louisville. Or also with moderation, the Renaissance manner could be combined with the Greek Revival to produce a work innocent of the usual incongruities of eclecticism, as in the School for the Blind and the Louisville Water Company Pumphouse complex. Even before the Civil War the Renaissance Revival bore buildings in which ornament suppressed architecture, as in the headquarters of the Falls City Terracotta Works, which may be excused (or at worse damned) for being a full-size display case for its products. Excessive ornament set the ideal for the great bulk of postwar building in Kentucky no less than elsewhere in the United States.

EPILOGUE

THE POSTWAR ARCHITECTURAL TRADITION

THE CIVIL WAR was a period characterized by disruption. It cleft the United States into North and South, separating industrial New England and the commercial middle states from the raw materials and export items produced in what became the Confederacy. It uprooted the economy and distorted the emotions on both sides. It severed a sequence of events that had been evolving in this country since before the American Revolution. The trials and struggles of that long half-decade from the beginning of 1861 until the late spring of 1865 wrought a great change in peoples' values. The united nation that emerged was quite different from that which entered the war. The centennial of independence, celebrated eleven years later by a world's fair at Philadelphia, the first capital, directed citizens' thoughts and feelings to the spectacular establishment of their democracy. Yet the people of 1876 were oriented differently from those who had gained independence. The early patriots—for all their opposition to the crown—were wholeheartedly English, having been born and reared as such. Their descendants, a century later, were more universal. They had become cognizant of and sympathetic to the ancient Greeks and Romans, the medieval cultures of western Europe, the Renaissance in Italy and elsewhere, and they had also become somewhat familiar with the cultures of Asia, Africa, and South America. This broader understanding was reinforced by teeming immigration. Henceforth people of taste were to bask in the light of several cultures simultaneously. The age of singular enthusiasms was over. In architecture, the particular

revivals of the antebellum period were superseded by the complex eclecticism of the Reconstruction era.

While eclecticism lacked the straightforward forms of the various revivals, it did cling to the traditional Western concept of architecture depending on an overlay of style(s) on structure. It did not, however, rely on direct derivation from historic monuments. Whereas a Greek Revival portico of wood adhered to the authentic form and proportion of the ancient marble original, its late-nineteenth-century equivalent received a manipulation of the components, achieving a new and different entity from the model. Such creativity produced many interesting and even attractive manifestations but missed the established bulk and symmetry of earlier architecture. The normal building had been a simple form with restrained details, a cubic mass with classic portal or portico, or a cruciform with prominent overhanging roof and traceried verandas. Inspiration for the new architecture in the age of emancipation was drawn from a few irregular villas built mostly during the decade before the war, in castellated and Italianate styles, having complex massing, with jutting towers, dormers, and chimneys, encircled by porches of various types, and expanding into porte cocheres and other protuberances. Later buildings were not only of even more restless forms but showed greater variety in color and texture. They combined a number of different kinds of stone, bricks processed for various surfaces, terra-cotta tiles, slates and shingles, and iron, bronze, tin, and lead ornaments. In these complicated compositions one saw mementos of pagan temples, Christian sanctuaries, royal palaces, exotic edifices, and playful references to incidental garden structures, tea houses, and amusement pavilions of diverse types.

New decorative motifs, other than from older architectural sources, were introduced. Carved heads, plant forms, and animal parts, formerly found only on furniture, appeared as wall ornaments. Cut-out stencils, flat arabesques and textile diaper patterns were translated into metal crestings and carved and modeled low-relief embellishments. Filigree and faceted work from jewelers' art were taken over for friezes and bandings. Decorative shapes derived directly from nature including flowers, trees, birds, insects, and other beings, were incorporated into the repertory. Even upholsterers' frills and pastry cooks' "gingerbread" were absorbed as building decor. Immersed in these details, structures were less architectural. Building "style" literally refers to the column—to its order or type. Designs from sources other than structural supports were bound to have tangential effects. Buildings sporting goldsmiths' and silversmiths' works, interior decorators' motifs, and naturalists' paraphernalia lost some of their architectural integrity. And with such focus on extraneous details, the once-sure sense of proportion was forfeited.

Eclecticism, comprising a variety of stylistic emphases with such names as "Queen Anne," Eastlake, and in modern times the Stick style, Colonial Revival (resulting from the Centennial at Philadelphia in 1876, and the McKim, Mead and White historic-architecture tour through New England a few years later), and the "neoclassical Florentine" (of the Columbian Exposition of 1893) persevered into the twentieth century. Still, some manifestations of the Colonial Revival and neoclassic were remarkably pure and distinguishable from the rank and file.[1] Also, the Romanesque Revival, which became popular after Henry Hobson Richardson designed and built Trinity Church in Boston during 1872-77, adhered to a massiveness that better related to the antebellum architectural tradition than other contemporary styles. This relation may be due to its abortive beginning at mid-century, or, more likely and despite its sometimes excessive elaboration to the simplicity and bigness of the forms of its prototype, which did not permit excessive articulation and borrowed little outside of its own domain.[2] Numerous examples of this individual late-nineteenth-

century style were to be found throughout Kentucky, especially in the larger cities.[3] The factor of exuberance, common to all postwar building vogues, was merely integrated differently into the Romanesque. Eclecticisim persevered after World War I in the adaptation of a host of quaint domestic prototypes. Among them were Old English, Normandy, Dutch, and Spanish, which was Americanized as the Monterey, and the ranch house. Meanwhile, the English bungalow had put in an appearance. Although originating in India, in the United States it took on Japanese characteristics; one phase was the Prairie House propagated by the Chicago School.[4] The bungalow constituted a popular form of housing, manifested in a wide variety of types, many of which were commonplace. But in its highest form, the bungalow was a creative artistic expression inspired by a movement that came from Europe as a reaction against eclecticism.

The break from stifling eclectic traditionalism began in the 1880s as what we now call Art Nouveau, although at the time it was known by various names in different places.[5] The style was centered in the decorative arts, though it embraced graphics, as in posters, and it tied in with impressionist painting. It included architecture largely through interior design, and its buildings often looked as though they had been turned inside out. Josef Hoffmann's Palais Stoclet (1905-11) in Brussels was one of its major monuments and seems to have laid the foundations for the International style that came out of a defeated Germany after World War I.[6] The International style was geometric to the point of being styleless, a look which the bungalow had avoided by embracing the ideals of rusticity, naturalness, and craftsmanship. The International made little impression upon Kentucky until well after World War II, when in the cities it figured prominently in the healing that covered the scars made by Urban Renewal during the late 1960s.

Styleless high-rise downtown buildings and sprawling suburban shopping malls have changed the character of the American landscape more drastically than any other phenomenon in two centuries. Many of these structures follow designs made for franchised outlets and chain stores, and facsimiles are put up all over the United States, if not the world. Architecture has been reduced to the nadir of anonymity, and examples do not merit inclusion in this or any other regional study.

The interruption to building caused by the Civil

War was essentially the terminus of a cultural tradition that existed before it. What came afterward was a different breed of being. Consequently we have been without a viable architecture for a longer time than that taken for it to evolve in the first place. Comparing the relatively few who lived in Kentucky during early times with today's millions and the scope of their building activities, we are struck by the realization that quality is not something that can be skimmed off the surface of tremendous output. True architecture is created out of ideal conditions and concentrated direction, behind which is a spiritual impetus that survives with difficulty under accelerated and congested conditions.

GLOSSARY

ABACUS: the square topmost member of a Doric capital

ACROTERIA [Greek pl.; sing. ACROTERIUM] summit or extremity ornaments on a pediment

AMPHIPROSTYLE: of a building, having columned porticoes at opposite ends

ANTA: a pier terminating a wall section

ANTEFIX: an eaves ornament that masks the end of a roof tile

ANTEPODIA [pl.]: projections of a platform or the basement of a building

ANTHEMION (Greek for flower): the "honeysuckle" motif

ARCHITRAVE: the first or lowest member of an entablature

ARCHIVOLT: the inner verticle molding around an arch

BACKBAND: the outer molding of the casing of a door or window

BARGEBOARD: a decorated member pendant to an overhanging gable

BAROQUE: in the flamboyant style of seventeenth-century European architecture

BEAD: a half- or three-quarters-round molding

BED MOLDING: a horizontal member at the junction of a wall or frieze and the soffit of a cornice

BELT COURSE: a horizontal flat projection on the upper part of a wall

BONNET: a rounded roof placed above a dome or ceiling

BRACKETED STYLE: of a building, having deep eaves upheld by a series of supports

CAMPANIFORM: bell-shaped

CAPITAL: the elaborated head of a column

CARPENTER GOTHIC: a phase of the Gothic Revival style carried out quite simply in wood

CAVETTO: a quarter-round concave molding; also called cove

CELLA: the enclosed part of a classic temple

CHAMFER: a surface formed by cutting away the edge of two perpendicular planes

CHEVET [French for head]: the vaulting over a polygonal or rounded end of a church interior

CHINKING: the filling of mud, rocks, and chips between members in a log wall

COLONNADE: a range of columns

COLONETTE: a small, slender column

CONSOLE: a bracket of classic pretentions, usually scrolled at either end

CORINTHIAN: the classic order distinguished by acanthus ornaments on column capitals

COPING: the capping of a wall that is without a roof

CORNICE: the projecting topmost member of an entablature, often used without architrave and frieze

COVED CORNICE: a cavetto

CROSSETTE: a double mitering of the outer molding forming a projection near the corner or base of a door, window, or fireplace casing

CROWN MOLDING: a projecting molding at the top of a cornice

CUPOLA: a cylindrical or polygonal roof superstructure with windows for admitting light

CURB ROOF: a gambrel or double-pitched gable roof

CYMATIUM [*kyma*, Greek wave]: a normal crown molding with a convex-concave profile

DADO: the space between the base and upper molding of a pedestal, or that between the baseboard and chair railing in a room

DATE CORBEL: a bracket at the base of a fire parapet giving the year of construction

DAUB: the mixture of mud and straw used for filling timber framing

DENTIL: one of a series of small blocks in an entablature resembling teeth

DISTYLE: having two columns

DOGTROT: a breezeway or open space between pens of a log house

DORIC: the common Greek order characterized by heavy channeled shafts and plain capitals

DRUM: any round member in a building, such as a column section or the base of a dome

ECHINUS: a round cushion form supporting the square abacus in a Doric capital

ENGAGED PIER: a classic support attached to a wall, an anta, or a pilaster

ENTABLATURE: the full crowning of a colonnade or wall, consisting of architrave, frieze, and cornice

ENTASIS: the swelling of a classic column about a third of the way up the shaft

FANLIGHT: a lunette, a half-round or half-elliptical opening filled with glass to admit light, often capping a doorway or complex rectangular window

FLANKER: a pavilion or other protruberance on the side or outer corner of a building

FLEMISH-BOND BRICKWORK: the pattern of bricks laid alternately with ends or sides exposed, whether horizontally or vertically

FLOUNDER ROOF: a single-pitched or shed roof

FRET, FRETWORK: an ornamental network of slender bars

FRIEZE: the middle member of an entablature

GABLE: the triangular space at the end of a pitched roof

GADROON, GADROONING: a decorative repeat pattern of stylized flower-petal forms

GIRT: the horizontal member in the outer frame of a building that supports the ends of the upper floor or ceiling joists

GAMBREL: a roof of two slopes, the lower of which is more steeply pitched

GORGE MOLDING: a cavetto

GREEK EAR: a side projection or crossette near the upper corner of a door, window, or fireplace casing, prevalent in Greek Revival architecture

GUTTA [Latin for drop; pl. guttae]: a small pendant conic ornament occurring in series

HEADER: the exposed end of a brick in a wall

HIP: the line of the outer angle formed by the meeting of two planes of a hipped roof

HIPPED ROOF: a roof that slopes inward from all sides

HOOD: a shelter over an opening

HOOD MOLD: an ornamental member over a door or window

IMPOST: an architectural section above a capital

IN ANTIS: between antas

IONIC: the classic order characterized by voluted capitals; associated with Ionia in Asia Minor

JACK ARCH: a flat support made up of voussoirs whose sides radiate from a common center

JERKINHEAD: a gable truncated by an upper hip section

JOIST: a horizontal floor or ceiling support

LAMB'S-TONGUE: a reverse-curve transition between the square and octagonal sections of a chamfered post

LEADER HEAD: a decorative funnel at the top of a downspout into which a roof gutter empties

LEVEL-CROWN VAULT: a vault whose summit maintains a constant height

LIERNE: a short rib in a Gothic vault that does not rise from the springing

LIGHT: a unit of a complex opening, as of a Palladian window

MERLON: one of the low intervals in a battlemented parapet

METOPE: the space between triglyphs in a frieze, sometimes filled with relief carvings

MODILLION: a block supporting the cornice that is more elaborate than a dentil and less so than a bracket or console

MUNTIN: a slender window bar supporting panes of glass

MUTULE: a projecting plate suspended from the cornice soffit over a triglyph or metope

NECKING: the treatment at the top of a column shaft beneath the capital

NOGGING: brickwork used to fill the spaces in a timber house frame

OCULUS [Latin for eye]: a round window or opening at the apex of a dome

ORDER: a combined column and entablature of a given style

PALISADE: a wall of adjacent upright posts; a stockade

PALLADIAN WINDOW: an opening having three lights of which the center one is arched; a motif associated with Andrea Palladio (1518-80)

PANTILE: an interlocking ceramic roof plate

PATERA: a circular ornament resembling a Greek wine cup

PEDIMENT: the triangular form of a classic gable

PEN: a room or storage-space unit in a log structure

PENDENTIVE: one of the concave triangular members over a square room rising to a horizontal circle or the base of a cylindrical cupola or dome

PENT: a small attached room or pavilion

PERISTYLE: a range of columns surrounding a building or courtyard

PIER: an upright support somewhat greater than a post and square or prismatic in form

PILASTER: an upright form projecting from a wall resembling a flattened column

PILASTRADE: a range of pilasters applied to a wall and treated as columns

PINRAIL: a horizontal board affixed to a wall at about eye level in which are set pegs for hanging various items

PRESS: a recessed cupboard for clothes with shelves and doors

PROSTYLE: of a building, having a portico spanning the front

PROTOMA: the forepart of a figure

RABBETED: a square-cut sinkage (rabbet) at the end or corner of a carpentry member to receive another piece joined thereto

RAKING BOARDS: planks at the top of a wall adjoining a sloping roof

RESPOND: a half column applied to the wall at the end of a colonnade

RINCEAU (PL. RINCEAUX): a continuous scrolled relief of intertwined stems and leaves

RUSTICATION: stonework in which blocks are made conspicuous by having beveled or rabbeted edges

SEGMENTAL ARCH: a curved support of less than half of a circle or ellipse with angles at the springing

SLEEPER: a timber laid horizontally as on the ground to support crosswise members

SOFFIT: the under side of an overhanging cornice, door, window, or staircase

SPRINGING: the base of an arch

STATION: a fortified house of the pioneer period

STRING: one of the sloping members of a stairway that supports the treads

TAENIA: the band in an entablature that separates the frieze from the architrave

TETRASTYLE: a portico having four columns

TORUS: a convex molding

TRABEATED [Latin trabs, a beam]: post-and-beam construction

TRIGLYPH: an abstract ornament in a frieze having three glyphs or channels

VAULT: a ceiling arched in various ways

VITRUVIAN: referring to Marcus Vitruvius Pollio, Roman authority on architecture of the first century B.C.

VOLUTE: having a spiral shape, as an Ionic capital or the end of a stair rail

VOUSSOIR: a wedge-shaped member of a masonry arch

WATER TABLE: a molded setback in exterior masonry, usually at the first-floor level

WATTLE: sticks inserted in a house frame to hold the "daub" (mud mixed with straw)

WINDER: a wedge-shaped step in a corner or a winding staircase

NOTES

1 LOG STRUCTURES

1. Jasper Danckaerts, a Dutch traveler, stayed overnight in a log house in 1679 described as "made according to the Swedish mode" (Harold R. Shurtleff, *The Log Cabin Myth* [Cambridge, Mass., 1939], 124).

2. J. Stoddard Johnston, *First Explorations in Kentucky,* Filson Club Publication 13 (Louisville, 1898), 55.

3. Victor Collot, *A Journey in North America* (Paris, 1826; Florence, 1924), 109.

4. Joseph Doddridge, *Notes on the Settlement and Indian Wars. . . .* (Wellesurg, Va., 1824; Pittsburgh, 1912), 99.

5. "Journey to Kentucky in 1775, Diary of James Nourse," *Journal of American History* 19 (1925): 256.

6. Ibid., 259.

7. Facsimiles of Benjamin Van Cleve's manuscript, typescript of the text, and a photocopy of the plan are reprinted in *Register of the Kentucky Historical Society* 28 (1930): 105-14, from a separate pamphlet by Willard Rouse Jillson, issued by the society in 1929.

8. Lewis Collins, *Historical Sketches of Kentucky* (Cincinnati, 1847), 453.

9. John D. Barnhart, ed., *Henry Hamilton and George Rogers Clark in the American Revolution* (Crawfordsville, Ind., 1951), 195.

10. W.W. Stephenson, "The Old Fort," *Register of the Kentucky Historical Society* 5 (1907): 47-50. Included is a perspective sketch of the enlarged fort.

11. See sketches made by John Dabney Shane from descriptions given by Martha Wymore and Josiah Colling, the State Historical Society of Wisconsin, in Clay Lancaster, *Vestiges of the Venerable City* (Lexington, 1978), 5; see also Bettye Lee Mastin, *Lexington 1779* (Lexington, 1979), 22.

12. Draper MSS 11S202, State Historical Society of Wisconsin, Madison.

13. James Truslow Adams, ed., *Album of American History* (New York, 1944), 1:138, 254; Hugh Morrison, *Early American Architecture* (New York, 1952), 181-83; Marshall B. Davidson, *Life in America* (Boston, 1951), 1:35.

14. Adams, *Album of American History* 1:349.

15. Samuel Wilson, Jr., "Colonial Fortifications and Military Architecture in the Mississippi Valley," *The French in the Mississippi Valley* (Urbana, Ill., 1965), 103-22.

16. Jane F. Babson, "The Architecture of Early Illinois Forts," *Journal of the Illinois State Historical Society* 61 (1968): 28-31.

17. Draper MSS 11CC130, State Historical Society of Wisconsin.

18. Richard W. Otis, *The Louisville Director for the Year 1832* (Louisville, 1832; repr., Louisville, 1970), 101-2.

19. C.A. Weslager, *The Log Cabin in America* (New Brunswick,

N.J., 1969), 336; Donald A. Hutshar, "The Log Architecture of Ohio," *Ohio History* 80 (1971): 177-78.

20. Information from Bettye Lee Mastin, Lexington.

21. A general account is that of Fred Kniffen and Henry Glassie, "Building in Wood in the Eastern United States," *Guideline* (National Recreation and Park Association) July-Aug. 1973, 41-52.

22. Henry Chandlee Forman, *The Architecture of the Old South: The Medieval Style, 1515-1850* (Cambridge, Mass., 1948), [9]-12; Ivor Noel Hume, *Martin's Hundred* (New York, 1982), 216-37.

23. Morrison, *Early American Architecture,* 258.

24. Clay Lancaster, *Ante Bellum Houses of the Bluegrass* (Lexington, 1961), 9.

25. Lincoln County Order Book, 1781-91, p. 178.

26. Information from George Stanhope Wiedeman II and Jefferson A. Wiedemann, whose father purchased the house in 1933 from Mrs. Sallie Payton (aged ninety-two), a descendant of Joseph Carroll; letter from John William Lancaster III to author, 22 Oct. 1964.

27. This plan has been reconstructed from measurements of the foundations made by the author on 30 July 1964; information about the openings and position of the stairways came from Mrs. Hugh Reynolds of Carrollton, Kentucky in a letter dated 23 Sept. 1964. The Reynolds family purchased the house from the Wiedemanns in 1942 and occupied it until it burned in 1949. They operated a riding academy on the grounds.

28. Willard Rouse Jillson, *Pioneer Kentucky* (Frankfort, Ky., 1934), 74.

29. Thomas A. Knight and Nancy Lewis Greene, *Country Estates of the Blue Grass* (Cleveland, 1904), 9.

30. Lewis W. McKee and Lydia K. Bond, *History of Anderson County* (Frankfort, Ky., n.d.), 17.

31. Gary Wheeler Stone, chief archaeologist at St. Mary's City, Maryland, discovered an advertisement in the 28 June 1794 issue of the *Kentucky Gazette* describing this property for sale as lot no. 63, "on which is a hewn log dwelling house 18 by 22 feet, with an addition of frame 16 by 18 feet." No mention was made, however, of a separate kitchen.

32. Gary Wheeler Stone examined the Rankin House on 29 Dec. 1971 and 1 Jan. 1972, before its removal, and made his notes available to the author. See also Bettye Lee Mastin, "Lexington's Oldest Open throughout Week," *Sunday Herald-Leader* (Lexington) 12 May 1972, 64-65.

33. C. Frank Dunn, "Fayette County Has 275 Houses That Were Erected before 1825," *Sunday Herald-Leader,* 23 May 1954, 38.

34. Simon Kenton built the first station in Mason County, which passed into oblivion long ago (Glenn Clift, *History of Maysville and Mason County* [Lexington, 1936], 1:44).

35. Mrs. Maude Ward Lafferty first made the author aware of

this house and accompanied him to the site in 1951. Miss Helda Trelkeld, former president of the Mason County Historical Society, corresponded about it in 1964. Afterward Mrs. Andrew Duke assumed the task of amicable correspondent and guide.

36. Mercer County Deed Book 1, pp. 115-16.

37. Fayette County Court Book, CoCt B, 153-55, 159, 161; CirCt B, 434; CoCt 7, p. 333; CoCt Y, 179.

38. Mercer County Deed Book 3, pp. 406-7.

39. Bettye Lee Mastin pointed out that this may have been a prevalent feature in Lexington. Urban Renewal projects destroyed three examples on High Street in 1969; three were still in existence in 1988. See *Sunday Herald-Leader*, 28 July 1968, 73, and 12 Jan. 1969, 54.

40. The plan was inscribed, "Chaumière des prairies the humble residence of David Meade in the County of Jessamine and State of Kentucky November 12th 1800," Library of the University of Virginia.

41. Henry J. Peet, ed., *Chaumière Papers* (Chicago, 1883), 55-56.

42. Dr. Herbert Livingston of Asbury Theological Seminary conducted excavations of the foundations for verification of the accuracy of the Meade plan and the location of the brick pavilion in relation to the early buildings (letter of 15 Mar. 1976). See articles by Bettye Lee Mastin, *Sunday Herald and Leader*, 19 Nov. 1975, D-3; Mary Cronan Oppel, "Paradise Lost: The Story of Chaumière des Prairies," *Filson Club History Quarterly* 56 (1982): 201-10.

43. William Henry Perrin, *History of Bourbon, Scott, Harrison, and Nicholas Counties, Kentucky* (Chicago, 1882), 48-50.

44. J. Winston Coleman, Jr., *Historic Kentucky* (Lexington, 1967), 87; Lois L. Olcott, "Public Architecture of Kentucky before 1870," *Antiques* 55 (1974): 835.

45. Information from Mrs. Maude Ward Lafferty, Lexington, interview 1951.

2 FRAME CONSTRUCTION

1. Reprinted in Julius P. Bolivar MacCabe, *Directory of the City of Lexington and County of Fayette for 1838 & '39* (Lexington, 1838), 6.

2. Joseph Charless published almanacs in Lexington from 1803 through 1808 for "Kentucky, Tennessee and Ohio." That of 1806 contains the first printed city directory of Lexington, listing 273 people, of whom 12 were stone or brick layers, and 11 were carpenters, store or house joiners.

3. François André Michaux, *Travels to the Westward of the Allegany Mountains, in the States of Ohio, Kentucky and Tennessee, etc., 1801-1803* (Paris, 1804: London, 1805), 54-55.

4. Memorandums of a Tour Made by Josiah Espy in the States of Ohio and Kentucky and Indiana Territory in 1805 (Cincinnati, 1870), 8, 15.

5. James Elliott Defebaugh, *History of the Lumber Industry of America* (Chicago, 1906-7), 2:6-9.

6. Edward Williams, *Virginia, More Especially the South Part There, Richly and Truly Valued* (London, 1650), [77-78].

7. *Kentucky Gazette*, 11 May 1793, 4; 9 Apr. 1796, 3; 12 July 1797, 2; 26 July 1797, 1.

8. Michaux, *Travels to the Westward*, 57; George W. Ranck, *History of Lexington* (Cincinnati, 1872), 185.

9. *Kentucky Gazette*, 9 Oct. 1806, 3.

10. Fortesque Cuming, *Sketches of a Tour to the Western Country, Through the States of Ohio and Kentucky . . . Commenced at Philadelphia in the Winter of 1807, and Concluded in 1809 . . .* (Pittsburgh, 1810), app. H, 406.

11. Henry McMurtrie, *Sketches of Louisville* (Louisville, 1819; repr., Louisville, 1969), 134-35.

12. *Kentucky Gazette*, 27 Dec. 1788, 1.

13. Ibid., 4 Oct. 1794, 4.

14. Ibid., 27 Apr. 1801, 3; 10 Jan. 1804, 2.

15. Ibid., 19 Apr. 1797, 1; 7 May 1802, 3.

16. Ibid., 26 Mar. 1802, 3.

17. Michaux, *Travels to the Westward*, 57. West sold the machine for $10,000. Models of both it and a steamboat of his design were deposited in the Patent Office; they were destroyed when the British burned Washington in 1814 (Robert Peter, *History of Fayette County, Kentucky* [Chicago, 1882], 380). Currently the Patent Office has records of two machines for cutting nails, both issued to West on 2 July 1802, but, of course, the contents are unknown because of the fire (W.C. Umhau, Office of the Commissioner of Patents, to author, 28 June 1965).

18. Barlow made the first steam locomotive in the western country in 1827; it could pull a heavily laden car up an incline of 80 feet to the mile. Later (1841-51) he constructed the celebrated planetarium used in teaching astronomy at Transylvania University. The self-feeding nail and tack machine was sold to a group of Massachusetts capitalists (Peter, *History of Fayette County*, 381).

19. *Kentucky Gazette*, 12 Sept. 1809, 4.

20. The name came from that of the land belonging to the father of Tristram Shandy, a fictional character in Laurence Sterne, *The Life and Opinions of Tristram Shandy* (London, 1760-65), 4:205.

21. Marcus Whiffen, *The Eighteenth-Century Houses of Williamsburg* (Williamsburg, Va., 1960), 174, [102].

22. Thomas W. Bullitt, *My Life at Oxmoor* (Louisville, 1911) contains various descriptions, floor plans, and photographs.

23. Bettye Lee Mastin, "Spring Hill Is Thought to Be Unique in State," *Sunday Herald-Leader*, 16 June 1968, 78; Kathryn Owen, *Old Houses and Landmarks of Clark County, Kentucky* (Lexington, 1967), 21.

24. Dunn, "Fayette County Has 275 Houses That Were Erected before 1825."

25. *The Biographical Encyclopaedia of Kentucky* (Cincinnati, 1878), 551; Edna Hunter Best, *Sketches of Washington, Mason County, Kentucky* (Washington, Ky., 1936), 2, 8.

26. Mrs. Andrew C. Duke of Maysville to author, 26 July 1967.

27. Restoration of the house in 1936 and the apothecary shop in 1959 was carried out under the direction of C. Julian Oberwarth, architect, of Frankfort.

28. H.A. Scomp, *A Historical Sketch of the Old "Mud Meeting House" Prepared for the Centennial Celebration* [25 Aug. 1900], (Harrodsburg, Ky., [mid-1930s]), 10-23.

29. Richard W.E. Perrin, "'Fahwerkbau' Houses in Wisconsin," *Journal of the Society of Architectural Historians* (Mar. 1959): 27-33. The Moravian Meeting House, Oley, Pennsylvania, is illustrated in Morrison, *Early American Architecture*, 542.

30. Scomp, *Historical Sketch*, 34-36.

31. On 23 Apr. 1807 Henry Banta conveyed to his son-in-law Peter Cozine Banta the tract of 30¾ acres on which the latter built his home (Mercer County Deed Book 6, 263). The author is indebted to the historians Mrs. Rebecca Conover and Mrs. Frances Keightley, Harrodsburg, for information about Peter C. Banta and John Cozine and their houses.

32. Mercer County Deed Book 5, pp. 522-23.

33. J. Winston Coleman, Jr., *The Springs of Kentucky* (Lexington, 1955), 13-15.

34. *Kentucky Gazette*, 22 May 1809, 3.

35. Collins, *Historical Sketches of Kentucky*, 480.

36. Richard H. Collins, *Historical Sketches of Kentucky* (Covington, Ky., 1874), 2:157.

37. Cuming, *Sketches of a Tour*, 152.

38. Carl W. Condit, *American Building Art: The Nineteenth Century* (New York, 1960), 87-88.

39. Roger Hale Newton, *Town and Davis, Architects* (New York, 1942), 42-44.

40. Entry for the Ithiel Town bridge proposed for Louisville was found in a day book in the A.J. Davis Papers at the New York Public Library by Dr. Patrick Snadon.

41. Samuel W. Thomas, ed., *Views of Louisville since 1766* (Louisville, 1971), 148.

42. Condit, *American Building Art*, 155-56, 312 n. 8, 316 n. 5; Howard Curry, *High Bridge: A Pictorial History* (Lexington, 1983), 20-33.

3 STONE CONSTRUCTION

1. Charles Henry Richardson, *The Building Stones of Kentucky* (Frankfort, Ky., 1923).

2. John J. McGee, "The McGee Family," *Register of the Kentucky Historical Society* 38 (1940): 314-15.

3. The tombstone in the Boggs family graveyard east of the house is inscribed, "Settled this place Feb. 18, 1784."

4. Letter from Dr. F.C. Lewis of Jackson, owner of the house, 1 Aug. 1967. Dr. Lewis also supplied material on Morgan's Station and the stone house, including a copy of letter (18 Feb. 1958) from Miss Madge B. Harding of Indianapolis, a descendant of Ralph and Priscilla Morgan; plats of the fort and environs in the eighteenth century; and numerous photographs taken during the 1967 renovation.

5. The builder's name and the date, "October 11, 1794," are incised in the plaster on the east end of the cellar of the Trabue residence (Mrs. Willis Field, "A Few Pioneer Homes of the Kentucky River and Grier's Creek in Woodford County" [Talk presented before the Gen. Calmes Chapter of the Daughters of the American Revolution, typescript lent by Mrs. Field, ca. 1942.]).

6. The existence of the porch on the north side is assumed from chamfered posts, matching those of the south porch, found by the owners, Mr. and Mrs. Edward C. O'Rear.

7. *The Biographical Encyclopaedia of Kentucky* (Cincinnati, 1878), 143.

8. Fayette County Burnt Records, 5:392. The record is incomplete, the description of the land not included. The Scott property is in Jessamine County, which was separated from Fayette in 1798. Information from Mrs. Frank S. Jackson (a great-granddaughter of the builder) of Farmington, Mich., and Mrs. Charlotte Dunkman of Lexington.

9. Bennett H. Young, *A History of Jessamine County, Kentucky* (Louisville, 1898), 79.

10. Forman, *The Architecture of the Old South*, [89], [93], [153], [161], and [184].

11. Mrs. J. Vimont Layson of Millersburg to author, 31 May 1967. Also see Bettye Lee Mastin, "One by One, the Stone Houses Go Down," *Sunday Herald-Leader*, 6 Aug. 1972, 84.

12. J. Winston Coleman, Jr., "Historic Kentucky: Valley Farm, Franklin County," *Sunday Herald-Leader*, 12 Apr. 1964, 39.

13. Charles Morse Stotz, *The Early Architecture of Western Pennsylvania* (New York, 1936), 52-56, 68-71.

14. Examples are the William McClintock House on Collier's Pike (abandoned when visited by author in 1968), and the Henry Thompson House (1785-90), with additions, illustrated in Carolyn Murray Wooley, "Kentucky's Early Stone Houses," *Antiques* 55 (Mar. 1974): 594.

15. Curtis W. Harrison of Lexington to author, May 1967, quoting the late Mrs. Sallie Steele Taylor of Nicholasville.

16. Curtis W. Harrison to author, Dec. 1967.

17. William E. Railey, *History of Woodford County* (Versailles, 1938; repr., 1968), 115, 214.

18. Joan Kay, "Woodford County Home Comes to Life Again," *Louisville Courier-Journal and Times*, 31 Oct. 1971, G-2.

19. Michaux, *Travels to the Westward of the Allegheny Mountains*, 55.

20. John Melish, *Travels in the United States of America in the Years 1806 and 1807, and 1809, 1810 and 1811* (Philadelphia, 1812), 2:180-81.

21. Cuming, *Sketches of a Tour*, 170-71.

22. Nelson County Deed Book 2, pp. 139-40. George M. Harding to author, 8 Oct. 1977.

23. Sarah B. Smith, *Historic Bardstown* (Shepherdsville, Ky., 1968), 10.

24. *Kentucky Gazette*, 16 Feb. 1788, 2.

25. *Daily Lexington Transcript*, 3 Aug. 1883, 2.

26. Thomas, *Views of Louisville since 1766*, 22.

27. Cuming, *Sketches of a Tour*, 151.

28. Melish, *Travels in the United States of America*, 2:200.

29. George W. Ranck, *"The Travelling Church": An Account of the Baptist Exodus from Virginia to Kentucky in 1781 under the Leadership of Rev. Lewis Craig and Capt. William Ellis*, booklet from a paper read before the Filson Club (Louisville, 1910).

30. Best, *Sketches of Washington*, 3.

4 BRICK BUILDING

1. Robert Johnson, *The New Life of Virginia* (London, 1612), D2.

2. Forman, *The Architecture of the Old South*, [22-23], [28].

3. An example is at Sugar Tree Grove on the north side of the Winchester Pike about five miles east of Lexington.

4. *Kentucky Gazette*, 25 Feb. 1797, 3; 12 Aug. 1797, 3.

5. Ibid., 12 July 1797, 2.

6. Ibid., 31 May 1788, 2; 20 Dec. 1788, 3; 14 Feb. 1789, 1; 20 Mar. 1804, 3.

7. Ibid., 12 Oct. 1793, 3.

8. Ibid., 30 July 1811, 3.

9. One of the proprietors, Christopher Greenup, advertised in the 26 Apr. 1790 issue of the *Kentucky Gazette*, for "Stone Masons, Carpenters, Quarriers, Wood Cutters and other Laborers, to work at the Slate-creek Iron-works" (p. 2). See also J. Winston Coleman, Jr., "Old Kentucky Iron Furnaces," *Filson Club History Quarterly* 31 (1957): 227-42.

10. *Kentucky Gazette*, 12 Dec. 1809, 1.

11. Ibid., 14 Apr. 1792, 4; 23 Jan. 1800, 3; 2 Oct. 1804, 2.

12. Cuming, *Sketches of a Tour*, 160-65.

13. Melish, *Travels in the United States of America* 2:184.

14. Fayette County Deed Book C, 271, 24 Jan. 1800.

15. Probably built after Isabella Lake sold the property to John Carty, 21 Nov. 1807 (Fayette County Deed Book C, 192).

16. Charles G. Talbert, "William Whitley, 1749-1813—Part II," *Filson Club History Quarterly* 25 (1951): 214-15. On Filson's map *Kentucke* (1784) the symbol for "Whitleys" is that for a fort or station.

17. Bettye Lee Mastin, "Whitley Home Is Self-built Memorial, *Sunday Herald-Leader*, 16 June 1957, 34.

18. A floor plan and elevation showing these addenda are included in Rexford Newcomb, *Old Kentucky Architecture* (New York, 1940), pl. 7.

19. Mary L. Williams, "William Whitley Built First Brick House, First Race Track in State," *Lexington Leader*, 17 Apr. 1957, 32.

20. Thomas Tileston Waterman, *The Mansions of Virginia, 1706-1776* (Chapel Hill, N.C., 1945), 196.

21. Samuel W. Thomas, "The History and Restoration of 'Locust Grove' Near Louisville, Kentucky, Built ca. 1790," *Register of the Kentucky Historical Society* 65 (1967): 271. Also see Samel W.

Thomas, "The Restoration of Locust Grove," *Western Pennsylvania Historical Magazine* 48 (1965): 145–50.

22. Fayette County Deed Book C, 159.

23. Waterman, *Mansions of Virginia*, 152-55, 200-1, 215, 219.

24. Cassius Marcellus Clay, *The Life of Cassius Marcellus Clay* (Cincinnati, 1886), 19-20.

25. Stone belt courses, stringers at first-floor level, and keystones over windows are to be found in Lexington on the Dr. Walter Warfield House (1806) on the southeast corner of Short and Upper streets, and William Palmateers Sign of the Green Tree Tavern (before 1812), 574 West Main Street.

26. Waterman, *Mansions of Virginia*, [72].

27. Rexford Newcomb, *Architecture in Old Kentucky* (Urbana, Ill., 1953), pl. 39A.

28. E.I. Thompson, owner of Oakland during the 1970s, to author.

29. Marsha Bottom, "A Harrodsburg Landmark," *Kentucky Heritage*, Winter 1972, 27.

30. The Baptist Church purchased the land in 1819 from John and Nancy Burford (Mrs. W. Henry Graddy, Versailles, Ky., to author, 1973).

31. Cuming, *Sketches of a Tour*, 162.

32. MacCabe, *Directory of the City of Lexington*, 15.

33. Three doors are shown in the representation of the building on J.T. Palmatary's "View of the City of Lexington, Ky.," published in Cincinnati in 1857. Although known to be inaccurate regarding some other buildings, it provides the only known contemporary pictorial record.

34. Rebecca Wilson Conover, ed., *Through Two Hundred Years* (Harrodsburg, Ky., 1974), 89.; Mary Waters, "Morgan Row's Happy Ending," *Courier-Journal Magazine*, 23 May 1965, 42-46.

35. Edward Hungerford, *The Story of the Baltimore and Ohio Railroad, 1827-1927* (New York, 1928), vol. 1, facing p. 54; Lawrence Grow, *Waiting for the 5:05* (New York, 1977), [27]; and Kincaid A. Herr, *Louisville and Nashville Railroad, 1850-1963* (Louisville, 1964), 70-71.

36. *Kentucky Reporter*, 10 Feb. 1830, 2; 17 Feb. 1830, 2. A total of $792,900 was raised by subscription.

37. *Lexington Observer and Reporter*, 25 Apr. 1833, 4.

38. Ibid., 28 Jan. 1835, 3; 21 Oct. 1835, 3.

39. "Built L. and N. depot building, Lexington, Ky., cost $16,000" (McMurtry advertisement in John Lethem, *A Review of Lexington, Kentucky, As She Is* [New York, (1886)], 102).

40. Clay Lancaster, "Death of a Depot," *Courier-Journal Magazine*, 24 May 1959, 24, 26-27. Union Depot is pictured in Grow, *Waiting for the 5:05*, 17.

41. Dan M. Bowmar, Sr., "Time Rolls On in Downtown Lexington, but Not by Train," *Lexington Leader*, 6 Mar. 1969, 29.

5 PLEASANT HILL AND SOUTH UNION

1. Edward Deming Andrews, *The People Called Shakers* (New York, 1953; repr., New York, 1963), 13, 18-69; Marguerite Fellows Melcher, *The Shaker Adventure* (Princeton, 1941; repr., Old Chatham, N.Y., 1973), 3-20, 23-56. Shaker communities were located at Watervliet and New Lebanon, N.Y.; Enfield, Conn.; Hancock, Harvard, Shirley, and Tyringham, Mass.; Canterbury and Enfield, N.H.; and Alfred and New Gloucester (Sabbathday Lake), Me. Branches and missions were founded at Canaan and Sodus Bay, N.Y.; Ashfield, Cheshire, Richmond, and Savoy, Mass.; Gorham, Me.; Philadelphia, Penn.; White Oak, Ga.; and Narcoossee, Fl. Inland Shaker communities were to be at Union Village, North Union, Watervliet (Beulah), and Whitewater, Ohio; West Union (Busro), Ind.; and Pleasant Hill and South Union, Ky.

Missions at Darby and Straight Creek, Ohio, did not long survive.

2. Andrews, *People Called Shakers*, 70-93; Melcher, *Shaker Adventure*, 67-83; Thomas D. Clark and F. Gerald Ham, *Pleasant Hill and Its Shakers* (Pleasant Hill, Ky., 1968), 4-16.

3. "The Origin and Progress of the Society at Pleasant Hill," 84-85, Harrodsburg Historical Society; Samuel Turner's Journal, 1806-36, entries during 1808, Western Reserve Historical Society Collection, Cleveland, Ohio.

4. Samuel Turner's Journal, entries during 1809.

5. The ministry at Pleasant Hill to New Lebanon, 13 Apr. and 21 Oct. 1812, Western Reserve Historical Society.

6. Letter from the ministry at Pleasant Hill to New Lebanon, 15 Apr. 1812, Western Reserve Historical Society.

7. Samuel W. Thomas and Mary Lawrence Young, "The Development of Shakertown at Pleasant Hill," *Filson Club History Quarterly* 49 (1975): 237.

8. Hazel Spencer Phillips, *Traditional Architecture, Warren County, Ohio* (Lebanon, Ohio, 1969), 121. The meetinghouse in Union Village was burned down by local firemen in practice exercises at the request of the owners in 1965.

9. Young members wanted to introduce Robert Owen socialism into the society and have the ministry elected by the membership, and the old guard wanted them appointed by the hierarchy. When the latter prevailed, many left the organization.

10. Members of the Junior Order were located away from the Senior Class until they had proved their steadfastness and were transferred to the older group.

11. *Church Record in Three Books*, Book C, 50, 56, 58, 59, 64, 73, 93, 472, Harrodsburg Historical Society; "A Journey to Kentucky in the Year 1872," *Shaker Quarterly* 4 (1965): 117-18; obituary in Shaker journal (Filson Club) of Dr. James L. Ballance under date 10 Jan. 1879; James C. Thomas, "Micajah Burnett and the Buildings at Pleasant Hill," *Antiques* 48 (1970): 600-5.

12. The meetinghouse at Whitewater, Ohio, is of brick, but it is a later building than that at South Union (Herbert Schiffer, *Shaker Architecture* [Exton, Pa., 1979], 180).

13. Tommy Hines, director, Shakertown at South Union, to author, Mar. 1989.

6 THE FEDERAL PERIOD

1. *Kentucky Gazette*, 27 June 1795, extra edition.

2. Ibid., 25 Apr. 1798, 3.

3. Ibid., 30 Jan. 1810, 3; The copy in Avery Library, Columbia University, is lacking twenty plates and the binding seems not to have been tampered with. It is possible that the copy to reach Lexington was imperfect too—though unlikely short forty plates and still salable.

4. *Kentucky Gazette*, 27 Mar. 1810, 4.

5. Lancaster, *Ante Bellum Houses of the Bluegrass*, figs. 61, 92, 188.

6. *Kentucky Gazette*, 27 July 1813, 4.

7. The copy is signed in front, "Mathias Shryock's Book bought May the 4 1802—Price 16/0—Mathias Shryock," and in back Mathias wrote his name again. Under it his son wrote, "Gideon G. Shryock July 1st 1821." Mr. Morgan also procured in Louisville a copy of the sixth edition of Benjamin's *The American Builder's Companion* (Boston, 1827), and an 1817 edition of Owen Biddle's *The Young Carpenter's Assistant*, discussed previously. Dr. Samuel W. Thomas, to author, 10 Aug. 1965, and Frederick L. Morgan to author, 18 Aug. 1965.

8. Elizabeth M. Simpson, *Bluegrass Houses and Their Traditions* (Lexington, 1932), 50, (ill.).

9. Newcomb, *Architecture in Old Kentucky*, 84.

10. Newcomb, *Old Kentucky Architecture* (New York, 1940), pls. 60-64.

11. *Kentucky Gazette,* 7 May 1802, 3.

12. Ibid., 13 Mar. 1815, 3.

13. Ibid., 21 Dec. 1793, 4.

14. Ibid., 30 July 1805, 4.

15. Ibid., 19 Sept. 1809, 3.

16. Ibid., 2 Dec. 1816, 3.

17. Identified by Warren P. Brown, Jr., administrator, French Panoramas of the Golden Age, Columbus, Georgia, letters of 24 Feb. and 11 Mar. 1973 to author, and letter of 21 Mar. 1973 to Stanley D. Petter, Jr., Hurricane Hall.

18. Elizabeth Patterson Thomas, *Old Kentucky Homes and Gardens* (Louisville, 1939), 79. Other sets of the hunting scene are on the walls of the John A. Andrews House (1818) in Salem, Mass.; the parlor from the Eagle House Inn, Haverhill, Mass., built in 1818, in the Metropolitan Museum of Art in New York City; and fragments in a Virginia room near Washington, D.C. (R.T.H. Halsey and Elizabeth Towers, *The Homes of Our Ancestors* [New York, 1937], 210-11).

19. Mrs. Mildred Cohen of Lexington, who owned a photograph of Alfred Cohen made in Danville in 1867, to author, 1948. In it he looks to be about fifty years old.

20. Mrs. Willis Field of Lexington, a granddaughter-in-law of the owner of Airy Mount, to author, 1941.

21. Edward B. Allen, *Early American Wall Paintings* (New Haven, 1926), fig. 88.

22. *Kentucky Gazette,* 20 June 1839, 3.

23. Edna Talbott Whitley, *Kentucky Ante-Bellum Portraiture* (Richmond, Va., 1958), 669-73. For accounts of early easel painters in the region, see also Samuel Woodson Price, *Old Masters of the Blue Grass* (Louisville, 1902).

24. Mrs. Juliet Brewer, Lexington, to author, 1963.

25. *Kentucky Gazette,* 6 July 1793, 4.

26. Ibid., 21 Dec. 1793, 4.

27. Ibid., 19 Dec. 1795, 4.

28. Ibid., 11 June 1811, 3; 3 Sept. 1811, 3; 20 Apr. 1813, 3; 11 July 1814, 3; 18 Dec. 1815, 3.

29. Ibid., 1 May 1815, 3.

30. Ibid., 5 Oct. 1802, 4.

31. Ibid., 4 Sept. 1810, 4. John Melish reported on his visit of 1811 that among the manufactories of Lexington was "an oil-cloth factory" (Melish, *Travels in the United States of America* 2:187).

32. Elizabeth M. Schenk, editorial assistant, *Encyclopaedia Britannica,* to author, 30 Aug. 1965.

33. Clay Lancaster, "Jefferson's Architectural Indebtedness to Robert Morris," *Journal of the Society of Architectural Historians* 10 (Mar. 1951): 3-10.

34. Talbot Hamlin, *Benjamin Henry Latrobe* (New York, 1955).

35. *The Story of St. Joseph's Proto-Cathedral and Its Paintings* (n.p., n.d.), contains information reportedly furnished by Rogers's great-granddaughter, who also claims that the architect made two trips to France to "perfect his plans for the Cathedral." According to recent research on John Rogers by Mrs. Edith S. Bingham, however, the trips were made in 1821 and 1824-25 to secure contributions to help complete and furnish the cathedral.

36. *Kentucky Gazette,* 17 Mar. 1812, 3.

37. Ibid., 1 Aug. 1814, 3.

38. Rob Morris, *The History of Freemasonry in Kentucky* (Louisville, 1859), 277.

39. Bettye Lee Mastin, "Architectural Landmark Now Home Again," *Sunday Herald-Leader,* 25 Jan. 1970, 34.

40. The corbel was originally at the base of the south parapet. After demolition of the house, it was squared off and used as a cornerstone of Mammoth Garage, Main Street facing Rose in Lexington. The date was altered to "1812."

41. Mrs. Willis (Elizabeth Shryock) Field to author, 1941.

42. Bill, dated 15 Dec. 1804, in Transylvania University Library, doc. no. 1805-40.

43. *Kentucky Reporter,* 17 Dec. 1814, 3.

44. The house built for Perry W. Gaugh in 1841 stands at 331 North Broadway.

45. *Kentucky Gazette,* 11 Dec. 1804, 3.

7 THE GEORGIAN SURVIVAL STYLE

1. Lancaster, *Vestiges of the Venerable City,* [135], 208.

2. Newcomb, *Old Kentucky Architecture,* pl. 80 (called the "Crittenden House"). Photograph taken before present fanlight muntins were installed.

3. John Brown, in Philadelphia, mentions his desire to return to Kentucky to get on with his plans, "particularly those for Building" in a letter to Harry Innes, in Frankfort, 2 Apr. 1796 (Library of Congress; typed copy in the Kentucky Historical Society).

4. Deering Davis, *Annapolis Houses* (New York, 1947), frontis., 40-45.

5. Whiffen, *The Eighteenth-Century Houses of Williamsburg,* 126-28.

6. Patricia Watlington, "The Building of 'Liberty Hall,'" *Register of the Kentucky Historical Society* (1971): 313-18.

7. Banister Fletcher, *A History of Architecture on the Comparative Method,* 15th ed., (New York, 1950), 820-21; Thomas Tileston Waterman, *The Mansions of Virginia, 1706-1776* (Chapel Hill, N.C., 1945), 264, 266; Harold E. Dickson, *A Hundred Pennsylvania Buildings* (State College, Pa., 1954), 9; Wayne Andrews, *Architecture in New York: A Photographic History* (New York, 1973), 5, 7.

8. Contract dated 6 Nov. 1840 in Rowan Papers, Federal Hill, Bardstown, Ky. David H. Hall, preservation coordinator for Bardstown, suggests that the brevity of the Rowan-Moore contract may indicate Moore's familiarity with the house by his having been the original house joiner. Hall has published a series of seven articles on Federal Hill in the *Kentucky Standard.*

9. Collins, *Historical Sketches of Kentucky,* 292.

10. Lancaster, *Ante Bellum Houses of the Bluegrass,* 56-57.

11. *Kentucky Gazette,* 16 Jan. 1806, 3.

12. George Ord, *Supplement to the American Ornithology of Alexander Wilson* (Philadelphia, 1825), 131-35.

13. J. Winston Coleman, Jr., *The Court-Houses of Lexington* (Lexington, 1937), 17, 25-30.

14. Minute Book 1, p. 104, 27 July 1812, Transylvania University.

15. Morrison, *Early American Architecture,* 466, 470, 555.

16. *Kentucky Gazette,* 11 Sept. 1818, 3.

17. *Kentucky Reporter,* 13 May 1829, 2.

18. *Transylvania University Journal of Medicine,* vol. 2 (1829), 201.

8 THE GEOMETRIC PHASE

1. Newcomb, *Architecture of Old Kentucky,* 59.

2. Ibid., fig. 9. Measured drawings by the Historic American Buildings Survey are deposited in the Library of Congress.

3. Fayette County Deed Book M, 401.

4. Fayette County Deed Book M, 26; C. Frank Dunn, "Old Houses of Lexington," 72-78, manuscript in the Kentucky Historical Society. Frankford.

5. The concluding deed to the property from John Maxwell to John Pope, 26 Apr. 1814, Fayette County Deed Book 7, pp. 79-80.

6. The Latrobe-Pope correspondence is in the Maryland His-

torical Society Baltimore, Ma.; and research by Bettye Lee Mastin, Lexington.

7. Hamlin, *Benjamin Henry Latrobe*, fig. 25. The original plan is in the Library of Congress, Washington, D.C.

8. Albert Simons of Charleston, S.C., pointed out this example and subsequently provided plans prepared for its completion.

9. The direction of the staircase was ascertained by the spiral of the lower end of the handrail, and reported in Lancaster, "Latrobe and the John Pope House," *Gazette des Beaux Arts* 29 (1946): 213-24. It had been removed and was being stored, along with columns, curved doors, and other decorative details in the cellar of the James Wyant residence in Transylvania Park, Lexington. They were examined by the author in July 1942.

10. Charles Kerr, "An Historic Dinner," *Lexington Herald*, 15 Apr. 1917, retail section, 2, 11.

11. Floor plans of the house during the Woolfolk regime have been restored from written descriptions, a sketch plan of the first floor, and photographs furnished by Miss Mamie B. Woolfolk of Memphis, Tennessee, in letters to the author, 24 Aug. and 7 Sept. 1942.

12. Mercer County Deed Book 18, pp. 408-9.

13. Whiffen, *The Eighteenth-Century Houses of Williamsburg*, 169.

14. Ibid., 172; Thomas Tileston Waterman, *The Early Architecture of North Carolina* (Chapel Hill, N.C., 1941), 90-97.

15. Calvin M. Fackler, *Historic Homes of Boyle County, Kentucky* (Danville, Ky., 1959), 22-23.

16. *Kentucky Gazette*, 24 Apr. 1815, 3.

17. C. Frank Dunn, "Fayette County Has Its 'Ghost Town' in Sandersville on Georgetown Pike," *Sunday Herald-Leader*, 1 Feb. 1953, 54.

18. Fayette County Deed Book CoCt A, 279; Deed Book 5, pp. 301-3; Deed Book 7, p. 368.

19. One of the photographs is from a glass negative made by Dr. Alfred Peter and now in the J. Winston Coleman, Jr., collection; the other is in the collection of Dr. W.O. Bullock. Both collections are now in the Transylvania University Library. The photographs show late-nineteenth-century side porches. Neither show the balustrade over the front mass represented in the early drawing reproduced in Lancaster, *Vestiges of the Venerable City*, fig. 15.

20. Henry J. Peet, ed., *Chaumière Papers* (Chicago, 1883), 55-56.

21. Ibid., p. 55.

22. William Leavy, "Memoir of Lexington and Its Vicinity," *Register of the Kentucky Historical Society* 41 (1943): [250]-53.

23. William Robards, the first owner after Meade, offered "CHAUMIERE. ONE OF THE HANDSOMEST Improved places in Kentucky FOR SALE" (*Kentucky Gazette*, 2 Mar. 1837, 3); Bettye Lee Mastin, "Friend Made Prophetic Query about Chaumière des Prairies," *Saturday Herald and Leader*, 29 Nov. 1975, D-3.

24. Thomas, *Old Kentucky Homes and Gardens*, [135].

25. C. Frank Dunn, "Historian Challenges Claim Whitley House State's Oldest . . . ," *Lexington Leader*, 25 Aug. 1952, 6. That Lewis was living on the land in 1788 is not proof that the present brick house was built at that time.

26. Clay called it "the most elegant [house] in the city" (Clay, *Life of C.M. Clay* 1:74).

27. Fayette County Deed Book CoCt E, 149.

28. The Grange: Newcomb, *Old Kentucky Architecture*, pls. 49-50. Forest Hill: Fackler, *Historic Homes of Boyle County, Kentucky*, 30-31.

29. John Speed Smith House: A.B. Davis, "139-Year-Old Richmond House Being Razed," *Lexington Leader*, 18 July 1957, 6. Sugar Grove: Coleman, *Historic Kentucky*, 110-11.

30. Jefferson County Deed Book K, 516, 3 Dec. 1816.

31. A photograph of the house before renovation, see Thomas, *Views of Louisville since 1766*, 35.

32. Henri Walbert, *Residences et plantations dans les vallées de l'Ohio . . .* (Paris, 1948), pls. 5, 6.

33. Dunn, "Old Houses of Lexington," 143-45.

34. Fayette County Deed Book CoCt, O, 80. Purchased for $1,062.50 in 1827, it sold for $5,000.

35. Waterman, *Mansions of Virginia*, 97.

36. Mrs. Eva A. Harrison, Kansas City, Mo., to author, 6 Oct. 1964. Mrs. Margaret S. Williams related to author, 4 Sept. 1964, that her father, John Steele, purchased the farm in 1869 from James A. McCampbell, who had bought it from the Singletons, but no deed to the property predating this sale can be found.

37. Clay Lancaster, "The Egyptian Hall and Mrs. Trollope's Bazaar," *Magazine of Art*, Mar. 1950, 94-99, 112.

38. William Bullock, *Sketch of a Journey through the Western States of North America, from New Orleans, by the Mississippi, Ohio, City of Cincinnati and Falls of Niagara, to New York, in 1827 . . .* repr. in Reuben G. Thwaites, ed., *Early Western Travels, 1748-1846* (Cleveland, 1905), 19:113-114, 138-39.

39. Conteur, "History of a Famous Old Landmark," *Enquirer* (Cincinnati), 5 Dec. 1920, 4.

40. Walter Rankin, *Historic Augusta and Augusta College* (Augusta, Ky., 1947), 8.

9 CLASSICISM

1. Mercer County Deed Book 3, p. 267; Deed Book 4, p. 477; Deed Book 7, p. 246; Deed Book 8, p. 168.

2. Morrison, *Early American Architecture*, 259-60.

3. Mercer County Will Book 11, p. 477.

4. This plan was identified as the source of Farmington by Milton L. Grigg of Charlottesville, Va., and Fiske Kimball concurred (Fiske Kimball, "Jefferson's Designs for Two Kentucky Houses," *Journal of the Society of Architectural Historians* [Oct. 1950]: 16). The original plan was drawn by Jefferson in pencil on brown-lined coordinate paper, and reproduced in Fiske-Kimball, *Thomas Jefferson, Architect* (Boston, 1916), pl. 191. Obviously that drawing was not sent to Kentucky, but the supposition is that one like it, or very nearly like it, was.

5. Mrs. Willis Field and the last owners, Mr. and Mrs. Earl Clough, supplied data to author, 1941.

6. Fayette County Will Book 1, p. 291; Deed Book 4, p. 198; Deed Book 16, p. 58.

7. Fayette County Deed Book 10, p. 152, 25 Mar. 1823.

8. Related to the author by Mrs. John Johnstone, daughter of H. Howard Gratz, an owner of White Cottage.

9. It is odd that the outline of White Cottage does not appear on the detailed plan of the city of Lexington on the *Topographical Map of the Counties of Bourbon, Fayette, Clark, Jessamine and Woodford, Kentucky, From Actual Surveys, Revised and Corrected by L.A. & G.W. Hewitt* (New York, 1861). The view of Lexington looking southwest by Ehrgott and Krebs (1871) shows White Cottage with a porch on the back, but its exact form cannot be determined.

10. Rebecca Conover and Elizabeth Gabhart stated that the date of 1812 was found in restoring the kitchen fireplace, and that of 1813 was scratched on plaster in the closet under the stairway (conversations with author, 1985).

11. Lancaster, "Jefferson's Architectural Indebtedness to Robert Morris," 7, 10.

12. Claude-Nicholas Ledoux, *L'Architecture Considérée sous le Rapport de l'Art des Moeurs et de la Législation* (Paris, 1804).

13. Dr. Joseph Pryor supplied photographs taken of White

Cottage when a hospital, and Mrs. Carolyn Bosworth Brown a set of snapshots made in 1935. The addition and rear gallery were gone and part of the roof had collapsed when the house was first examined by the author in 1937. Measurements for the accompanying plans were made after demolition had begun in the summer of 1940.

14. Bettye Lee Mastin, "Lane's End Pleasant Lawn Is on Tour," *Sunday Herald-Leader*, 18 May 1969, 88.

15. Leaflet on the Gano House prepared by Richard N. Smith II and John E. Kunkel, Covington, 1968. Relevant material is also in the Kenton County Public Library.

16. Isaac Ware, *The Four Books of Andrea Palladio's Architecture* (London, 1738); repr., New York: Dover, 1963), bk. 2, pls. K and L, etc.

17. Samuel Gaillard Stoney, *Plantations of the Carolina Low Country* (Charleston, 1938), 146-47.

18. William B. O'Neal, *Architecture in Virginia* (New York 1968), 30-31.

19. Bettye Lee Mastin, "Architectural Landmark Now Home Again," *Sunday Herald-Leader*, 25 Jan. 1970, 34.

20. Bettye Lee Mastin, "Kentucky's First Governor Gave Grassland Acreage to His Son," *Sunday Herald-Leader*, 20 July 1958, 47.

21. Bettye Lee Mastin, "Old Calumet Is Woodford House," ibid., 5 July 1958, 10.

22. Simpson, *Bluegrass Houses and Their Traditions*, 104.

23. A photograph of Auvergne is reproduced in Thomas, *Old Kentucky Homes and Gardens*, p. 70; one of Bucknore was printed in the *Lexington Leader*, 3 Sept. 1952, 3.

24. *Acts Passed at the Second Session of the Thirtieth and the First Session of the Thirty-first General Assembly for the Commonwealth of Kentucky*, Frankfort, 1823, p. 149.

25. Record Book of the Medical Department, 9, Transylvania University.

26. *Kentucky Gazette*, 20 Apr. 1827, 3.

27. *Transylvania University Journal of Medicine* 1 (1828): 301-2.

28. Mrs. Ellen Heber Dearing, Louisville, to author, 28 July 1964.

29. *Report of the Committee appointed to enquire into the condition of the Louisville Hospital. To which is Added, The Report & Petition of the Managers of Said Institution* (Frankfort, Ky., 1824), 1, 2.

30. Ballou's Pictorial Drawing-Room Companion, 18 Oct. 1856, 249. This and a view of the opposite facade from Richard Edwards, ed., *Edward's Directory . . . for 1867-8* (Louisville, 1868), 106, are reproduced in Thomas, *Views of Louisville since 1766*, 47. Edward's view shows the same side of the building as the Staffordshire plate. This series includes the main building of Transylvania University, indicating a date in the 1820s.

31. His Highness Bernhard, Duke of Saxe-Weimar Eisenach, *Travels through North America during the Years 1825 and 1826* (Philadelphia, 1828), 2:132.

32. Theo B. White et al., eds., *Philadelphia Architecture in the Nineteenth Century* (Philadelphia, 1953), pl. 1.

33. The contract between the state commissioners, and Matthew Kennedy and James Ware for building the statehouse, signed 9 Apr. 1814, declares in its first sentence that the work is to be "agreeably to a plan furnished by said Kennedy." This undated contract (to Kennedy and Ware) for the carpentry work, and a certificate of work done on the building, dated 16 Sept. 1816, were found by James D. Birchfield and purchased for the University of Kentucky libraries on 29 Nov. 1987. Except for frequent references to trim for arches, and staircase banisters and railings, these documents give no clue to the appearance of the building (James D.

Birchfield, "Select Acquisitions," *Kentucky Review* 8 [Fall 1988]: 76-80).

34. Bayless E. Hardin, "The State-Houses of Kentucky," *Register of the Kentucky Historical Society* 43 (1945): 179-80.

35. Richard H. Collins, *History of Kentucky* (Covington, Ky., 1874), 2:249. Gideon Shryock, born in 1802, would have been twenty-one years old when the second statehouse burned.

36. C. Julian Oberwarth, Frankfort, Ky., to author, 26 Oct. 1965.

37. Hamlin, *Benjamin Henry Latrobe*, 237-44.

38. Curtis D. MacDougalt, *Hoaxes* (New York, 1958), 105.

10 THE GREEK REVIVAL STYLE

1. Howard Major, *The Domestic Architecture of the Early American Republic: The Greek Revival* (Philadelphia, 1926), 29.

2. Hamlin, *Benjamin Henry Latrobe*, pl. 2.

3. Ibid., pls. 12, 13; fig. 12.

4. Ibid., pl. 23.

5. Ibid., 216-18.

6. Clay Lancaster, "Major Thomas Lewinski: Emigré Architect in Kentucky," *Journal of the Society of Architectural Historians* 11 (Dec. 1952): 12-[20].

7. The doorway of the Miller-Kerrison House at 138 Wentworth Street, Charleston, S.C., includes the transom design as well as the enframement from the Lafever plate. See Clay Lancaster, "Builder's Guide and Plan Books and American Architecture from the Revolution to the Civil War," *Magazine of Art*, Jan. 1949, 19, fig. 6.

8. James Stuart and Nicholas Revett, *The Antiquities of Athena* (London, 1830), vol. 4, sec. 3, pl. 2.

9. Gideon Shryock to his parents, 21 Oct. 1823; letter was in the possession of Mrs. Willis (Elizabeth Shryock) Field of Lexington.

10. Agnes Addison Gilchrist, *William Strickland, Architect and Engineer, 1788-1854* (Philadelphia, 1950), pls. 5-13.

11. *Kentucky Reporter*, 1 Jan. 1827, 1.

12. Ibid., 7 Feb. 1827, 3.

13. [Theodore Bell, M.D.], obituary in the *Courier-Journal*, 22 June 1880, 4.

14. *Atkinson's Casket. Gems of Literature, Wit & Sentiment* (Philadelphia) 12 (Dec. 1833): 553. This description is almost identical to one in a letter from Gideon Shryock to Robert M. Scott of Lexington, dated 15 Feb. 1833, reprinted in Elizabeth S. Field, "Gideon Shryock, His Life and His Work," *Register of the Kentucky Historical Society* 50 (1952): 117-18.

15. From an interview which appeared in the *Courier-Journal*, undated clipping in the collection of Mrs. Field. Charles G. Shryock died in 1910.

16. Clay Lancaster, "New York City Hall Stair Rotunda Reconsidered," *Journal of the Society of Architectural Historians* 29 (Mar. 1970): 33-39; H.J. Birnstige, *Sir John Soane* (London, 1925), pls. 12-13.

17. See n. 15.

18. *Kentucky Gazette*, 17 Aug. 1837, 2.

19. Theodore Laist, "Two Early Mississippi Valley State Capitols," *Western Architect* (May 1926): 53-58; George W. Donaghey, *Building a State Capitol* (Little Rock, Ark., 1937), 6.

20. Minute Book 1, p. 21, 10 Dec. 1827, Transylvania University.

21. Doc. 1827-U-49, Transylvania University archives.

22. Doc. 1830-U-4, Transylvania University archives.

23. Although not shown in the view by Seth Eastman in Lewis Collins, *Historical Sketches of Kentucky* (Cincinnati, 1847), 264, the triglyphs appear in the view of Morrison College on the cover of W. Ratel's march, *The Ashland Quick Step*, published in 1844.

Dr. Charles E. Brownell of the University of Virginia has noticed a number of features in Shryock's work that bypass Strickland's and resemble Latrobe's, such as the use of arched openings and domes. Both are included in the Kentucky State House, and there are blind arches on the flanks of Morrison College. A possible model for the college building may be the center pavilion in Latrobe's proposed design for the New York City Hall (1802). It has a hexastyle portico on a high basement with great antepodia flanking the front steps. The order of the portico, however, is Corinthian, and, in Roman fashion, two bays deep. Inasmuch as the design was rejected, it is difficult to ascertain how Shryock might have become familiar with it.

24. Minute Book 1, p. 266, 31 Aug. 1832, Transylvania University.

25. Minute Book 1, p. 330, 24 Apr. 1834, Transylvania University.

26. L.F. Johnson, *The History of Franklin County, Ky.* (Frankfort, Ky., 1912), 92.

27. Newcomb, *Architecture in Old Kentucky*, pl. 50.

28. Samuel W. Thomas, "An Enduring Folly: The Jefferson County Courthouse," *Filson Club History Quarterly* 55 (1981): 317.

29. W.N. Haldeman, "The Court House," in *The Directory of 1844-45* (Louisville, 1844), 70; Charles K. Needham, "Some Historical Notes Relating to the Courthouse of Jefferson County" (Paper read before the Filson Club, Louisville, 3 Jan. 1927), 12; Thomas, "An Enduring Folly," 311-43.

30. Charles B. Seymour, "A History of the Jefferson County Courthouse" (Paper read before the Filson Club, Louisville, 8 Jan. 1921).

31. Justus Bier, "Adding to Courthouse Called Ruinous to Architectural Gem," *Courier-Journal*, 25 Mar. 1945, sec. 3, p. 1.

32. *Family Magazine* (Cincinnati, 1841), 358.

33. Lunsford P. Yandell, *History of the Medical Department of the University of Louisville, An Introductory Lecture, Delivered November 1st, 1852* (Louisville, 1852), 31.

34. Joan Titley, librarian of the Kornhauser Memorial Medical Library of the University of Louisville, to author, 29 Mar., 12 Apr., 26 July, and 18 Aug. 1967.

35. This discovery was made and the Dakin drawings were identified by Arthur Scully, Jr., author of *James Dakin, Architect: His Career in New York and the South* (Baton Rouge, La., 1973), 26-32.

36. Having a similar facade as the Louisville bank was the Long Island and Atlantic National Bank, which stood until the mid-1950s at 53-55 Fulton Street on the perimeter of Brooklyn Heights, New York, also the location of an academy, three churches, and a stone arch by Minard Lafever.

37. "New Life for Old Buildings," *Preservation News*, 1973, Supplement, [1/].

38. James Patrick, *Architecture in Tennessee, 1768-1897* (Knoxville, 1981), 4, 5, 31, 81, 109; Richard W. Otis, *The Louisville Directory of 1832* (Louisville, 1832), 154-55.

39. Huntley Duprey, "The French in Early Kentucky," *Filson Club History Quarterly* (1941) 15:100.

40. Johnson, *History of Franklin County*, 124.

41. "Travels in Hot Weather," *Western Monthly Magazine* (Cincinnati, 1834), 2:592-95.

42. *Kentucky Yeoman* (Frankfort), 15 June 1843, 3.

43. *Lexington Observer and Reporter*, 14 June 1845, 3.

44. J. Winston Coleman, Jr., *The Springs of Kentucky* (Lexington, 1955), 84-85, 96-97.

45. Beatrice St. Jullien Ravenel, *Architects of Charleston* (Charleston, S.C., 1945), [188].

46. *Records of the Proceedings of the Board of Trustees for the Transylvania Seminary and University*, 6:9, 23, 26, 45, 62.

47. Dr. Robert Peter, *History of the Medical Department of Transylvania University* (Louisville, 1905), 162-63.

48. *Lexington Observer and Kentucky Reporter*, 15 Aug. 1840, 3.

49. J. Winston Coleman, Jr., *Lexington during the Civil War* (Lexington, 1938), 23, 41-42.

50. "Georgetown's Historic Giddings Hall to Be Made Administration Building," *Lexington Leader*, ca. 1969, undated clipping in the author's file.

51. Constance M. Greiff, ed., *Lost America: From the Atlantic to the Mississippi* (Princeton, 1971), 13.

52. Johnson, *History of Franklin County*, 145.

53. Clay Lancaster, "Oriental Forms in American Architecture, 1800-1870," *Art Bulletin* 29 (Sept. 1947), 184. A receiving vault described as Egyptian was built in Cave Hill Cemetery, Louisville, in 1849. No picture of it is known to exist.

54. Fiske's Patent Metallic Burial Cases, advertisement with illustration in the *Kentucky Statesman*, 29 Mar. 1853 and subsequent issues.

55. Orlando Brown Papers, the Filson Club, Louisville, Ky.

56. M. Buxton Forman, "Georgiana Keats and Her Scrapbook," *Connoisseur*, Sept. 1945, 8.

57. Dorothy Thomas Cullen, curator and librarian of the Filson Club, to author, 6 Sept. 1967.

58. Dorothy Thomas Cullen, to author, 6 Sept. 1967.

59. Henry Caswell, *America and the American Church* (London, 1838), 214, 220.

60. Waterman, *Mansions of Virginia, 1706-1776*, [365-66, 373] (ill.).

61. Entry under 21 July 1846 in Maj. Thomas Lewinski's Account Book, formerly owned by Judge James H. Mulligan, later by W.K. Massie, now in Special Collections, University of Kentucky Library.

62. McMurtry to Gibson, 11 July 1848, McMurtry listed these improvements and included a sketch plan of the chamber floor (fig. 10.51). Courtesy of Mrs. Sarah Buckner, Lexington.

63. Fayette County Deed Book 4, 206.

64. Fayette County Deed Book 31, 415.

65. Woodford County Deed Book 5, 155, tract 3, 28 Nov. 1850.

66. Fayette County Deed Book 21, 257-58.

67. Marilyn Kilgus, "Page from Past Being Torn Out as Old Building Comes Down for School," *Lexington Leader*, 3 June 1953, 27.

68. See n. 6.

69. Rosamond Randall Beirne and John Henry Scarff, *William Buckland* (Baltimore, 1958), 60-61.

70. Lancaster, *Ante Bellum Houses of the Bluegrass*, 103-14.

71. Fayette County Deed Book 17, p. 507, 30 Mar. 1840.

72. Fayette County Will Book D, 375, 19 Apr. 1840.

73. Redwood Library was inspired by an elevation serving as headpiece to book 4 of Edward Hopkins's *Andrea Palladio's Architecture in Four Books* (London, 1736); Lancaster, "Thomas Jefferson's Architectural Indebtedness to Robert Morris," figs. 1-2.

74. Henry-Russell Hitchcock lists only two copies in his *American Architectural Books . . . Published in America before 1895*, 3d ed. (Minneapolis, 1946). These belong to the Library of Congress and the New-York Historical Society. Avery Architectural Library of Columbia University acquired one in 1947.

75. For instance, pls. 5 and 14 come from illustrations in Nicholson's *The Builder and Workman's New Directory* (London, 1824), following pp. xvi and xxx.

76. Mills Lane, *Architecture of the Old South, Virginia* (Savannah, Ga., 1987), 163, 166-68.

77. Roger Hale Newton, "'Sachem's Wood,' New Haven, Connecticut, One of the Earliest Greek Revival Mansions in the United States," *Old-Time New England*, Oct. 1942, 33-36.

78. Mrs. Martha Allen Porter, Lexington, to author, 1 Sept. 1964; Eugenia Blackburn, Kentucky Historical Society, to author, 7 Dec. 1964.

79. Scott County Deed Book 4, p. 403.

80. Scott County Deed Book 27, pp. 56, 400.

81. Elizabeth M. Simpson, *The Enchanted Bluegrass* (Lexington, 1938), 198.

82. Clay Lancaster, *Back Streets and Pine Trees* (Lexington, 1956), 44.

83. Barbara Hickey, "UK's Tapp Developing Museum of Early Life," *Lexington Leader*, 28 Nov. 1958, 18.

84. Lancaster, *Ante Bellum Houses of the Bulegrass*, 91-92.

85. Mrs. Joseph Kerr (granddaughter of C.W. Innes) to author, 5 May 1943.

86. Lancaster, *Ante Bellum Houses of the Bluegrass*, 95-96.

87. Simpson, *Bluegrass Houses*, 294.

88. The suggestion was made by architectural historian William Blair Scott, Jr., at the dedication of the historic marker in 1983. For additional information see Bettye Lee Mastin, "Early Plumbing Was Inspiration for Tales of Roof Garden at Susong Home in Scott," *Sunday Herald-Leader*, 17 Sept. 1967, 54.

89. Fayette County Deed Book 27, p. 230; Deed Book 26, p. 516.

90. Information from Dr. Alfred Peter.

91. Lancaster, *Ante Bellum Houses of the Bluegrass*, 98-99.

92. Mary Jane Gallaher, "Bonnie Scotland in the Bluegrass," *Courier-Journal Magazine*, 8 Oct. 1961, 20-23.

93. Russell I. Todd, *This Is Boone Country* (Louisville, 1968), 48; Miss Sarah Yancey Barker, Richmond, Ky., to author, 28 Feb. 1973.

94. Newcomb, *Architecture in Old Kentucky*, pls. 60A, 60B, and 61B.

95. Fayette County Deed Book 30, 386, 25 Oct. 1854.

96. *Kentucky Statesman*, 26 Sept. 1856, 2.

97. Ibid., 24 Dec. 1858, 1.

98. Mrs. Charles Clinton Calvert, Maysville, Ky., to author, 23 Mar. 1966.

99. Calvin M. Fackler, *Early Days in Danville* (Louisville, 1941), 228.

100. Newcomb, *Architecture in Old Kentucky*, pl. 57A.

101. Fackler, *Early Days in Danville*, 220-21.

102. Mary Hobson Beard, *Old Homes in and near Bowling Green, Kentucky* (Bowling Green, 1964), 37-38.

103. Fayette County Deed Book 25, 442, 585-86.

104. Simpson, *Bluegrass Houses*, 309.

105. Fayette County Deed Book 24, 50.

106. Helen C. Powell, ed., *Historic Sites of Harrodsburg and Mercer County* (Harrodsburg, Ky., 1988), 90-91.

107. Thomas, *Old Kentucky Homes and Gardens*, 159.

108. Interview with Miss Amelia Hamilton of Lexington, 9 Oct. 1954.

109. Bettye Lee Mastin, "Ancestor Built Blockhouse near Where House Stands," *Sunday Herald-Leader*, 23 May 1965, 74.

110. Bettye Lee Mastin, "Transitional Architecture Is Evidenced in Mt. Sterling Home of Mrs. Rhea Miller," *Sunday Herald-Leader*, 16 Feb. 1969, 64.

11 THE GOTHIC REVIVAL STYLE

1. Kenneth Clark, *The Gothic Revival* (London, 1928; repr., New York, 1964), 81.

2. William Mason, *Works of Thomas Gray, with a Memoir of His Life and Writings* (London, 1807), 2:239-401.

3. W.S. Lewis, "The Genesis of Strawberry Hill," *Metropolitan Museum Studies* 5 (1934-36): 57-92.

4. John Rutter, *Delineations of Fonthill and Its Abbey* (London, 1823); John Britton, *Graphical and Literary Illustrations of Fonthill Abbey* (London, 1823).

5. Clark, *Gothic Revival*, 58.

6. Ibid., 39-41.

7. Robert Furneaux Jordan, *Victorian Architecture* (Middlesex, 1966), 77-87.

8. Clay Lancaster, "The Architecture of Sunnyside," *American Collector* 16 (1947): 13-15.

9. Morrison, *Early American Architecture*, 64-68, 146-49, 154-56, 57-59, and 80-81. For southern examples: Forman, *The Architecture of the Old South*.

10. White, et al., *Philadelphia Architecture*, pl. 9.

11. Ibid., pl. 11.

12. *Port Folio*, Feb. 1811, after a drawing by Robert Mills. See Theodore Bolton, "Gothic Revival Architecture in America: The History of a Style," pt. 1, *American Collector* 17 (1948): 6, ill. 1.

13. A perspective view of old Saint Patrick's Cathedral is in D.T. Valentine, *Manual of the . . . City of New York* (New York, 1862), facing 156.

14. Everard Miller Upjohn, *Richard Upjohn, Architect and Churchman* (New York, 1939).

15. Newton, *Town and Davis, Architects*, 207-43, 264-303.

16. Issued serially, copies vary as to contents, at most including some thirty sheets (Hitchcock, *American Architectural Books . . . Published in America before 1895*, 29-30).

17. A.J. Downing, *The Architecture of Country Houses* (New York, 1850), 257.

18. Peter, *History of Fayette County*, 121.

19. *The Louisville Directory . . . 1832* (Louisville, 1832; repr., Louisville, 1970), 140. A sketch is reproduced in Clyde F. Crews, *The Faithful Image* (Louisville, 1986), 34.

20. George W. Ranck, *History of Lexington, Kentucky* (Cincinnati, 1872), 190-91.

21. This attribution is made in Robert L. Alexander, *The Architecture of Maximilian Godefroy* (Baltimore, 1974), 79-81; however, no confirmation has been found in contemporary diocesan papers.

22. Coleman, *Historic Kentucky*, 33, 39, 44 and 143; *Courier-Journal*, 27 Nov. 1973, 49.

23. J.R. Cowan, "The Hundred Years of Trinity Parish," *Daily Messenger*, 4 and 5 June 1929. Repr. in Fackler, *Early Days in Danville*, 194.

24. Ibid.

25. *Kentucky Gazette*, 7 Dec. 1837.

26. MacCabe, *Directory of the City of Lexington*, 13-14.

27. Reuben T. Durrett, *An Historical Sketch of St. Paul's Church, Louisville*, Filson Club Publication 5 (Louisville, 1889), 3.

28. Ibid., 4, 63.

29. Obituary of John Stirewalt, *Courier-Journal*, 22 Nov. 1871.

30. *Manual of the First Presbyterian Church* (Louisville, ca. 1916), 17-20.

31. *Lexington Observer and Reporter*, 3 Oct. 1846, 3.

32. Frances Keller Swinford and Rebecca Smith Lee, *The Great Elm Tree: Heritage of the Episcopal Diocese of Lexington* (Lexington, 1969), 247.

33. Elizabeth King Smith and Mary LeGrand Didlake, *Christ Church, 1796-1946* (Lexington, 1946), 49-50.

34. Bettye Lee Mastin to author, 29 May 1973; Mrs. Rebecca Smith Lee, historiographer of the Diocese of Lexington, to author, 18 and 27 Oct. 1973.

35. *Lexington Observer and Reporter*, 3 Nov. 1847, 3.

36. *The Centenary of the Church of Saint Martin of Tours, Louisville, Ky.* (Louisville, 1953), 1-3.

37. Clyde F. Crews, *An American Holy Land: A History of the Arch-diocese of Louisville* (Wilmington, 1987), 114, 137-38; *Louisville Directory for the Year 1832*. Credit to Whitestone for the spire is given in a biographic sketch in the *Courier-Journal*, 21-22 Mar. 1869, supplement, 2. And see Rathbun Associates and W. Brown Morton III, *Historic Structure Report, Cathedral of the Assumption* (Louisville, 1986).

38. "Little Historical Sketches," *After an Hundred Years, 1812-1912: Motherhouse and Academy of the Sisters of Charity of Nazareth* (Nazareth, Ky., 1912), [1-2]; Anna Blanche McGill, *The Sisters of Charity of Nazareth, Kentucky* (New York, 1917), 296-399.

39. Matt Spalding, *Bardstown, Town of Tradition* (Louisville, 1942), 47.

40. Abbey of Our Lady of Gethsemani, *Trappist Life: A Guide* (Gethsemani, 1946), 9-10.

41. Carl E. Kramer, *Capital on the Kentucky* (Frankfort, Ky., 1986), 137.

42. Edmund V. Gillon, Jr., *Victorian Cemetery Art* (New York, 1972), v-xiii, 150.

43. *Lexington Observer and Reporter*, 4 May 1849, 3.

44. Robert W. Scott, *Report of the Kentucky Agricultural Society to the Legislature of Kentucky* (Frankfort, Ky., 1857), 153.

45. Ibid.

46. "Note to John McMurtry, due Sept. 30, 1852, $1,296.00," (Peter, *History of Fayette County*, 121). "Built the large Fair Ground amphitheatre, destroyed during the war" (John McMurtry in the *Lexington Daily Press*, 2 June 1887, 2).

47. Coleman, *Lexington during the Civil War*, 26.

48. Samuel W. Thomas, *Crescent Hill Revisited* (Louisville, 1987), 19-22.

49. Fayette County Deed Book 30, 109; *Lexington Observer and Reporter*, 2 May 1857.

50. *Ballou's Pictorial Drawing-Room Companion*, 25 Aug. 1855, 121.

51. Burton Milward, "Ornate Gothic Structure Once Selected as Clay Memorial; Plan Was Discarded by Donors Because of Lack of Funds," *Sunday Herald-Leader*, 7 Apr. 1940, 4. Haly's advertisement, *Lexington Observer and Reporter*, 19 Dec. 1860, 4.

52. Cincinnatus Shryock is remembered mostly for his designs of the 1870s, including those for the Centenary Methodist Church on North Broadway and the First Presbyterian Church on North Hill Street, Lexington, and the main building of the old Central University in Richmond.

53. Interview with Cincinnatus Shryock's daughter. Mrs. Willis Field, 191; J. Winston Coleman, Jr., *The Squire's Sketches of Lexington* (Lexington, 1972), 47, 65.

54. Fayette County Deed Book 14, 238; Deed Book 11, 478.

55. Contract made 7 May 1867. See note on research by C. Frank Dunn in Newcomb, *Architecture in Old Kentucky*, 150. Notice of the completion of the building: *Kentucky Gazette*, 14 Aug. 1867, 3.

56. Fayette County Deed Book 23, 131.

57. Ibid., bk. 25, 442.

58. Ibid., bk. 22, 64, 228.

59. "Observations on Architecture," *Lexington Daily Press*, 27 May 1887, 1.

60. Interview with Mrs. Laura Hall Bohmer, late 1930s. The gates had been removed to her property on the Versailles pike.

61. Fayette County Deed Book 62, 520.

62. Downing, *Country Houses*, 59.

63. *Lexington Daily Press*, 2 June 1887, 2.

64. *Lexington Observer and Reporter*, 16 Sept. 1848, 3.

65. Fayette County Deed Book 21, 452.

66. Reproduced in Newton, *Town and Davis Architects*, pl. 13.

67. *Lexington Observer and Reporter*, 20 Jan. 1855, 1.

68. Mrs. Elley stated that the house would be completed by 1 Nov. (Mrs. Elley to Eugene Erwin, 22 Sept. 1851, University of Kentucky archives).

69. Print Department, the Metropolitan Museum of Art, New York City. Downing's first sketch had pantry-stair hall section at the front, and equisized dining and drawing rooms across the back.

70. Downing, *Country Houses*, 306.

71. Bettye Lee Mastin, "Aylesford House, Now Encircled by Lexington, Designed As Country Villa on Eight-acre Plot," *Sunday Herald-Leader*, 10 July 1960, 52-53.

72. Fackler, *Early Days in Danville*, 228-29.

73. Fackler, *Historic Homes of Boyle County*, 23.

74. W.P.A., *Kentucky: A Guide to the Bluegrass State* (New York, 1947), 287.

75. Fayette County Deed Book 33, p. 258.

12 THE ITALIANATE STYLE

1. Fiske Kimball, *Domestic Architecture of the American Colonies and of the Early Republic* (New York, 1927), 62, reproduced from the *American Magazine of Useful Knowledge* (1836).

2. Everard Miller Upjohn, *Richard Upjohn, Architect and Churchman* (New York, 1939), 68, 93, 137, 207.

3. Charles Lockwood, *Bricks and Brownstone* (New York, 1972), 132-33.

4. Fletcher, *History of Architecture*, 790, 800.

5. John Summerson, *Heavenly Mansions* (New York, ca. 1948), "The Vision of J.M. Gandy," 111-34.

6. G.L. Meason, *On the Landscape Architecture of the Great Painters of Italy* (London, 1828), 139-40.

7. Carroll L.V. Meeks, "Henry Austin and the Italian Villa," *Art Bulletin* 30 (1948): 166; J. Downing, *A Treatise on . . . Landscape Gardening* (New York, 1841), 314-15 (ill.).

8. Clay Lancaster, "Major Thomas Lewinski: Emigré Architect in Kentucky," *Journal of the Society of Architectural Historians* 11 (1952): 13-14, 20, nn. 2-8.

9. Elizabeth F. Jones, *Henry W. Whitestone: Nineteenth-Century Louisville Architect* (master's thesis, University of Louisville, 1974), 11-18; biographic sketch of Whitestone in the *Courier-Journal*, supplement, 21-22, Mar. 1869, 2.

10. Wilbur D. Peat, *Indiana Houses of the Nineteenth Century* (Indianapolis, 1962), 183-84; John T. Windle and Robert M. Taylor II, *The Early Architecture of Madison, Indiana* (Madison, 1986), 78.

11. "U.S. Marine Hospital," a report issued by the Historic Landmarks and Preservation Districts Commission (Louisville, 1976), 7. The author is in debted to an unpublished paper by William B. Scott, Jr., "The Louisville Marine Hospital," which is the product of extensive research in Washington.

12. George Yates, *The Morrissey Building: 130 Year Saga—1858-1988* (Louisville, 1988).

13. A.B. Young, *Plans of Public Buildings in Course of Construction under the Direction of the Secretary of the Treasury*, 2 vols. (Washington, D.C., 1855-56).

14. Ada Louise Huxtable, *Classic New York* (New York, 1964), 73-74.

15. Petition filed in the Louisville Chancery Court, 29 Apr. 1859.

16. Prof. Madison J. Lee, superintendent, Kentucky School for the Deaf, to Dr. G.M. McClure, 27 Mar. 1939. See also Charles Case, "Kentucky School for the Deaf Celebrates 150th Anniver-

sary, "*Sunday Herald-Leader,* 15 Apr. 1973, 5; and "Jacobs Hall, 1855-1975," leaflet published by the school, 1988.

17. Lancaster, *Back Streets and Pine Trees,* 64-65.

18. Constance M. Greiff, ed., *Lost America: From the Atlantic to the Mississippi* (Princeton, 1971), 49.

19. The Latrobe pumping station and William Rush's "Nymph" were the setting for John Krimmel's painting *Fourth of July* (1812), in the Philadelphia Academy of Fine Arts, reproduced in Talbot Hamlin, *Greek Revival Architecture in America* (New York, 1944), pl. 17. The Centre Square building was demolished in 1827; more than fifty years later the Philadelphia City Hall was erected on the site.

20. *Daily Louisville Democrat,* 24 Oct. 1860, 2.

21. An engraving of the complex from the 1865 *Louisville City Directory* is reproduced in Thomas, *Views of Louisville since 1766,* 105.

22. Pamphlet, *The Water Tower* (Louisville, 1982), to accompany graphic print issued by C.M. Whittle and Mark Bird.

23. Consolidated Illustrating Company, *Louisville of To-day* (Louisville, 1895), 131.

24. Bettye Lee Mastin, "Clay Villa Endured Vicissitudes" and "Clay Villa Has Known Sunshine, Shadow," *Sunday Herald-Leader,* 9 Jan. 1956, 46, and 8 Feb. 1970, 52.

25. Another example, Terrace Place, near Maysville, although eight-sided because of splayed corners, is a two-story pilastered Greek Revival house that is wider than it is deep and includes a low ell; it has nothing to do with the Fowler ideals.

26. Riley Handy, "Some Historic Architecture in Western Kentucky," *Antiques* 55 (Mar. 1974), 583-84.

27. Dr. Miles Williams, to author Sept. 1852.

28. Bettye Lee Mastin, "'Nicest Italianate Villa in U.S.' Is Named Cane Run—or Glengarry—and Now Sits Almost Deserted," *Sunday Herald-Leader,* 23 Nov. 1958, 8-9; Mastin, "House of Historic Interest Destroyed by Fire Here," *Lexington Leader,* 18 Feb. 1970, 3.

29. Entry in Lewinski's diary, 24 Apr. 1846: "Completed design for gardener's cottage for the Honbl. H. Clay."

30. "Barkley to Speak at Opening of Henry Clay Home April 12," *Sunday Herald-Leader,* 2 Apr. 1950, 46.

31. Lancaster, *Ante Bellum Houses of the Bluegrass,* 64; Fayette County Deed Book 35, 258.

32. Jones, "Henry Whitestone," 61-68.

33. Melville O. Briney, "The Town's Handsomest House Nearly a Century Ago," *Louisville Times,* 7 May 1953, 10.

34. The original plans, owned by the successor firm, Luckett and Farley, Architects, and used to prepare the first-floor layout shown in fig. 12.24, show a small dressing closet in the outer corner of "Mr. Ford's Room."

35. Fayette County Deed Book 35, p. 611.

36. Sloan, *Model Architect* 1:41.

37. *Lexington Daily Press,* 2 June 1887, 2.

38. Bettye Lee Mastin, "Lyndhurst was 'Welcome Home' Present," *Sunday Herald-Leader,* 28 Jan. 1962, 49.

39. Beard, *Old Homes in and near Bowling Green, Kentucky,* 55-56, 59-60.

40. Miss Margaret M. Hobson, interview with author, 16 Mar. 1973.

41. Bettye Lee Mastin, "Henry Besuden: A Legend in His Own Day," *Sunday Herald-Leader,* 5 Dec. 1971, 102.

42. Burton Milward, "Home of Cassius M. Clay Was a Magnificent Place," *Sunday Herald-Leader,* 13 Jan. 1957, sec. B, [1]; "'White Hall' Bought by State for Shrine," *Lexington Leader,* 30 July 1968, 2; Betty Tevis Balke, "Whitehall's Furnishings Coming Home," *Courier-Journal,* 20 Oct. 1968, sec. D, 1; Clay Lancaster, "The Metamorphosis of Clermont into White Hall," *Kentucky Review* 7 (1987): 5-28.

43. Bettye Lee Mastin, "Dr. Scott's Home to Open for Tour," *Sunday Herald-Leader,* 28 Apr. 1963, 60.

EPILOGUE: THE POSTWAR ARCHITECTURAL TRADITION

1. Some such designs came out of the McKim, Mead and White examination of New England Georgian houses in 1877.

2. The first Romanesque Revival building in the United States was Richard Upjohn's Church of the Pilgrims (1844) in Brooklyn Heights, New York. An early domestic scheme was by Cincinnati architect W. Russell West, included as design 20 in Downing's *Architecture of Country Houses.* Another appeared as design 10 in Sloan's *Model Architect.* Both are characterized as "Norman." Neither is known to have been built.

3. Samuel W. Thomas and William Morgan, *Old Louisville: The Victorian Era* (Louisville, 1975); Lancaster, *Vestiges of the Venerable City,* 109-46; Ann Bolton Bevins, "History in Towns: Georgetown, Kentucky," and Walter E. Langsam, "Louisville Mansions from the Civil War to World War I," *Antiques* 55 (Mar., Apr. 1974): 855-[869].

4. Clay Lancaster, *The American Bungalow* (New York, 1985), 17-40, 95-152.

5. Stephen Tschudi Madsen, *Sources of Art Nouveau* (New York, 1955), "Name and Conception," [75]-83.

6. For the Palais Stoclet see Werner J. Schwieger, *Wiener Werkstätte: Design in Vienna* (New York, 1984), 51-55, 155-61. The International style was fully realized in the work of Walter Gropius during the second decade of the twentieth century, and popularized by the Bauhaus founded in 1919. Siegfried Giedion, *Space, Time and Architecture* (Cambridge, Mass., 1943), 390-406.

INDEX

Metcalfe, John and Thomas: constructed McKee residence, 51
Methodist Episcopal Chapel, 82-83
Middletown: Head House, 54-56
Miller, John Clark: residence, 247
Millersburg: McKee House, 51-52; Miller House, 247
Mills, Robert: designed basic scheme for marine hospitals, 289
mills: John Bowman II, 13; Abraham Bowman, 16; early sawmills, 30; Joel DuPuy, 48; Croghan, 73
Mitchell, Stanislaus and Ignatus: builders of Maysville City Hall, 203
Moore, Alexander: work at Federal Hill, 124
Morgan, Frederic L.: owned Shryock copy of Benjamin's *Builder's Assistant,* 108
Morgan, Joseph: Morgan Row, 68; Morgan's Tavern, 83-84
Morgan, Ralph: residence, 47-49
Morrison, Col. James, 163; purchased Plancentia, 139
Morrison College, 194-95
Morton, William: residence, 144-45
Mound Cottage (J.T. Boyle residence), 277-79
Mount Airy (Col. Andrew Muldrow residence), 160-63
Mrs. Thomas' Candy Kitchen, 156
Mud Meeting House, Old, 37-39
Muldrow, Col. Andrew: built Mount Airy, 160-63
Mulkey Meeting House, Old, 27
murals: in early Kentucky houses, 111-14; in Riverview, 307

nails: early sources and types, 30-31
Nash, John: designed Cronkhill, 287
national historic landmarks: Pleasant Hill, 99; Liberty Hall, 123
Nazareth Academy: buildings, 260-61
Nelson, Rev. Samuel K.: built Forest Hill, 146
Nelson County Courthouse, 60-61
New York City: city hall stairway compared to that in third Kentucky statehouse, 193
Norman, John: builders' guides, 107
Norton, John: residence enlarged for Judge George Woolley, 301
Notman, John: designed Philadelphia Atheneum, 286

Oakland: Joseph Graves residence, 79-80
octagonal houses, 296-97
Odd Fellows Hall, Lexington, 266
Oldham, Edward: acquired Bayles House, 240-41
Old Mud Meeting House, 37-39
Old Mulkey Meeting House, 27
Olympian Springs, 41

Oxmoor: residence of Alexnder Scott Bullitt, 31-32; William C. Bullitt's addition, 147

Pain, William: mantel design related to Clermont, 77; builders' guides, 107
paint: color choice during late eighteenth, early nineteenth century, 115-16
Palladio, Andrea: villa plan used at Elmwood Hall, 155; designs recalled in facade of Gano House, 167; influence in England, 287
Papworth, John Buonarroti: planned Hygeia for William Bullock, 153
Paris, described in 1796, 29; Duncan Tavern, 59; cemetery gateway, 263
Patterson, Robert: built blockhouse at Lexington, 10
Paul, Peter: stone cutter, 110
Pernell, L.: builder of Maysville city hall, 203
Peter, Dr. Robert: commissioned villa design of Lewinski, 299
Pettit, William B.: residence, 228
Pindell, Thomas H.: built Bodley House, 134
Plancentia: Lewis Sanders residence, 139-40
Pleasant Hill: Shaker community, 88-99
Pleasant Lawn: Cohen murals in, 113-15; Daniel Jackson Williams residence, 165-66
Pope, Sen. John: residence, 134-38
Portland cement: from Kentucky source, 45
Preston, Mrs. Margaret: owned Ellerslie, 71
Preta, Marria: painting in Saint Joseph's Cathedral, 177-78
Price, Daniel Webster: renamed Coolavin Locust Grove, 149
Pugin, Augustus Welby Northmore: publications and designs, 250, 277
Pugin, Charles Comte de: collected designs of Gothic architecture, 249-50

Quarles, Roger: added to Hurricane Hall, 73-75

Rafinesque, Constantine Samuel: said to have landscaped White Cottage, 163
railroad: bridges, 44: Lexington and Ohio Railroad Station, 85-86; determined site of later South Union tavern, 102
Rankin, Dr. Adam: shared quarters with Dr. Epraim McDowell, 35
Rankin, Rev. Adam: log house, 17-18
Renaissance Revival style: early examples in America, 285; Nouveau Louvre, 286; examples in Kentucky, 291, 292-94, 302-3

Revett, Nicholas: joint author of *Antiquities of Athens,* 183; measured drawings of Sunium temple used for Jefferson County courthouse, 196
Richmond: mantel in Ezekiel Fields house, 109, 146; John Speed Smith House, 146; Rosehill, 187-88, 233-34
Ridgeway (Col. Henry Massie residence), 147-49
Riverview (Col. Atwood Gaines Hopson residence), 306-8
Roberts, O.P.: solicited architectural work, 118
Roebling, John A.: began railroad bridge at Shaker Landing, 44
Rogers, Isaiah: architect of Capital Hotel, 205-6; co-designer of spire of Cathedral of the Assumption, 259
Rogers, John: architectural work, 117: credited with Wickland, 131; architect of Saint Joseph's Cathedral, 176-77; builder of Bank of Louisville, 199; built Saint Thomas Church, 252-53
Roland, Hugh: designed Louisville Hotel, 200-202; Saint Louis Church, later cathedral, 259
Rose Hill (John Brand residence), 145-47
Rosehill: frontispiece after Dakin design, 186-87; Col. William Holloway residence, 233-34
Rowan, John: built Federal Hill, 123
Runyon, Dr. Guilford: built Honeysuckle Hill, 243-44
Russell, Christopher: builder of Maysville city hall, 203
Russell, Robert Jr.: built Warwick, 238; built Holy Trinity Church, 254

Saint Joseph's Cathedral, 176-79
Saint Martin of Tours, Church of (Louisville), 258-59
Saint Mary's Seminary (Baltimore): chapel, 253
Saint Paul's Church (Louisville), 255-56
Saint Peter's Church (Lexington), 255
Saint Thomas's Church, 252-54; compared to Saint Joseph's Cathedral, 177
Sanders, Col. Lewis: built Lewis Manor, 139
sawmills: early examples in America and Kentucky, 30
Sawyer, Joseph O.: associate architect on U.S. Marine Hospital, 289
Scott, Joel, II: remodeled Smith House, 54
Scott, John Two-Nine: residence, 50-51
Scott, Sir Walter, 249
Scowden, Theodore R.: designed Louisville Water Co. pumphouse, 293-94
Sedgeley (William Crammond residence), 250-51

Whitley, William: built Sportsman's Hill, 68-70

Whitney, Payne: purchased Fairlawn, 228

Wickland (Charles A. Wickliffe residence), 131-32

Wickliffe, Charles A.: built Wickland, 131

Wickliffe, Robert: portico of residence, 134

Wilgus, Asa: builder of John Pope House, 118, 134-35

Wilgus, G.D.: built Episcopal Burying Ground Chapel, 266

Williams, Daniel Jackson: built Pleasant Lawn, 165

Williams, Elias E.: architect of U.S. Post Office, Louisville, 290; Masonic Temple, 291

window glass: early use in Kentucky, 66; special order for Liberty Hall, 121

winery (Augusta), 62

Winslow, Hallett M.: co-builder of 1806 Fayette County Courthouse, 118, 127-28

Woodlands (Trotter-Erwin residence), 139-41

Woodlawn: notable woodworking, 109, 110

Woods, Archibald: built Woodsland, 81

Woodside (Henry Bell residence): compared to Ward Hall, 229

Woodstock (William Hayes residence), 78-79

woodwork, carved: in White Hall, 56; in Clermont, 77; in Oakland, 80; by Matthew P. Lowery, 109-110; in Warwick, 157; in Mount Airy, 161

Woolfolk, Joseph Sowyel: remodeled Pope House, 137

Woolley, Judge George: enlarged Norton Cottage, 301

Youngs, Isaac N.: plans of Kentucky Shaker villages, 99